Home Maintenance
Revised

Home Maintenance

By

WILLIAM WEISS

Bennett & McKnight
a division of
Glencoe Publishing Company

Glencoe Publishing Company
17337 Ventura Boulevard
Encino, CA 91316

85 86 87 VH 5 4

ISBN 0-02-664420-7
(Previously ISBN 0-87002-386-1)

Library of Congress Catalog No. 82-71388

Printed in the United States of America

Preface

HOME MAINTENANCE was written for the individual who is faced with repair and maintenance jobs around the home. This book deals with repairs of existing structures rather than the installation of new facilities. Mindful application of the information contained in this book can save the do-it-yourselfer time, money, and frustration when making household repairs. In addition, labor costs and the difficult task of obtaining professional mechanics are eliminated.

Many repair tasks in the home can be done by the person who has an understanding of basic repair procedures and some basic skills with tools. HOME MAINTENANCE presents common repair procedures in a clear, step-by-step manner with detailed instructions and numerous illustrations. Tools and materials that are needed to make the repairs are listed. Technical terms are explained as they appear in the chapter.

To prepare this book, the author has researched many sources, such as periodicals and technical publications. This text is also based on the author's own experiences as a homeowner, craftsman, and industrial arts educator. Each section of this book has been written with an eye to the practical approach to home maintenance. The capabilities and limitations of the average do-it-yourselfer are taken into account. Limits as to what the do-it-yourselfer should attempt are stated, and general building code requirements are given where necessary.

Readers who follow the instructions in these chapters can learn to:

- Develop a set of tools for home use and care for them properly.
- Organize a suitable home workshop.
- Skillfully use the tools needed in home repairs.
- Understand the basic materials used in home repair work and purchase these materials intelligently.

Table of Contents

CHAPTER 1

Tools

When you think of home maintenance, you usually think of tools. Tools are needed for nearly all home repairs. Many tools are expensive. Some are dangerous if not handled properly. Therefore it is important to have some basic understanding and information about tools. For a home repairs class, the school will probably supply most of the tools. If you plan to do repair work at home, you will need to buy your own tools.

Following are two lists. The first suggests a basic collection of tools. Anyone who regularly makes home repairs will often find need for these tools. The second list mentions tools you might want to add to the basic collection as the need arises and money is available.

The lists are by no means complete. Other tools will be mentioned later in this book as specific jobs are discussed. However, the worker with the tools listed here and the skills to use them properly has a solid foundation for home maintenance work.

BASIC HAND TOOLS

- 13-ounce claw hammer. Fig. 1-1.
- 4″ screwdriver, regular blade. Fig. 1-2.
- 6″ screwdriver, cabinet tip. Fig. 1-3.
- #1 and #2 point Phillips-head screwdrivers. Fig. 1-4.
- 9″ smooth plane. Fig. 1-5.
- Wood chisels: 1/4″, 1/2″, and 3/4″ sizes with plastic handles. Fig. 1-6.
- Utility knife with extra blades. Fig. 1-7.
- 12″ combination square. Fig. 1-8.
- 6′ push-pull or zigzag ruler with inch and metric markings. Fig. 1-9, 1-10.
- Handsaw, crosscut, 26″ length, 10 points.
- Nail set. Fig. 1-11.
- Hacksaw, adjustable, with extra 8″ or 10″ blades. Figs. 1-12, 1-13.
- Countersink, 1/2″, round shank.
- Hand drill, 1/4″ chuck. Fig. 1-14.
- Set of twist drills, 1/16″ to 1/4″.
- 8″ bit brace with ratchet. Fig. 1-15.
- Auger bits, 1/2″, 3/4″, and 1″ sizes. Fig. 1-16.
- Long-nose pliers with cutter, 6″ length.
- Combination pliers (slip joint), 7″. Fig. 1-17.
- Open-end adjustable wrench, 10″. Fig. 1-18.
- Stepladder, wooden, 6′.

The 1/4″ hand drill, the 8″ bit brace, and the auger bits can be replaced by the following:

- Electric drill, 1/4″ chuck. Fig. 1-19.
- Set of spade-type power wood bits, 1/4″ to 1″. Fig. 1-20.

In addition, the following tools extend your capabilities in home maintenance.

- Center punch. Fig. 1-21.
- Combination oilstone, 8″ x 2″ x 1″ (for tool sharpening).

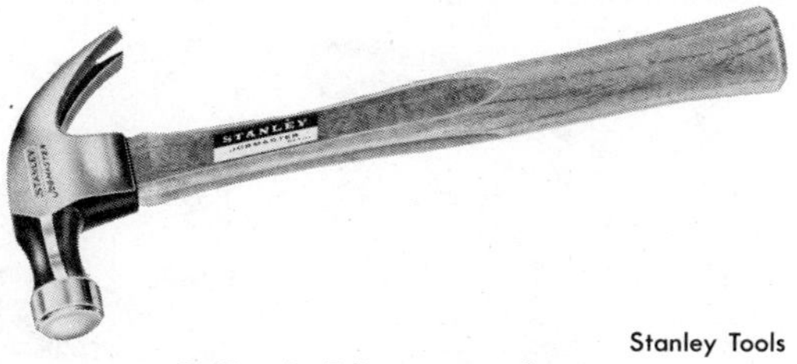

Stanley Tools

1-1. A 13-ounce claw hammer with wooden handle.

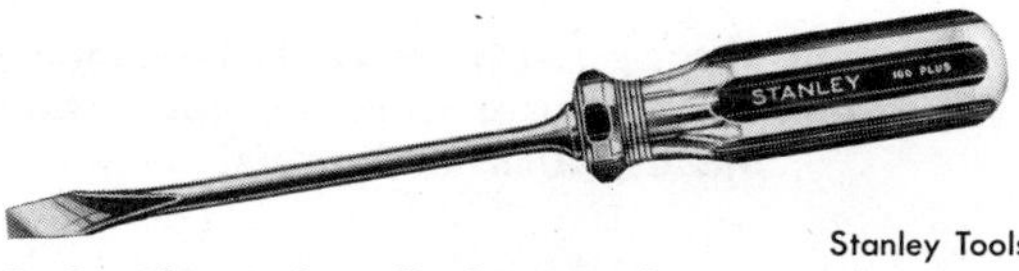

Stanley Tools

1-2. Plastic-handled screwdriver with a regular blade.

Stanley Tools

1-3. Cabinet-tip screwdriver.

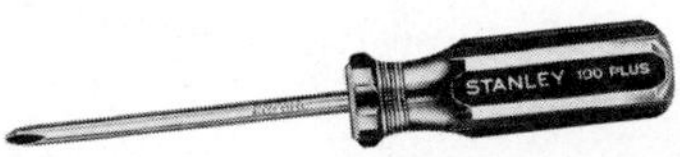

Stanley Tools

1-4. Small Phillips-head screwdriver.

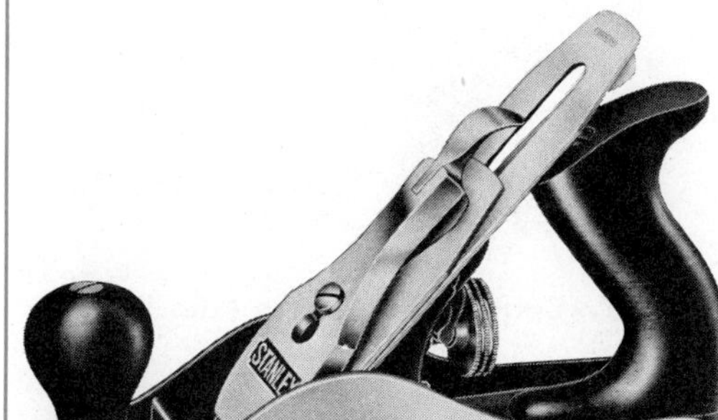

Stanley Tools

1-5. A 9″ smooth plane.

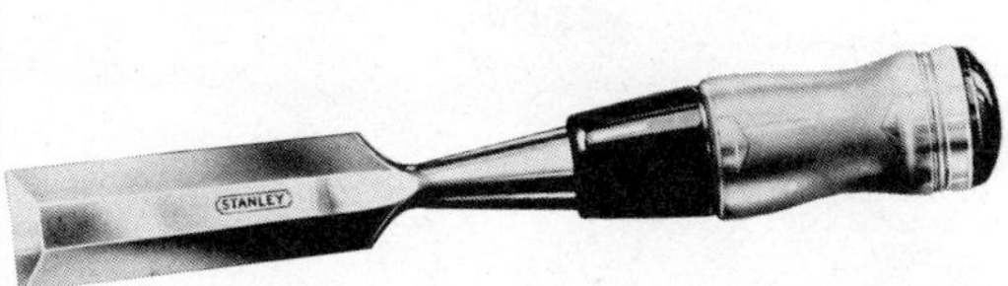

Stanley Tools

1-6. Wood chisel with plastic handle.

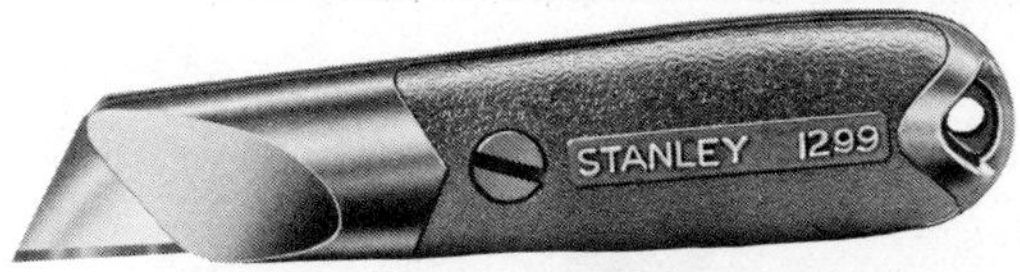

Stanley Tools

1-7. Utility knife with hollow aluminum handle to hold extra blades.

Stanley Tools

1-8. A 12″ combination square. There is a level on the handle and a scriber in the end of the handle.

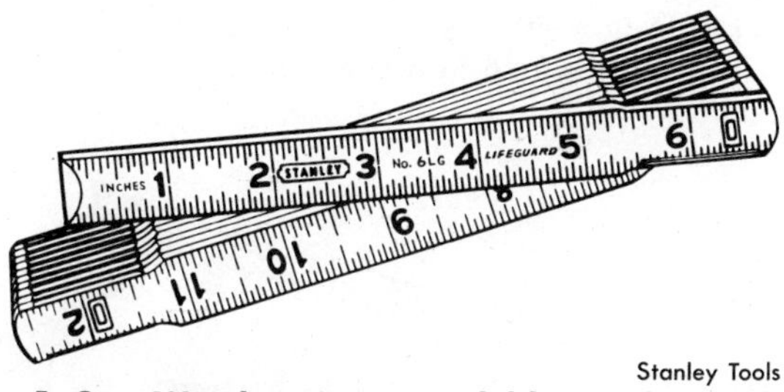

Stanley Tools

1-9a. Wooden zigzag, or folding, ruler, with inch markings.

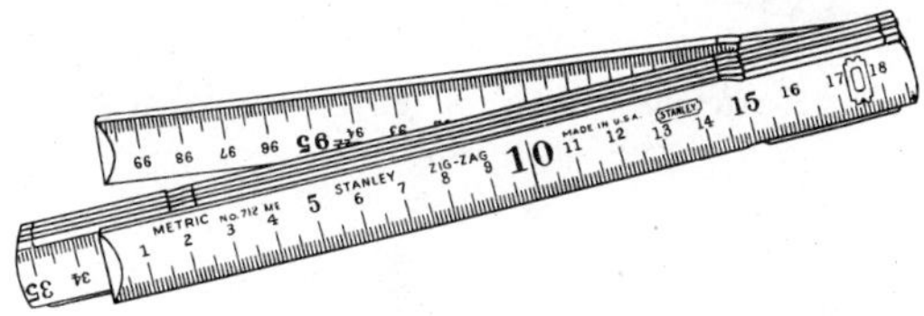

1-9b. A folding ruler with metric markings.

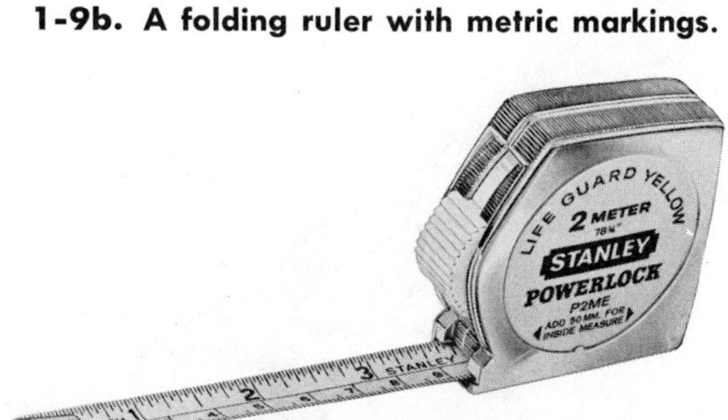

Stanley Tools

1-10. Push-pull ruler or measuring tape with both metric and inch markings.

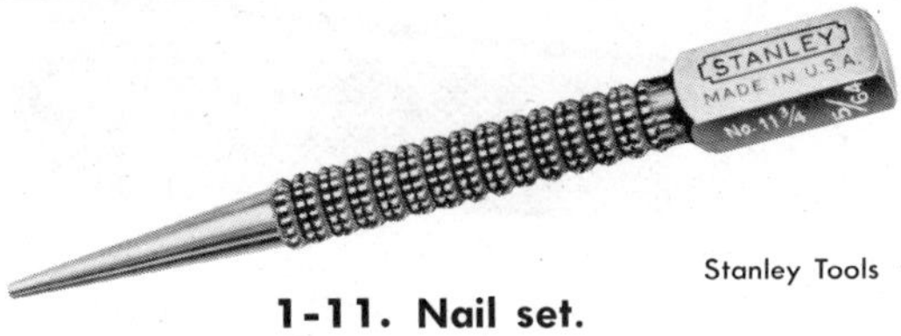

Stanley Tools

1-11. Nail set.

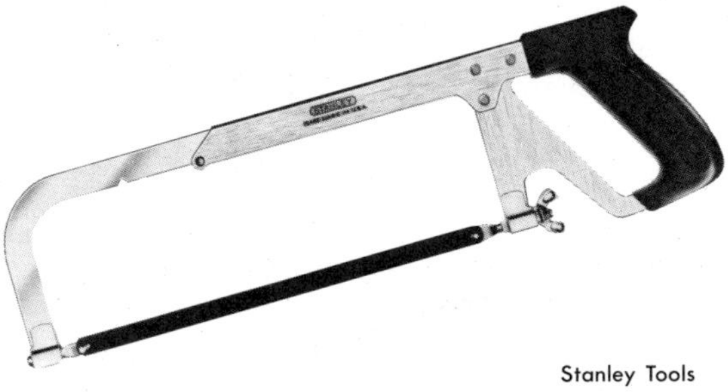
Stanley Tools

1-12. Adjustable hacksaw with a pistol-grip handle and knuckle protector.

Stanley Tools

1-13. Hacksaw with a simple pistol-grip handle.

Stanley Tools

1-14. Hand drill with hollow handle to hold extra twist drills.

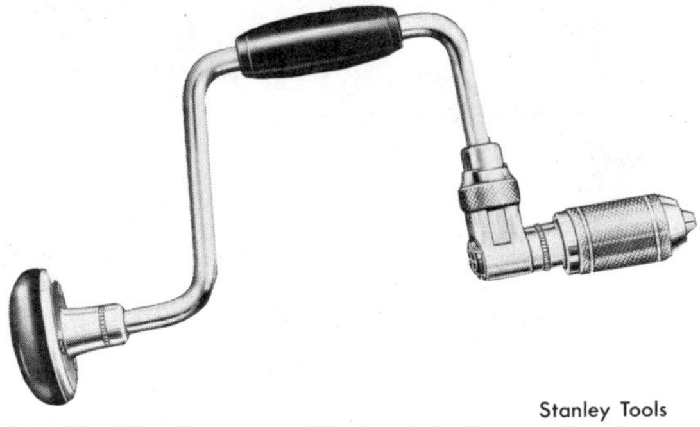
Stanley Tools

1-15. Bit brace with ratchet mechanism which enables the user to drill holes in tight places, such as corners.

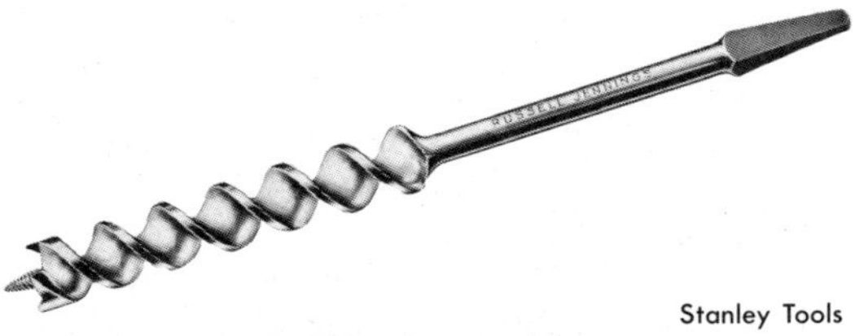
Stanley Tools

1-16. Auger bit.

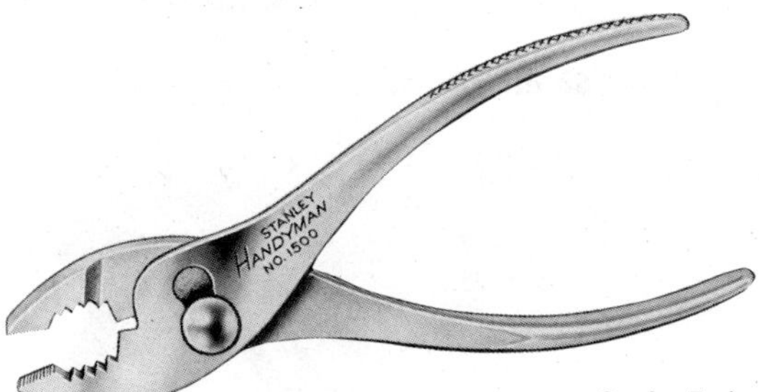

Stanley Tools

1-17. Combination pliers (slip joint).

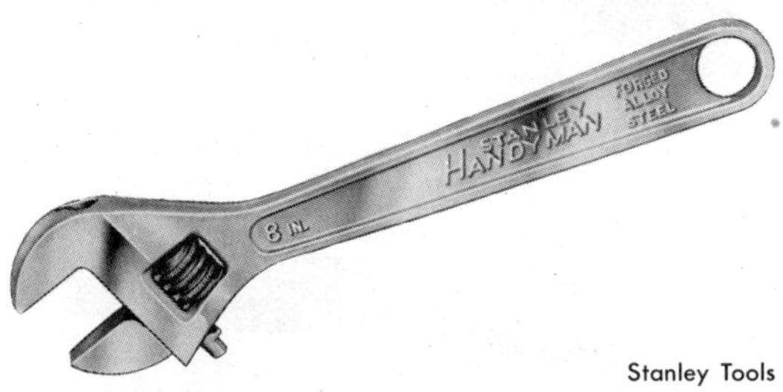

Stanley Tools

1-18. Open-end adjustable wrench.

Skil Corporation

1-19. A ¼″ electric drill.

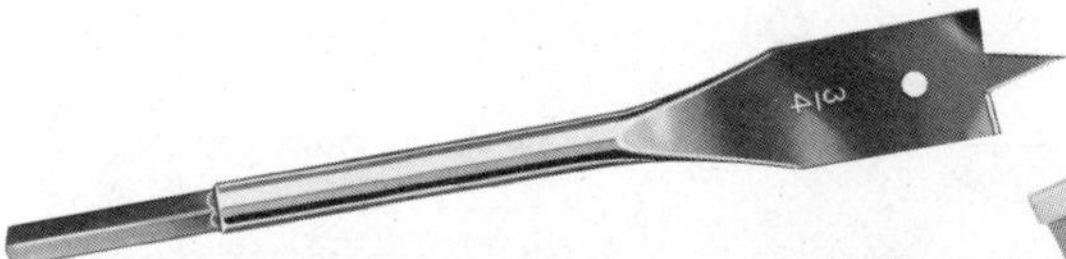

Stanley Tools

1-20. Spade-type power wood bit with ¼″ shank to fit into an electric drill.

Stanley Tools

1-21. Center punch.

1-22. Woodworking vise with a metal handle.

Stanley Tools

1-23. A cold chisel.

Stanley Tools

1-24. A backsaw which can be used in a miter box.

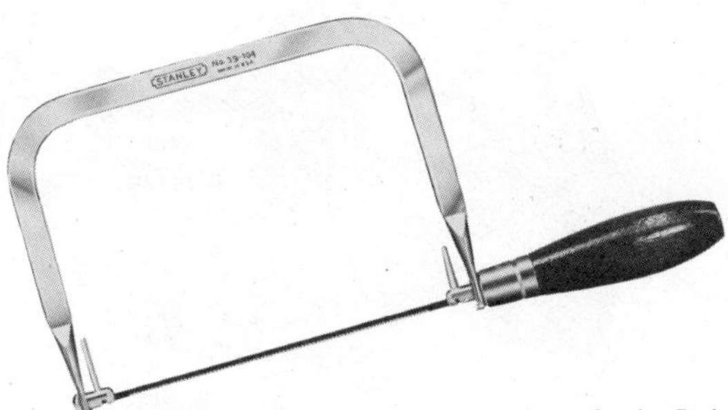

Stanley Tools

1-25. Coping saw with a wooden handle.

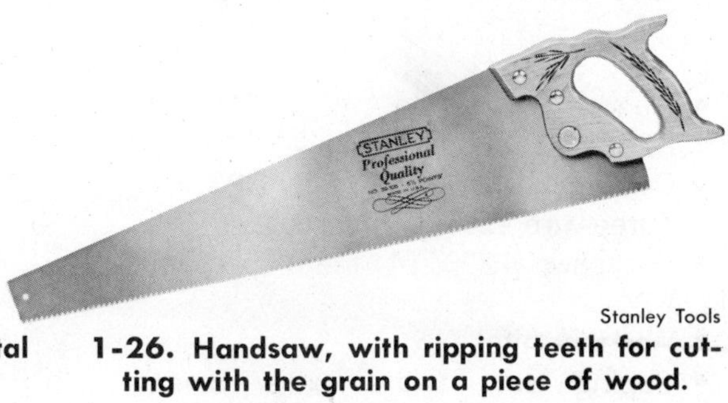

Stanley Tools

1-26. Handsaw, with ripping teeth for cutting with the grain on a piece of wood.

Stanley Tools
1-27. Flexible-blade putty knife.

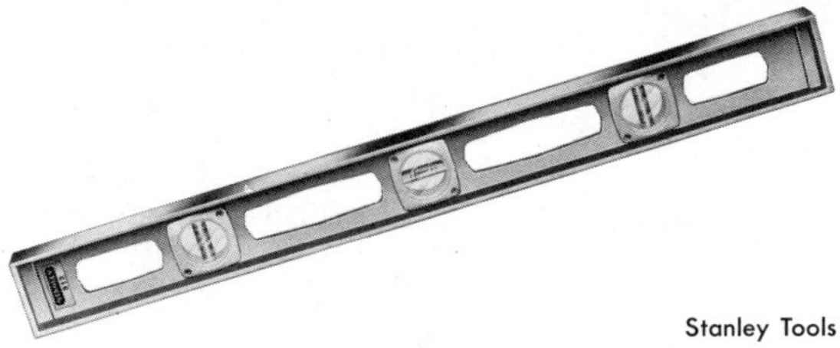

Stanley Tools
1-30. An aluminum level.

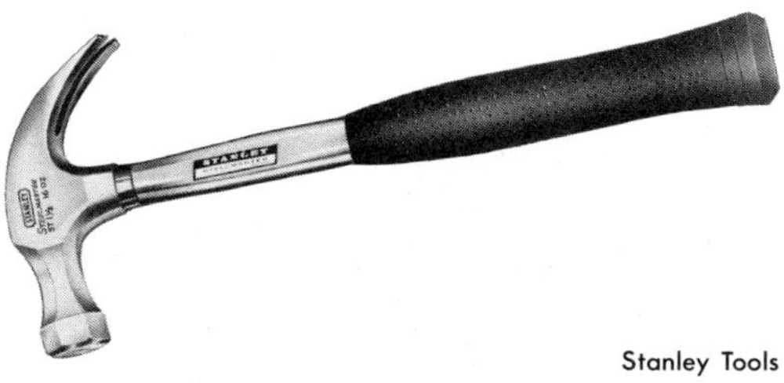

Stanley Tools
1-28. All-steel 16-ounce claw hammer.

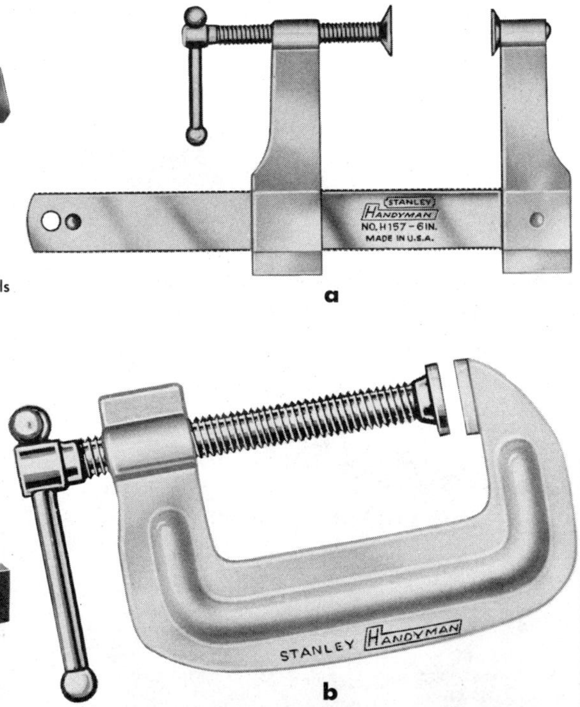

Stanley Tools
1-31. Two types of C-clamps. The adjustable one (a) can be quickly opened to any size up to 6″.

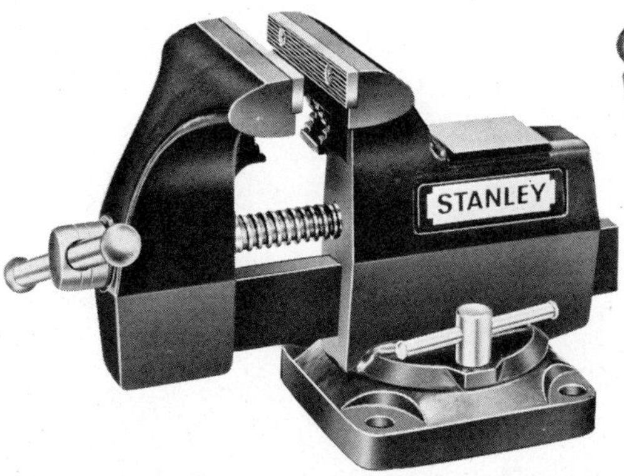

Stanley Tools
1-29. Metalworking vise with a swivel base.

• Woodworking vise, 4″ x 10″ jaws. Fig. 1-22.
• Cold chisel, $\frac{3}{4}$″ width. Fig. 1-23.
• Three-wire extension cord, 25′.
• Backsaw, 12″, 14 teeth per inch. Fig. 1-24.
• Wooden miter box.
• Coping saw (with extra blades). Fig. 1-25.
• Handsaw, rip, 26″, 5$\frac{1}{2}$ points. Fig. 1-26.
• Propane torch with spark lighter.
• Putty knife, 3″ blade. Fig. 1-27.
• #3 point Phillips-head screwdriver.
• 16-ounce claw hammer. Fig. 1-28.
• Metalworking vise, 3$\frac{1}{2}$″ jaws. Fig. 1-29.
• Level, aluminum, 18″. Fig. 1-30.
• 2 C-clamps, 6″. Fig. 1-31.

TOOL SELECTION

When walking through your local hardware store or tool supply store, you can find hundreds of tools and gadgets for use in the home.

The Right Tool for the Right Job

If you are going to buy a tool, your selection should be based on three factors:

- *Need for the tool.* Either you have a repair job that requires immediate use of this tool, or you anticipate using it for repair jobs in the near future.

- *Usefulness.* You should ask yourself these questions: Will this tool be useful often enough to make buying it worthwhile? Is there another less expensive tool that is not as difficult to use and will do the job as well?

- *Skill of the user.* Be sure that you will be able to handle the tool effectively before you buy it. If you have never used such a tool before, ask a salesclerk or other knowledgeable person to explain its use. The same is true if you are taking a course in home repairs. Whenever you are not sure how to use a tool, ask the instructor. Using a tool incorrectly may damage the tool or the object you are repairing. It could even be dangerous.

Your local library probably has many good books on home repairs and the use of tools and machines. Select a book that explains the use of a specific tool in detail, and do some reading on the subject. Then, a little practice should improve your skill in operating the tool.

How to Select the Proper Tools

There are often several choices of tool sizes. Claw hammers, for instance, are made in various weights, such as 13- and 16-ounce heads. To select the proper weight hammer for your use, you should know that a 16-ounce hammer is fine for driving 2″ nails, but too heavy for driving small brads. A 13-ounce hammer is a better choice for both jobs if you plan to purchase only one hammer.

Most manufacturers offer two lines of tools: one for the amateur and another for workers in the building trades. The builders' line of tools is usually of better quality, will probably withstand harder use, and in the case of edged tools, will stay sharp longer. A very important decision when purchasing tools is choosing between a good one and one of poor quality. A well-made tool always has the manufacturer's name on it because the company is proud of the product. There is usually a guarantee or warranty on the tool.

Observe the construction of the tool carefully. Hold it in your hand. A hammer, for example, should feel comfortable when you hold it by the handle. It should feel balanced so that it can be swung with ease. And a saw handle should fit your hand, with the saw blade long enough so you will not pull the blade out of a piece of wood on the up-stroke when sawing.

The criteria for selection of power tools are the same as those for regular tools. In addition, you should consider the safety factors built into each machine. Many portable power tools, for example, are made of high-impact plastic, which offers double insulation against electric shock. Fig. 1-32. A

1-32. Double insulation protects the tool user from shock.

Rockwell International

metal-encased tool requires a three-wire electric cord with a three-pronged plug.

Some types of portable power tools have safety guards. A portable circular saw, for instance, should have a good blade guard which will slide back to expose the blade gradually as you cut into a piece of wood, and then snap back over the blade when you remove the saw from the wood. A portable circular saw should also have a dust chute that deflects the sawdust to one side, away from the face of the operator.

Sometimes a more expensive power tool will give you more versatility. A three-speed saber saw can cut more types of material than a single-speed saw, for example. An electric drill with a variable speed control will allow you to drill into a masonry wall at slow speed or into a piece of wood at high speed. A larger motor for a table saw will give added cutting power for thick lumber, and help prevent the saw from stalling in the middle of a heavy board.

PORTABLE POWER TOOLS

Portable Electric Drill

Probably the most commonly used electric tool for home repair is the portable drill. Fig. 1-33. It is made in several sizes, of which the 1/4″ and 3/8″ are the most popular. Fig. 1-34. Many accessories fit this drill so that it will do much more than just drill holes. A variable speed control allows the operator to select any drilling speed by squeezing the trigger. Some drills have a reversible feature, which at slow speed and with a screwdriver bit, enables you to drive or remove screws. Fig. 1-35.

The term *size* in electric drills refers to the capacity of the chuck; that is, the largest size drill bit the chuck will hold. A 1/4″ drill will hold any accessory or twist drill that has a shank no larger in diameter than 1/4″. Heavy duty drills, of 1/2″ and larger sizes, are usually used for industrial purposes. Fig. 1-36. They also have a slower running speed than the 1/4″ drill.

Twist drill bits for electric drills are available individually or in sets. Fig. 1-37. For

1-33. A 1/4″ drill made of high-impact plastic.

Rockwell International

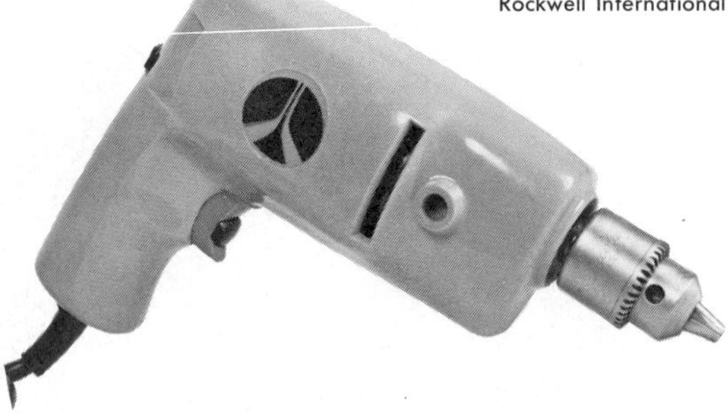

1-34. A cordless 1/4″ drill is available from some manufacturers.

Rockwell International

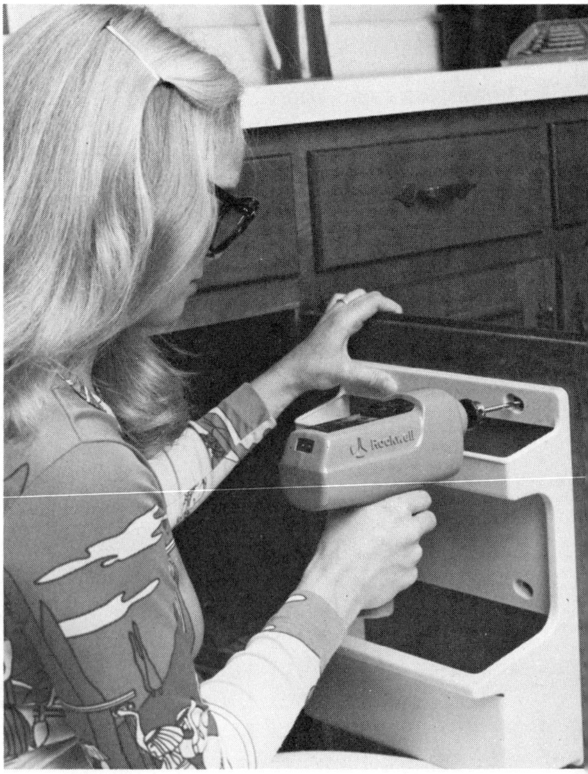

Rockwell International

1-35. Some drills have attachments which enable you to drive or remove screws.

Rockwell International

1-36. Heavy-duty electric drill.

1-37. Set of twist drills. It includes two masonry drills and a center punch.

Skil Corporation

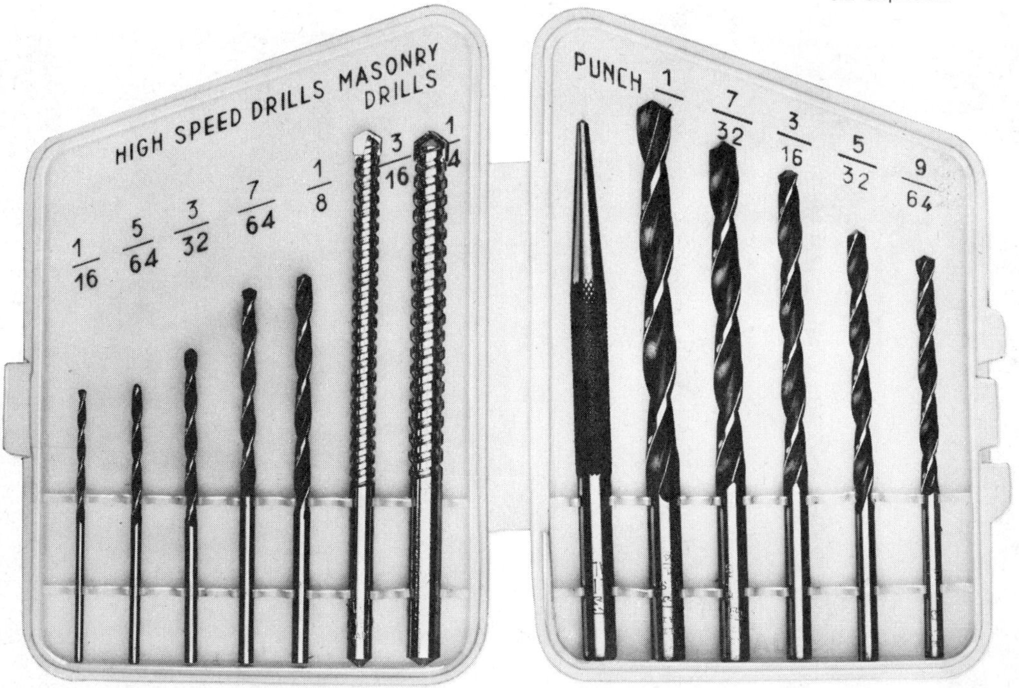

Rockwell International

1-38. Disk sanding attachment for a 1/4″ electric drill.

1-39. When drilling into metal or masonry, protect your eyes with safety glasses. Goggles would be even better.

Rockwell International

Rockwell International

1-40. Portable belt sander equipped with vacuum attachment and bag to collect sawdust.

1-41. Hold a belt sander firmly when sanding a wooden surface.

Rockwell International

example, you can buy a $\frac{1}{16}''$ to $\frac{1}{4}''$ set in a plastic or metal case. These drill bits are made of either carbon steel or high-speed steel. High-speed bits are for drilling metal. The type of drill used for making larger holes in wood is called a spade-type wood bit. These are available in fractional sizes and may be purchased individually or in sets. They fit into a $\frac{1}{4}''$ drill and can be used at high speed.

Other accessories available for electric drills include:

- Paint mixer.
- Disk sander (for rough sanding only). Fig. 1-38.
- Wire brush.
- Grinding wheels.
- Polishing wheels.
- Slow-down attachment for screwdriver bit.
- Hole saws.
- Masonry drills.

SAFETY RULES FOR OPERATING ELECTRIC DRILLS

When using a portable drill there are several safety rules to remember.

- A metal-encased drill must have its three-pronged plug put into a grounded outlet to avoid the possibility of electric shock to the operator.
- Never work with the drill (or any electrical equipment) on damp ground or on a wet floor.
- Whenever possible, clamp the object to be drilled to your bench. Never hold in your hand the object that you are drilling.
- Wear goggles or safety glasses when drilling into metal or masonry. Fig. 1-39.
- Don't wear loose clothing (such as a tie or scarf) when using the drill. Roll up your sleeves, or button the cuffs of your shirt, to prevent loose cloth from getting wrapped around the drill bit or the chuck when working.

Portable Belt Sander

A belt sander is used for smoothing wood and metal surfaces. It can be used for rough work or, with a fine grit belt, for finish work. It is a heavy machine, and therefore easier to handle on large horizontal areas. Many portable belt sanders come equipped with attachments to vacuum up wood dust as the sander produces it. Fig. 1-40.

Belts for the sander are available in a variety of sizes to fit any machine model. The belts are backed with cloth and coated with abrasives such as emery, garnet, or aluminum oxide.

Each type of belt sander will include instructions for replacing belts, adjusting the belt tension, and lubricating the machine. In general, all sanding machines operate in a similar way.

- Hold the belt sander firmly so that the movement of the belt will not pull the machine away from you. Fig. 1-41. It is unnecessary to bear down on the sander because the weight of the machine is enough to allow the belt to cut away at the surface to be sanded.
- Keep the machine moving constantly when it is running, or it will wear a trench in the surface of the material.
- Start with a coarse belt, gradually changing to a medium and then to a fine belt, until you have achieved a smooth surface.
- It is best to start and stop the sander when it is off the object being sanded to prevent marring the work surface.

SAFETY RULES FOR OPERATING BELT SANDERS

- Do not allow the machine to run over the electric cord when you are working.
- Do not tilt the sander, or the edge of the belt will cut into the object being sanded.
- After replacing a belt and adjusting the tension, turn the sander on briefly to insure that the belt is firmly attached.
- Do not wear loose clothing which might get caught in the machine.
- To prevent damage to the object being sanded, keep the sander moving over the work surface.

Rockwell International

1-42. Clamps are used to hold the abrasive paper in place over the sole plate of this orbital sander.

1-43. A heavy-duty orbital sander.

Rockwell International

Rockwell International

1-44. A vibrating sander.

1-45. Saber saw with a 45-degree tilting base that will make bevel cuts at various angles. A variety of blades can be used in this saw.

Rockwell International

1-46. Cutting a piece of paneling with a saber saw. Notice the straightedge held in place with C-clamps.

Orbital and Vibrator Sanders

Because orbital and vibrator sanders remove very small amounts of surface material (in contrast to belt sanders), they are used as finishing sanders. It is possible to get a very smooth surface using these machines. But unlike the belt sander, which has a continuous belt, these sanders have a flat sole plate containing a soft pad. The abrasive paper is held in place on the sole plate with two clamps. Fig. 1-42. (Sheets of abrasive paper can be bought in packages already cut to the proper size for the machine, or you can cut a 9″ by 11″ sheet of abrasive paper into the right size pieces.)

An orbital sander moves in a circular motion. Fig. 1-43. A vibrating sander moves from side to side very slightly and is therefore capable of removing very little of the surface with its abrasive action. Fig. 1-44. The orbital sander is more versatile because it can use many types of abrasive papers for sanding, and several kinds of pads for polishing.

In using these machines keep them flat on the work. To sand very rough wood, move the machine across the grain. This removes surface material faster. To finish the surface so that it is smooth and free of scratches from the abrasive, the final sanding must be done with the grain (that is, in the same direction as the grain), first with medium and then with fine abrasive paper.

SAFETY RULES FOR OPERATING ORBITAL AND VIBRATOR SANDERS

- Always read the manufacturer's instructions before you start to use the machine.
- Do not tilt an operating sander or you will mar the surface of the work.
- To prevent the abrasive paper from being torn off, be sure it is securely clamped over the plate on the sander.
- Always start with the coarsest abrasive paper, working gradually to very fine paper.

Saber Saw

A saber saw is a portable electric jigsaw. It has a pointed blade which is used to cut curves. With the aid of a rip fence, it can be used to cut straight lines. A rip fence is a metal guide that permits the operator to cut strips of wood of even width. The guide bears against the straight edge of a board. It is adjustable to width. The blade of the saber saw moves rapidly up and down with the teeth on the blade facing up. Fig. 1-45. There are many varieties of blades available for this machine that will cut wood, plastic, wallboard, paper, and even metal. Fig. 1-46.

This saw can be used to make both inside and outside cuts. The work is clamped down so that the part to be cut overhangs the workbench or the sawhorses that support the material. Follow the pencil lines you have made, but cut on the waste side of the lines so that they remain visible. With some practice you can cut close to the lines, leaving a smooth edge that requires little filing or sanding.

To make an inside cut—for example, the inner part of a circle—drill a hole in the area to be cut. The hole must be large enough to contain the saw blade so that you can start the cut from this point. If it will be necessary to make sharp turns, the blade you put into the saw must be a narrow one (wide blades make wide turns; narrow blades can make tighter turns). When cutting around a curve, slow down the forward movement of the saw. Curves must be cut gradually or the blade will get too hot, burn out, or break off. There is also available a special blade which will cut through the surface of the wood, making its own entrance cut when the saw is tilted upward.

SAFETY RULES FOR USE OF A SABER SAW

- The area under the material you are cutting must be clear. Keep the electric cord, the workbench, and your fingers away from the area where the blade will cut through.
- The saber saw must have a three-pronged plug, or be constructed of nonconductive plastic, to prevent electric shock to the operator.
- Make adjustments only when the saw is not plugged in.
- Do not attempt to touch a saber saw blade immediately after use. The blade will be hot.
- When buying new saw blades, purchase those with the same screw holes or notches that the old ones have. This can prevent the blades from working loose and falling out while the machine is running.
- When replacing a blade in the saw, make sure the blade is straight and the screws holding it are tight.

Portable Circular Saw

The portable circular saw is an electrical replacement for the handsaw. The great variety of available saw blades (see *Saw Blades,* p. 24) permits the circular saw to be used for cutting wood both across and with the grain and for cutting different materials such as plastic laminates, masonite, and asbestos. Gauges on the saw allow the operator to adjust for depth of cut and blade angle. For example, the saw can be set for a 45-degree angle. One saw accessory, the rip fence, will allow you to cut long pieces of wood to a specified width. Fig. 1-47.

Saws come in different sizes which correspond to the diameter of the blades. For example, there are 6½″, 7″, and 8″ saws. The larger ones have more powerful motors and are capable of cutting through heavier lumber. Some saws have chutes which shoot sawdust out to the right. Fig. 1-48. (These, of course, would be impractical for a left-handed person. The dust would be directed toward the operator's face.)

1-47. Portable circular saw with a rip fence attached to the base.

Skil Corporation

Be sure the circular saw is unplugged while all gauges and other accessories are adjusted. The work should be supported on sawhorses so that the area under the saw blade will be clear of obstructions. Fig. 1-49. Plug the saw into a grounded outlet, and, holding the saw firmly, press the trigger. In a few seconds, when the saw comes up to full speed, move the saw along the pencil line which you have marked previously on the wood. Cut on the waste side of the line. Support the waste piece with your hand as you finish cutting it off. If the blade binds (stops) in the middle of the cut, turn the machine off immediately or it will "kick back". That is, the saw will buck out of the wood. When you finish the cut, stop the machine before you put it down again.

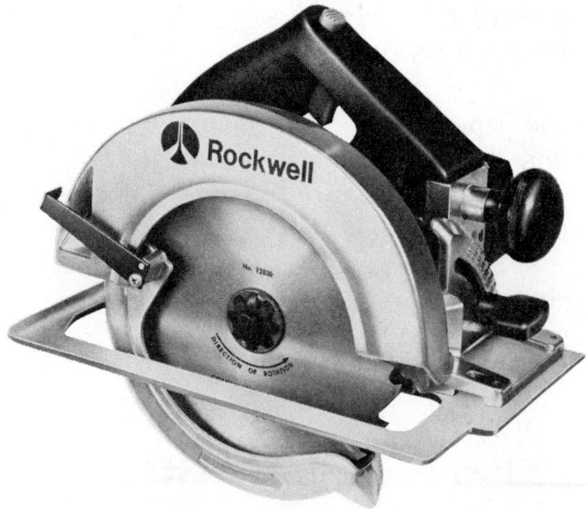

Rockwell International

1-48. This portable circular saw has a dust chute in the upper blade cover behind the blade.

1-49. The work should be supported on sawhorses. The area under the saw blade must be free of obstructions.

Rockwell International

SAFETY RULES FOR USE OF A CIRCULAR SAW

• Wear goggles or safety glasses when using the saw to protect your eyes from dust and chips.

• Keep the power cord clear of the saw to prevent cutting it.

• Select the right saw blade for the job you are doing. Keep the blades sharp. They will cut cleaner and not bind or cause a "kickback".

• The work must be supported by saw-horses or a workbench so that the area underneath it is clear of obstructions.

• Make all adjustments when the saw is unplugged.

• Follow the manufacturer's instructions for the use and lubrication of the saw. Make sure the blade guard is clean and lubricated so that it moves back and forth over the blade easily.

STATIONARY POWER TOOLS

The Table Saw

The table saw is a circular saw on a stand. Fig. 1-50. It is a versatile machine which can be used to cut wood, masonite, plastic, and soft metal. It can rip, crosscut, miter, dado, cut tenons, tapers, and grooves, and make moldings of various shapes. An assortment of accessories, including a dado head, (Fig. 1-51) various types of blades, a feather board, a tenoning jig, and a molding head with cutters, are available. These accessories will enable you to do many kinds of woodworking for a home.

Size of a circular saw is designated by the diameter of the blade it uses. Common sizes are 8″, 9″, and 10″. The bigger the blade, the larger the horsepower of the motor necessary to run the saw.

1-50. A 10″ circular saw on a stand. The blade will be covered by the transparent plastic guard.

Rockwell International

EQUIPMENT

A saw is usually purchased with a miter gauge, a rip fence, and a motor. Fig. 1-52. You can buy a stand for the saw or make your own at home. You may also buy extension wings to make the saw table larger, to facilitate the handling of large sheets of plywood or other bulky materials. The circular saw is usually sold with a combination blade which will either rip or crosscut wood. In addition, you should buy a blade guard, a vital safety device for the circular saw operator.

SAW BLADES

There are several types of blades available for a circular saw. The blade for your saw must be the correct diameter. It must also have the right size hole to fit the arbor of the machine. (The arbor is the revolving shaft that holds the blade.) Using a blade too large in diameter for the saw, or with a hole too big for the arbor, can cause an accident to anyone near the saw.

Types of blades available for a table saw are listed here, with the purpose of each explained.

• *Crosscut blade.* Used to cut wood across the grain.

• *Hollow-ground blade.* Also called a

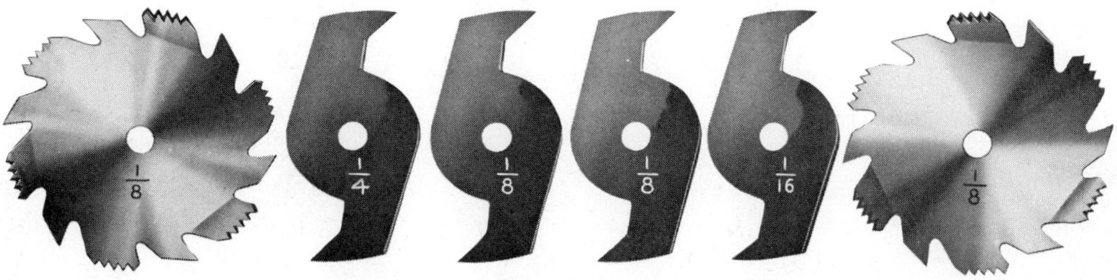

Rockwell International

1-51. Parts of a dado head. The largest dado this set can cut is $^{13}/_{16}$″. It goes on the arbor of a circular saw just like a saw blade.

planer blade, it is thinner toward the center than it is near the teeth. Fig. 1-53,a. It is used for smooth cuts such as those often needed in cabinetmaking.

- *Ripping blade.* Used to cut with the grain of the wood. Fig. 1-53,b.
- *Combination blade.* A blade for all types of cutting. It will either rip or crosscut stock. It is unnecessary to change the blade for each operation. Fig. 1-54.
- *Plywood blade.* Has many small teeth which will cut through plywood leaving no splinters along the edges. Fig. 1-54.
- *Carbide-tipped blade.* The various blades mentioned above may be purchased with carbide tips. Carbide, a very hard ma-

Rockwell International

1-52. Crosscutting a piece of wood on a 9″ circular saw. Notice that the wood is pushed into the moving saw blade with the miter gauge.

1-53. (a) A hollow ground combination, or planer blade, that will either rip or crosscut. (b) A ripping blade used to cut with the grain of the wood.

Rockwell International

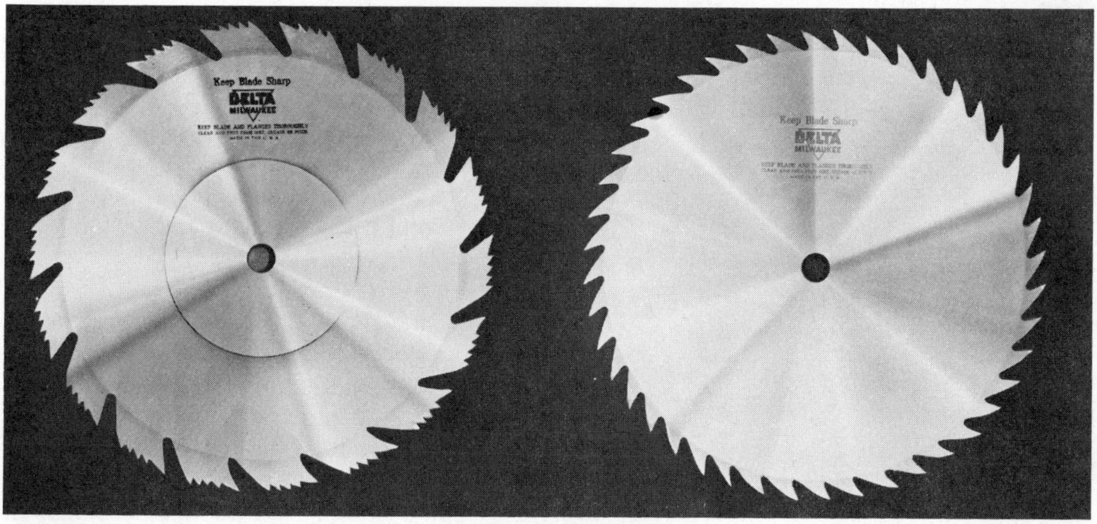

a b

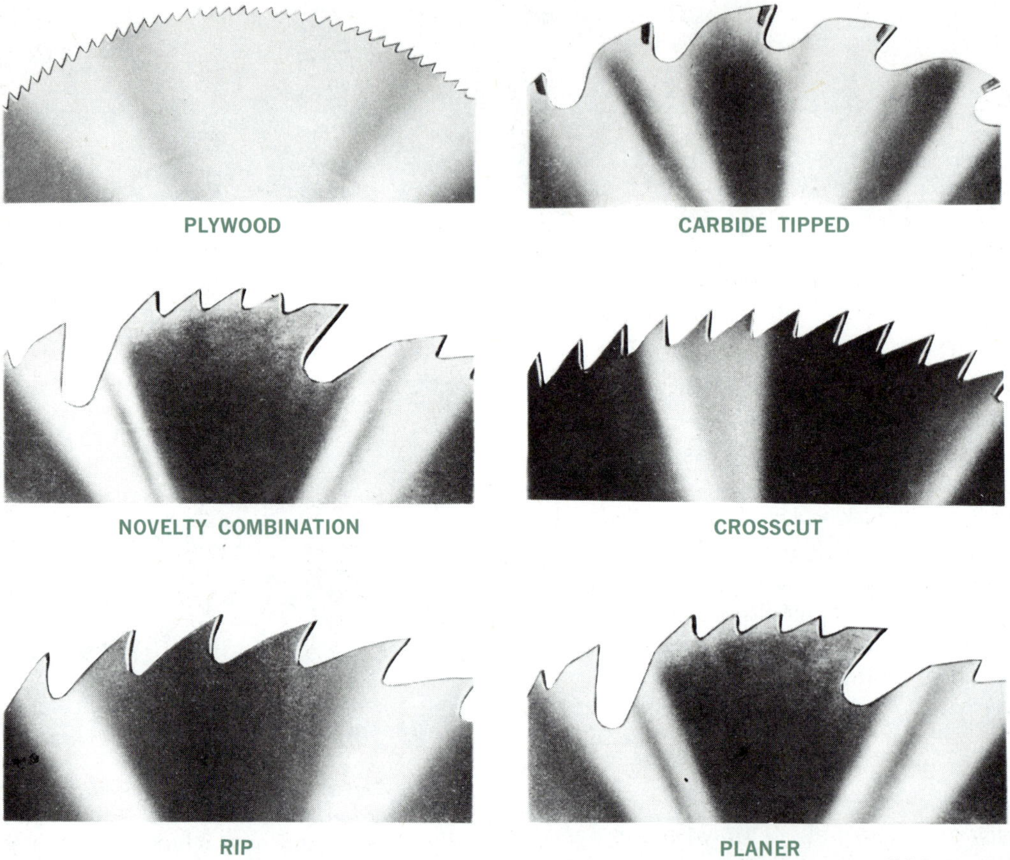

Skil Corporation

1-54. Six types of circular saw blades useful in home maintenance.

Rockwell International

1-55. Miter gauge.

terial, is brazed to each saw tooth, so that the blades can be used to cut materials which would burn out an ordinary saw blade. Because they maintain a sharp edge, these blades are used in industry to cut such materials as plastic laminates and other composition materials. Fig. 1-54.

PARTS OF A TABLE SAW

The major parts of a table saw are:

- *Table.* A piece of smoothly machined steel on which the material being cut rests. Parallel to the saw blade on the top are two grooves in which a miter gauge slides back and forth.
- *Miter gauge.* The wood is held against the gauge and slid into the moving blade to

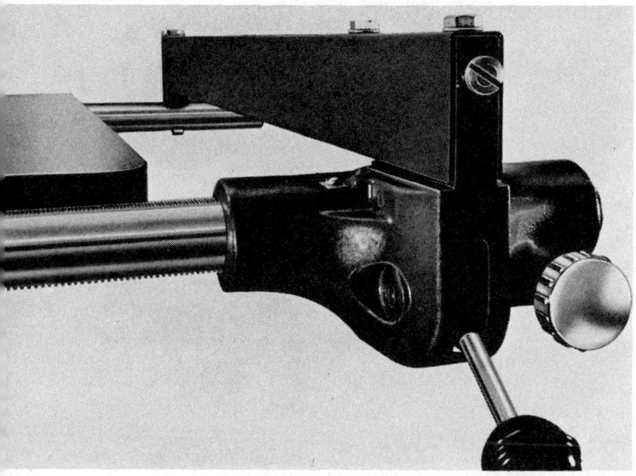

Rockwell International

1-56. Rip fence.

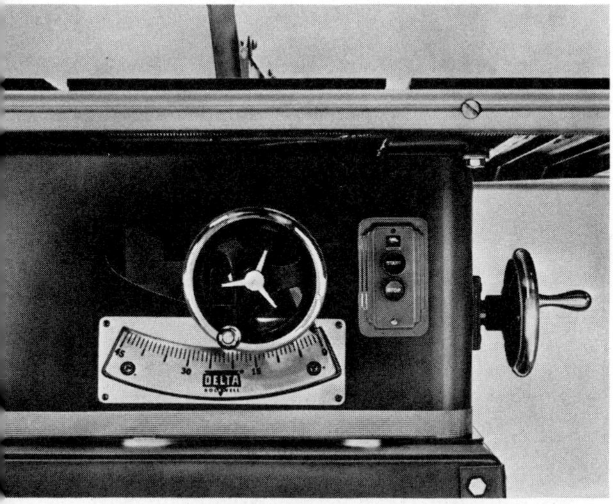

Rockwell International

1-57. Blade-raising handle, on the front of the saw, next to the control switch. On the right side of the saw is the blade-tilting handle. The scale showing the angle of the blade is on the front of the machine.

crosscut a piece of stock. Fig. 1-55. A stop rod can be put on the miter gauge so that a number of pieces can be cut exactly the same size. The gauge can be set for any angle from 90 to 30 degrees.

• *Rip fence.* This is clamped to bars connected to the table. It can be moved along the table to any distance from the blade. Fig. 1-56. This allows the operator to rip pieces of wood to specific widths.

• *Throat plate.* The piece that covers the opening in the center of the table through which the blade appears. It is removable and can be replaced by other plates designed for dado heads and molding heads.

• *Guard.* Covers the blade so that the operator's hands cannot get too close to it. It may also include a splitter and an anti-kickback device. The splitter keeps the saw kerf open, thus preventing the blade from being pinched by the wood, which would cause the blade to bind.

• *Blade-raising handle.* Raises the blade to any height above the table. Fig. 1-57. It has a locking knob which secures the blade at the desired height while the saw is running. The blade should be raised so that it projects about $\frac{1}{8}''$ above the piece of material being cut.

• *Blade-tilting handle.* A handle on the side of the saw. It lets the operator tilt the blade and adjust it to the angle shown on the scale at the front of the saw. Usually the blade can be tilted from 90 to 45 degrees.

• *Table extension wings.* Extensions, bolted to the edges of the saw table, increase the table size to hold large sheets of material such as plywood and masonite.

SAFETY RULES FOR USE OF A TABLE SAW

• Use the proper size wrench when removing the arbor nut from the saw. Do not hold the blade with your hand. Instead, use a piece of scrap wood against the blade to keep it from moving.

• Never raise the saw blade more than $\frac{1}{8}''$ above the top surface of the wood to be cut. The less blade exposed, the less chance of being cut by it.

• Use a push stick, made from scrap wood and kept near the saw, when ripping a piece of wood when the fence is set to less than 6″ from the blade.

• Don't use the miter gauge and the rip fence at the same time when cutting a piece of stock to length. The material will get caught between the blade and the fence and will "kick back" at the operator.

• Change the blade and make machine adjustments with the machine unplugged.

• When using the table saw, never stand directly behind the blade. Stand a little to one side of the blade.

• Keep your hands away from the moving saw blade at all times. Do not reach over the revolving blade to grab a piece of wood.

• Use the correct blade for the job you are doing. If you do not want to change blades, install a combination blade on the saw.

Radial-Arm Saw

Similar to the circular saw but more versatile, the radial-arm saw will do many different woodworking operations with accessories you can buy for it.

It is available in sizes according to its blade diameter. Common sizes that would be useful in a home workshop are 9″ and 10″ blades.

1-58. A 10″ radial-arm saw on a stand.
Rockwell International

EQUIPMENT

The radial-arm saw, a guide table, and a fence are sold as one unit. Fig. 1-58. Motor and controls are within the machine. Additional equipment includes a stand, dado head, molding head, shaper-jointer fence, and a planer head for surfacing lumber. You could make your own stand to hold the machine, plus a larger auxiliary table to allow the saw to handle large panels more easily.

SAW BLADES

The same types of saw blades are available for the radial-arm saw as are available for the portable and stationary circular saws (p. 24).

PARTS OF A RADIAL-ARM SAW

This machine is more complicated than the table saw. It therefore has more adjustment handles. Following is a list of major radial-arm saw parts and their uses.

• *Table.* A sturdy base for the material being cut or shaped that includes an adjustable fence.

• *Overarm or radial-arm.* Supports all the parts of the saw. It can be moved 360 degrees with the track along which the saw unit moves, making it possible to set the saw for angle cuts.

• *Yoke.* Holds the motor and the blade; can be rotated 360 degrees. For ripping, the yoke is turned so that the blade is parallel to the fence. The handle is used to pull the saw across a piece of wood when crosscutting. Figs. 1-59, 1-60.

• *Elevating handle.* Raises or lowers the saw unit to adjust the blade to the proper height.

• *Column.* The upright steel column on which the saw overarm swivels.

• *Blade guards.* Cover the blade for protection of the operator.

• *Arm track.* Attached to the overarm on some models of radial-arm saws. The saw moves back and forth on this track instead of directly on the overarm.

• *Motor controls.* A switch box with "on" and "off" buttons, usually located on the forward end of the overarm, where the operator can find it easily.

• *Anti-kickback fingers.* A rod, containing two movable fingers which hold the material being cut and prevent it from being moved toward the operator.

• *Sawdust spout.* A dust chute which sends the sawdust out to one side. It adjusts to direct the dust away from the operator.

Before operating any equipment, read the manufacturer's instructions and study the diagrams enclosed with the saw. Also, there are probably many books on the use of woodworking machines in your local library.

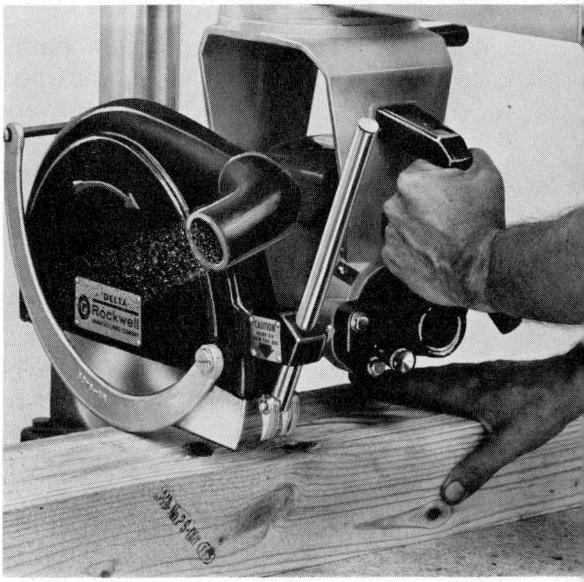

Rockwell International

1-59. Crosscutting a piece of wood on the radial-arm saw. Note the sawdust spout, blade guard, and the anti-kickback fingers.

SAFETY RULES FOR THE RADIAL-ARM SAW

• Before you use the saw, read the manufacturer's directions for its use and maintenance.

• Keep your hands away from the revolving blade. Do not reach under the blade. If you have to reach something near the blade, turn off the machine and wait for the blade to come to a complete stop.

• Make all adjustments on the machine when it is stopped. The blade should be changed only when the saw is unplugged.

• Use a push stick when ripping wood where the space between the fence and the blade is 6″ or less.

• When setting up the saw for ripping, make sure the saw blade will rotate upward toward you. The guard should be lowered so that it clears the wood by at least $\frac{1}{8}$″ on the end of the saw nearest you.

• Turn on the saw and allow it to reach full speed. Then allow the saw blade to enter the wood steadily. Do not try to force the blade to cut too fast.

1-60. Front view of a radial-arm saw showing the yoke, the handle, the motor, and the blade housing. This saw has steel legs bolted to its base to form a table.

Rockwell International

Electric Grinder

A grinder is a stationary machine that is used in the home workshop to sharpen tools. Grinders can be purchased with various diameter wheels. However, the larger wheels, such as the 7″ one, require electric motors with greater horsepower to turn them. Some common wheel diameters and thicknesses are: 4″ x $\frac{1}{2}$″, 5″ x $\frac{1}{2}$″, 6″ x $\frac{3}{4}$″, and 7″ x 1″.

Grinding wheels for sharpening tools are made of aluminum oxide. Wheels can be purchased in various grits. For example, a 60-grit wheel is a medium grade; a 120-grit wheel is fine in texture. Since most electric grinders have two wheels, one could be coarse and the other medium or fine. Wheels are also made with various size holes to fit the arbor on your grinder. When replacing wheels, it is important to buy the right size wheel with the correct arbor hole. Machine instructions will specify the wheel sizes that are safe to use with that particular grinder.

ACCESSORIES

A grinder should have an adjustable tool rest and a safety shield for each wheel. The safety shields cover most of the wheel edge and stop fragments and sparks from hitting the operator. Also, a water container attached to the machine is handy for cooling the tool frequently while it is being ground. This prevents the metal from overheating and losing its hardness. Fig. 1-61.

Some of the more expensive grinders are sold with pedestals, adjustable lights, safety shields with attached lights, and a honing wheel mounted on the grinder top. A plane-iron grinding attachment and a drill grinding attachment may also be purchased. Although most grinders are motorized, belt driven grinders can be bought. For the latter, a separate motor is necessary. The motor is attached to the pulley on the grinder with a V-belt and a V-belt pulley. A 1725 RPM, $\frac{1}{3}$ or $\frac{1}{4}$ horsepower motor will power these grinders as shown in Fig. 1-62.

Rockwell International

1-61. An electric grinder with safety eye shields, adjustable tool rests, and a removable cooling-water container.

1-62. A belt driven grinder. The motor is connected to the pulley on the grinder with a V-belt.

SAFETY PRECAUTIONS FOR OPERATING AN ELECTRIC GRINDER

- Wear safety glasses or goggles when using the grinder, even when the machine has its own safety shields. Fig. 1-63.
- Follow the manufacturer's directions when buying grinding wheels for your grinder.

Rockwell International

1-63. Grinder with adjustable lamp, and eye shields over each grinding wheel.

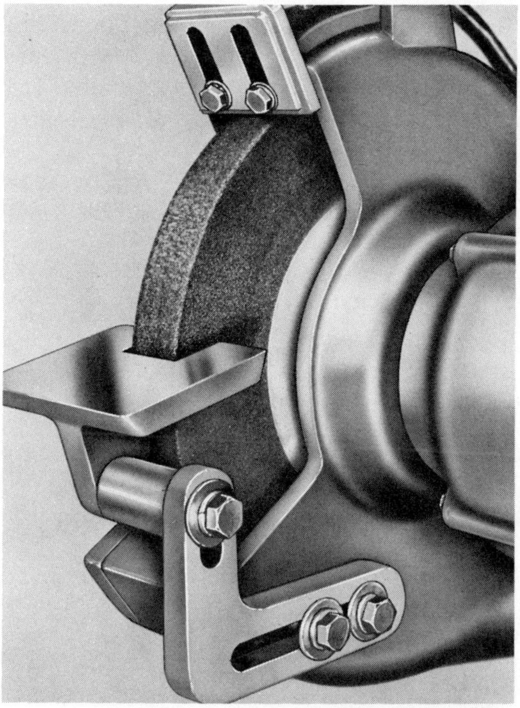

Rockwell International

1-64. The adjustable tool rest should be set close to the edge of the grinding wheel so that tools being sharpened will not get caught between the wheel and the rest.

- When grinding tools, keep a filled water container nearby. Dip the end of the tool into the water frequently to avoid overheating the tool.
- Check a grinding wheel before you install it to be sure it has no cracks. A cracked wheel will fly apart when it is revolving on the grinder.
- When working at the grinder, do not wear loose clothing. It can get caught on the arbor or on one of the wheels.
- Adjustable tool rests should be no more than $1/4''$ from the edge of the wheels. Fig. 1-64. A larger space would allow the edge of the tool being sharpened to get caught between the tool rest and the wheel.
- Whenever possible, use the edge (rather than the side) of the wheel for grinding. Keep the tool moving from side to side across the wheel to avoid burning the tool and to avoid cutting a groove in the edge of the grinding wheel.
- Use causes the edges of grinding wheels to become misshapen. A wheel dresser may be purchased to true the wheels. Before you attempt to use the dresser, however, read the instructions carefully. Then be sure to wear goggles when dressing the wheels.

METRICS IN HOME MAINTENANCE

As the United States converts to the metric system of measurement, the tools and materials used in home maintenance will be made in metric sizes. You can already find metric measurements on some items. A gallon of paint, for example, is also labeled "3.785 liters." (After conversion, however, paint will probably be sold in 4-liter cans, not 3.785-liter cans.)

Eventually tools, fasteners, lumber, plywood, wallcoverings, and many other items used in home maintenance will be available in metric sizes. Such items as paint, varnish, and cement will be sold in metric units.

At present, however, most of the tools and materials you will use are still made according to the customary measurement system as given in this book. Metric measurements are given wherever they will be useful. The conversion charts on drawings and the tables of metric standards will help you become familiar with the metric system. At the same time, the customary measurements will be practical for actual repair work.

CHECKUP

1. Make a list of the hand tools that you have at home. How does it compare with the list of basic hand tools in this chapter?
2. Check your power tools. Do you have the equipment needed for operating them safely (guards, safety goggles, etc.)?
3. Using the criteria of *need, usefulness,* and *skill,* what tools could you add to your collection?

CHAPTER 2

Care of Tools and Equipment

The care of home maintenance tools and equipment is important to insure successful repair work. Well-maintained tools are also safe tools. For instance, a sharp chisel is less likely to cause injury because it cuts *into* a piece of wood instead of sliding over its surface.

To keep tools in good condition, use them for their proper purpose.

- Do not improvise: a screwdriver should not be used as a chisel or a pry bar. You can't cut through nails in a piece of wood with a crosscut saw without damaging the teeth of the saw.
- Tools should be put away properly after use. Wipe them with an oily cloth and hang them on a tool board, or put them in some other dry storage facility.

REMOVING RUST FROM TOOLS

Tools that have not been properly cared for can be restored in most cases. Cleaning them up, sharpening them, perhaps installing a new handle or some other new part will put them back into workable condition. The first step in restoring a metal tool to a useful condition is removing any rust and dirt.

Rust can be removed from tools with chemical rust removers. These are applied, left on for a specified time, then removed from the metal. The rust, which is loosened, comes off with the chemical. An old toothbrush is helpful for getting the chemical into hard-to-reach areas.

Another way to remove rust from metal is with steel wool or emery cloth, and some turpentine or benzine. The turpentine or benzine on the abrasive helps loosen the dirt and grease and washes off the loose rust removed by the abrasive.

A wire brush attached to an electric drill or grinder will also help loosen rust and will polish the surface of the tool. Wear safety glasses or goggles when using a revolving wire brush, because sometimes rust and pieces of the brush break off and fly around.

SHARPENING EDGED TOOLS

The following tools and supplies are needed to sharpen most of the edged tools used in home maintenance:

- Combination oilstone, 8″ x 2″ x 1″. (One side is rough and the other side is fine.) Fig. 2-1.

2-1. Oilstone and can of light machine oil.

2-2. Tool edge that needs grinding.

2-3a. Grinder with a special jig for grinding plane irons and chisels.

2-3b. Another view of the same grinder.

2-4. Square the cutting edge of the tool on the grinder.

2-5. The proper angle for grinding out the nicks on a chisel.

- Oilcan filled with light machine oil. Fig. 2-1.
- Electric grinder with one coarse aluminum oxide wheel and one medium or one fine wheel.
- Container with water (kept on or near the grinder).
- Piece of scrap soft wood.
- One or two clean rags.

Tool Grinding (Sharpening)

The condition of the tool's edge dictates what step you must first take to restore its cutting ability. Fig. 2-2. If the edge has nicks in it or if the original bevel has been destroyed by improper sharpening, then the tool must be ground until the edge is back to its original shape, with no imperfections.

Most of the grinding you will do freehand; that is, holding the tool to be sharpened, rather than using a jig to hold the tool. The tool rest on the grinder is the only support needed. With some practice you should be able to grind a beveled edge to the proper angle. Steps in grinding an edged tool, such as a woodworking chisel, cold chisel, plane iron (Fig. 2-3), knife or hatchet, are as follows:

1. Square the cutting edge of the tool by placing it on the tool rest and grinding it on the edge of the wheel. Fig. 2-4. Check the results with a combination square. Dip the edge of the tool in water frequently to avoid overheating and possibly drawing the temper (hardness) out of the metal.

2. Adjust the tool rest at the coarse wheel so that you can hold the tool at the proper angle. Fig. 2-5. Hold the tool with both hands comfortably and try out this position before you turn the grinder on.

3. Holding the tool at the proper angle, grind out the nicks. Move the tool constantly from side to side to avoid burning the metal. Fig. 2-6. (If the steel turns blue you have overheated it. Do not forget to dip the tool into water frequently.) Grind the bevel evenly until the tool has a sharp edge and all the nicks are out.

4. For double-edged tools, such as a cold chisel or a hatchet, grind one bevel and then turn the tool over and grind the other bevel to the same angle. Fig. 2-7 (a). Study the original angle of the bevel to make sure that you are not changing the shape of the tool. A cold chisel should have a slightly rounded edge as shown in (b) of Fig. 2-7.

Honing Edged Tools

After the tool has been ground so that the edge is free of nicks, it is *honed*. Fig. 2-8. Sometimes, a tool edge is dull but does not need grinding, so it is honed on an oil-

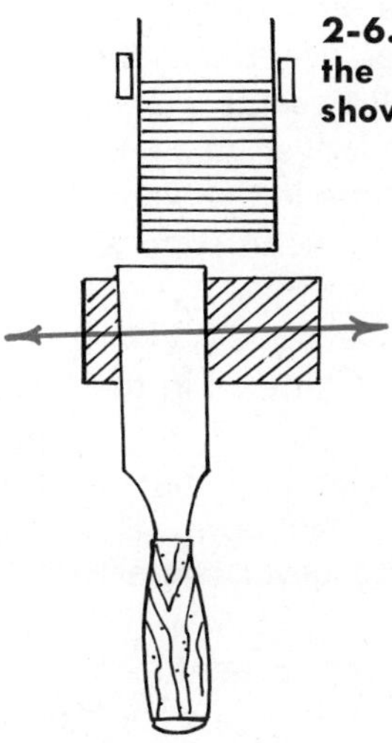

2-6. To avoid overheating the steel, move the tool constantly from side to side, as shown in this top view of the grinding wheel.

2-7. (a) Correct angle for grinding a cold chisel. (b) The slightly rounded edge.

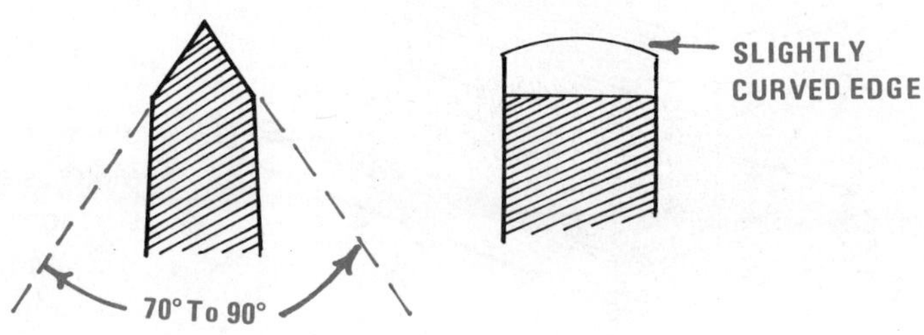

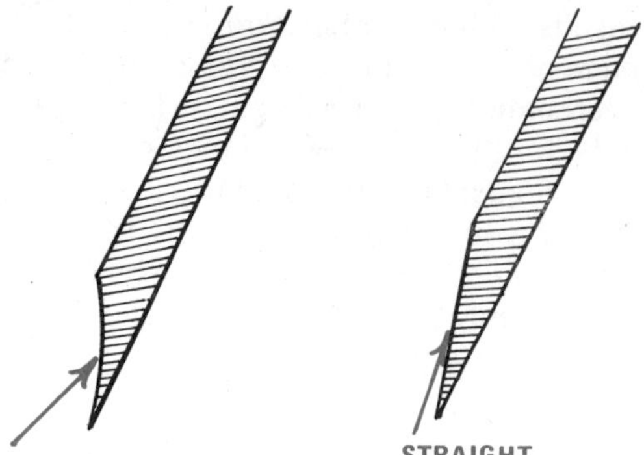

2-8. The proper bevels on wood chisels and plane irons.

2-11. Honing the flat side of a woodworking chisel to remove the wire edge.

2-9. Hold the chisel with both hands. The bevel should be down on the oilstone.

2-10. The back-and-forth and the figure-eight movement for honing a tool on a stone.

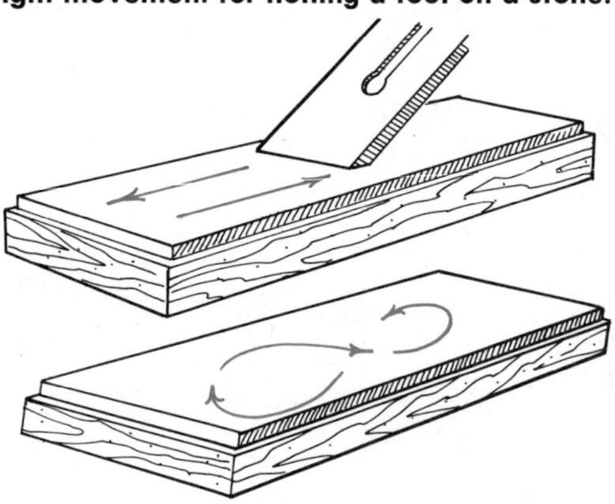

stone. *Honing* means rubbing a steel tool on a sharpening stone (oilstone) until a keen edge is achieved. A few drops of light machine oil are applied to the stone. The oil acts as a lubricant and helps float the tiny pieces of steel out of the stone as the tool is sharpened. If the tool needs a great deal of honing, start on the coarse side of the stone and finish honing on the fine side.

Use the entire surface of the oilstone to avoid wearing a groove in it. After use, wipe the stone with a rag to remove the oil and metal residue. (If you allow this residue to remain on the stone, eventually the surface of the stone will become glazed and clogged, and it will no longer do a good cutting job.) Store the stone in a covered box.

Honing a tool to get a keen edge is done as follows:

1. Make sure that the stone is clean. Put a few drops of light machine oil in the middle of the stone.

2. Grasp the tool with both hands and place it on the stone, bevel down. Fig. 2-9. Make sure that all the bevel contacts the surface of the stone.

3. Move the tool over the entire stone, spreading the oil. Use a back-and-forth or a

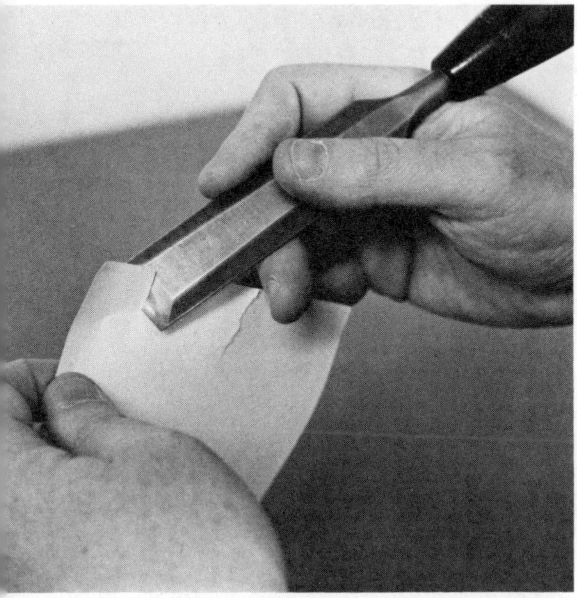

2-12. Testing a chisel for sharpness with a piece of paper.

2-13. Slicing into a piece of soft wood to remove a wire edge.

figure-eight movement, with only light pressure. Fig. 2-10. Keep the tool bevel in contact with the stone. It will take some practice to keep from rocking or changing the angle of the bevel. Add a few more drops of oil if the stone becomes dry.

4. Check the bevel of the tool to see if the edge is sharp, and that the bevel angle has not been changed. When you have completed the honing of the tool on the fine side of the oilstone, the cutting edge will have a wire edge on it.

5. If the tool has only one bevel, as in the case of a woodworking chisel or a plane iron, turn it over on the flat side and rub it on the fine side of the stone two or three times. Fig. 2-11. Then reverse it to the beveled side and hone it two or three times. Repeat until the wire edge is worn off. Test the sharpness of the tool by trying to slice the edge of a piece of paper. Fig. 2-12.

Another way of removing the thin wire edge is by slicing into a piece of soft wood with the tool. The wire edge will remain in the wood. Fig. 2-13. This is done after honing both the beveled and the flat side of the tool once or twice.

6. If a tool, such as a hatchet, has two bevels, hone both bevels equally. Hone on the coarse, then on the fine side of the oilstone. Fig. 2-14. The wire edge will be worn off when the second bevel is honed.

2-14. Correct shape of a hatchet bevel.

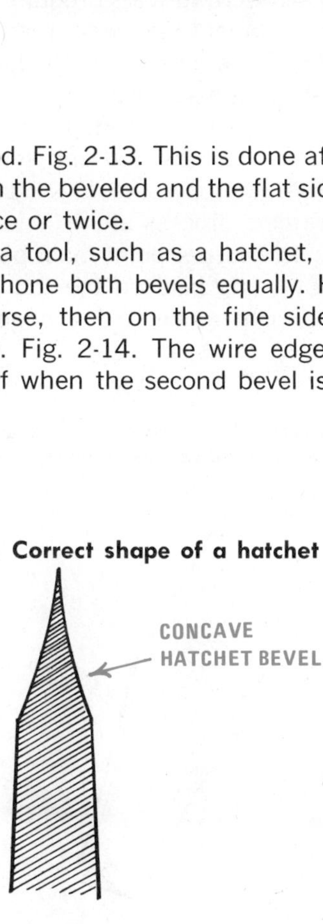

REMOVING A MUSHROOMED HEAD FROM A COLD CHISEL OR A CENTER PUNCH

With usage, the head of a cold chisel or a center punch may become spread out, or mushroomed, from hammer blows. Fig. 2-15. Because such a misshapen head is dangerous (some of the metal can fly off when hit with a hammer) it should be restored to its original shape. Use the coarse wheel on your grinder to shape a bevel on the head of the tool.

2-15. Mushroomed head on a cold chisel.

SHAPING SCREWDRIVER POINTS

Screwdrivers with standard blades are usually the only type that can be sharpened in the home workshop. Other kinds, such as Phillips-head screwdrivers, require special grinding equipment that is not readily available for the home. The grinder is the correct tool for shaping a screwdriver.

A screwdriver point needs reshaping because it becomes rounded and sometimes nicked from improper use. Fig. 2-16. Steps in the grinding process are:

1. The screwdriver point must be ground straight by being held on the tool rest exactly at a right angle to the edge of the wheel. Fig. 2-17. Use the fine or medium wheel and grind off as little metal as possible. Look to make sure that the end of the point is square.

2. Grind the sides of the point so that they are parallel to one another. Adjust the rest on the grinder so that you can hold the screwdriver against the wheel to obtain this parallel shape. Fig. 2-18. Both sides must be ground equally until the point is the right thickness to fit a screw slot. Use another

2-16. A screwdriver point in poor condition. Notice the rounded corners and the nick in the edge.

2-17. Grinding a screwdriver point straight across by holding it at right angles to the wheel.

screwdriver of the same size for a model, or, if one is not available, use a screw to test the thickness of the newly shaped point. Make sure the point fits squarely into the screw slot. Fig. 2-19. If it does not, it will slip and chew up the head of the screw.

2-18. Holding the screwdriver on the tool rest so that the sides of the point can be ground parallel to one another.

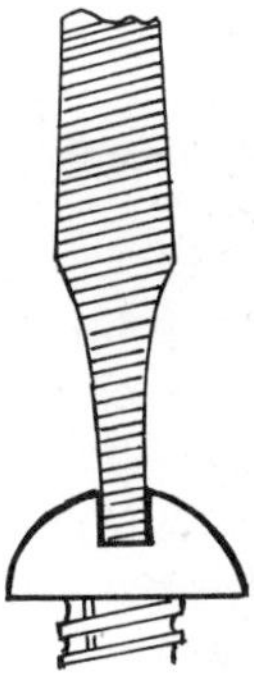

2-19. A screwdriver point should fit properly into a screw slot.

SHARPENING AUGER BITS

An auger bit should stay sharp for a long time if it is stored in a protective case between uses. Also, to protect the bit when boring into a piece of wood, make sure the bit does not come in contact with a nail or any other metal which would dull the cutting edges or break the feed screw (point). A light coat of oil after use will keep an auger bit from getting rusty.

To sharpen an auger bit, you need either a 6″ three-cornered file or an auger-bit file. Fig. 2-20. Of the two, the auger-bit file is better for the job because it is designed specifically to get into the small spaces on a bit. Spurs (scoring nibs) and cutting lips are the only parts that can be sharpened. Fig. 2-21. If the feed screw is damaged, the bit will not pull itself into the wood to begin boring, and is therefore useless.

To sharpen spurs:

1. Hold the auger bit against a solid object, such as the edge of a table, with the feed screw pointing up.

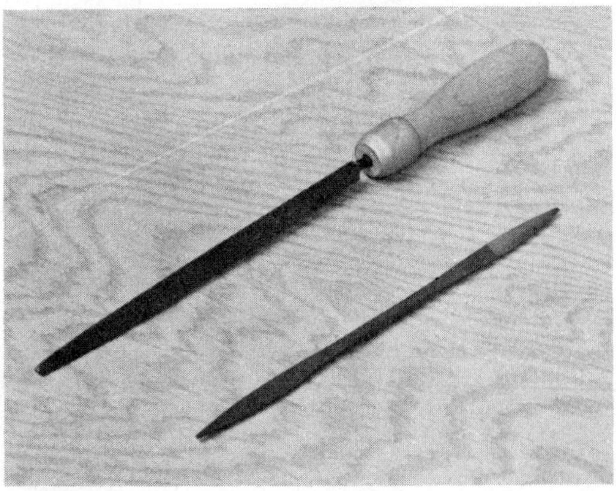

2-20. A 6″, three-cornered file with a handle, and an auger-bit file.

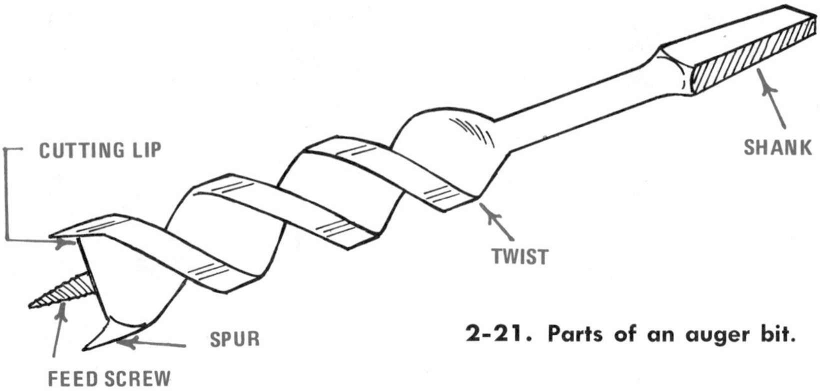

2-21. Parts of an auger bit.

2. File the inside surfaces of the spurs, first one, then the other. Fig. 2-22. Check them with your finger for sharpness along the top and the edges. File off as little metal as possible, keeping the spurs to their original shape. Both spurs should be the same length.

Cutting lips are easier to sharpen because they are flat.

1. Hold the auger bit down on a solid surface with the feed screw facing down. The bevel on each cutting lip is now facing up. File each bevel to a chisel-like edge. Fig. 2-23. Be sure to file the same amount on both lips so that they will cut into the surface of a piece of wood on the same level.

2. Check the edges with your finger carefully to be sure that they are sharp. Any wire edge that is formed will be removed when you use the auger bit again.

2-22. Sharpening spurs with an auger-bit file.

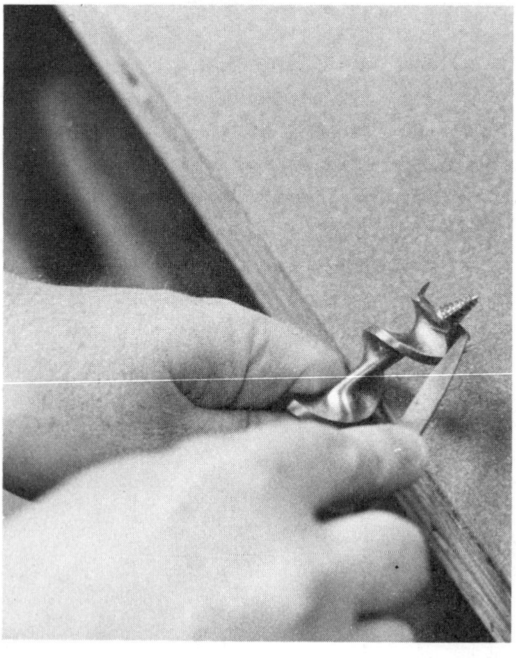

2-23. Filing a chisel-like edge on the cutting lips of a bit.

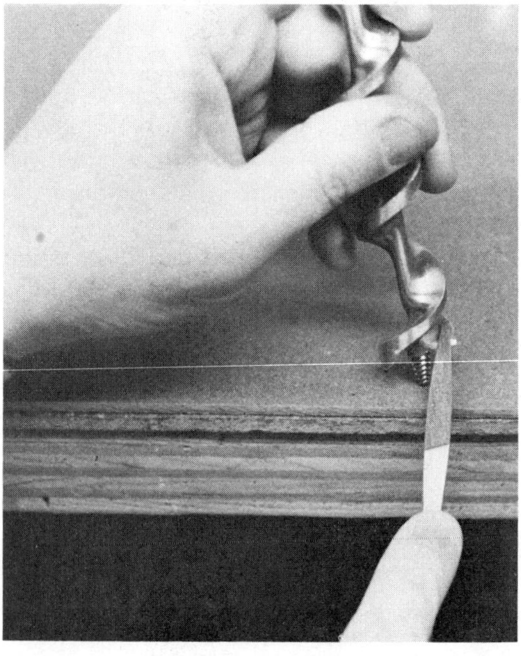

SHARPENING TWIST DRILLS

When the cutting edges of a twist drill are dull and the bit will no longer cut through the material you are drilling, it is time to regrind the drill bit. This may be done with a drill-sharpening attachment on a grinder, or it can be done freehand. Most of you will probably use the latter method.

The cutting edges of a twist drill are ground at 59 degrees. Both edges must make the same angle with the *axis* (an imaginary line which runs through the center of the drill). Fig. 2-24. The cutting edge has a 12-degree clearance behind it, as shown in the diagram. Failure to grind the drill to these specifications will result in poor cutting, and the drill will probably break. Cutting edges must be the same length so that the drilled hole will not be enlarged or distorted.

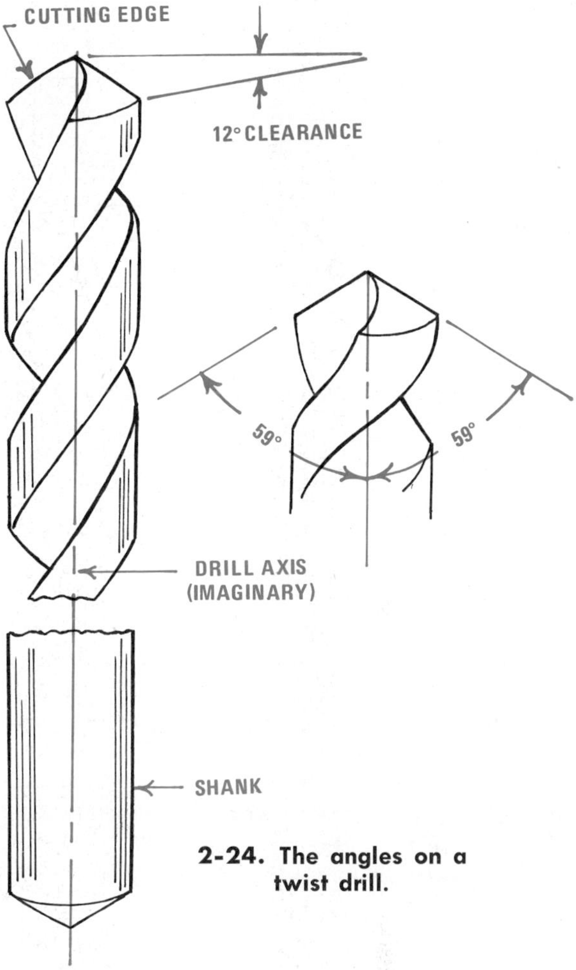

2-24. The angles on a twist drill.

Grinder Method

The drill bit is one of the most difficult tools to sharpen, requiring some practice before you can do it easily and properly. Drill-sharpening attachments for grinders are available. Use the medium wheel on the grinder and follow instructions that come with the attachment.

Freehand Method

These are the steps for freehand grinding of a twist drill:

1. Fill the water container and place it near the grinder. Adjust the tool rest on the medium wheel so that you can place your hand on it to hold the drill in position.

2. Hold the twist drill between the thumb and fingers of your hand, as shown. Fig. 2-25. (The other hand holds the shank of the drill. The hand holding the drill nearest its tip is the one that is placed on the tool rest.)

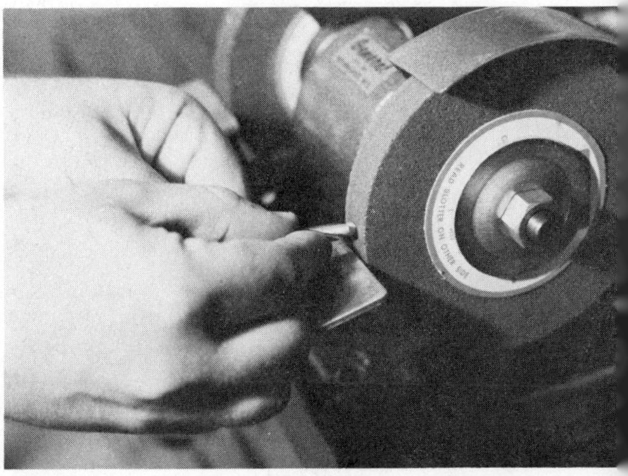

2-25. Holding a twist drill against the grinding wheel.

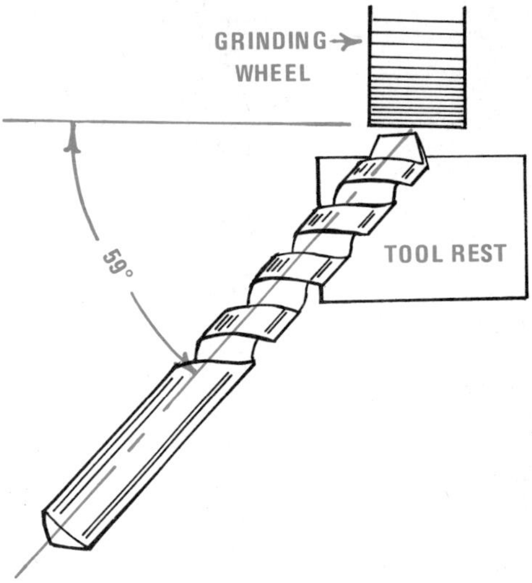

2-26. Top view of grinding wheel, showing the center axis of the drill making a 59-degree angle with the edge of the wheel.

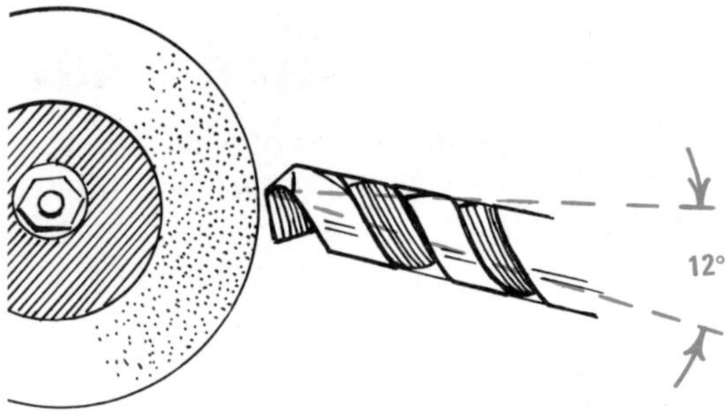

2-27. The end of the drill is 12 degrees lower than the cutting edge when grinding.

3. The center axis of the drill should make an angle of approximately 59 degrees with the edge of the grinding wheel. Fig. 2-26. The end of the drill shank should be slightly lower than the cutting edge—about 12 degrees lower—to give the drill clearance, as shown in Fig. 2-27.

4. Carefully place the end of the drill against the grinding wheel so that one cutting edge is horizontal and making contact with the revolving wheel. Slowly lower the shank end toward the wheel, twisting the drill clockwise in your fingers at the same time. Fig. 2-28. Use light pressure, dipping the drill in water after each pass on the wheel to avoid overheating. Fig. 2-29.

5. Turn the drill over so that the other cutting edge is horizontal, and repeat the procedure. Make the same number of passes on the grinding wheel for each edge. Count them as you make them. Unless a drill is in very bad condition, two or three passes should be sufficient to make its edges sharp.

6. Check the accuracy of your grinding by comparing the drill's shape with that of a new one. The cutting edges must be the same length, at the proper angle, and the edge must have a clearance of 12 degrees.

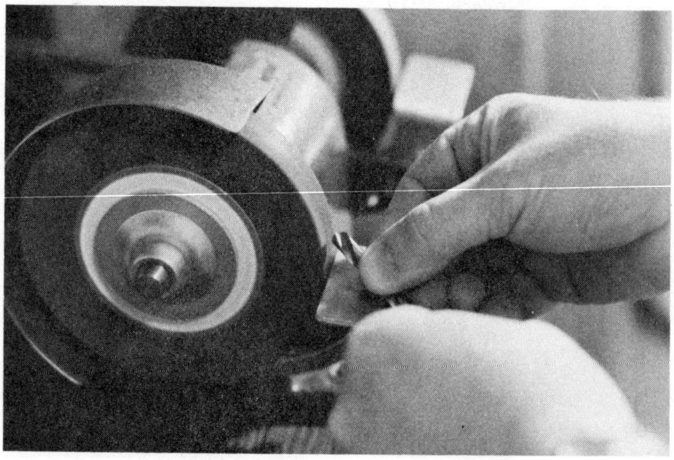

2-28. Lower the shank, twisting the drill clockwise against the moving grinding wheel.

2-29. Dipping the drill in water to prevent overheating.

SAW SHARPENING

Sharpening of handsaws and circular-saw blades by hand requires special tools and considerable skill. It is a tedious job, one that is probably best done by a professional who has a saw-filing machine. A saw sharpening service will *set* the teeth (bend them so that alternate teeth are slightly out to the right or left) and resharpen saws perfectly. Cost is rather nominal compared to the work required for you to do the job yourself, by hand. If some teeth are broken on the saw, a sharpening service can cut an entirely new set of teeth on it.

REPLACING A HAMMER HANDLE

A broken hammer handle can be replaced and the hammer restored to use. A cracked handle should also be replaced because it could break during use. The tools necessary for this operation are:

- Woodworking vise.
- Electric drill.
- 10″ rasp or coarse file.
- 8″ flat second-cut file.
- Solid or drift punch.
- Wooden mallet.
- Hacksaw with blade.
- ½″ wood chisel.
- Hammer.

The steps in replacing a hammer handle are as follows:

1. To remove the broken handle from the hammer head, clamp the head in a vise. With a hacksaw, saw off the old handle close to the head. Fig. 2-30. (A hacksaw is best for

2-30. Saw off the broken handle close to the hammer head with a hacksaw.

2-31. Drill two holes in the old handle.

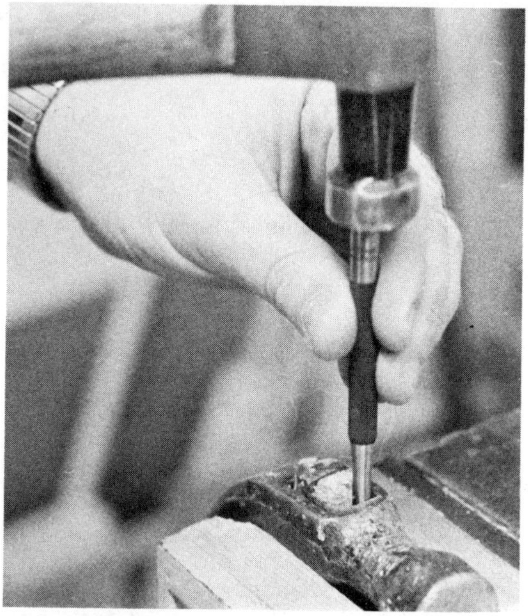

2-33. Drive out the metal wedges and the remaining parts of the old handle with a solid punch.

this job since you don't have to worry about damaging the saw teeth if you touch the neck of the hammer.)

2. Drill a couple of holes in that portion of the old handle that remains in the eye of the hammer, (the hollow part in the head through which the handle fits). Fig. 2-31. Drive the metal wedges out with a punch. Fig. 2-32. (Save them because they can be used again.) Drive out the remaining pieces of the handle with a solid punch or a piece of metal rod. Fig. 2-33.

3. Obtain a new handle to fit the hammer head. Fig. 2-34. Handles are available for any size hammer (by weight), and any type, such as a ball-peen, claw, or tack hammer. Some handles come with a hardwood wedge and two metal wedges. With others, the wedges are sold separately.

4. The end of the new handle has to be shaped to fit the eye of the hammer. This is done with a rasp or a coarse file. Fig. 2-35. First insert the handle into the hammer to see whether it fits. To test for fit, drive the handle into the head lightly with a mallet. Fig. 2-36. When you remove the handle, check any marks made by the eye of the hammer for locations where material must be shaved off. Always take the same amount off each side so that the handle will go into the hammer straight.

Stanley Tools

2-32. A solid punch.

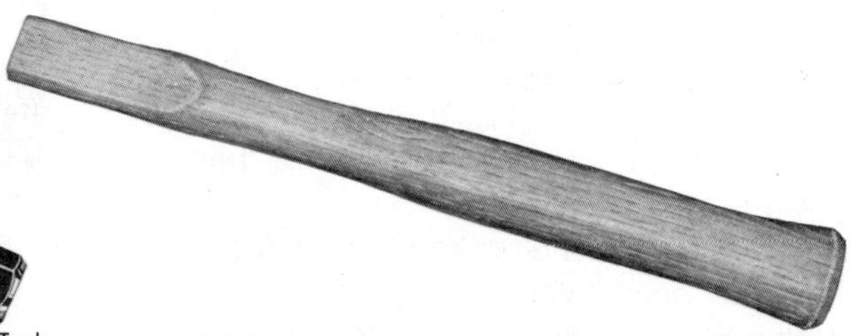

Stanley Tools

2-34. A new claw-hammer handle.

2-35. Shaping the new hammer handle to fit, using a rasp.

5. When the handle has been shaped properly, it is driven into the head for a tight fit. Strike the end of the handle with a mallet to seat it properly. Don't hit the end of the handle with a hammer or you may splinter it. Look to make sure the handle is in the head straight, not leaning to one side.

6. If part of the handle projects above the top of the hammer head, saw off the excess with a hacksaw. Fig. 2-37. With a wood chisel, cut slits in the top for wedges. Fig. 2-38. Insert the wedges in the new han-

2-36. Inserting the new handle into the eye of the hammer to check the fit.

2-37. Sawing off the part of the handle that protrudes above the top of the hammer head.

dle the same way they were put into the old handle. A hardwood wedge goes down the center, with the two metal wedges at right angles to it. Drive the wedges in so that the tops are level with the handle top. Fig. 2-39.

7. File the top of the handle to make it level with the top of the hammer head. Use a second-cut file. Fig. 2-40. Wedges and handle should be smooth. Fig. 2-41.

If the handle on an old hammer feels loose, drive the wedges down a little with a punch. If this does not help, soak the hammer in a pail of water overnight. The wooden handle will swell and tighten up. If the handle is so loose that a wedge falls out, replace it with a larger wedge.

2-38. Cutting slits in the top of the handle for wedges, using a wood chisel and a hammer.

2-39. Driving in the new metal wedges with a hammer.

The same procedure for replacing a hammer handle can be used to replace a hatchet or an ax handle. If you are doing this repair at home, be sure to buy the right handle for the tool. If in doubt about which to buy, take the tool to the hardware store when you shop for a new handle.

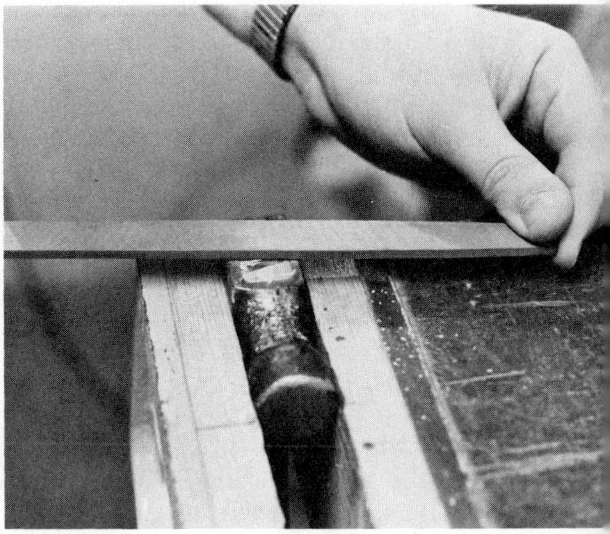

2-40. Filing the excess from the handle and the wedges until they are smooth and level with the top of the hammer head.

2-41. The completed job, showing the placement of the wedges in the new handle.

CARING FOR POWER TOOLS

Periodically all power tools should be wiped clean with a rag to remove all sawdust, dirt, and grease. Remove rust on bare metal parts with steel wool or fine emery cloth. To protect a circular-saw table from rust, and to make it easier to slide lumber on it, coat the table with paste wax and buff it. Coating the shoe or baseplate of a saber saw or a portable circular saw with wax allows the tool to move more easily over wood and offers protection against rust.

Check lubrication specifications in the tool manufacturer's instructions. Some machines with sealed bearings never need to be lubricated.

Make sure saw blades are sharp. If a circular-saw blade needs to be sharpened, take it to the nearest saw-sharpening service. All blades should be free of rust and dirt. Keep them lightly oiled to protect them when they are not being used.

Inspect the electric cords on all machines. If you notice a break in the insulation on the cord, tape it with electrical tape. Fig. 2-42. If a plug is broken or looks faulty, replace it with the proper plug.

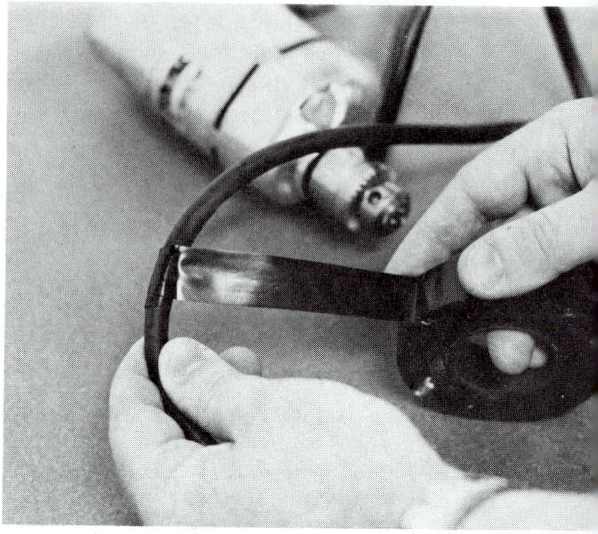

2-42. Using plastic electrical tape to repair a break in the insulation of a portable drill power cord.

CHECKUP

1. Why is it important to take good care of your tools?
2. Check your tools. Are any of them in need of sharpening, cleaning, or repairs?
3. What should you do to keep power tools in good condition?

CHAPTER 3

Plumbing Repairs

This chapter deals with simple plumbing repairs you can make in the home. Serious problems, such as pipe breakage, should be taken care of by a plumber. New fixtures and additions to the plumbing system should be installed by a plumber. Four basic plumbing tools you will find necessary for home maintenance are:

- Clean-out auger, or plumber's snake. Fig. 3-1.
- Plunger, or force cup.
- Hex wrench, or adjustable locknut wrench. Figs. 3-2, 3-3.
- Faucet reseating tool. Fig. 3-4.

These tools, together with a screwdriver and an adjustable open-end wrench (Fig. 3-5), will be all you need to complete the repairs described in this chapter.

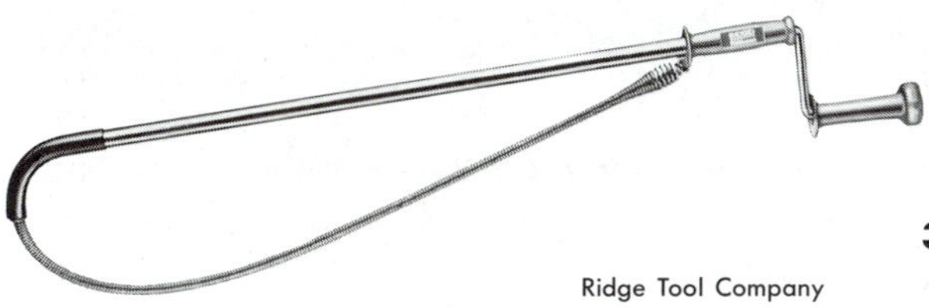

Ridge Tool Company

3-1. A clean-out auger.

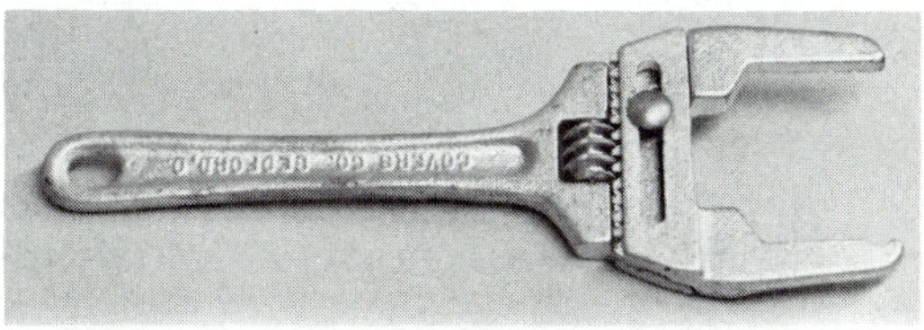

3-3. An adjustable locknut wrench.

3-2. A hex wrench.

Ridge Tool Company

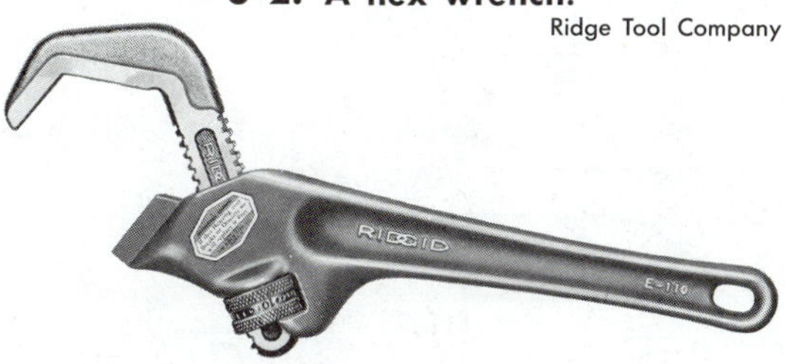

3-4. One type of faucet reseating tool, with extra cutters.

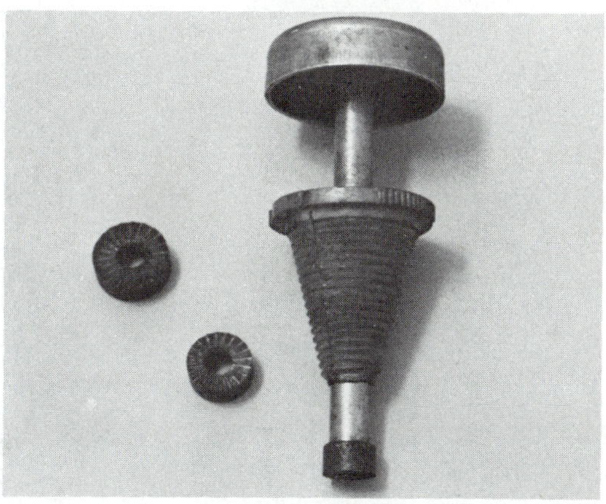

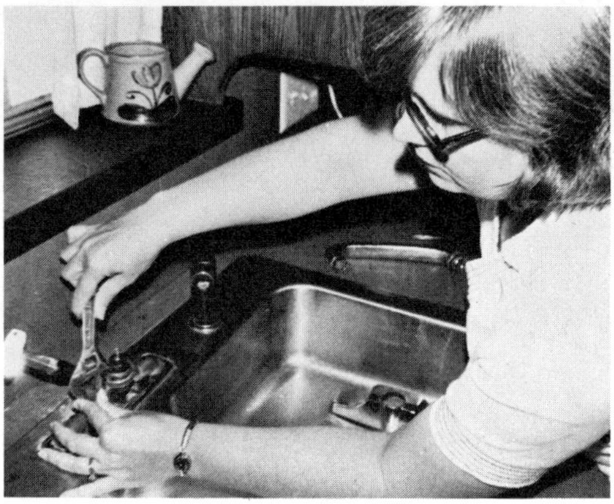

Oklahoma Industrial Arts News
Photograph by Emmett Osgood
3-5. An adjustable open-end wrench is one of the tools you will need for plumbing repairs.

REPAIRING A LEAKY FAUCET

The modern faucet, also called a compression faucet, is found on sinks, laundry tubs, bathtubs, showers, and outside hose connections. Fig. 3-6. When the faucet drips or operates poorly, one of three problems exists:

- The washer needs to be replaced. (The faucet drips and makes vibrating noises.)
- The packing must be replaced. (Water escapes around the faucet stem.)
- The faucet needs reseating. (Replacing the washer does not stop the dripping, or the washer wears out in a very short time.)

Note: Washerless faucets are difficult to repair. When they fail to operate properly, a plumber should be consulted.

3-6. Sectional view of a compression faucet. Notice the relationship between the washer and the seat.

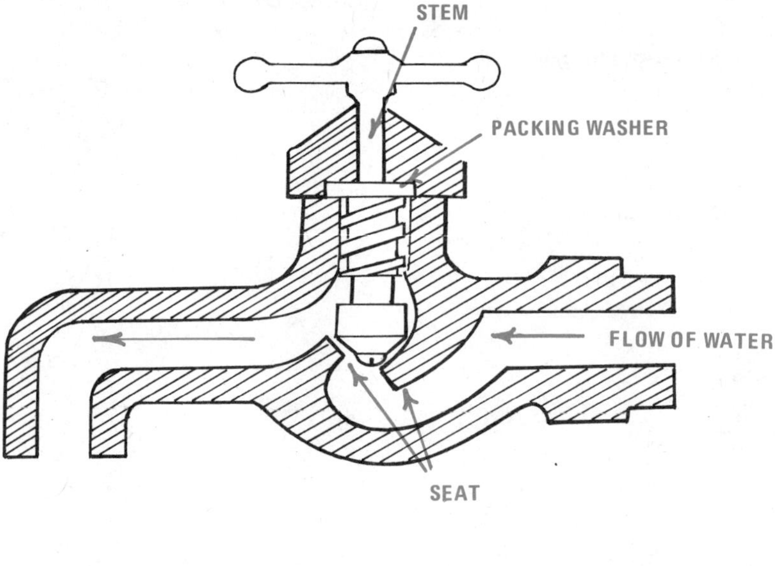

Replacing a Washer

An assortment of faucet washers should be kept in the workshop. When you replace a faucet washer, be sure to put back the same size and shape washer (beveled or flat) that was removed from the faucet. Neoprene, or rubber, washers, available in hardware stores, can be used for both hot and cold water faucets.

These steps must be followed to replace a faucet washer:

1. Close the shut-off valve that controls the flow of water to the faucet. If the faucet does not have an individual shut-off valve, turn off the main cold-water valve in the basement or utility room.

2. Remove the handle from the faucet stem. It is held on the stem by a screw which may be hidden by a decorative metal cover. Pry the cover out of its recess in the handle with a small screwdriver to get to the screw. Figs. 3-7 through 3-9. On some outside faucets the handle is wedged onto the stem. To remove the handle, tap it underneath with a wrench. Remove the cap nut from the faucet by turning it counterclockwise with an adjustable open-end wrench. Fig. 3-10. You can cover the cap nut with adhesive tape to protect the metal from becoming scratched by the wrench.

3-7. Pry the decorative cover out of its recess in the handle of the faucet.

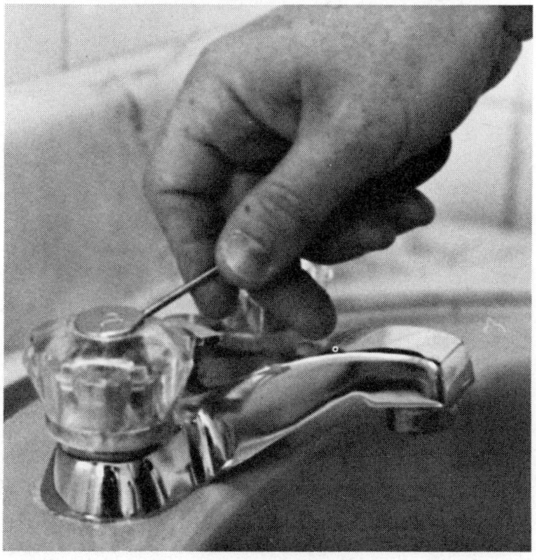

3-8. Remove the handle from the faucet stem by loosening the screw that holds it in place.

3-9. Lift off the handle.

3-10. Loosen the cap nut and the stem from the faucet by turning it counterclockwise with an adjustable open-end wrench.

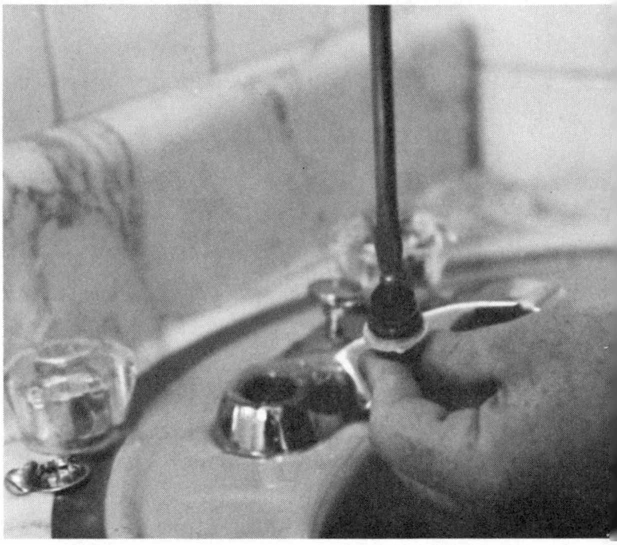

3-12. Use a screwdriver to remove the bib screw that holds the old washer in place.

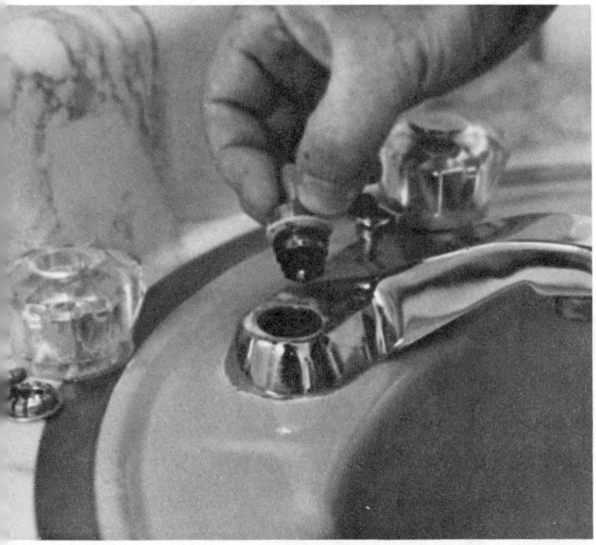

3-11. Remove the cap nut and the stem with your fingers.

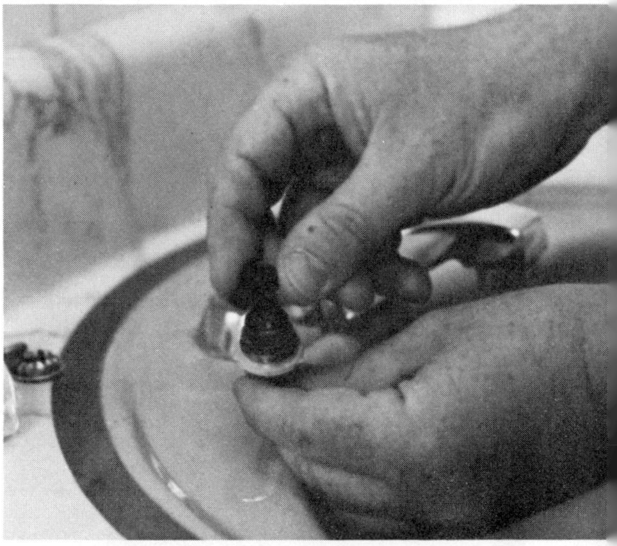

3-13. Put a washer into the recessed seat on the end of the stem and replace the bib screw.

3. If the cap nut is not part of the stem, unscrew the stem from the faucet body by turning it counterclockwise until it is free. Fig. 3-11. The washer is held in its seat at the end of the stem by a brass bib screw.

4. If the washer is worn—that is, if the faucet seat has cut into the washer and reduced it in size—use a screwdriver to remove the bib screw that holds the washer in place. Fig. 3-12. Remove the washer and check the size marked on it. Select a new washer of the same size and shape (beveled

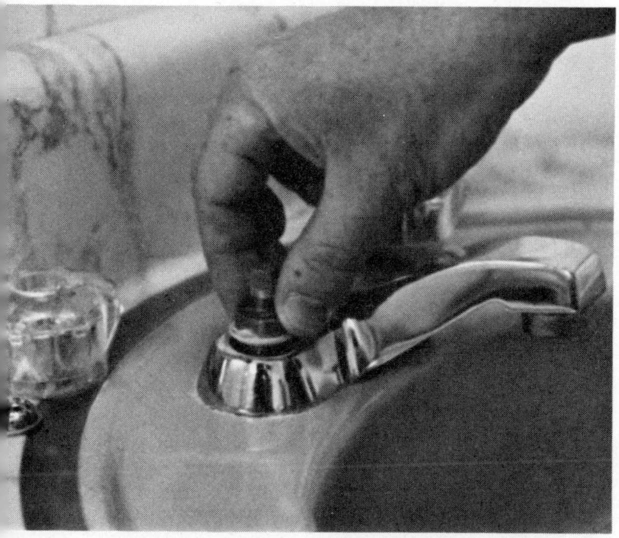

3-14. Put faucet parts back in place when the repair has been completed.

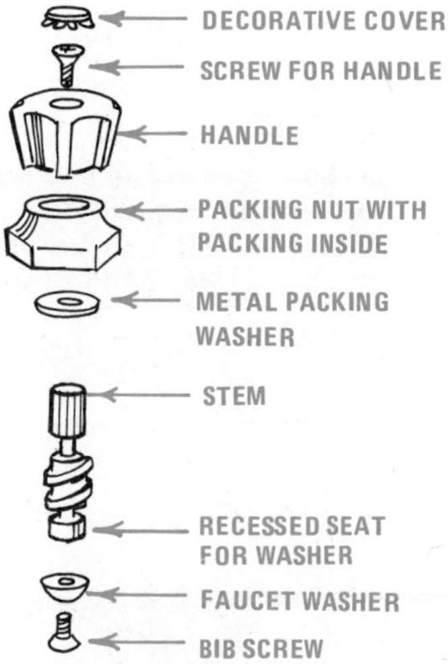

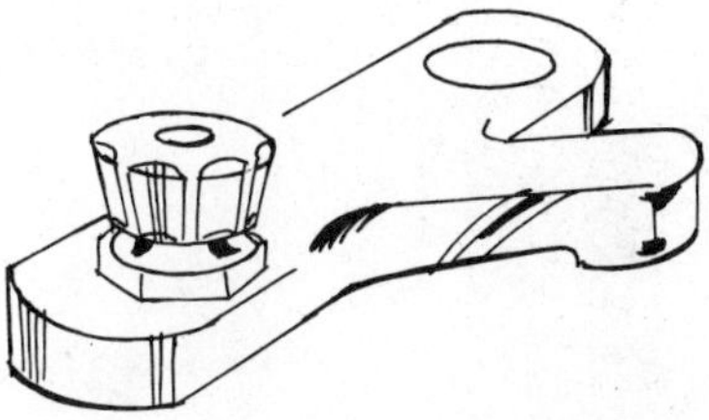

3-15. Parts of a typical compression faucet.

or flat) from the supply of washers and place it on the stem. Place the side with the size marked on it against the seat of the stem. If you do not see the size marked on the old washer, compare diameters of the old and new washers. Test the fit of the new one by putting it into the recessed seat on the end of the stem. Fig. 3-13. If the bib screw is broken or partially worn, replace it with a new screw. (These can be bought wherever washers are sold.) If the bib screw breaks before you get it out, cut away the washer around the remaining part. Use a pair of pliers to grab the shank of the screw and turn it out.

5. After installing the new washer, put back the stem, cap nut, handle, and the decorative metal cover. Fig. 3-14. Tighten the cap nut with the wrench just enough so the water will not leak from under it. Over-tightening will strip the threads. (Be sure to put the decorative cover back on the proper faucet; the one marked HOT on the hot-water faucet, for example.) When all parts have been replaced, turn on the water valve. Check to see that the faucet is operating properly and that the dripping has stopped. Fig. 3-15.

Replacing Faucet Packing

If water is leaking out around the stem of the faucet, the packing in the cap nut must be replaced. Several varieties of stem packing can be bought in small coils. Two or three turns of this coiled packing around the stem under the packing nut (cap nut) will compress into a solid packing when the nut is tightened. The following steps explain how to replace the packing on a faucet.

1. Turn off the valve that controls the flow of water to the faucet.

2. Remove the faucet handle first, then the cap nut (as explained in the section dealing with replacing a washer). Fig. 3-16. Slip the cap nut off the stem to find the packing. Some faucets have a metal packing washer on top of the packing that helps to compress it. Fig. 3-17. You do not have to remove this washer unless it has to be replaced because of damage.

3-16. Loosen the cap nut on an outside faucet with an adjustable open-end wrench. The faucet handle can be used to turn the stem out of the faucet body.

3-17. Cap nut and the packing washer on the faucet stem.

3-18. Wrap two or three turns of coiled packing around the stem. Then cut the portion used from the rest of the coil.

3-19. Using a faucet reseating tool. The handle, cap nut, and stem have been removed.

3. Pull out the remains of the old packing and replace it with two or three turns of coiled packing around the stem. Cut off the rest of the coil. Fig. 3-18. Replace the cap nut on the stem and tighten it in place. Then put the handle back and tighten the screw that holds it. If there is a decorative cover over the handle screw, replace it. Turn on the water valve and check for leaks around the stem.

Reseating a Faucet

As shown in the faucet diagram (Fig. 3-6), the washer makes contact with the faucet seat as the stem is turned down. If the seat is corroded or rough, it will wear away the faucet washer very fast and cut it up so that the faucet will begin to drip. Some faucets have removable seats which, by using a special tool, can be taken out of the faucet body and replaced. If the seat cannot be removed, an inexpensive faucet reseating tool can be used to cut the metal seat so that it is smooth once more. The reseating of a faucet is done as follows:

1. Turn off the shut-off valve for that faucet.

2. Take the faucet apart (as explained in the section on replacing a washer). Do not remove the washer or the bib screw.

3. After the stem is removed, examine the seat of the faucet inside the faucet body. If the seat is rough, it must be resurfaced or smoothed with a reseating tool or seat dresser. Fig. 3-19. (There are many varieties of reseating tools. Each comes with its own particular directions for use.) Basically, the tool is screwed onto the top of the faucet body in place of the cap nut, with the cutter on the end of the tool stem pressed against the faucet seat. The handle on top of the tool is turned so that the cutter removes metal from the seat. Be careful to remove very little metal. Take off just enough to leave the surface smooth.

4. Remove the reseating tool and reassemble the faucet. Turn the shut-off valve on again and test the faucet for drips.

TOILET-TANK REPAIRS

If the parts of a toilet tank do not function properly, the tank will overfill, water will be wasted, and you will hear the continuous noise of the water trickling through the overflow pipe or outlet valve in the tank.

All of the parts in the toilet tank can be replaced if necessary. Fig. 3-20. Some replacements are difficult and require a plumber to do the work, but there are a few repairs that you can make yourself. Spare parts are available at hardware and plumbing supply stores.

Repairing the Intake Valve System

1. Remove the lid of the toilet tank. If the water in the tank is so high that it is flowing over the top of the overflow pipe, (Fig. 3-20) something is wrong with the intake valve system.

2. A plastic or metal float ball floats on top of the water at the end of a rod. Fig. 3-21. The ball closes the intake valve when it is raised to the water's highest point in the tank.

If the float develops a leak and some water gets inside, the ball will not float high enough to close the intake valve. To check it for leaks, unscrew it from the rod and shake it to hear if there is water inside. If there is, replace the float ball with a new one. The new one will screw onto the rod just as the old one did. If the rod is bent or corroded, replace that too.

If the ball is all right and it is just riding too high on the water, bending the rod (float-ball arm) downward a little will lower the water level in the tank.

3. If float ball replacement is unnecessary, or if a new one does not stop the water

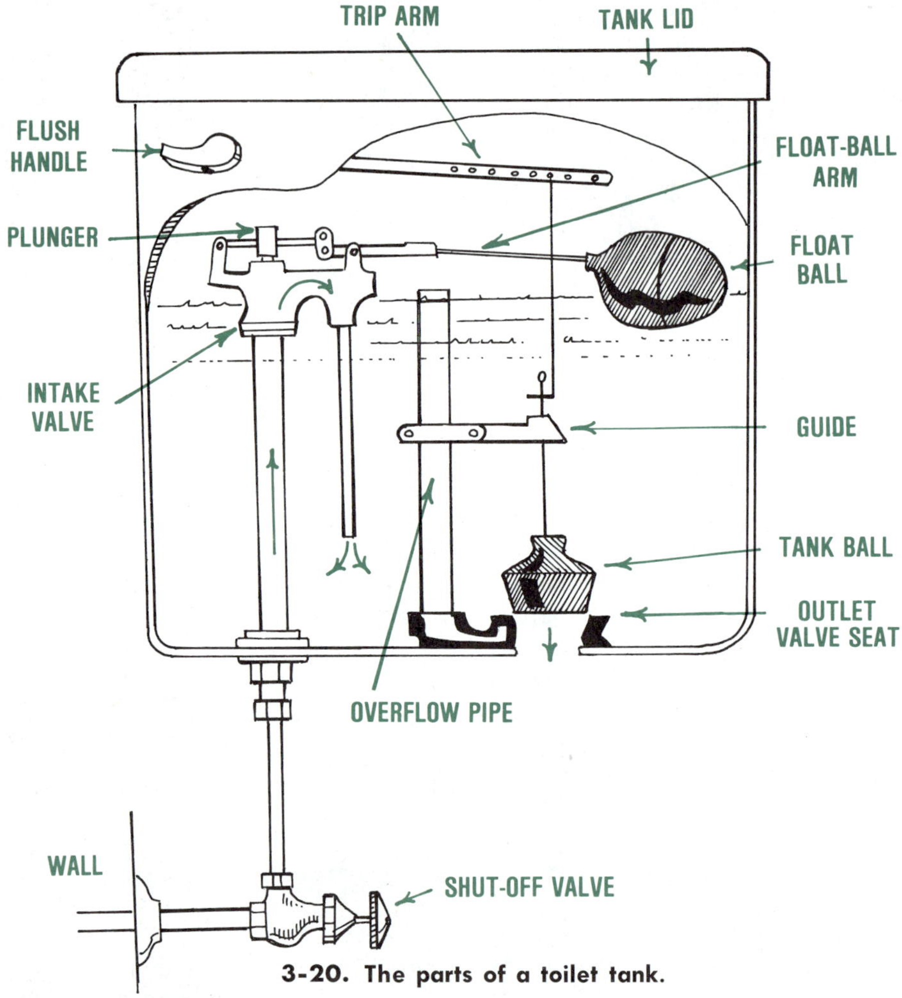

3-20. The parts of a toilet tank.

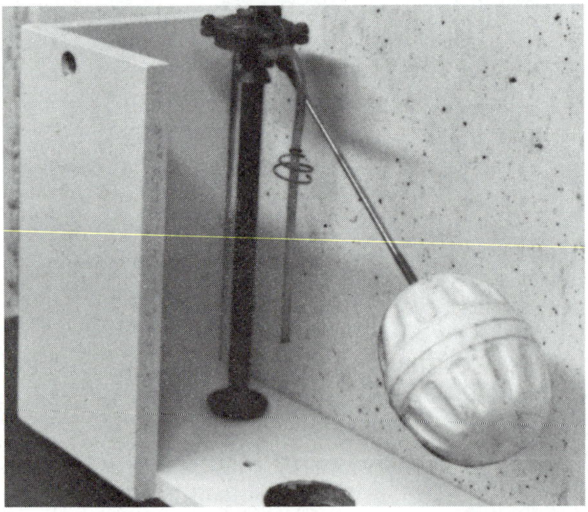

3-21. An intake valve system in a toilet tank, showing the intake valve, the float-ball arm, and the float ball.

overflow, the next step is to check the intake valve itself. The valve contains a washer which fits against a seat to shut off the flow of water. The washer is held in place by a screw at the end of the plunger on top of the valve. On many intake valves the washer is easy to replace. Before you do this, however, turn off the water with the shut-off valve located beneath the toilet tank. If you do not have such a valve, turn off the main cold-water valve. To empty the tank so that you can work, flush the toilet. The tank will not refill with the valve turned off.

4. Check the float arm and the levers that move the plunger in the intake valve to see that they are operating properly. Disconnect these and lift the plunger out of the intake valve carefully. Remove the washer from the end of the plunger with a screwdriver. Replace the washer as described in the section dealing with faucet repair. Be sure to replace the washer with one of the same size and shape. If the valve seat below the washer is rough, it cannot be resurfaced with a reseating tool. Have a plumber replace the entire intake valve.

Repairing the Outlet Valve

If the toilet tank never seems to fill up and stop running, the trouble could be the outlet valve. That repair problem is corrected in the following way.

1. Check the rubber tank ball that closes the outlet opening in the tank bottom. Fig. 3-20. After a time this tank ball becomes deformed and waterlogged so that it does not work properly. If this ball does not sit directly on the valve seat, water will continuously escape through that valve.

2. Check all the parts that lift the tank ball (Fig. 3-22): the flush handle on the outside of the tank, the trip arm to which it is connected, the lift rods (one of which is screwed into the top of the ball), and the guide for the lift rod which keeps the rod straight and the tank ball in the proper place. (On some toilet tanks the tank ball is raised with a chain connected to the trip arm.) These parts must all work smoothly. If one or more do not, replace them. Adjust the guide if the lift rod is out of line. Clean with steel wool any part that is covered with grit or is beginning to corrode.

3. If the outlet valve still allows water to trickle out of the tank into the toilet bowl after you have checked all the parts, replace the old tank ball with a new one. First, turn off the water. Flush all the water out of the tank. Unscrew the old tank ball from the lift rod and replace it. Replace the lift rod, too, if it is badly bent or corroded.

4. If the rim of the valve seat is corroded and roughened the tank ball will not seat itself well. When you replace the tank ball, clean the rim with some steel wool or fine emery cloth to make it smooth again. Turn on the water and flush the toilet a few times to see that it is working properly.

3-22. An outlet valve system, showing the flush handle, lift rods, guide for the rods, tank ball, and seat for the tank ball. See also Fig. 3-20.

CLEARING CLOGGED PLUMBING FIXTURES AND DRAINS

An outgoing water system takes waste water from sinks, bathtubs, and other fixtures out of a house into septic tanks or sewers. The plumbing system within a building contains a number of traps which prevent sewer gases (emitted from decaying materials) from entering the house through sink and tub drains. These traps also allow access to the various pipes in a drainage system in case an object becomes lodged in it beyond the drains.

There are two types of traps: external and internal. The external trap is not a part of the fixture. A sink, for example, has a trap located underneath. An internal trap is located inside the fixture itself, as in the case of a toilet bowl.

The external trap is a curved piece of pipe, sometimes containing a clean-out plug which can be removed. Fig. 3-23. The trap may be in the shape of an *S* or a *P*. It traps solid material and also retains some water. The water acts as a seal to keep out sewer gases. Water can move through the trap, but since some water always remains in it, gases cannot back up into the drainpipe from the septic tank or sewer.

Cleaning an Exterior Trap That Has a Clean-Out Plug

1. Put a pail under the clean-out plug. As soon as you loosen the plug with a wrench, the water in the trap will pour out into the pail. Remove the plug. Solid material that is clogging the drain should fall out. You may need an adjustable locknut wrench or a hex wrench to open the plug if your open-end wrench will not fit. *Caution:* If a chemical drain cleaner was used in trying to clear the drain, some of the chemical may still be present in the water and debris that pours out of the trap. Be careful that this material does not get on your skin or clothing. Do not use a metal pail.

2. Use a piece of stiff wire, such as a bent coat hanger, to scrape out any of the solid material that remains in the trap. To see if the trap is clear, run a little water from the sink into the drain before reinserting the plug. The water should come through the clean-out plug opening into the pail underneath. If the obstruction is farther along in the pipe (past the trap), you can use the clean-out opening as an access to the pipe. Put a clean-out auger into the trap and run it through the pipe.

3. Replace the plug. Be careful not to injure the threads. If there is a washer, remember to put it back too. If the washer is damaged, replace it with a new one. Tighten the plug with a wrench, but do not overtighten it. Turn the water on to check whether the drain is clear and to make sure that there is no dripping from the clean-out plug. If it drips slightly, tighten the plug a little more.

Cleaning a Swing Trap

A swing trap has no clean-out plug. Fig. 3-24.

1. To clean out the trap, loosen the slip nuts on each end of the trap with an adjust-

3-23. A *P* trap with a clean-out plug.

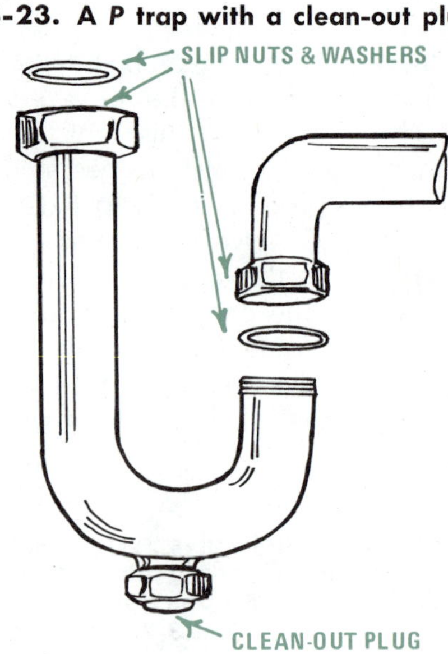

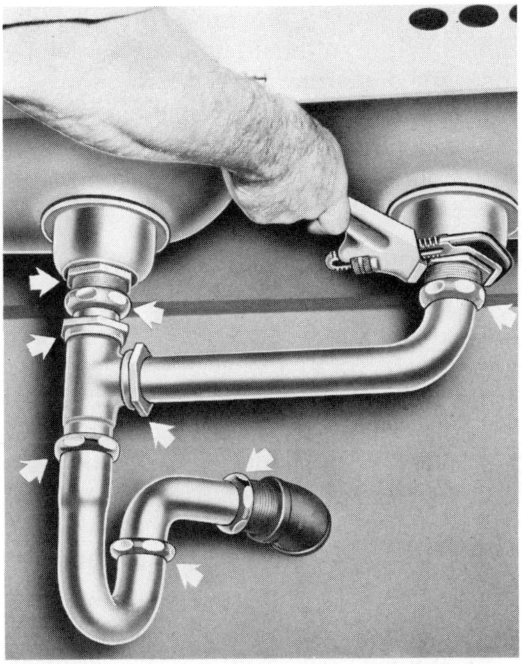

Ridge Tool Company

3-24. Pipes under a double sink. The arrows show the places where a hex wrench or a locknut wrench can be used to open slip nuts. It also shows an *S* trap without a clean-out plug.

3-25. A locknut wrench being used to open the slip nut on a trap. When both nuts are open, the trap can be removed.

able locknut wrench or a hex wrench. Fig. 3-25. Remove the entire piece. (Be sure to place a pail underneath the fixture.) Turn the trap over. The water and solid waste material will pour out of the trap into the pail. Run a wire through the trap to make sure it is clear.

2. Replace the trap by holding it in position and tightening the slip nuts with your fingers. Make sure the washers fit into the slip nuts correctly. Start the threading of the slip nuts carefully to avoid stripping the threads. Hand-tighten the two slip nuts first and then use a wrench to complete the job. Run water to make sure that the trap does not leak at the joints.

Clearing a Clogged Drain with a Plunger

A sink, toilet, or bathtub drain can sometimes be unclogged with a plunger, or force cup. The procedure is as follows:

1. Fill the sink or tub with two or three inches of water. (A toilet bowl will already have water in it.) For better suction, stuff a towel or a rag in the overflow hole of the sink or tub. Fig. 3-26.

2. Place the rubber force cup over the drain opening. Fig. 3-27. Move the handle up

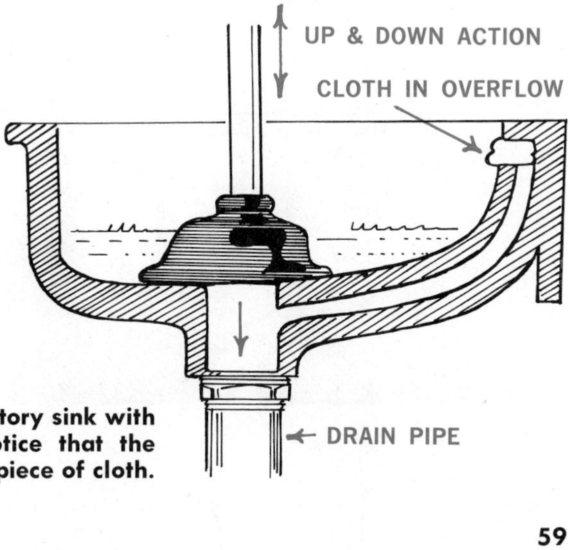

3-26. Sectional view of a lavatory sink with a plunger over the drain. Notice that the overflow hole is stuffed with a piece of cloth.

3-27. Using a plunger in a kitchen sink. Fill the sink with 2 or 3 inches of water.

and down hard a few times. Remove the rubber cup from the drain and see whether the water flows down the drain.

3. If the water does not drain quickly, repeat the procedure with the plunger until the drain is clear. Wash off the plunger before putting it away.

Using Chemicals to Clear a Drain

In place of using a plunger, or after using one without success, you may use a drain-cleaning chemical to dissolve grease and other obstructions in a sink or bathtub drainpipe. (Such chemicals cannot be used for toilets because they will damage the porcelain bowl.) Do not use crystal drain cleaners in garbage disposers or plastic pipes. These cleaners generate heat when mixed with water, and the heat damages disposers and plastic plumbing.

Read the directions on the chemical container carefully. These chemicals are poisonous. They can burn your skin and eyes and can harm the finish on a sink or tub if they are not properly used. Wear rubber gloves and goggles when using these caus-

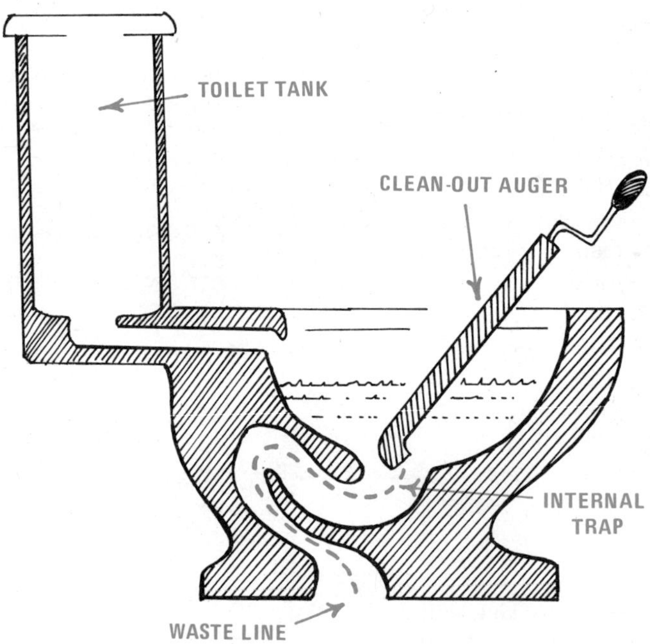

3-28. Clean-out auger being used to unblock a toilet. The diagram shows the internal trap in the bowl.

tic chemicals. Never use a plunger in the fixture until after the chemical has gone down the drain and the drain has been thoroughly flushed with cold water.

Using a Clean-Out Auger to Clear a Drain

A clean-out auger (Fig. 3-1), or plumber's snake, as it is sometimes called, can be used to unclog a sink, bathtub, or toilet bowl. There are several varieties of these augers available, including a short closet auger and a drain auger which comes in various lengths. A clean-out auger is a long, flexible wire enclosed in a short length of tubing. The wire is available in lengths ranging from 3′ to 25′. A crank on the end near the tube allows the wire to be turned Augers have a wire corkscrew on the end to facilitate breaking through solid material which is blocking drainage. To use a snake to unclog a plumbing fixture (Fig. 3-28), follow these steps:

1. Put the end of the wire into the drain. While turning the crank, snake the wire through the drainpipe and the trap. Turn the crank slowly with one hand and hold the tube with the other. (Sometimes better access to the blockage can be achieved by snaking the wire through the clean-out opening in the trap itself.)
2. Move the wire in through the pipe as far as it will go. If it meets resistance and the auger refuses to go through the obstruction after several attempts, it will be necessary to call a plumber to remove the obstruction.
3. Before putting the clean-out auger away, clean off the wire and tube with a rag or with running water. If it is a self-contained auger, wind the wire back into the tube after it has been cleaned.

TOILET SEAT REPLACEMENT

A broken or worn toilet seat can be replaced, using only an adjustable open-end wrench in the following way:

1. Check the nuts and bolts holding the toilet seat hinge in place on the back of the bowl rim. Most toilet seats have cadmium-plated bolts with plastic nuts so that they cannot rust in place. If the nuts are metal, however, they may have some rust in the threads making them difficult to remove. If checking these bolts is difficult because there is little room to get behind the toilet, hold a small mirror underneath the back of the toilet bowl to show you the condition of the two bolts.
2. Adjust the wrench to fit the nuts. Turn them clockwise to remove them from the bolts. Be careful not to chew up the plastic nuts with the wrench before you get them off. Once the nuts are loosened, you can sometimes turn them by hand. After both nuts are off, lift the toilet seat from the bowl rim.
3. If the nuts are metal and do not loosen with reasonable effort with the wrench, put some penetrating oil on the threads in and around the nut. Let the oil work itself into the threads for a few minutes. They should loosen. (Be careful not to hit the toilet bowl with the wrench as it can crack or chip the ceramic.)
4. Remove the nuts from the new toilet seat. Put the seat in place on the toilet bowl with the bolts through the holes in the rim. Hand-thread the nuts onto the bolts until they are tight. Use a wrench to tighten them a little more, but be careful not to use excessive pressure which might crack the bowl rim.

TEMPORARY REPAIR OF A LEAKING PIPE

Several kinds of materials are used in the manufacture of pipe for household plumbing, including copper, brass, iron, and plastic. Even a tiny pinhole in a water pipe allows a great deal of water to escape because the contents of the pipe are under pressure. The pipe will eventually have to be replaced by a plumber, but a temporary repair will stop the leak. The procedure for repairing a leaky pipe is:

1. Turn off the main cold-water valve. This will reduce the water pressure and cut off the flow of both hot and cold water. (Some water remaining in the pipe will still leak out.) Open the hot and cold water faucets on the lowest level in the house to empty the pipes (for example, open the washing machine or laundry tub faucets in the basement).

2. Measure the approximate diameter of the leaking pipe by holding a ruler up to the pipe. Obtain a sleeve clamp for that pipe diameter. A sleeve clamp consists of a metal patch in two halves and a rubber gasket. The clamp is held together over the pipe with machine screws and nuts. Fig. 3-29. Cover the leak with the piece of rubber and

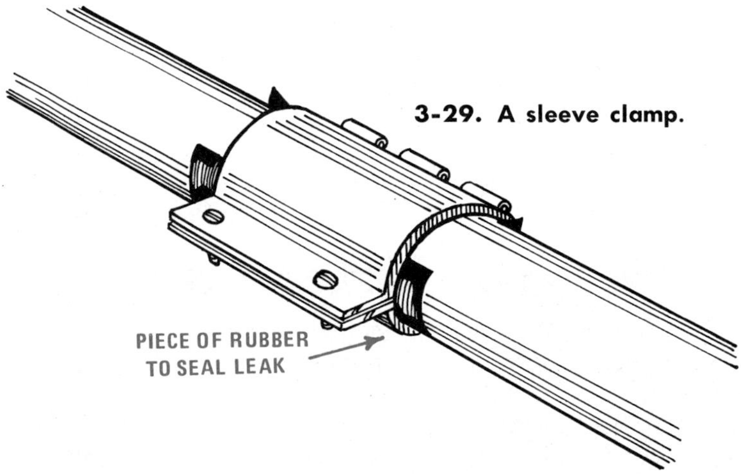

3-29. A sleeve clamp.

3-30. Hose clamp for a pipe 1 9/16″ to 2½″ in diameter.

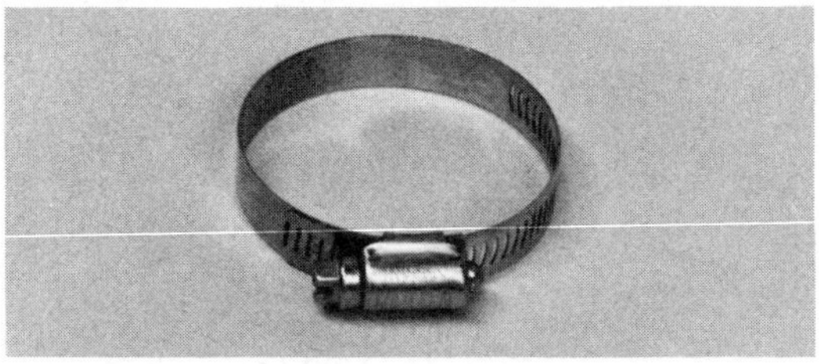

3-31. Hose clamp and a piece of rubber used to stop a pipe leak.

clamp it in place by tightening the screws on the sleeve with a screwdriver.

3. If the hole is very small, it is possible to stop the leak with a hose clamp and a piece of rubber gasket material such as a piece of tire patch. Fig. 3-30. Hose clamps come in various sizes, and you can get one to fit the diameter of any leaky pipe. Fig. 3-31. Hose clamps are opened and tightened with a screwdriver.

4. You can also use epoxy patching materials to repair small leaks. Instructions for use come on the package.

5. After the leak has been stopped, turn on the main water valve again. Be sure to close the faucets you opened earlier.

THAWING FROZEN WATER PIPES

During cold weather, water in pipes in unheated dwellings, or in unheated sections of a home such as crawl spaces, may freeze solid. Water expands as it freezes, and it can split an iron pipe. Even flexible copper pipe will expand somewhat and perhaps split.

To prevent pipes from freezing, wrap them in insulation which you then tape in place. Special pipe insulation can be purchased at hardware stores.

There are a limited number of methods for thawing a pipe. You can wrap rags around the pipe and pour hot water on them. Or you might use an electric hair dryer to thaw sections of the pipe. Fig. 3-32. Be sure to start on a section of the pipe close to the frozen part. Slowly work your way into the frozen section. (The frozen section will feel very cold to the touch and may have frost on it.)

Using an open flame, such as a propane torch, to thaw a pipe is dangerous. If the pipe and the water get too hot, steam will build up inside the pipe and cause it to explode. If, however, you do use a torch on a pipe, open the faucet nearest the frozen

3-32. Using an electric hair dryer to thaw sections of a frozen pipe.

section and start thawing out the pipe near the faucet. Fig. 3-33. Gradually work your way along the pipe with the torch. The open faucet will help to reduce the dangerous steam pressure buildup.

Another safety precaution for thawing frozen pipes with a torch is to never heat the pipe to a temperature hotter than you can comfortably touch with your bare hand. Always start thawing at a part of the pipe that is not frozen and work up to the section that is frozen. Remember, thawing frozen pipes is a slow, gradual process.

3-33. Thawing a pipe with a propane torch is dangerous. To avoid excess steam buildup, open a nearby faucet and start thawing out that section of frozen pipe closest to the faucet.

CHECKUP

1. Inspect the plumbing in your home. Are any repairs needed? If so, what are the correct repair procedures?
2. What are the functions of traps in a plumbing system?
3. What are the advantages and disadvantages of chemical drain cleaners? Do you think it is better to use tools (plunger, snake, etc.) or chemicals to clear a clogged drain?

CHAPTER 4

Plaster and Dry-Wall Repair

The interior walls of most homes are either dry-wall or plaster construction. Dry-wall construction uses gypsum panels covered with paper. The panels are fastened to the studs, then taped and cemented with wallboard compound to give a smooth appearance at seams and corners.

Homes with plaster walls have the plaster applied in two coats to a cement base, over wire lath or gypsum lath (gypsum board containing holes that is nailed to the studs). The cement is applied, filling the holes in the lath and forming a firm foundation for the second and finish coats of plaster, which can be either smooth or textured.

You should know how to repair wall surfaces to prepare them for repainting or for redecorating with wall coverings. This repair or preparation of wall surfaces is the first step in any interior paint job.

REPAIRING CRACKS IN PLASTER WALLS

Tools and materials necessary to repair cracks include:

- Flexible putty knife with 3″ blade. Fig. 4-1.
- Spackling compound (either powdered or prepared).
- Container for mixing spackling compound (such as a disposable aluminum pie plate).
- Pointed can opener (for opening cracks).
- Abrasive paper, medium grade.

These are the steps in making the repairs:

1. Remove all loose plaster using the pointed end of the can opener as a scraper. Undercut a wedge-shaped opening in the wall so that the spackling compound will hold. Fig. 4-2.

2. Wet the area to be patched with a rag or a sponge to prevent water absorption by

4-1. Flexible-blade putty knife.
Red Devil, Inc.

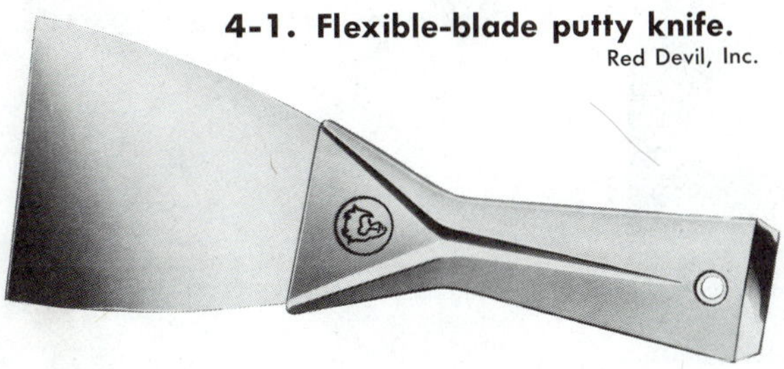

4-2. Sectional view of a plaster wall, showing the wedge-shaped opening cut into it.

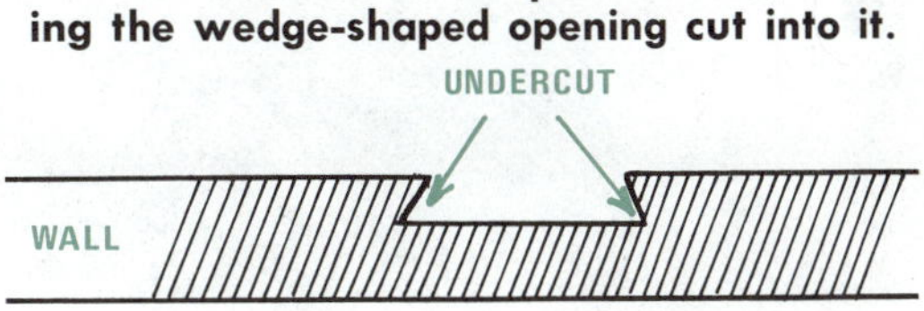

the old plaster from the new material. If the patch dries out too rapidly, it will powder or crack.

3. Mix approximately the amount of spackling compound needed to fill the cracks. Mixing instructions are on the package. The compound should be the consistency of a thick paste. An aluminum pie plate makes a good disposable mixing container. (Prepared compound is also available.)

4. Using a flexible-blade putty knife (Fig. 4-3), fill the crack with spackling compound so that it is slightly higher than the rest of the wall. Fig. 4-4. (The material will shrink as it dries.)

5. After the spackling compound is dry (it usually takes several hours), rub the patch

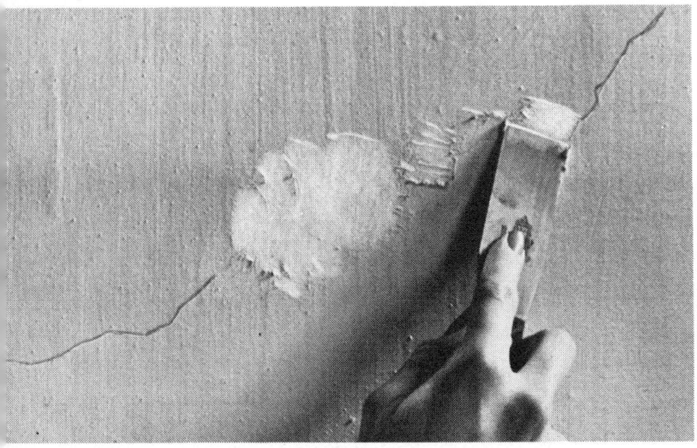

Benjamin Moore and Co.

4-3. Filling a wall crack with spackling compound.

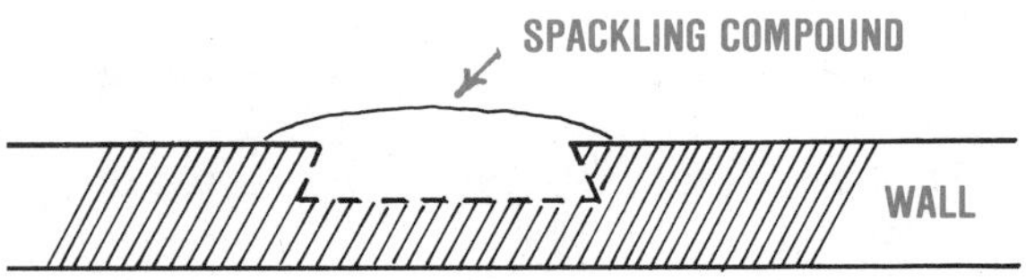

4-4. The crack is filled with spackling compound until it is slightly higher than the rest of the wall.

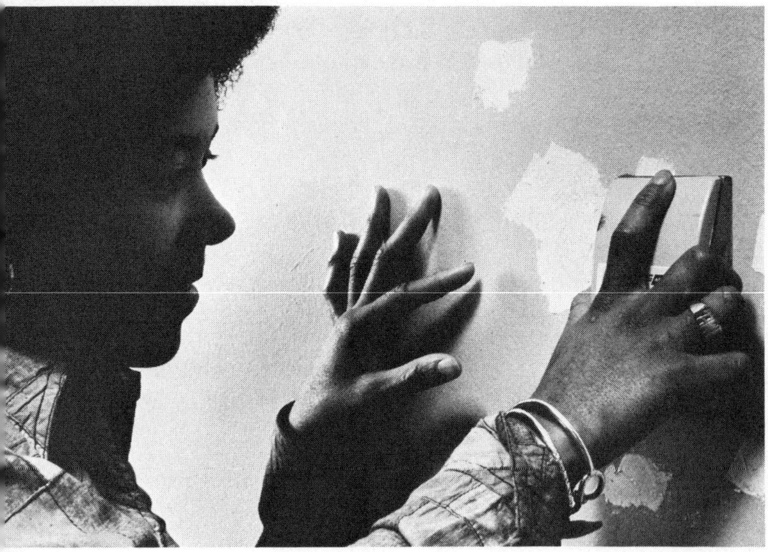

National Paint & Coatings Association

4-5. Using a sanding block to level patches in plaster.

with abrasive paper until it is level with the wall. A block of wood with a piece of abrasive paper wrapped around it or a sanding block works well for this. Fig. 4-5.

6. Your tools should be washed off with water as soon as the job is finished. Otherwise the compound will harden on them and be difficult to remove.

—REPAIRING A SMALL HOLE IN A PLASTER WALL—

Repair of extensive damage to a plaster wall should be done by a professional plasterer. However, you can repair a small hole (less than 3″) by following these steps. The tools for this repair job are the same as those for repairing cracks. You will also need some old newspaper or steel wool.

1. Remove all loose plaster with a flexible putty knife. Fig. 4-6. Check to see that the lath under the plaster is solid.

2. Moisten the area. Fill the hole with several coats of spackling compound. Be sure to allow each coat to dry before applying the next. Dampen the surrounding area between coats.

3. If the damage extends through the lath, you have to build up a foundation for the spackling compound. This may be done by stuffing wads of old newspaper or steel wool into the hole to form a solid base. Fig. 4-7. Then apply the first coat of compound. Do not try to fill up the hole all at once. Let the previous coat dry; then wet the area and put on the next coat. Build up the coats until the area is slightly higher than the rest of the wall. Let the final coat dry overnight.

4. Sand the compound level with the surrounding area, using a wood block with a piece of abrasive paper wrapped around it.

Benjamin Moore and Co.

4-6. Removing loose plaster with a putty knife.

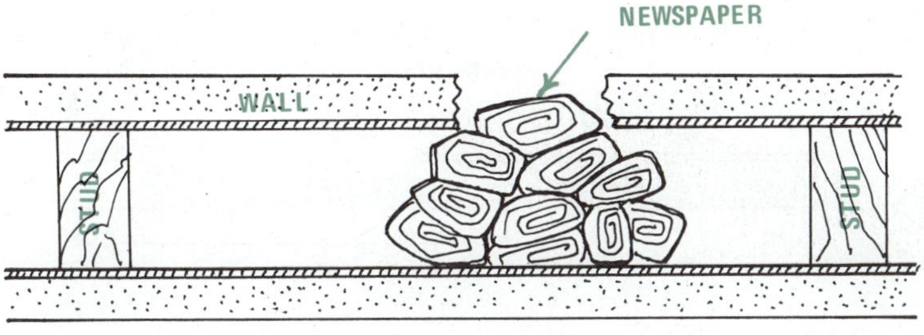

4-7. Sectional view of a small hole in a plaster wall. The hole has been stuffed with newspaper to form a base for spackling compound.

REPAIRING DRY-WALL CRACKS

Tools and materials for repairing cracks in plasterboard, or gypsum board, are the same as those for repairing cracks in plaster walls. The steps are the same, except you must be careful not to damage the paper covering on the plasterboard by dampening it too much.

PATCHING A SMALL HOLE IN DRY WALL

The following tools and materials are needed to complete the repair of a small hole in a plasterboard wall.

- Flexible putty knife with 3″ blade.
- Spackling compound (either powdered or prepared).
- Wallboard compound.
- Container for mixing spackling compound (such as an aluminum pie plate).
- Utility knife.
- Ruler (zigzag or push-pull).
- Piece of plasterboard or wire lath.
- String.
- Medium abrasive paper.
- Piece of wood, such as a dowel.
- Hand drill and small drill bit.
- Tin snips (shears).

The procedure for repairing dry wall is:

1. Remove any loose dry-wall material from around the edges of the hole with a utility knife. Cut the hole to a rectangular shape, if possible.

2. Cut a piece of scrap plasterboard to a rectangle a little larger than the size of the hole. The width of the piece should be less than the length of the hole in the wall so that you can slip the piece inside the wall later. Drill a small hole in the center of this patch and slip a loop of string through it. Knot the string on the end so that it will not pull through the hole in the patch.

3. Apply wallboard compound around the inside of the hole on the back of the wallboard. If the hole is too small to get both your hand and the putty knife through, use your fingers to apply the compound.

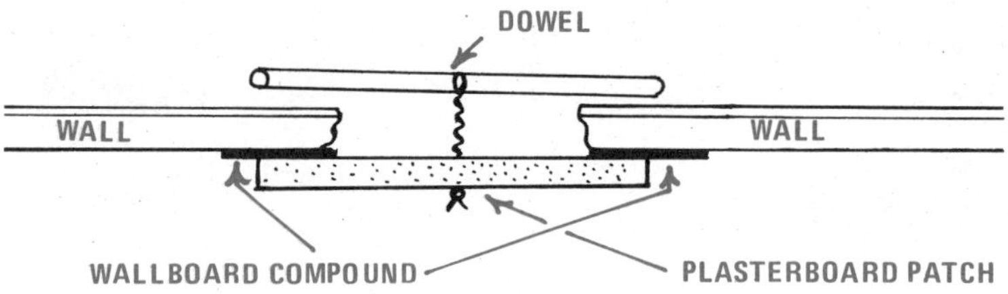

4-8a. Plasterboard patch can be held in place with a piece of string and a dowel.

4-8b. The hole in the plasterboard wall was built up with wallboard compound and spackling compound after the patch was in place.

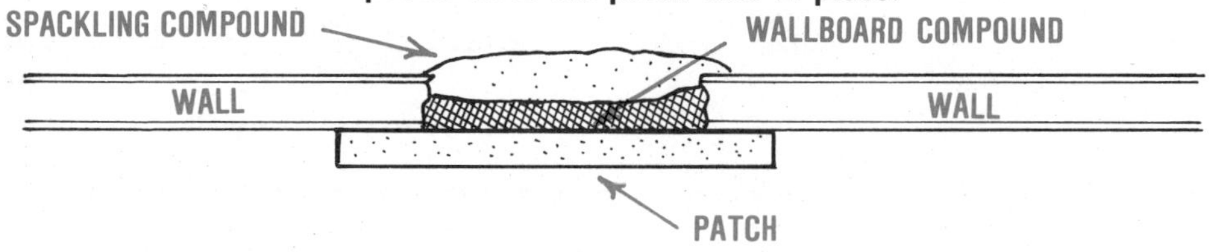

Stanley Tools

4-9. A pair of tin shears.

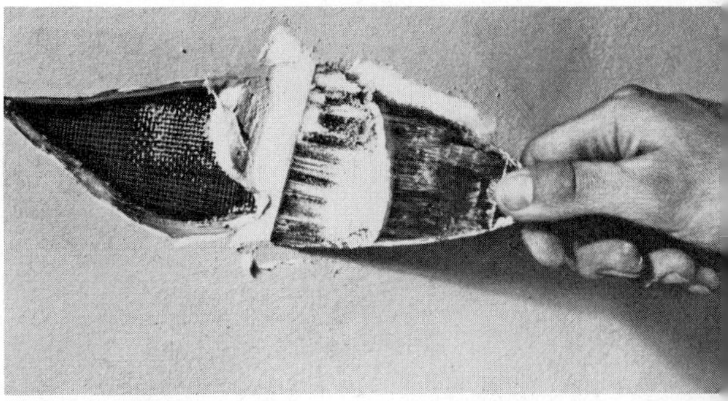

Benjamin Moore and Co.

4-10. Applying wallboard compound to a wire-lath patch in a plasterboard wall.

4. Slip the rectangular plasterboard patch through the hole in the wallboard. Using the string to keep it from falling, move the patch into position. It should cover the entire opening and be imbedded in the wallboard compound behind the wall. Pull the string tight and tie it around a piece of dowel, or any small piece of wood which is longer than the hole in the wall. This works like a tourniquet, the wood against the wall on the outside keeping the patch in place on the inside of the wall. Fig. 4-8a.

5. When the patch is firmly in place and the compound dry, cut the string and remove the wood. Apply some wallboard compound to the hole to partially fill it in. Allow this to dry.

6. Dampen the area around the patch. Mix the spackling compound. Fill in the hole so that it is slightly higher than the rest of the wall. Fig. 4-8b. You may need two coats of compound to do this.

7. When the compound is dry (overnight), sand the area even with the surrounding wall.

Instead of plasterboard as a patch, you can use a piece of wire lath. Because it is flexible, lath is easier to insert into the wall. With tin shears, cut it somewhat larger than the hole. Fig. 4-9. Use the same method as described for a plasterboard patch to hold it in place while the wallboard compound dries. Apply a coat of wallboard compound to the wire lath and push some of the compound through the lath. Fig. 4-10. When it dries it will be a firm foundation for the coats of spackling compound needed to build up the area to the same level as the existing wall.

REPAIRING A LARGE HOLE IN DRY WALL

The necessary tools and materials are:

- Utility knife.
- Flexible putty knife with 3″ blade.
- Perforated reinforcing tape.
- Wallboard compound.
- Straightedge.
- Medium abrasive paper.
- Plasterboard nails.
- Zigzag or push-pull ruler.
- Claw hammer.
- Plasterboard.

The steps in patching a large hole in a plasterboard wall are as follows:

1. First cut the hole into a rectangle with a sharp utility knife. Then cut back the wallboard to expose half the width (about $\frac{3}{4}$″) of the 2″ x 4″ studs on or near the ends of the opening. These partially exposed studs will serve as a nailing surface for the patch.

2. Measure the thickness of the existing wallboard. Select a piece of plasterboard

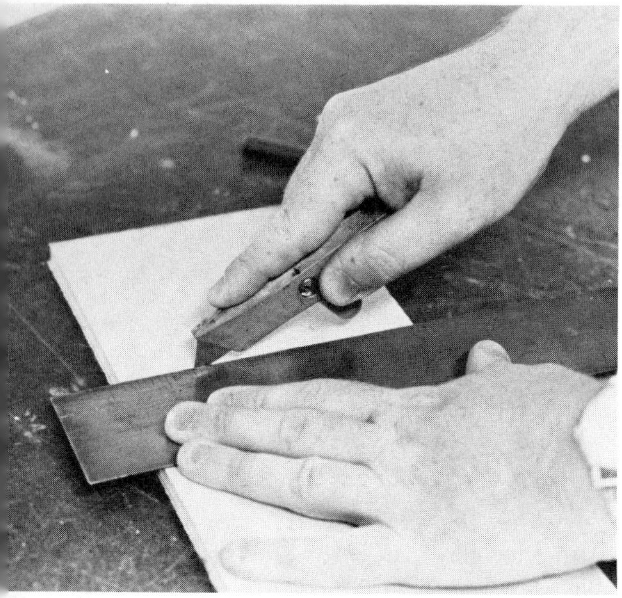

4-11. Scoring one face of a piece of plasterboard with a utility knife and a straightedge.

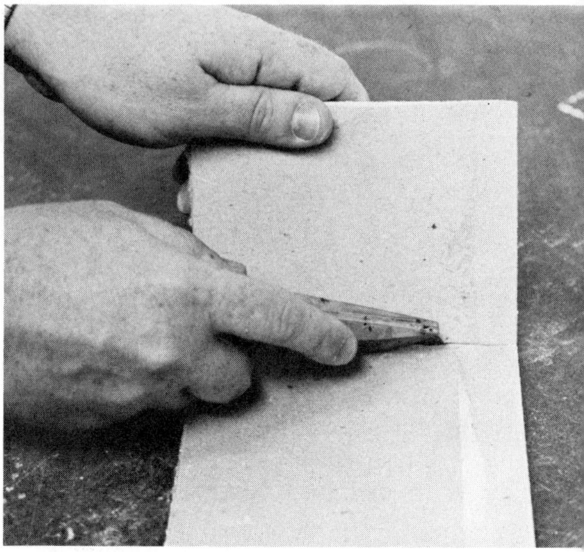

4-12. After snapping the plasterboard by bending it in the opposite direction from the scored face, cut through the resulting crease on the other side with a utility knife.

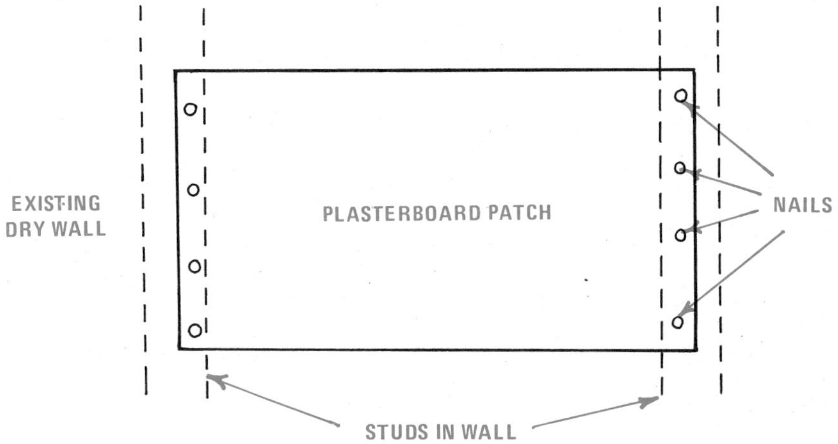

4-13. Front view of a plasterboard patch nailed in place on a wall.

4-14. Sectional view of a plasterboard wall that has been patched. The patch is even with the rest of the wall surface.

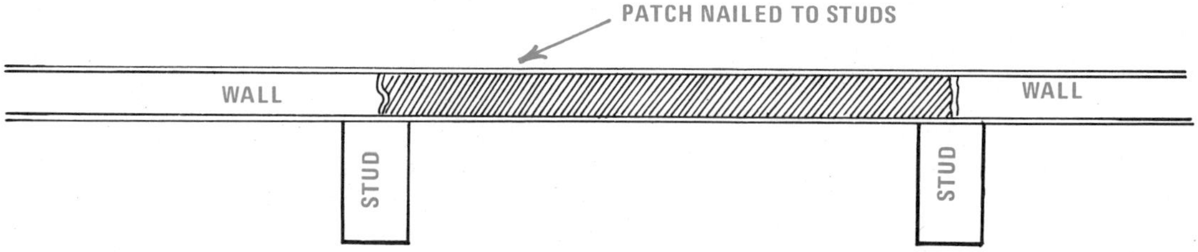

which is the same thickness and cut it so that it fits the opening. (Using a piece of $\frac{1}{2}''$ plasterboard as a patch when the wall is made of $\frac{3}{8}''$ material would make the repair job quite noticeable.) To cut a piece of plasterboard, measure out the piece you need and mark it in pencil. Cut one line at a time. First score one paper face of the material with a utility knife and a straightedge. Fig. 4-11. Turn it over and bend the board in the opposite direction from the cut until it snaps. With the board folded at about 90 degrees, you will see a crease in the uncut paper face. Cut through this with a utility knife and the piece will break off evenly. Fig. 4-12.

3. Place the new piece of dry wall into position. Using plasterboard nails every six inches, fasten the patch in place by nailing into the studs. There must be a nail near each corner. Drive the nails slightly below the surface, but do not damage the paper face of the plasterboard. The patch should be flush with the surface of the existing wall. Fig. 4-13, 4-14.

4. Use a putty knife to spread a 3″ strip of wallboard compound on all four seams. Place strips of perforated reinforcing tape over the compound so that one-half the width of the tape is on each side of the seam. Smooth the tape into the compound with the putty knife to get rid of wrinkles and air pockets under the tape. Allow to dry.

5. Apply a thin coat of wallboard compound over the tape, allowing the edges of the compound to "feather out" past the tape so that they blend with the wall surface. Allow the compound to dry overnight and then lightly sand any high spots.

6. Remove the dust with a rag or brush.

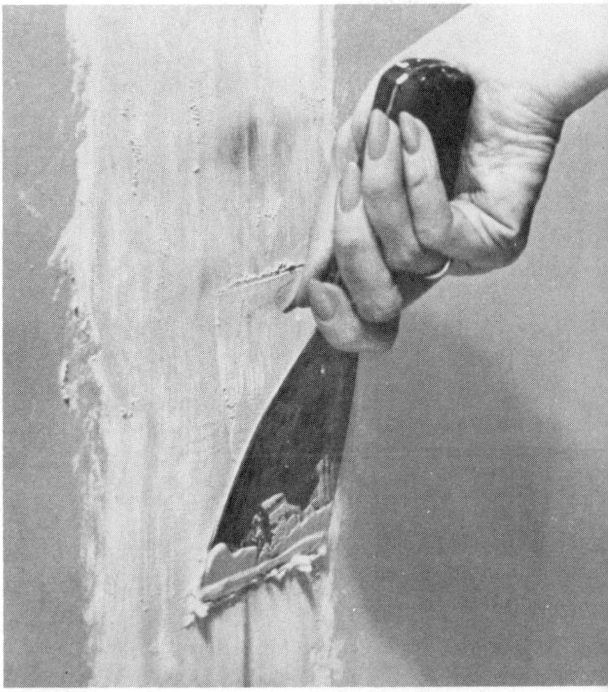

Benjamin Moore and Co.

4-15. Applying wallboard compound over a taped seam with a wide putty knife.

Apply another coat of compound over the first one. Fig. 4-15. The strip of compound should now be about six inches wide, feathering out at the edges. When this has dried thoroughly, sand it lightly, blending the repaired section with the wall surface.

Practice in applying wallboard compound and in taping seams will increase your skill enough so that just a little sanding is needed to achieve a seam which disappears into the surrounding area. Once primed and painted to match the wall, the patch will not be noticeable at all.

CHECKUP

1. What tools and materials do you need to repair cracks in plaster walls? Dry wall?
2. What is lath?
3. What causes cracks and holes in walls? Can you think of ways to prevent such damage?

CHAPTER 5

Redecorating with Paint

WHAT TO USE . . . AND WHERE

	Flat Paint	Semigloss Paint	Enamel	Casein	Interior Varnish	Shellac	Wax (Liquid or Paste)	Wax (Emulsion)	Stain	Wood Sealer	Floor Varnish	Floor Paint or Enamel	Aluminum Paint	Sealer or Undercoater	Metal Primer	Latex Types
Plaster Walls & Ceiling	√·	√·		√										√		√
Wallboard	√·	√·		√										√		√
Wood Paneling	√·	√·			√	√	√		√	√						√·
Kitchen & Bathroom Walls		√·	√·											√		
Wood Floors						√	√	√·	√·	√	√·	√·				
Concrete Floors							√·	√·	√			√				√
Vinyl & Rubber Tile Floors							√	√								
Asphalt Tile Floors								√								
Linoleum						√	√	√			√	√				
Stair Treads						√			√	√	√	√				
Stair Risers	√·	√·			√	√			√	√						
Wood Trim	√·	√·			√	√	√		√					√		√·
Steel Windows	√·	√·											√		√	√·
Aluminum Windows	√·	√·											√		√	√·
Window Sills					√											
Steel Cabinets	√·	√·													√	
Heating Ducts	√·	√·											√		√	√·
Radiators & Heating Pipes	√·	√·											√		√	√·
Old Masonry	√	√		√									√	√		√
New Masonry	√·	√·												√		√

√· Black dot indicates that a primer or sealer may be necessary before the finishing coat (unless surface has been previously finished).

National Paint & Coatings Association

5-1. Different interior surfaces also require different kinds of finishes.

EXTERIOR AND INTERIOR PAINTS

Painting a house interior is often done for decoration, to make rooms look better. Exterior painting, although certainly done to make a house look better, also serves a more important purpose: it protects the surface from the weather.

Interior paint, in addition to its decorative qualities, also protects a wall from dirt and grease. Some interior paints are washable. There are basically four types of interior paint: oil, alkyd, latex, and calcimine, which is an inexpensive, water-soluble mixture of

WHAT TO USE . . . AND WHERE

	House Paint (Oil)	Transparent Sealer	Cement Base Paint	Exterior Clear Finish	Aluminum Paint	Wood Stain	Roof Coating	Roof Cement	Asphalt Emulsion	Trim and Trellis Paint	Awning Paint	Spar Varnish	Porch and Deck Paint	Primer or Undercoater	Metal Primer	Latex Types	Water-Repellant Preservatives
Clapboard Siding	✓•				✓									✓		✓•	
Brick	✓•	✓	✓		✓									✓		✓	
Cement & Cinder Block	✓•	✓	✓		✓									✓		✓	
Asbestos Cement	✓•													✓		✓	
Stucco	✓•	✓	✓		✓									✓		✓	
Natural Wood Siding & Trim				✓		✓						✓					
Metal Siding	✓•				✓•					✓•					✓	✓•	
Wood Frame Windows	✓•				✓					✓•				✓		✓•	
Steel Windows	✓•				✓•					✓•					✓	✓•	
Aluminum Windows	✓•				✓					✓•					✓	✓•	
Shutters & Other Trim	✓•									✓•				✓		✓•	
Canvas Awnings											✓						
Wood Shingle Roof						✓											✓
Metal Roof	✓•														✓	✓•	
Coal Tar Felt Roof							✓	✓	✓								
Wood Porch Floor													✓				
Cement Porch Floor													✓			✓	
Copper Surfaces												✓					
Galvanized Surfaces	✓•				✓•					✓•		✓			✓	✓•	
Iron Surfaces	✓•				✓•					✓•					✓	✓•	

✓• Black dot indicates that a primer or sealer may be necessary before the finishing coat (unless surface has been previously finished).

National Paint & Coatings Association

5-2. Different kinds of exterior surfaces need different kinds of paints or coatings.

chalk and glue. Water-base paints dry quickly; tools clean up with soap and water. In the case of latex paints, colors are subdued and come in pastel shades. Oil-base paints will dry overnight. Tools must be cleaned with paint thinner or turpentine. Oil-base paints are tougher than water-base paints in washability and durability. Paints are available in flat (no shine) finish, gloss enamel (shiny) finish, and semigloss enamel (dull shine) finish. Fig. 5-1 shows the types of finishes to use on different interior surfaces.

Exterior paint forms a protective coating or film which keeps moisture from affecting the siding materials on a house. Exterior paint must be flexible, or elastic, enough to allow for expansion in heat and contraction in cold. Exterior paint wears by *chalking;* that is, the top surface turns to powder and is washed away by rain and snow. There are three basic types of exterior paint: oil-base, alkyd (oil-base paint with alkyd resins), and latex (water-base). Each of these paints has advantages and disadvantages. Which paint is best for a home depends on the home's location and the climate. A reliable paint dealer can give advice about which type to use. Fig. 5-2 shows which coatings to use for different outside surfaces.

PAINT BRUSHES

How to Choose Brushes

Good brushes, properly cared for, will last many years. Select them for the specific paint job you are planning. Generally, for most painting around the home, you will need a 4″ wall brush, a $1\frac{1}{2}$″ sash brush (Fig. 5-3), and a 2″ trim brush (Fig. 5-4).

If you use latex paint on some parts and oil-base paint on others, you will need a set of brushes for each type of paint. It is hard to clean brushes used in oil paint well enough to use them in latex paint. Traces of the old paint always seem to remain in the heel, where the bristles meet the ferrule, no matter how well you clean the brush.

When choosing brushes, look for these indications of quality:

- The handle should be shaped to fit the hand comfortably, and the brush should feel balanced.
- Bristles should be long and springy, either pure hog bristles or nylon bristles. Nylon bristles have tiny split (flagged) ends. When selecting a brush, tug on the bristles; very few should come out in your hand.
- There should be a tapered wooden plug in the center of the bristles. It should be visible if you spread the bristles like a fan.

5-3. An angular sash brush for painting windows.
Benjamin Moore and Co.

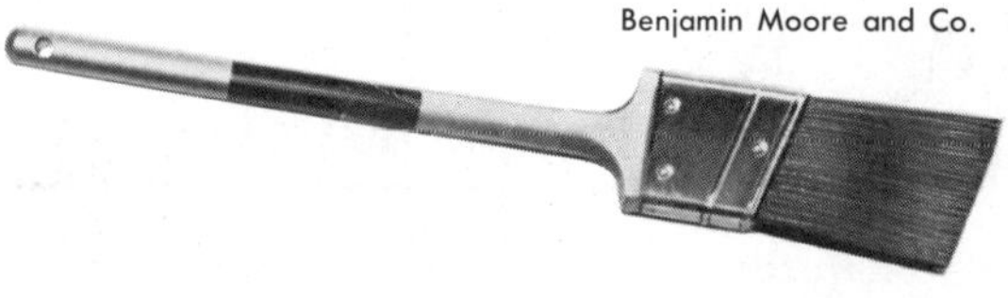

5-4. A wall brush, and a smaller trim brush.
Benjamin Moore and Co.

• The handle should be firmly fastened to the metal ferrule with round-headed nails.

How to Use a Paint Brush

Hold the paint brush the way you hold a pencil when you write. The brushing motion comes either from the wrist or the elbow, depending upon how wide an area you are trying to cover. Dip the bristles no more than one third into the paint. Tap the bristles against the side of the can two or three times to remove excess paint.

Work from unpainted areas toward areas you have just painted. Brush the paint out in a back-and-forth movement, either up and down or across, to make a smooth surface. Enamels (those with glossy or semigloss finishes) should be brushed on horizontally first, then lightly leveled off vertically, in even strokes. Paint one surface (one wall) at a time. Be careful to cover the entire surface. Avoid painting over areas which have already started to dry.

5-5. Spin the brush between the palms of your hands to remove excess water.

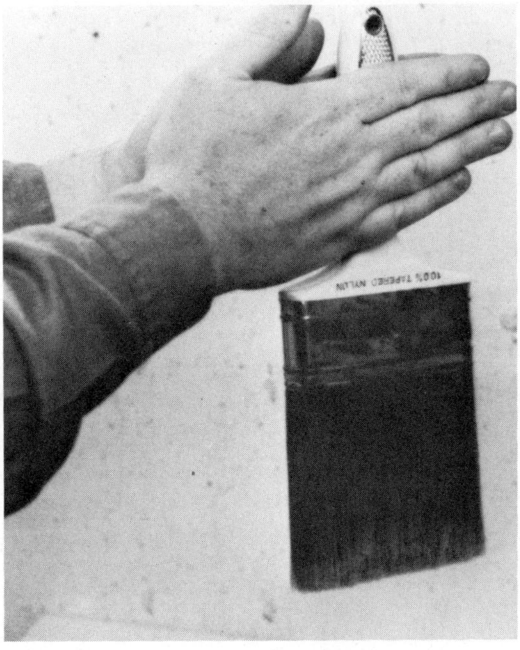

Cleaning and Caring for Paint Brushes

When you are through with a paint job, all the tools must be thoroughly cleaned. Brushes not cleaned properly will be stiff and useless the next time you need them.

To clean a brush used in latex (water-based) paint:

1. Squeeze out excess paint along the inside of the paint can. Work out remaining paint by brushing pieces of old newspaper.

2. Wash the brush in warm water, using a little soap if you wish. Rinse until the water runs clear. To help dry the brush, spin the handle between the palms of your hands. Fig. 5-5.

3. Use a brush comb to straighten the bristles. Fig. 5-6. Hang the brush by the handle to dry. Then wrap the bristles in heavy paper to keep out dust. Figs. 5-7, 5-8. Store the brush in a cool, dry place. Mark the wrapper with the word *latex* so that you will not use the brush later for oil paint.

A brush used in oil paint must be cleaned with a spirit solvent. Paint-can labels will tell you which solvent to use. Usually turpentine

5-6. A brush comb is used to straighten bristles.

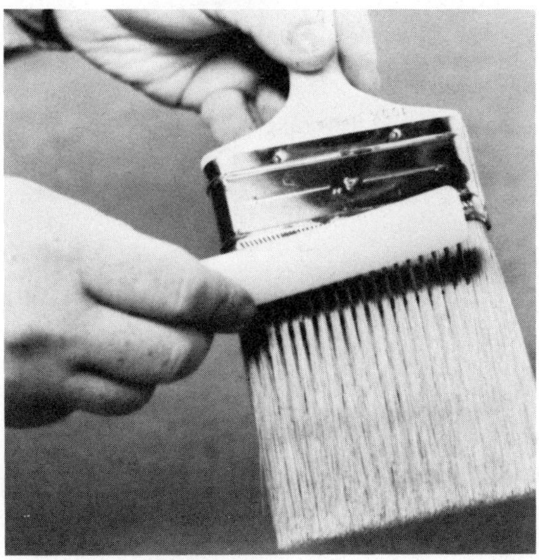

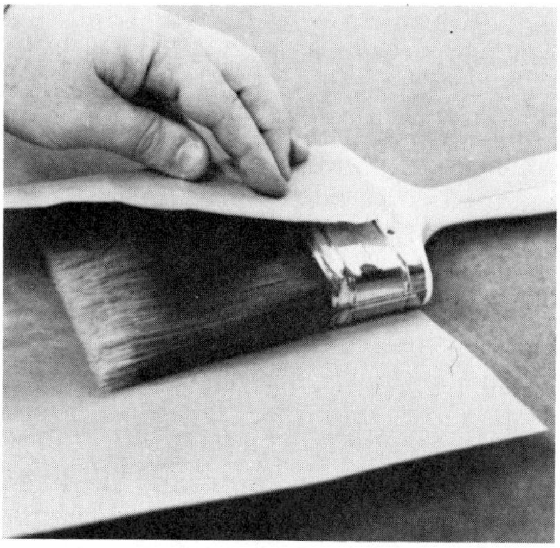

5-7. Wrap the brush in a piece of heavy paper after it is dry.

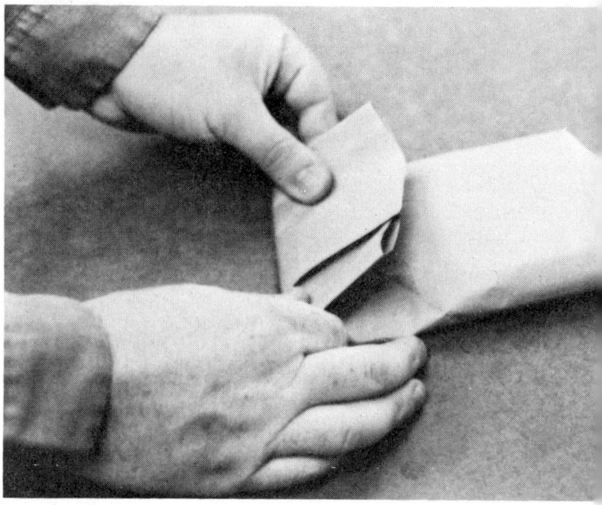

5-8. Fasten the wrapped brush with tape or a rubber band.

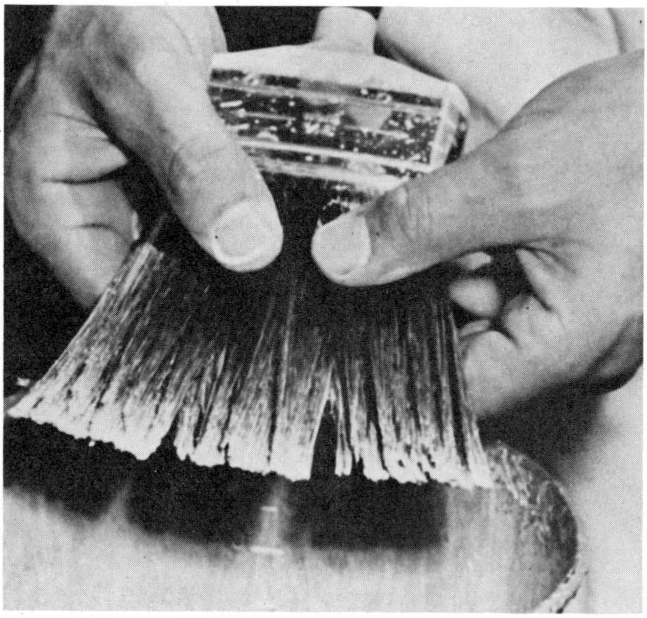

Benjamin Moore and Co.

5-9. After you soak the brush in solvent, make sure that there is no paint left between the bristles.

or paint thinner will do the job. The cleaning procedure is as follows:

1. Tap and squeeze the excess paint from the brush along the inside of the paint container. Remove as much of the paint as possible by brushing sheets of newspaper.

2. Stand the brush in a container of solvent, making sure the solvent reaches as far as the metal ferrule on the brush. If possible, hang the brush in the solvent so that the bristles do not touch the bottom of the container. Let the brush stay in the solvent overnight.

3. The next day, remove the brush from the solvent and spin the remaining solvent out of the brush. Hold the brush handle

between the palms of your hands and spin it rapidly. Hold the brush inside a large container, such as a waste can, when spinning it. This will keep the solvent from getting on you and the surrounding area.

4. Wash the brush in lukewarm water and detergent to remove any remaining solvent and paint. Fig. 5-9. Rinse until the water is clear. Again spin the brush to remove the water. Use a brush comb to straighten all the bristles, and hang the brush to dry.

5. When the brush is dry, wrap it in heavy paper. Store it in a cool, dry place. Mark the brush wrapper *oil paint* so that you do not use it for latex paint.

If you are going to use a brush in oil paint again the next day, it is not necessary to clean it. You can wrap it in aluminum foil to keep it soft, or you can hang the brush in a can of solvent. If the brush will not be used for a few days, the container of solvent should be capped to prevent the paint thinner from evaporating. When you are ready to paint again, spin out the solvent and wipe the brush clean with a rag.

After you have cleaned the oil paint brush and are ready to store it, you can saturate the bristles with linseed oil to keep them pliable. Then wrap the brush in heavy paper and put it in a dry place.

ROLLERS FOR PAINTING

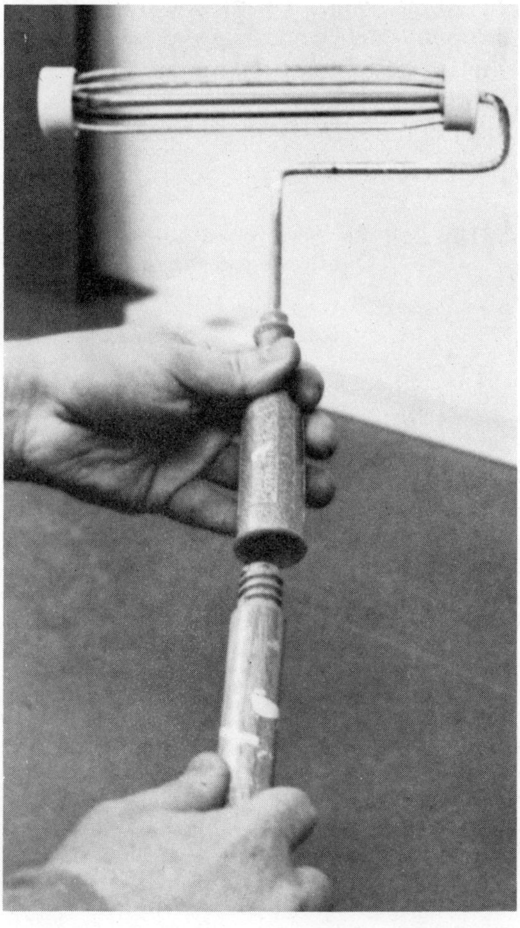

5-10. The handle of a roller frame should be threaded so that an extension pole can be screwed into it.

Choosing a Roller

Rollers have two parts, a frame and a cover. Frames are available in several widths, the most popular being the 7″ and the 9″. The roller handle should be threaded to allow an extension pole to be screwed into it. Fig. 5-10. Extension poles make it possible to reach ceilings without a ladder.

Roller covers, made in sizes to fit the frames, are available in various materials suitable for different paints, such as oil or latex. Fig. 5-11. The specific uses are listed

Benjamin Moore and Co.

5-11. A roller frame with a cover in a roller pan. The tray on the pan is used to keep the roller out of the paint when it is not in use.

on the wrapping material for the individual covers. Roller-cover materials and their purposes are:

- Wool—oil-base paints.
- Polyurethane, a foam synthetic—enamels on smooth surfaces.
- Mohair—for thin coats of latex and oil-based enamels.
- Frieze fabric, (looped yarn attached to roller)—for textured effects on walls.
- Lambskin shearling—oil-base paints on rough surfaces.
- Polyester fiber—exterior paints, latex or oil.
- Modacrylic fiber—rough surfaces, latex or oil.
- Nylon—latex paint, any type of wall surface.

In addition, various other special kinds of rollers are available. These include narrow trim rollers, corner rollers, segmented rollers for pipes, and doughnut-shaped rollers for the edges of outside house siding.

Using a Roller

Select the proper roller cover and slip it onto the roller frame. You can use the roller tray as it is, or you can line it with a purchased plastic liner or with aluminum foil.

In places where a roller cannot reach, such as corners, near baseboards, and where the ceiling meets the walls, use a brush. This must be done before roller application of paint.

Pour paint into the roller pan to a depth of about $1\frac{1}{2}''$. Dip the roller into the paint and move it up the sloping part of the pan until the roller cover is evenly loaded with paint. Fig. 5-12. Be careful not to overload the roller.

Pass the roller over the wall surface in up-and-down movements. Overlap the first stroke with part of the second. Roll the paint on an area 3′ or 4′ wide. Fig. 5-13. Go over any parts not covered by paint the first time you did that area. Then, go on to the next 3′ or 4′ area to be painted until you have completed that wall or ceiling. Dip the roller into the pan again when it no longer contains enough paint to cover the surface evenly.

When painting exterior siding, select a roller of the same width as the siding. Use a

5-12. Dip the roller into the paint. Move it upward along the sloping part of the pan to coat the roller cover evenly with paint.

Benjamin Moore and Co.

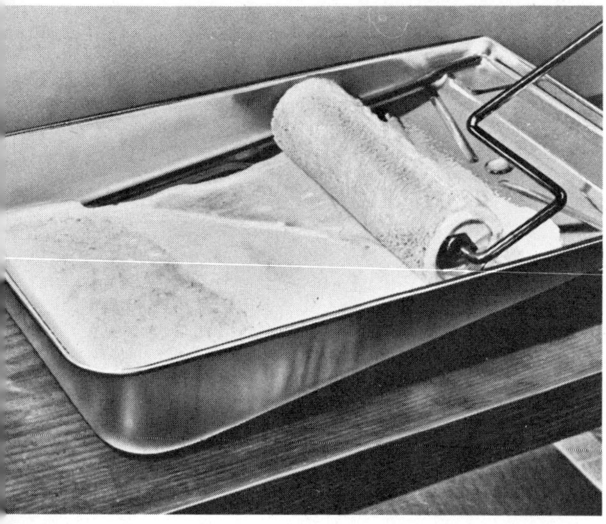

5-13. Roll an area about 3′ or 4′ wide. Overlap each stroke.

Benjamin Moore and Co.

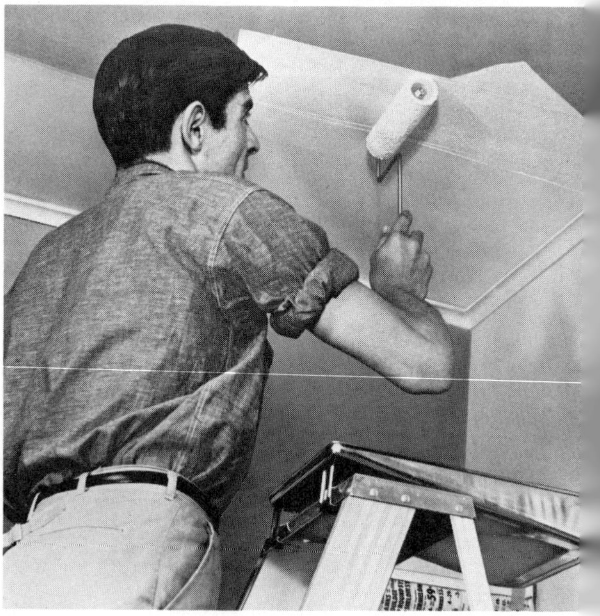

9″ roller for flat siding. Material with a short nap, such as polyester, is good for smooth siding. Long-nap roller covers are needed for rough surfaces like cedar shakes, masonry, and stucco. Fig. 5-14. Read the label on the wrapper of the roller cover to determine which cover you should use for a particular type of siding. Generally, a longer nap makes it easier to get paint into all the uneven spots on rough siding. Use horizontal strokes for smooth siding and vertical strokes for shingles, cedar shakes, and vertical siding such as board-and-batten.

Cleaning the Roller and Pan

If the roller pan still has paint in it after you finish, pour it back into the paint can. Then carefully remove the liner (if you used one) from the pan and dispose of it. If you did not line the pan, wipe out the excess paint. For oil-base paint, pour a little solvent into the pan. Using a couple of rags, clean out all the paint until the pan is clean. If you used latex paint, rinse the pan in warm running water. Dry the pan with a cloth or paper towel. Don't forget to clean the paint drips and spots from the outside of the pan.

To clean the roller cover, first work out the excess paint by rolling it out on newspaper until no more paint shows. Slip the cover off the frame and soak it in the appropriate solvent (listed on the paint label) until it is clean. Soak a cover used for oil-base paint in a pan full of paint thinner. You can clean a cover used in latex paint under a faucet. Fig. 5-15.

After a roller cover has soaked several hours, squeeze out the excess solvent with your hands, or with a brush comb and roller cleaner. For a cover used in oil paint, you must wash out the paint thinner with soap and water. Rinse it under a faucet until the water is clear. Squeeze out the excess water and put the cover away to dry.

After a cover is dry, put it back in its original wrapper or in a plastic bag and mark the outside with the words *oil paint* or *latex.*

Some paint usually leaks in around the ends of the roller frame. The frame may be wiped with a rag and some solvent or washed in water, depending on the type of paint used.

5-14. Painting a brick wall with a roller.
Benjamin Moore and Co.

5-15. Clean a roller cover used in latex paint under running water. Squeeze the water out of the cover with your hands.
Benjamin Moore and Co.

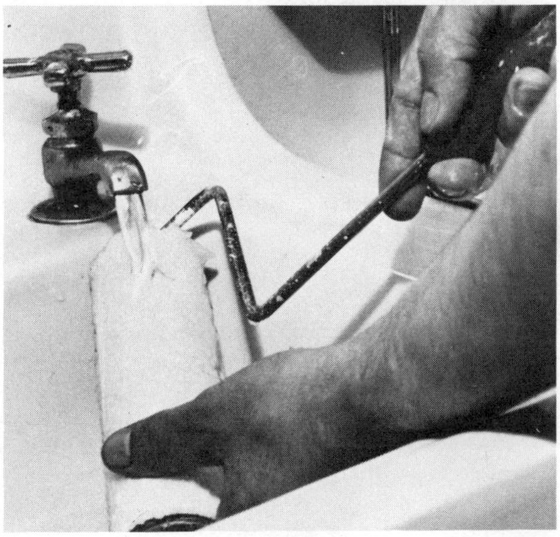

HOW TO USE A LADDER

There are two types of ladders that you are likely to use for painting or repair work: the stepladder and the extension ladder. Owning a stepladder is very helpful, since it can be used a great deal, both inside and outside the house. However, an extension ladder proves useful only occasionally for outside repairs and painting jobs. If you do not need an extension ladder often, you might consider renting rather than buying one.

To prevent accidents, remember these safety rules:

- Carry a ladder horizontally. The middle, or balance point, of a long ladder should rest on your shoulder. Fig. 5-16. To move an extension ladder a short distance, however, such as along a wall, carry it vertically along the wall. (Be careful not to hit windows when you do this.)
- Never climb an extension ladder above the third rung from the top. Some people prefer to have the last rung of the ladder at no less than shoulder height.
- When working from an extension ladder, hold the ladder with one hand or hook a leg over a rung. Fig. 5-17a. Your paint can should be hung from a special hook on the ladder, made for that purpose so that you don't have to hold the can in your hand. Fig. 5-17b.
- Place the ladder carefully so that you do not have to overreach to get to your work. Obviously, overreaching on a ladder is dangerous.
- Extension ladders usually have two sections (top and bottom). To insure rigidity

5-17a. Hook a leg over one rung to help hold you up.

5-16. Carry a ladder horizontally. The balance point of the ladder should be on your shoulder.

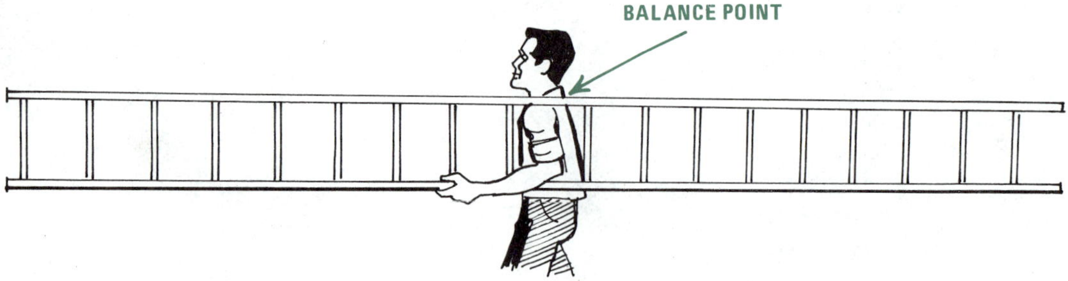

of the ladder, overlap the sections as follows: 3′ for a 36′ ladder, 4′ for a 48′ ladder, and 5′ for up to a 60′ ladder.

- The base of an extension ladder should be placed a distance of one quarter of the ladder's vertical height away from the wall. For example, if the height of the ladder is 16 feet, the base of the ladder should be 4 feet out from the wall. Fig. 5-18.
- The top of a ladder should extend at least 3 feet above the roof if you are going to use the ladder to climb onto the roof.
- A ladder should have a solid, level, non-skid footing. Outside, if the ground is soft, use wide pieces of wood under the ladder feet.
- Don't lean extension ladders against window panes, or on easily broken siding,

Benjamin Moore and Co.

5-17b. When working on an extension ladder, hold the ladder with one hand. Your paint can should be hung from the ladder on a special hook.

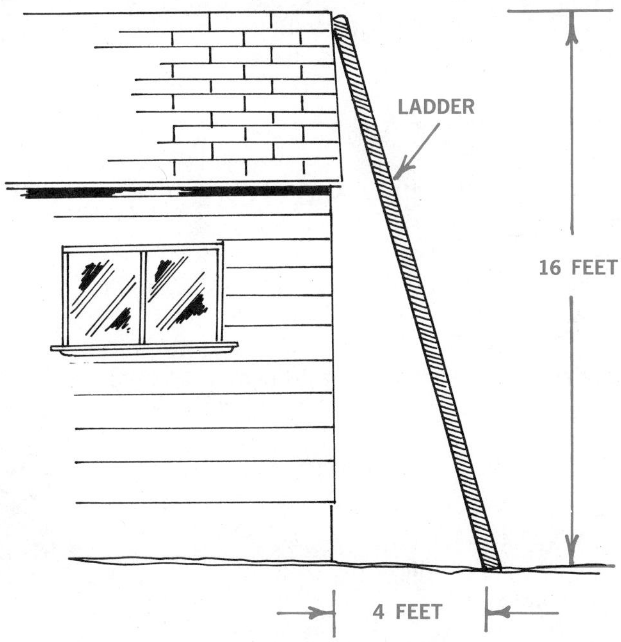

5-18. The base of an extension ladder should be placed from the wall a distance equal to one quarter of the vertical height of the ladder.

Customary	Metric
4′ 16′	1.2 m 4.8 m

such as asbestos shingles. The combined weight of you and the ladder could break these materials. To prevent such damage, use a *ladder stand-off*. This device, which attaches to the ladder, has arms that keep the ladder away from the wall.

- If you place a ladder in front of a door, lock the door. This prevents someone from opening the door suddenly and knocking you off the ladder.
- Always climb facing the ladder. Never climb backwards.
- Check the condition of the ladder before using it. With wooden ladders make sure that there are no cracks or broken pieces. Check to insure that all rungs are tight and free of wet or slippery material before attempting to climb. The bottoms of your shoes should also be dry and clean.
- To raise an extension ladder, lay the ladder on the ground with one end against the base of the wall. Fig. 5-19. Lift up the other end by one of the rungs and walk toward the wall, grasping other rungs as you move along. Fig. 5-20. The ladder will now be vertical; so you just have to move the foot of the ladder away from the wall the required distance (one quarter the height).

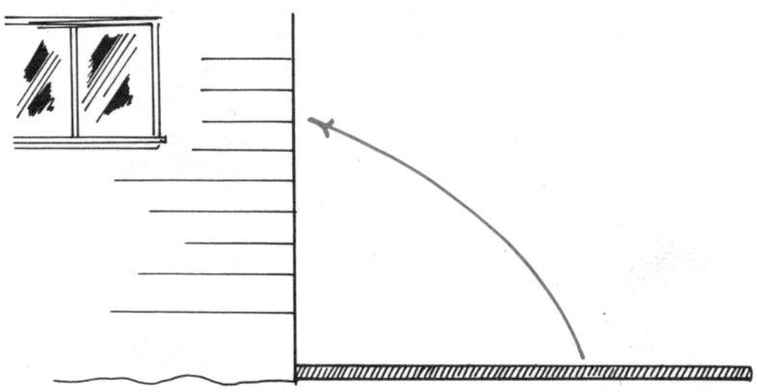

5-19. To raise an extension ladder start by putting one end on the ground against the foot of the wall.

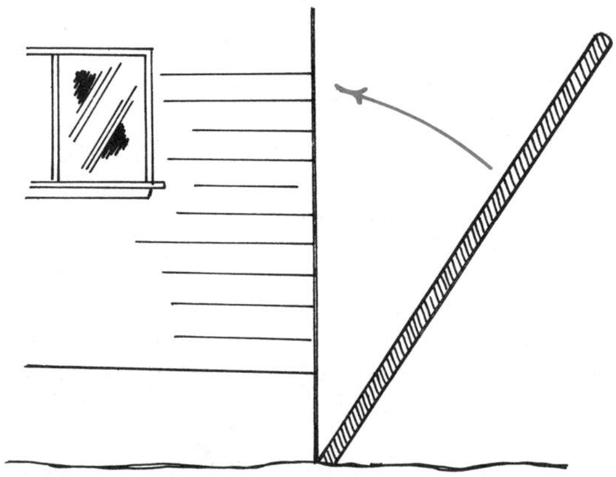

5-20. Lift up the other end of the ladder and walk toward the wall with it. Then move the foot of the ladder away from the wall the proper distance.

PREPARATION OF EXTERIOR SURFACES

Before the actual painting of a house begins, the surfaces must be prepared. Preparation is very important if the paint job is to last. Failure to prepare areas for painting can cause paint to crack and peel in a short time.

Materials

- Hammer.
- Nail set.
- Putty (for filling nail holes; linseed oil putty works well).
- Putty knife.
- Abrasive paper, coarse or medium grade.
- Orbital sander, or disk sanding attachment on electric drill.
- Wire brush.
- Galvanized nails to replace missing nails. Galvanized nails won't rust.
- Scraper. Fig. 5-21.
- Caulking gun with extra caulking cartridges.
- Glazing compound.
- Primer and a 2″ brush, for undercoating and sealing.

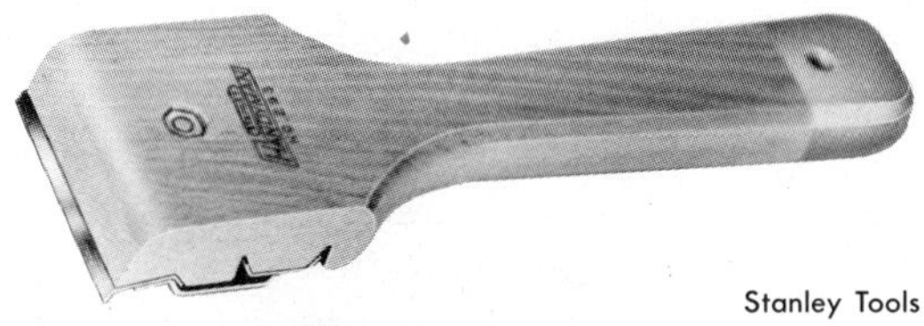

Stanley Tools

5-21. Paint scraper.

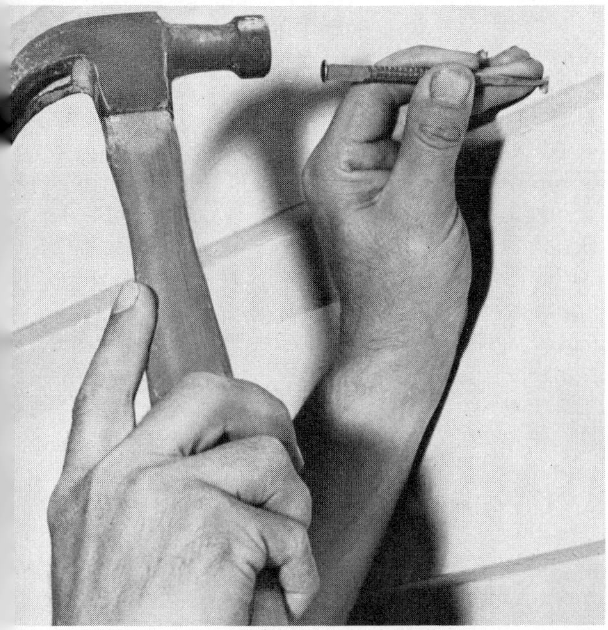

Benjamin Moore and Co.

5-22. Set down all the nails that are showing in the siding and trim. Spot prime the nail holes.

• Shellac and a 2″ brush, for sealing knots.

Procedure

1. Put drop cloths under the area you will paint. Tie shrubs back out of the way.

2. Set up the ladder on sound footing. Try to take as much equipment as you will need up the ladder to avoid many up-and-down trips.

3. Remove any items, such as the mailbox, outside lights, and shutters, that may get spattered while you are painting.

4. Make all needed repairs. Replace rotted trim and broken shingles. Renail loose siding. Use a nail set to drive the nailheads below the surface. Fig. 5-22. Spot prime all the nail holes and fill them with putty. The back of new trim should be primed before it is installed. Then the front must be primed. Use the type of primer recommended by the paint manufacturer. (See Chapter 11 for information about exterior carpentry repairs.)

5. Seal with shellac all knots and other places where pitch has oozed out of the wood.

6. Scrape off loose paint with a hand scraper, putty knife, or wire brush. Fig. 5-23. Smooth rough surfaces with sandpaper (Fig. 5-24), an orbital sander, or the disk sanding attachment of an electric drill. Sand or wire-brush the old paint that is still

5-23. Scrape off loose paint.

Benjamin Moore and Co.

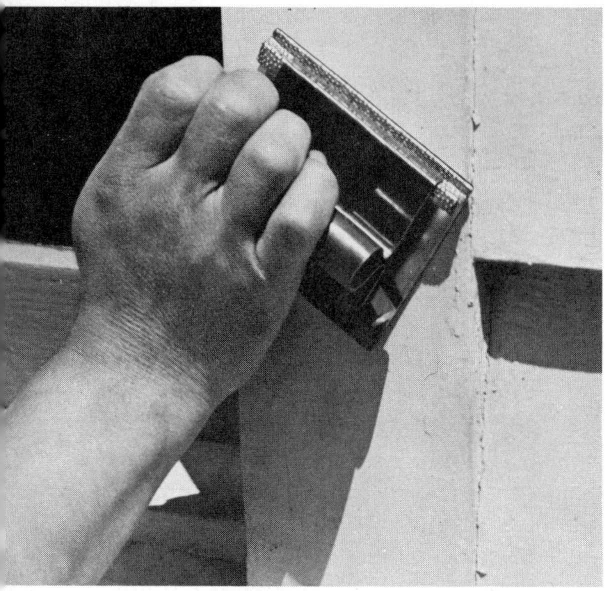

Benjamin Moore and Co.

5-24. Smooth rough surfaces with sandpaper. A sandpaper holder is used here to sand window trim.

5-25. Clean the dust and dirt from siding with a cloth.

Benjamin Moore and Co.

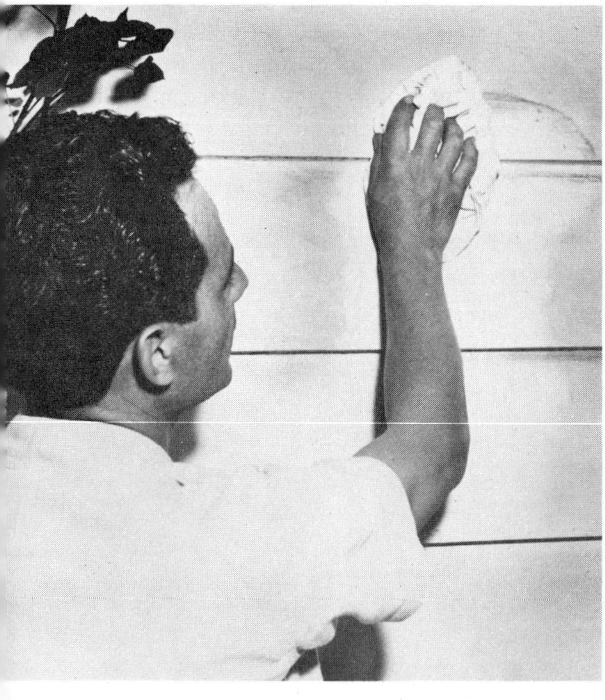

shiny. Such paint may be found in protected areas, such as under the eaves.

7. Clean and prime the outside of gutters and downspouts before painting them. Scrape and wire-brush the gutters to remove rust and peeling paint.

8. Clean all dust and dirt from surfaces to be painted with a cloth or a stiff brush. All siding must be free of dirt. Fig. 5-25.

9. Dried and cracked putty around window glass should be removed and replaced with new compound. Fig. 5-26. (See Chapter 10.)

10. Caulk around windows, doors, and other areas where caulking is loose. First scrape out loose caulking with a putty knife. Brush out any dust or dirt. Then run a bead of caulking, making sure it gets into the space evenly, without any gaps. Fig. 5-27. Caulking is needed wherever two different materials join. For example, it is used where a door or window frame meets the siding, or where a chimney meets the siding or the roof.

11. Prime (undercoat) all areas where bare wood is showing. Prime over new caulking too. Use a primer that is recommended for the paint you are using. When it is dry, you are ready to paint.

PREPARING MASONRY SURFACES

Powdery and peeling areas of masonry must be cleaned completely. A wire brush or a hand scraper will do this job well. Clean out the cracks and fill them with patching cement. Let the cement dry overnight.

PREPARING METAL SURFACES

Remove any grease or dirt from the metal with paint thinner. Remove rust, scale, and peeling paint with a wire brush. Go over new metal surfaces with steel wool to roughen them so that paint will adhere better. Before painting a galvanized surface, coat it with a primer made for that purpose. (You can ask a paint salesperson which primer is correct for the metal you are painting.) Two thin coats of primer usually cover better on a metal surface than one thick coat.

Benjamin Moore and Co.

5-26. Dried up window putty should be removed. Replace it with new glazing compound applied with a putty knife.

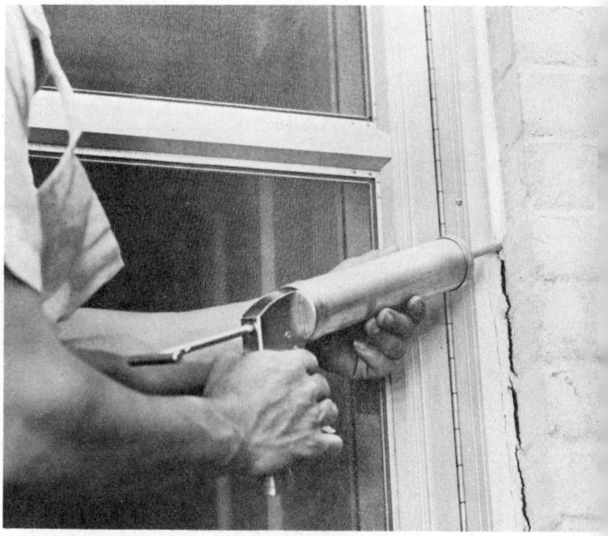

Benjamin Moore and Co.

5-27. Scrape out loose caulking and replace it. Here a caulking gun is used to apply new caulking.

MATERIALS FOR EXTERIOR PAINTING

- Extension ladder, long enough to reach eaves.
- Stepladder.
- Drop cloths for covering shrubs, walks, and parts of house.
- Exterior house paint. Fig. 5-28.
- Trim paint.
- Solvent (paint thinner for oil-base paint).
- Paint buckets. (Paper or plastic disposable buckets are convenient.)
- Paint can hook (to hang paint cans on ladder).
- Clean rags.

HERE ARE SOME SUGGESTED COLOR SCHEMES FOR YOUR HOME:

If your house has shutters, paint the trim the same color as body of house—or white. If not, use these suggested colors for trim.

If the roof of your house is 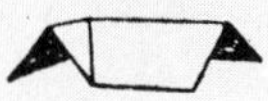	You can paint the body 	. . . and the trim or shutters and doors															
		Pink	Bright red	Red-orange	Tile red	Cream	Bright yellow	Light green	Dark green	Gray-green	Blue-green	Light blue	Dark blue	Blue-gray	Violet	Brown	White
GRAY	White	X	X	X	X	X	X	X	X	X	X	X	X	X	X		
	Gray	X	X	X	X		X	X	X	X	X	X	X	X	X		X
	Cream-yellow		X		X		X		X	X							X
	Pale green				X		X		X	X							X
	Dark green	X				X	X	X									X
	Putty			X	X				X	X			X	X		X	
	Dull red	X				X		X						X			X
GREEN	White	X	X	X	X	X	X	X	X	X	X	X	X	X	X	X	
	Gray			X		X	X	X									X
	Cream-yellow		X		X			X	X	X						X	X
	Pale green			X	X		X		X								X
	Dark green	X		X		X	X	X									X
	Beige				X				X	X	X		X	X			
	Brown	X				X	X	X									X
	Dull red					X		X		X							X
RED	White		X		X				X		X			X			
	Light gray		X		X				X								X
	Cream-yellow		X		X						X		X	X			
	Pale green		X		X												X
	Dull red					X		X		X	X						X
BROWN	White			X	X		X	X	X	X	X		X	X	X	X	
	Buff				X				X	X	X					X	
	Pink-beige				X				X	X						X	X
	Cream-yellow				X				X	X	X					X	
	Pale green								X	X						X	
	Brown			X		X	X										X
BLUE	White			X	X		X					X	X				
	Gray			X		X						X	X				X
	Cream-yellow			X	X								X	X			
	Blue			X		X	X					X					X

National Paint & Coatings Association

5-28. This chart can help you choose the colors of paint to use for the body of the house and the trim.

- Paint stirrers, wood or metal.
- 4″ wall brush. Fig. 5-29.
- 2″ trim brush. Fig. 5-29.
- 2″ sash brush (optional).
- Roller pan or tray with plastic or aluminum foil liner.
- Roller with cover (7″ or 9″) and extension poles.
- Doughnut roller for doing the edges of siding (optional).
- Trim roller, 3″ (optional).
- Pad applicator (7″ or 9″) for shingles or shakes.

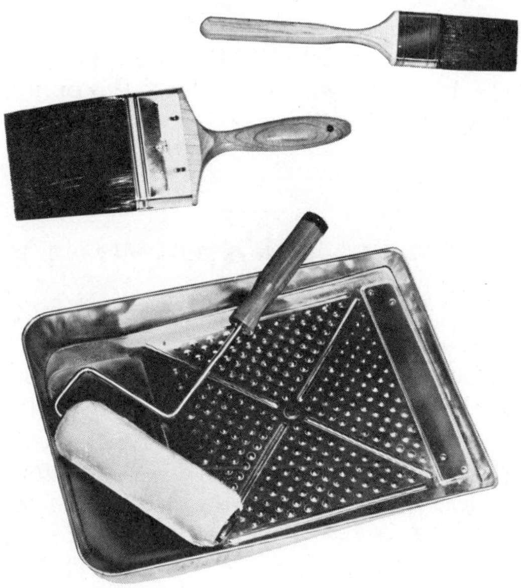

Benjamin Moore and Co.

5-29. A 2″ trim brush, a 4″ wall brush, and a roller pan and roller covered with lambskin shearling for rough surfaces.

ESTIMATING HOUSE PAINT

To estimate the amount of paint you will need, do the following:

1. Measure the home's perimeter (the distance around the house).
2. Measure the height of the siding up to the roofline.
3. Multiply the perimeter by the height to obtain the square feet of outside wall area.
4. If the house has gables, figure the area of each gable as follows: multiply the height of the gable from the eaves by $\frac{1}{2}$ the width of the gable. Add the area of the gables to the outside wall area.
5. On the paint can label, you will find the estimated coverage. Fig. 5–30. Divide this number into the total area to be painted. For example, if the label states that 1 gallon of paint will cover 500 square feet and the

5-30. Read the paint can label to find the estimated coverage.

National Paint & Coatings Association

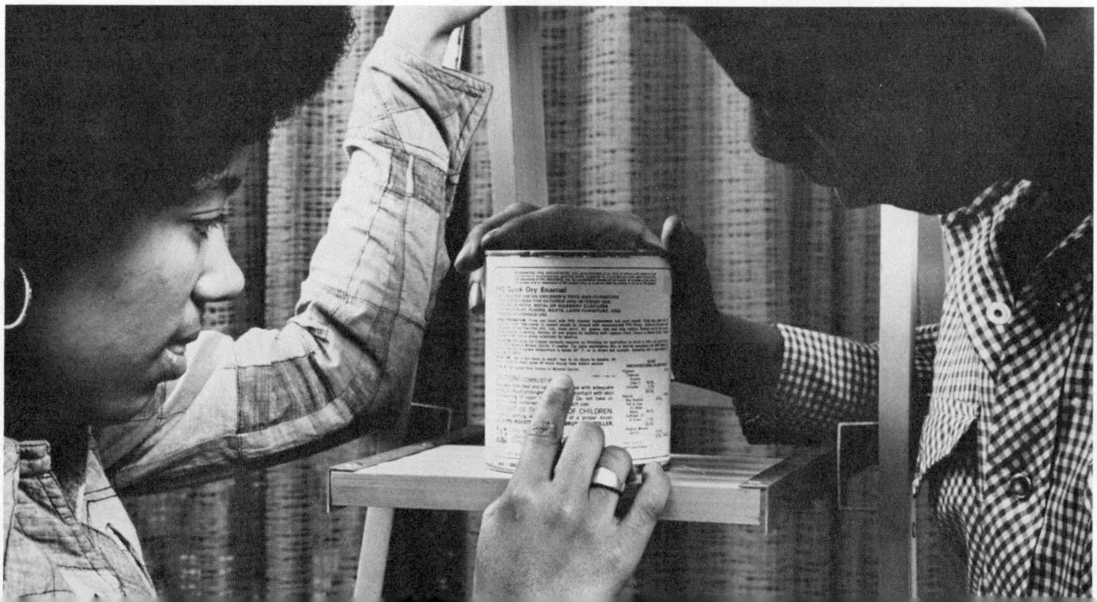

area to be painted equals 1440 square feet, you will need about 3 gallons of paint. For the trim, you will need $\frac{1}{8}$ to $\frac{1}{5}$ of this amount.

6. Remember, the amount figured will be for one coat of paint. For two coats, double the amount.

APPLYING EXTERIOR PAINT

1. There are three ways to apply paint to the outside of a home. You can use brushes, rollers, or pad applicators. The latter are synthetic foam pads containing many nylon fibers. The pads will coat a rough cedar shake or a striated asbestos shingle in one or two strokes without missing any of the ridges. These pads come in different sizes and are disposable.

2. Stir the paint thoroughly. A stirrer is usually included free with paint that you buy. Using a lifting motion, bring the pigment up from the bottom of the can with each stroke. When the paint is thoroughly stirred, pour it from one can to another a couple of times to complete the mixing.

If you are using oil paint that has been standing around in the workshop for a long time, it will probably have a skin on top. Remove the skin with a piece of wood and dispose of it. The paint must then be thoroughly mixed. Pour off the oil that has risen to the top into another container. Stir the remaining paint with a lifting motion while gradually pouring the extra oil back into the paint. Then pour the paint from one can to another to complete the mixing.

3. Brush on the paint, working it out from side to side. Fig. 5-31. Do the seam or the edge of the siding first, then coat the remaining surface. Fig. 5-32. Feather the ends of the brush strokes so that there will be no lap marks.

If you use a roller, apply the paint in even strokes. Use a brush or doughnut roller to do the edges of the siding. A trim roller (narrow width) can be used for narrow areas. Pad applicators are used to coat each individual shingle. Use an extension pole on rollers and pad applicators when possible, to avoid having to climb a ladder.

4. Paint from the top down. Do the highest parts (eaves and gutters) of the house first. Fig. 5-33. Work out a systematic way to avoid going up and down and moving the ladder too often.

5-31. Brush the paint out well, working from side to side.
Benjamin Moore and Co.

5-32. Paint the seam or edge of siding first. Then paint the rest of the surface.
Benjamin Moore and Co.

5. Complete the trim last. If possible remove shutters for painting. Window sash is painted first, then the frame and sill. Leave the windows open after you are through. Otherwise, the paint on the sill and sash may dry them shut.

6. After you are finished, clean your painting tools. Store leftover paint in tightly closed cans. Remove all the drop cloths from sidewalks and shrubs. Clean up any paint spills with solvent and a stiff brush.

Benjamin Moore and Co.

5-33. Paint from the top down. Do the gutters and eaves first.

PREPARATION FOR INTERIOR PAINTING

1. Remove as many pieces of furniture as possible from the room to be painted. Furniture too large to be removed can be moved into the center of the room and covered with drop cloths.

2. All curtains, drapes, shades, venetian blinds, pictures, and area rugs should be removed. Use a screwdriver to remove switch plates, outlet covers, doorknobs, and other hardware. Fig. 5-34. Drop ceiling light fixtures so that they hang by the wiring. Tie plastic bags loosely over the canopy and bulb to protect them from paint spatters.

3. Wash soiled or greasy walls with a detergent and water. Fig. 5-35. Rinse with clear water. Kitchen walls and ceilings especially need washing because smoke and grease from cooking cling to them. The walls must be clean so that paint will adhere to them.

5-34. Use a screwdriver to remove switch plates, outlet covers, and other hardware.

Benjamin Moore and Co.

5-35. Wash soiled or greasy walls. Use detergent in a bucket of water. Sponge and rinse with clear water.

Benjamin Moore and Co.

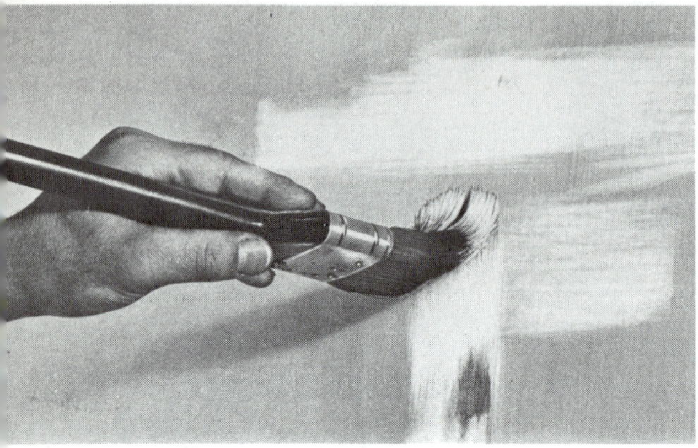

Benjamin Moore and Co.

5-36. Spot prime all repaired areas.

Benjamin Moore and Co.

5-37. Scrape off loose paint around woodwork and sand the area smooth. Prime all bare spots.

4. Fill all cracks, holes, and other surface imperfections. (Wall repair is discussed in Chapter 4.) Set down all wallboard nails with a nail set and hammer, and fill the holes. Spot prime all repaired areas with an interior primer or with the same paint you will use on the walls. Fig. 5-36.

5. Scrape off loose paint around woodwork and sand the area smooth. Fig. 5-37. Prime all bare spots.

MATERIALS FOR INTERIOR PAINTING

Benjamin Moore and Co.

5-38. Some materials for an interior paint job.

The following is a list of supplies for inside painting. Fig. 5-38.

- Spackling compound for wall repairs.
- Putty knife for wall repairs.
- Mixing pails. (Disposable plastic or paper pails are handy.)
- Newspapers for covering floors and furniture.
- Drop cloths.
- Wall paint (usually flat finish).
- Trim enamel (usually semigloss).
- Solvent mineral spirits for oil paint.
- Abrasive paper, medium grade.
- Stepladder.
- Clean rags.
- Roller tray, or pan.
- 7″ or 9″ roller with cover.
- Sash brush, $1\frac{1}{2}$″.
- Trim brush, 2″.
- Wall brush, 4″.
- Sponge, detergent, and bucket for washing walls.

ESTIMATING WALL PAINT

Use the following procedure to estimate the amount of paint needed.

1. To find the wall area of the room, multiply the room's perimeter (the distance around the room) by the ceiling height. Check the paint can label to find the estimated coverage. Divide this amount into the wall area to find the number of gallons of paint needed for one coat.

For example, the room may be 10′ x 15′ with 8′ ceilings. The perimeter would be 50′. The wall area would be 400 square feet. If 1 gallon of paint covers 450 square feet, you will need only 1 gallon to cover the walls with one coat of paint.

2. To find the ceiling area, multiply the length by the width. Figure the amount of paint needed by using the method described in Step 1.

3. To estimate trim paint, figure $\frac{1}{4}$ pint for each window and frame and $\frac{1}{2}$ pint for each door (one side) and frame. You will also need paint for the baseboard. If you are giving the trim two coats of paint, double these amounts.

INTERIOR PAINTING PROCEDURE

1. Assemble all painting tools and materials. Make sure the brushes and rollers are clean.

2. Stir the paint thoroughly, bringing the paint up from the bottom of the can with a lifting motion of the stirrer. Pour the mixed paint from one can to another a couple of times to complete mixing.

3. Paint the ceiling first. Fig. 5-39. If you are using a roller, use a trim brush to paint

Benjamin Moore and Co.

5-39. Paint the ceiling first. Use a trim brush to paint the corners where the ceiling meets the walls.

Benjamin Moore and Co.

5-40. Fill in the large wall areas with a wall brush.

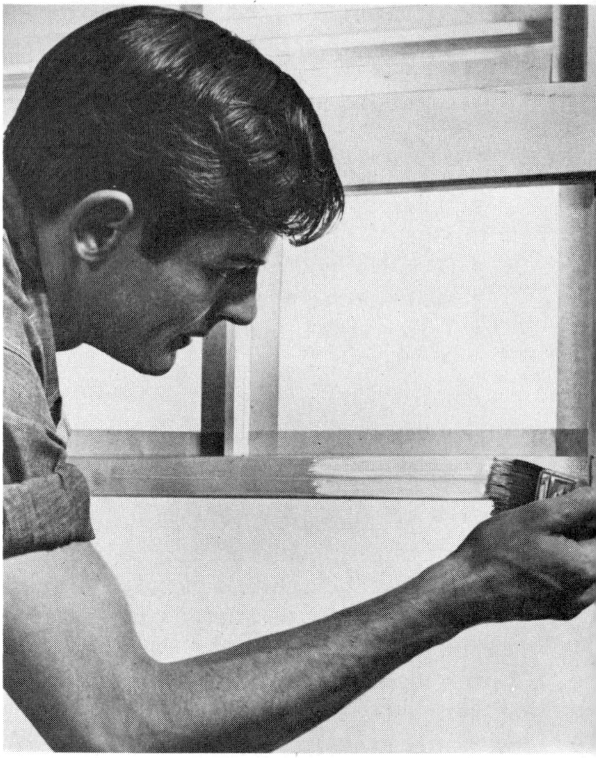

Benjamin Moore and Co.

5-42. Paint the upper sash first, then the lower sash.

5-41. Use masking tape on window panes to do a neater job when painting the sash.

Benjamin Moore and Co.

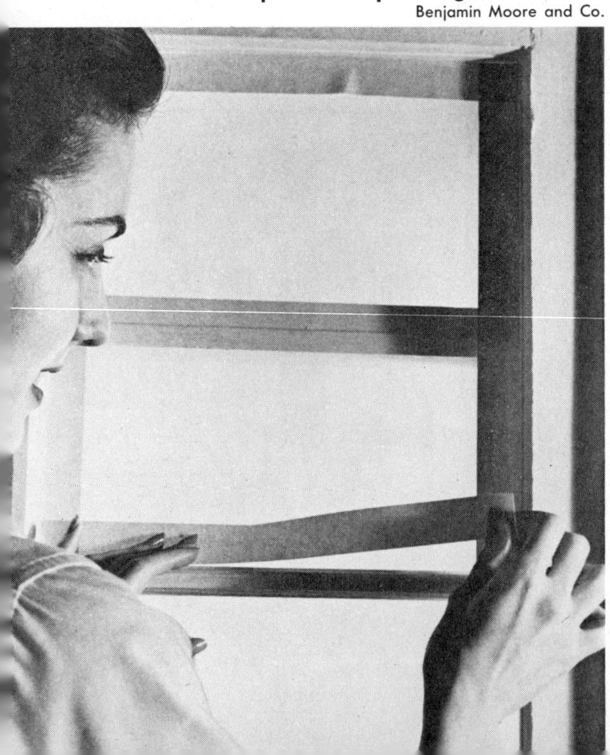

5-43. Hold a piece of cardboard or plastic against the bottom edge of a baseboard to protect the floor or carpet from paint.

Benjamin Moore and Co.

the corners where the ceiling meets the walls. Paint in a 3′ or 4′ strip across the narrowest dimension of the ceiling. Then go back and paint the next strip before the edge dries so that there will be no lap marks.

4. Two people painting a room as a team often work well. One person paints corners and edges with a brush, while the other fills in large areas with either a brush or roller. Fig. 5-40. Start painting walls at the top and work down in 3′ strips.

5. The trim is done next. Enamels used to paint woodwork are flowed on with horizontal strokes, then lightly leveled off with even, vertical strokes. Work quickly because enamel sets quickly.

6. Use masking tape on window panes for a neater job when painting window sash. Fig. 5-41. (Remove the tape *carefully* before the paint is dry.) Any paint that gets on the glass can be removed with a razor blade when the paint is dry. Paint the upper sash first, then the lower sash. Fig. 5-42. Next, paint the window frames and the sill. The window sill should be given two coats.

7. Paint the doors next, starting with the faces of the door, then finishing the edges. On a paneled door, the panels are painted first, starting at the top.

8. Baseboards are painted after all the other trim is done. Hold a piece of thin cardboard or plastic against the bottom edge of the baseboard to protect the floor or the carpet from paint. Fig. 5-43. A trim guard for this purpose may be purchased in any paint or hardware store. Another method is to use a dustpan to hold wall-to-wall carpeting away from the baseboard while you paint. Do not let drop cloths or newspapers rub against baseboards until the paint is dry.

9. Clean your painting tools with the proper solvent. Store unused paint in tightly closed cans. Do not clean up the room or move the furniture back until the paint has completely dried, to avoid marring the walls. When the paint is dry, replace all the hardware and rehang the pictures, shades, and blinds.

CHECKUP

1. What functions do interior and exterior paints serve?
2. What are the three basic types of exterior paint? The four basic types of interior paint?
3. Why is it important to prepare a surface before painting it?

CHAPTER 6

Redecorating with Wallcoverings

TYPES OF WALLCOVERINGS

The term *wallcoverings,* as discussed in this chapter, means any paper- or textile-backed materials which are pasted to walls. Many types of wallcoverings are available. Stores selling paint and wall coverings have many sample books available for you to look through. You will probably see, from the great variety of books available, that the term *wallpaper* does not accurately describe the kinds of materials available.

Wallcoverings fall into these categories for both paper-backed and textile-backed materials:

- Prepasted—glue is already on the back; it is activated by wetting the back of the roll with water.
- Self-adhering—you have to pull a backing paper off to expose the adhesive.
- Vinyl-covered—front surface is vinyl-coated to make it washable.
- Foil-coated.
- Plasticized—front surface is impregnated with plastic to make pattern washable.
- Flocked—design is covered with a synthetic flock.

Some rolls of wallcovering are sold *untrimmed.* This means that the selvage edge has not been cut off by the manufacturer. Most are available pretrimmed, however. (Trimming the strips at home is a difficult and time-consuming task.) The description of the wallcovering in the sample book will give such information, as well as price and size of rolls.

ESTIMATING WALLCOVERING

When you look through wallcovering sample books, you will notice that many of them include a chart for estimating the amount of wallcovering needed. The book will also tell you available widths (usually 24 to 28 inches) and how much coverage can be expected from a single roll. For example, a roll 5 yards long may cover 30 square feet.

If there is no chart, the required amount of wallcovering can be estimated as follows:

1. Measure the width and height of the walls to be covered. Multiply the width by the height of each wall to obtain its square footage (area). Add the areas of all the walls to be covered to obtain the total square footage.
2. Measure the window and door openings. Figure the total square footage of these openings the same way you figured that of the walls.

3. Subtract the total square footage of the windows, doors, and other large openings from the total wall square footage. The answer is the total area to be covered in that room.

4. Consult the information section of the wallcovering sample book for the number of square feet one roll will cover. Divide that figure into the total figure for the room. Round off to the next full roll. Be aware that when using a patterned wallcovering you must allow for some waste when matching patterns. It is sometimes handy to order an extra roll to allow for such waste.

5. If the paper is sold in only double or triple rolls, divide the number of single rolls necessary by two or by three to determine the number of double or triple rolls you need. You will probably get more usable wallcovering in a double or a triple roll.

WALL PREPARATION

Preparing a Painted Wall or a New Wall

1. Repair any cracks, dents, or holes as explained in Chapter 4.

2. Spot prime any bare spots on dry wall or plaster with primer or paint. Be sure to prime all spackled patches also.

3. If walls are dirty or greasy, wash them down with a detergent and water. Rinse them off if necessary.

4. New dry wall must be primed before any wallcovering can be put on. Otherwise, the covering will be difficult to remove later without ruining the dry wall.

Preparing a Wallpapered Wall

1. Inspect walls carefully to see that the old wallcovering is in good condition. Reglue any loose edges or ripped portions of the covering with a small amount of paperhanger's paste or white glue. Press and rub these areas flat with a clean cloth to remove any air bubbles. Let the pasted area dry for 24 hours to be sure of good contact.

2. Apply new wallcovering over old only if there are fewer than three layers on the wall and if they are in good condition.

If you want to remove old wallcovering, there are several methods. These are discussed in the following sections. The method to use will depend partly on the type of wallcovering. For example, strippable wallcovering can be removed simply by carefully pulling it away from the wall. (See "Removing Textile-backed Wallcoverings.")

Removing Old Wallcoverings with a Steamer

1. Rent a wallpaper steamer. Fig. 6-1. These are electrically heated machines that build up steam. The steam softens the old paste, making it easy to remove the wallcovering. The only preparation a steamer requires is to be filled with water. Get instructions from the shop that rents you the machine.

2. Cover the floor under the wall with a drop cloth or newspapers.

3. Start at the bottom of the wall because the rising steam will loosen the material above. A ceiling that has a covering on it will also be loosened by the rising steam.

4. A steamer uses a flat pan with a long hose attached to it. Steam comes from the flat pan. Hold the pan for a minute or two against the old paper that you wish to remove. Then shift it to another area while

6-1. Electric wallcovering steamer.
Warner Manufacturing Co.

you slip a putty knife under the softened wallcovering and remove it. Remove all small pieces of covering that are left, or they will dry and harden on the wall. Continue in this manner, removing the material that has been softened by the steam, until the entire wall is completed.

5. Wash down the stripped walls with hot water and a sponge to remove all the old glue. Sand off any remaining small pieces of wallcovering. Fill cracks and dents with spackling compound. If there are rough areas, sand the wall smooth with medium-grade abrasive paper.

Removing Wallcovering by Soaking

1. Cover the floor with a drop cloth or newspapers.

2. Apply hot water to the wall with a cloth or a sponge, continuing until the glue loosens. Start from the top of the wall and work downward.

3. Use a wide putty knife to loosen the wallcovering. Usually, only one layer at a time can be removed with this method.

Removing Wallcovering with a Wallpaper Stripping Knife

A wallpaper stripping knife is a tool that uses replaceable blades similar to razor blades. Follow these steps:

1. Slit the wallcovering horizontally with a sharp razor blade or razor knife so that you cut through the layers of wallcovering to the paint on the surface of the wall.

2. Press the end of the stripper knife against the wall with one hand. Force the edge of the blade under the slit in the wallcovering. Hold the handle of the knife with the other hand.

3. Push the tool upward. Use quick strokes as you keep the blade close to the surface of the wall. Strips of the old wallcovering will be shaved off the surface with each upward stroke.

4. Areas of the wall where pieces of wallcovering remain can be stripped clean if you apply hot water with a sponge or cloth to soften the paste. Then use the wallpaper stripping knife on these areas again.

Chemical Wallcovering Removers

These are paper-wetting agents which contain a detergent that cuts through dirt and grease. The remover then soaks through the wallcovering. Follow the manufacturer's instructions for using these chemicals.

1. Cover the floor with a drop cloth or newspapers.

2. When the wallcovering is soaked through and the glue on the back is softened, strip off the material carefully with a putty knife. Do not dig into the wall with the knife.

Removing Plastic-coated Wallcoverings

These wallcoverings have a nonporous protective coating that is sometimes hard to break. If, after testing the wallcovering with water you determine that its plastic coating will not allow the penetration of water or steam, you must break the surface in one of the following ways:

- Sand the area with medium or coarse abrasive paper.
- Scrape the surface with a cheese grater.
- Slash the surface, criss-cross fashion, with a razor blade.

Follow with a thorough soaking with hot water, working from top to bottom, or use a steamer. Remember to cover the floor with a drop cloth or newspapers before you begin.

Removing Textile-backed Wallcoverings

Many types of wallcovering are made with textile backings. Such wallcoverings are heavy; so they cover minor imperfections on the wall. Another advantage of textile-backed wallcoverings is that they can be stripped off a wall, usually without soaking or steaming. Pulling the covering off the wall does little or no damage to the wall surface. To remove textile-backed wallcoverings, follow these steps:

1. Pull the cloth-backed covering off the wall. Pull to one side, not straight out.

2. Soak any stubborn spots with hot water, or steam them off.

3. Wash the wall with hot water to remove the glue. Sand any rough spots with medium-grade abrasive paper.

TOOLS AND MATERIALS FOR HANGING WALLCOVERINGS

- Paste brush. Fig. 6-2.
- Smoothing brush. Fig. 6-2.
- Two plastic buckets.
- Cheesecloth for straining the paste.
- Water box of cardboard or plastic (for prepasted wallcoverings). Fig. 6-3.
- Clean cloths.
- Newspapers to cover pasting surface on worktable.
- Razor knife and extra single-edge razor blades. Fig. 6-4.
- Worktable, at least 2′ x 6′ (a piece of $\frac{1}{2}$″ plywood on sawhorses or a metal utility table).
- Sponge.
- Seam roller. Fig. 6-5.
- Pencil.
- 36″ metal straightedge.
- Push-pull ruler or measuring tape.
- Wallpaper paste (use the kind recommended by the wallcovering manufacturer).
- Stepladder.
- Wallcovering in single, double, or triple rolls.
- Sharp scissors, to cut and trim.
- Chalk line reel, or line with a plumb bob (weight). Fig. 6-6.
- Paint stirrer for mixing paste.

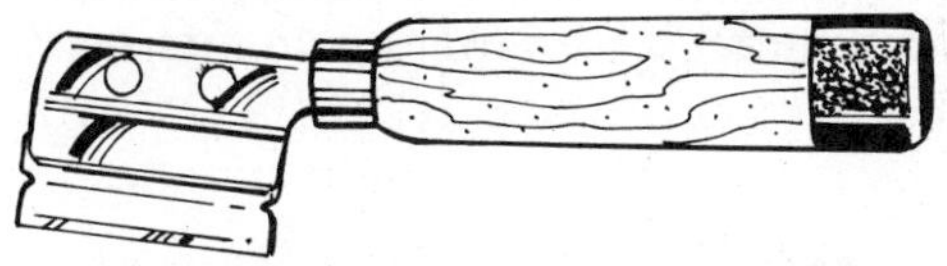

6-4. Razor knife for single-edged blades.

Warner Manufacturing Co.

6-2. Paste brush (left), and a smoothing brush.

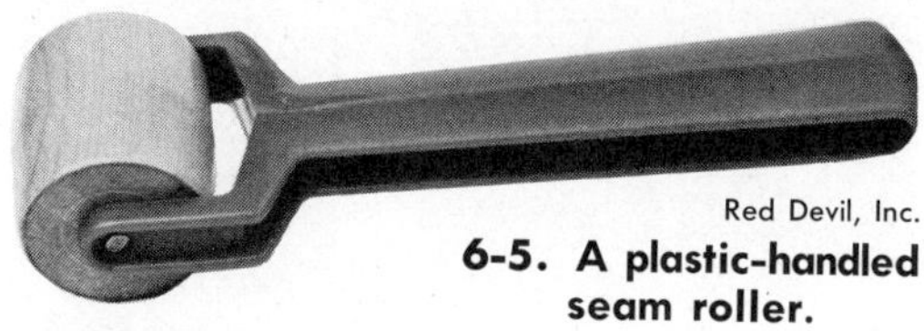

Red Devil, Inc.

6-5. A plastic-handled seam roller.

6-3. A cardboard water box.

Warner Manufacturing Co.

6-6. A chalk line reel. The case acts as a plumb bob, or weight, so that you can make a true chalk line on a wall.

Stanley Tools

HANGING WALLCOVERINGS

1. Prepare the wall surfaces as discussed earlier in this chapter under "Wall Preparation." Remove all outlet and switch plates and any wall decorations. This will make it easier to apply the wallcovering. (These objects can be replaced after the wallcovering is up.) Unroll each roll, inspect it for damages or printing errors, then reroll.

2. The first strip will be placed at one corner. The edge of this strip will act as a guide line for the next strip. Therefore it is very important that the first strip be straight. Snap a chalk line from the ceiling to the floor, using either a chalk line reel or a plumb bob and a string covered with chalk. Fig. 6-7. The first strip will be placed along this line and extended about ½″ around the corner.

To snap a chalk line follow these steps:

- Chalk the line.
- Measure the width of the wallcoverings and subtract ½″ for overlap on intersecting wall.

6-7. Snap a chalk line on the wall to insure that the vertical edge of the first strip will be straight.

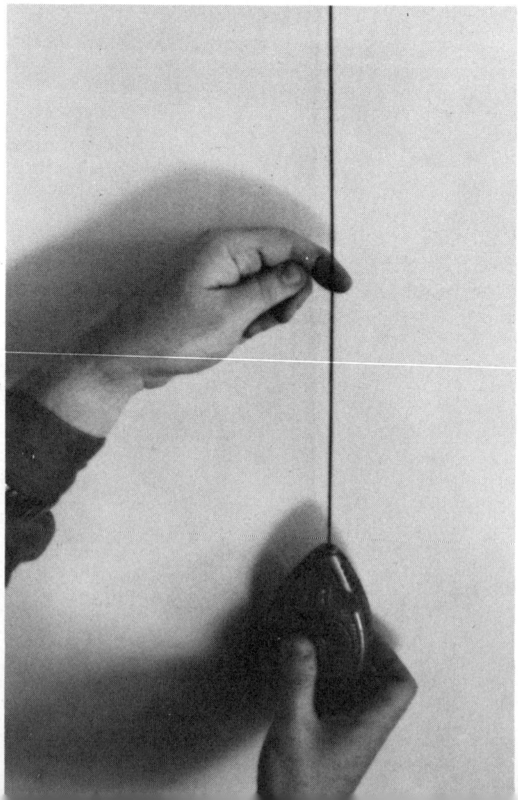

- Mark one wall near the ceiling with this measurement, starting at any corner.
- Tack the end of the plumb bob line to the wall at the mark and let the plumb bob hang freely.
- When the plumb bob stops swinging and is perfectly still, press the plumb bob gently against the wall with one hand.
- With your other hand, grasp the line between the thumb and index finger and gently pull it towards you about 4″ to 6″ from the wall.
- Release the line and allow it to snap once against the wall.
- Remove the tack.

3. Cover your worktable with a layer of newspaper. Each time you finish putting paste on a strip, replace the newspaper with a fresh layer before you lay down a new strip of wallcovering. By doing this, you will avoid getting paste on the printed side of the wallcovering.

4. Mix the paste in a plastic bucket. The package directions will tell you how much water to add. The paste should have the consistency of heavy cream. Spread a piece of cheesecloth over the top of another bucket and strain the paste through the cheesecloth. The paste should not have any lumps because these will show under the wallcovering.

5. Set up the stepladder where the first strip will be placed. On the ladder put a seam roller, a clean dry cloth, damp sponge (to remove excess paste), the smoothing brush, and the razor knife. Taking these items up with you will save the time and trouble of looking for them later. Measure the wall height with the measuring tape or the push-pull ruler.

6. Put the wallcovering on the worktable, pattern side down, and unroll it the length of the table. Allow 2 inches extra at both the top and the bottom of the wall height measurement. For example, on an 8′ wall, measure and mark off 8′4″. Make a light pencil mark near the edge of the mate-

rial to mark the length to be cut. Use a straightedge and a razor blade, or a pair of scissors, to cut the wallcovering to length.

7. Keep the paste and paste brush handy on the worktable. Apply paste to the back of the material with the paste brush, being careful not to miss any spots, *especially the edges.* Fig. 6-8. Make sure that there are no lumps of paste on the wallcovering. Do not put too much paste on the wallcovering; just enough to coat the back is sufficient. Cover the bottom two thirds of the strip with paste. Fold the strip down to the end of the paste area. Move the rest of the strip up on the table, taking care not to get paste on the pattern side. Paste the remaining one-third of the strip, which will be the top portion. A short strip (5 feet or less) may be folded almost in half, leaving the top 3 inches unfolded. Fold lightly. *Do not press down* or you will crease the strip.

8. Lightly pick up the wallcovering strip by the corners of the TOP edge, with the printed side facing you. Take the strip up the ladder and position it on the wall along the chalk line, overlapping about 2 inches of wallcovering onto the ceiling. Smooth out the paper with strokes from left to right, using a brush or cloth, to make the strip adhere to the wall. Fig. 6-9. Then release the folded section of the material so that it drops against the wall in front of you.

6-8. Apply paste to a wallcovering strip with a paste brush. Be careful not to miss any areas.

Starting at the top center of the strip, smooth the wallcovering, working from the center outward and from top to bottom. Take care that no bubbles are left under the material. Fig. 6-10. If the strip moves away from the chalk line, it can be slid over slightly to meet the line. If it must be moved more than a little, pull the material away from the wall and place it again.

When the strip is in position, wipe off any paste that is left on the surface. Use a damp

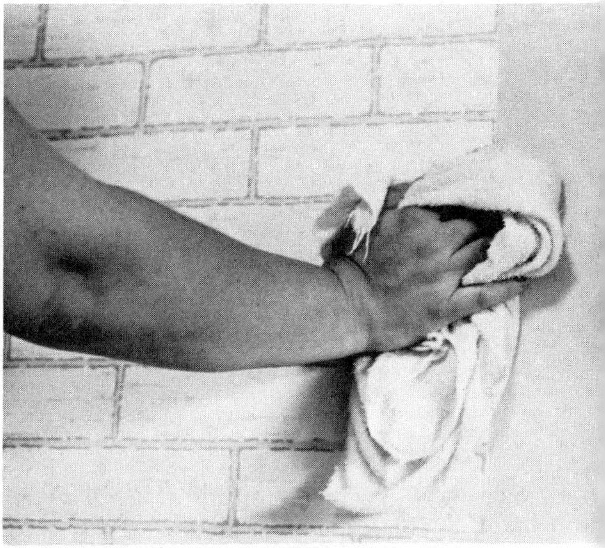

6-9. Apply pressure with a clean, dry cloth or a smoothing brush to make the strip adhere to the wall.

6-10. Starting at the top center of the strip, smooth the wallcovering from left to right and from top to bottom. Be careful to work out air bubbles from the material.

cloth or sponge for vinyl-faced or textile-backed covering. When using uncoated paper or foil-faced paper, wipe off the paste immediately with a slightly damp cloth. Use light pressure and very few strokes to prevent the paper from tearing at the edges. Use the smoothing brush or a cloth to force the strip tightly into all joints and corners. Inspect the strip on the wall from different angles to see if there are any bubbles.

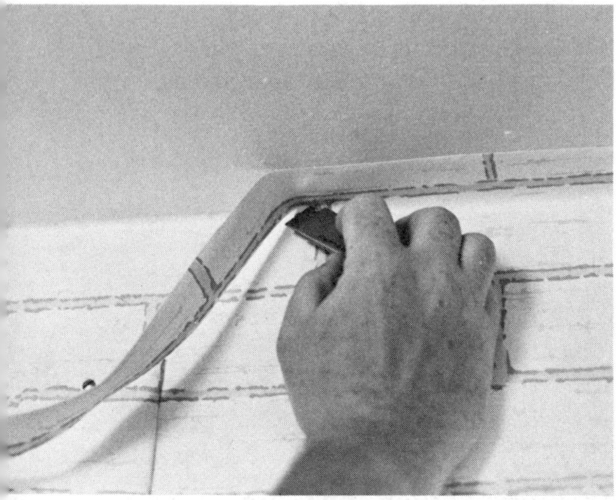

6-11. When you trim the strip along the ceiling, be careful to cut a straight, clean line.

9. If you allow the strip to set for at least 15 minutes (but not until the glue is thoroughly dry) before trimming, it will be easier to cut. Trim the top and bottom with a sharp razor blade. When you trim against the molding on the wall, be careful to cut in a straight, clean line. Fig. 6-11. A metal trim guide is useful for making straight cuts.

10. Put a new layer of newspaper on the worktable. Otherwise paste from the old newspapers may get on the printed side of the next strip.

11. Before cutting the next strip, take the roll of wallcovering up the ladder with you. Unroll a foot or two of the material. Hold it up alongside the first strip and match up the patterns at the top, near the ceiling. Make a small pencil mark on the strip at the spot where the wall meets the ceiling.

6-12a. Roll the seams with a seam roller after the strip has set for at least 15 minutes.

6-12b. Using a seam roller and a smoothing brush.

Oklahoma Industrial Arts News
Photograph by Emmett Osgood

12. Lay the roll on the worktable with the pattern side up. Starting at the pencil mark, measure off the height of the wall. Add two inches at the top and bottom for adjustments. Cut the strip with a razor blade and a straightedge or a pair of scissors. Apply paste to this strip and proceed to fold and apply the wallcovering as described in Steps 7 and 8.

13. Position the second strip so that its edge butts against the edge of the first strip. Release the folded section of the strip and begin smoothing out the covering with a cloth or smoothing brush. Check to be sure that the edges butt tightly but do not overlap. If you find that the pattern cannot match perfectly all along the edges, make sure that it at least matches at eye level. Smooth out the bubbles, starting at the top and working from the center toward the edges. Wipe off any paste that gets on the printed side of the wallcovering.

14. Allow this strip to set for at least 15 minutes. Roll the seams with the seam roller, using firm pressure. Fig. 6-12. Wipe any paste from the seam roller. Then trim the top and bottom of the strip with a sharp razor blade. (When the blade becomes dull, dispose of it safely in an old jar or other container with a cover.)

15. If there is an electrical switch or outlet in the area where the wallcovering is placed, cut an *X* in the strip with a razor blade as you smooth the strip over the opening. Feel the space with your fingertips to locate the opening.

When the wallcovering is dry enough to trim, cut out the wallcovering over the electrical box with a razor blade or scissors. Fig. 6-13. To insure that the plate will cover the cut edges, do not cut the paper past the edges of the box. Fig. 6-14.

16. When you come to a large opening, such as a doorway or window, the procedure is as follows. Place the strip on the wall in the correct location, matching the patterns. Lightly mark off the doorway opening on the strip with a pencil, allowing 3 extra inches from the top of the doorframe and 3 extra inches from the inside of the doorframe. Lay the material on the worktable and use a straightedge to draw the two lines on the wallcovering. Cut away the excess material to reduce the weight of the wallcovering and

6-13. Cut out the wallcovering over the electrical box with a razor blade or scissors.

6-14. Do not cut past the edges of the outlet or switch box. Remove the cutout piece of wallcovering.

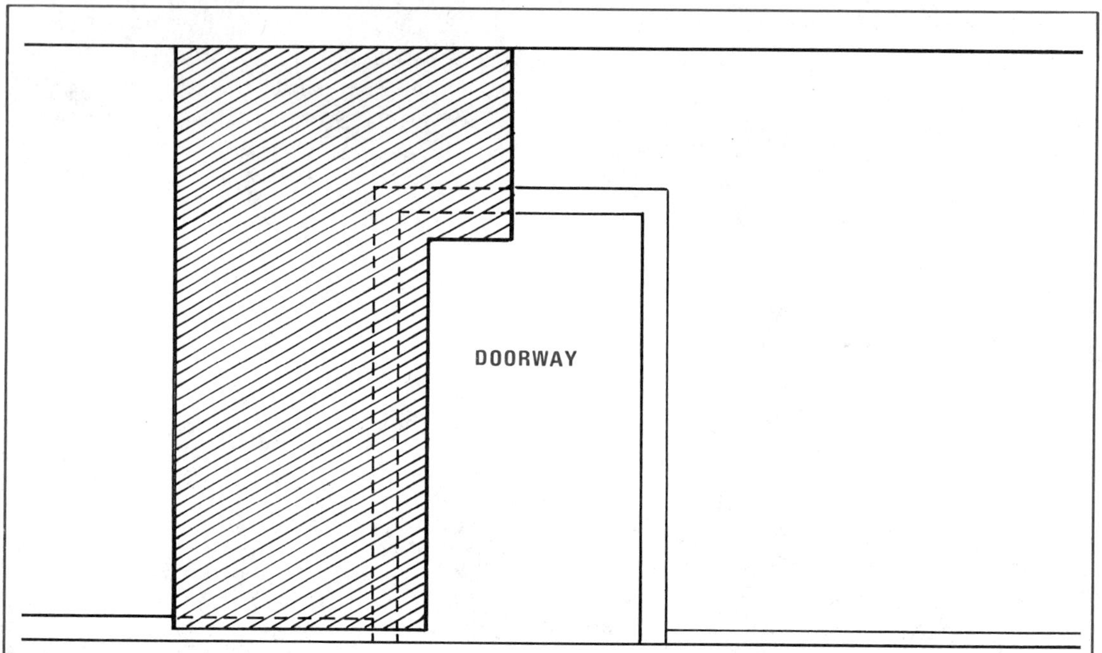

6-15. Placement of the strips over a window or doorway. Cut away excess material to make it easier to handle the strip of wallcovering.

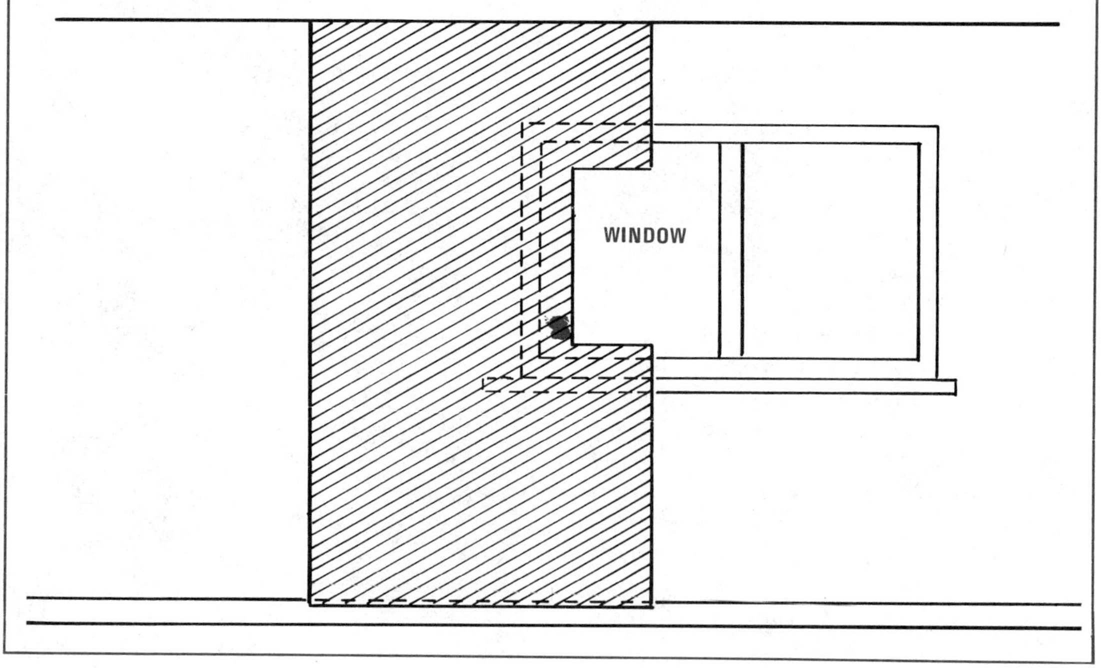

make it easier to handle. Fig. 6-15. (Save all cutout portions.)

A window is handled in a similar way except that 3 extra inches must be allowed from the bottom of the window apron (the part of the window trim under the sill).

Apply paste to the back of the strip and then adhere it to the wall. Smooth out the strip up to the casing and over it. Where the casing meets at a corner, the material must be cut so that the covering lies flat. Smooth the material along the top of the casing, then diagonally slash the corner of the wallcovering where it overlaps the casing so that you can push down the material along the side of the casing. Use the smoothing brush to tap the strip firmly into the corners formed by the casing and by the wall.

Allow the strip to set until it is dry enough to trim. Then carefully cut around the door or window frame. Wipe off the paste from the casing with a damp cloth or sponge.

To cover a kitchen soffit with nothing on the wall underneath, add the height and depth of the soffit to the wall measurement when cutting the strip. Paste on the wallcovering in one complete unit, matching patterns. To cover a soffit with a cabinet underneath, anticipate where the pattern will match to the wall that is closest to the soffit. Cut the strip to match patterns at that point. Be sure to include 6 inches extra at the bottom of the soffit to tuck underneath between the soffit and the top of the cabinet. Fig. 6-16.

If you notice a completed seam not adhering well, pull the wallcovering back a little, put some paste on your fingertip and run it up and down the seam. Press the seam down with a dry rag. Wipe off any paste that has been squeezed out.

Special Problems

If you should see a bubble under the wallcovering after the strip cannot or should not be moved, stick the bubble with a pin in an inconspicuous spot on the pattern. Push the air out of the bubble through the hole. Or, if the glue is still wet, pull the strip back from

6-16. Trimming wallcovering to fit over a kitchen soffit.

the edge carefully, in line with the bubble. Smooth the bubble toward the edge with a dry cloth until the entire strip of wallcovering is flat.

If you should cut a strip too short, save it even if it has paste on it. You may be able to use it later over a window or a doorway.

When you come to a corner, continue the strip around it. On an inside corner use a cloth or a smoothing brush to get the strip tightly in place.

Applying wallcoverings to a ceiling is a difficult job. It should be attempted only in a very small room, such as a kitchen or bathroom. Paper the ceiling before you do the walls. Snap a chalk line on the ceiling so that the side and edges of the first strip will extend down on the wall 1 inch. To snap a chalk line on the ceiling, measure off the required amount in two places on parallel edges of the ceiling. Tack the line in one place. Stretch it across to the other mark. Hold the end of the line in place and snap the line.

To get around easily while applying wallcovering to a ceiling, it is helpful to have a walking plank (a heavy board the same length as the short dimension of the room that is placed across two sawhorses). The technique for applying wallcoverings to ceilings is similar to that used for walls.

Keep most of the pasted section folded so that each strip is easy to handle. Smooth out the first portion with a brush. Use your other hand to hold the rest of the strip up. Then hold the attached section of the strip to the ceiling with a roll of wallcovering as you unfold the remainder of the pasted strip. Smooth this out with the brush quickly. When you cover the walls, the wall strips will come up to the place where the walls meet the ceiling, overlapping the ceiling strips.

ALTERNATE TECHNIQUES FOR HANGING WALLCOVERINGS

Each type of wallcovering requires a slightly different hanging technique. For instance, textile-backed coverings are not as fragile as paper-backed coverings, which cannot be rubbed or handled roughly because they will tear or crease. Application of some foil requires that the paste be put on the wall instead of the back of the strips. Prepasted coverings require that you immerse the strips in water, either in a water box or other large container, to wet the glue. Once the paper is wet, it must be handled very carefully.

Read the manufacturer's application instructions in the sample book from which you select the wallcovering. Often there are instructions on the wrapper of each roll. Additional information may also be obtained from the salesperson.

The instructions given here suggest that you cut each strip to length and hang it before cutting a new strip. You may, of course, prefer to measure and cut the first strip, then match and cut all the remaining strips while the first is on the worktable. If you choose this method, put up each strip in order, using the pasting and trimming techniques discussed in this chapter.

CHECKUP

1. Many types of wallcoverings are available. In choosing wallcovering for your home, what are some of the points you might consider?
2. Why must new dry wall be primed before wallcovering is put on?
3. When can you apply new wallcovering over old? When is it better to strip off the old wallcovering?

CHAPTER 7

Redecorating Floors

WOOD FLOORS

Wood floors are made of such materials as oak, maple, birch, or pine. Oak is the most popular wood used for finish flooring. The finish flooring is installed over a subfloor of plywood panels or long boards. Finish flooring may be long planks or parquet blocks. The long planks are either square edged or tongue and grooved. All the nailing on tongue-and-grooved planks is done through the tongues so that it cannot be seen when the floor is completed. Fig. 7-1.

A wood floor may need to be recoated with a finishing material to restore its original luster and color. In this case dirt and marks must be removed before a new coat of finish is applied. If a floor is in such bad condition that the finish is worn through, it must be sanded down to the raw wood and completely refinished.

Renewal of a Wood Floor Finish

1. Wash the floor with a strong wood floor stripping product or a paint cleaner. This will remove dirt, old wax, and many of the marks on the floor but will not harm the original finish. Fig. 7-2. Use a mop or a cloth to apply this liquid. It may be necessary to rub some of the stubborn spots with coarse steel wool. Rinse the floor thoroughly with clear water until all the stripper has been removed. Allow the floor to dry overnight.

2. When the floor is dry, inspect it to see whether all the dirt and marks are gone. If there are any heel marks left, lightly sand

Customary	Metric
4″	102 mm

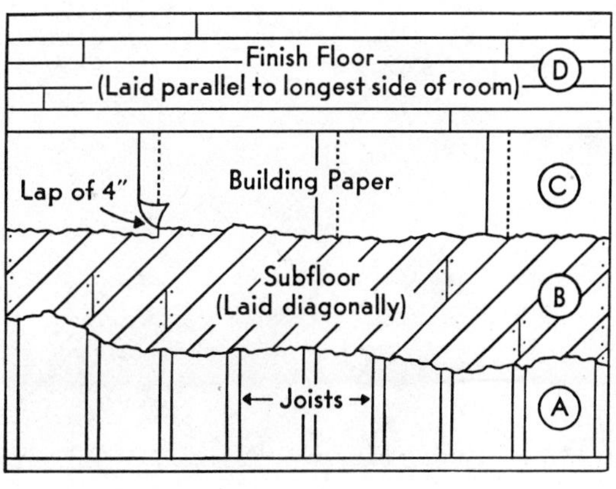

National Oak Flooring Manufacturers' Association

7-1. A cutaway view of a floor showing the construction details: A. The floor beams or joists. B. The subfloor. C. The building paper. D. The finish floor which is refinished and repaired as needed.

them off with fine steel wool or fine sandpaper. Remove any dust with a vacuum cleaner and then a cloth dampened with paint thinner.

3. Coat the sanded bare spots on the floor with a good floor finish—either varnish or a plastic finish. Read the label on the can to make sure that the new material is compatible with the old finish on the floor. Allow the coated areas to dry overnight or for the length of time stated on the container label. You can use a wide brush or a lamb's-wool wax applicator to apply the finish. Fig. 7-3.

4. Coat the entire floor area with the finishing material. Be careful to plan ahead so that you do not have to step on the wet finish in order to get out of the room. Open the windows, if possible, to get adequate ventilation while you are working and while the finish is drying. Allow the floor to dry overnight. Block off all doorways so that no one will walk on the new finish.

Refinishing a Wood Floor

A floor that must be completely refinished has to be sanded down to the bare wood first. After sanding the floor, you may want to stain it darker than the previous finish or bleach it lighter. You can also fill the pores of an open-grained wood like oak. Any broken or loose floorboards should be fixed before the floor is refinished.

Benjamin Moore and Co.
7-2. Wash the floor with a strong floor stripping product or a paint cleaner to remove dirt, wax, and heel marks.

Benjamin Moore and Co.
7-3. Coat the entire floor with the finishing material using a wide brush or a lamb's-wool wax applicator.

REPAIRS

Loose boards can be renailed with long finishing nails. The nails must be driven below the floor's surface with a nail set. The nail holes can then be filled with wood putty. After the putty is sanded smooth and the floor is refinished, the nail holes will be invisible.

If a section of the flooring is damaged, that section can be removed and replaced. Cut out the damaged portion of the floor in the following way:

1. Mark off the area to be removed using a combination square and a pencil. Fig. 7-4. Do not try to cut lengthwise through the middle of a board, but rather plan to cut on a seam in the flooring.

2. Drill entry holes on the ends of the boards to be taken out. Fig. 7-5. Using a chisel, cut through the ends of the boards as close to the line that you drew as possible. Fig. 7-6. Use the chisel to split out one board. Then pry out the others with a chisel or a wrecking bar. To make the opening

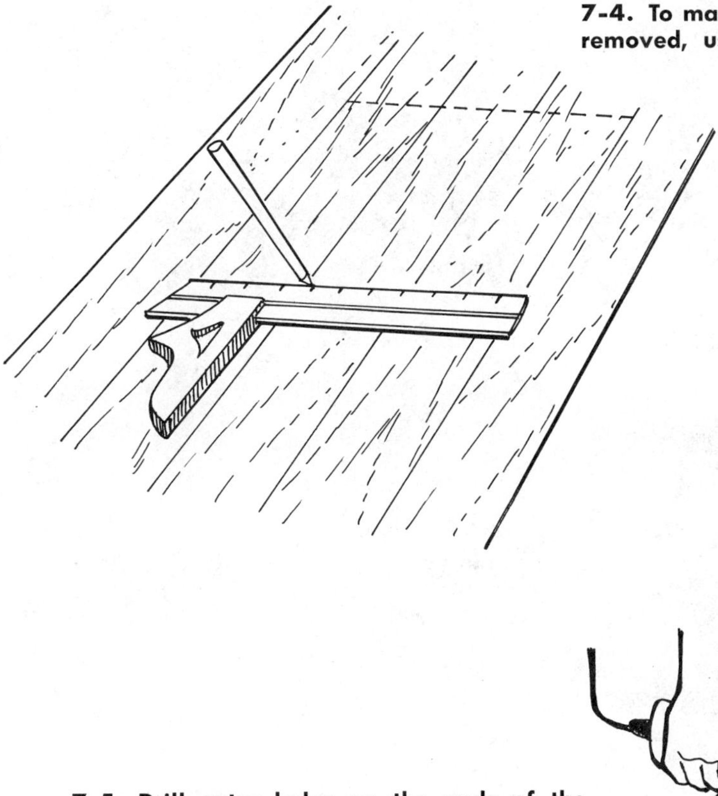

7-4. To mark off the area of the floor to be removed, use a combination square and a pencil.

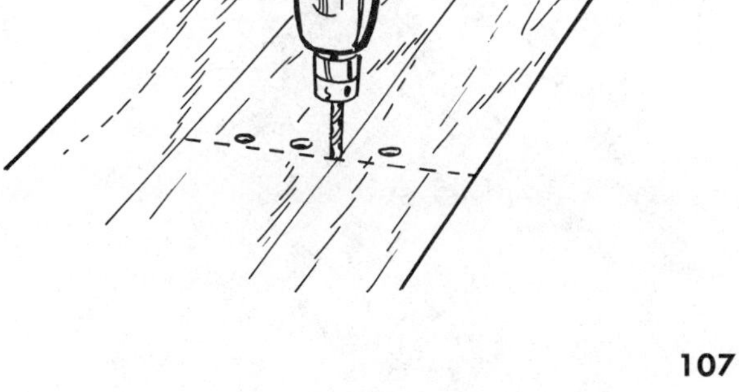

7-5. Drill entry holes on the ends of the boards that are to be taken out.

7-6. Use a chisel and a hammer to cut out the damaged floorboards close to the line that you drew on the flooring. In this photo you can see the subfloor under the tongue-and-grooved finish flooring.

7-7. Use a portable circular saw with the blade set to the thickness of the finish floor to cut the opening straight. Here the subfloor can be seen through the opening.

Weyerhaeuser Co.

7-8. Nail down the tongue-and-grooved flooring on an angle through the tongues.

7-9. Remove the bottom half of the groove on the last board to be replaced.

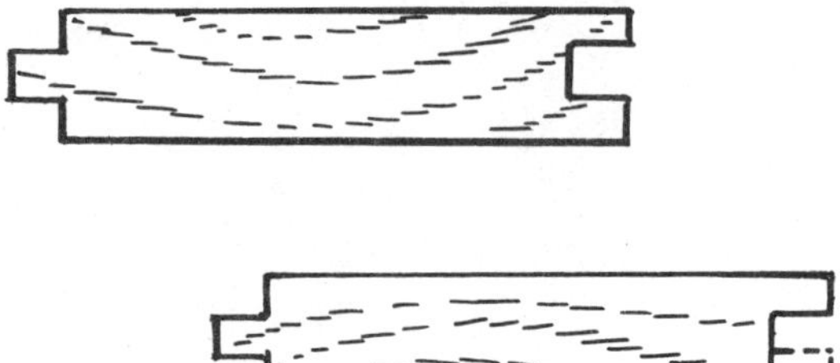

straight, use a portable circular saw with the blade set to the thickness of the finish floor. Fig. 7-7. Be careful not to damage any of the good floorboards near this area.

3. Cut the new floorboards to the proper length so that they fit the space tightly. Be sure that they are the same width as the old flooring.

If the flooring is of the tongue-and-groove type, the bottom half of the groove must be removed on the last board to be replaced. The others can be nailed through the tongue on an angle so that no nails will show. Fig. 7-8. Use a sharp wood chisel to remove the bottom part of the groove on the last board. Fig. 7-9. Then force it into place carefully so that it does not split. Nail it through the face with long finishing nails. Set the nails down. Fill nail holes with putty.

If the floorboards have a square edge, they must all be nailed down with finishing nails, the nails set down, and the holes filled with wood putty.

PREPARING AND FINISHING AN OLD FLOOR

1. Inspect the floor. Set down any nails that are sticking up so that they will not tear the abrasive belts on the sanding machine.

2. Obtain a power sanding machine for the main floor area and an edging machine so that you can sand the floor up to the baseboard molding. Figs. 7-10, 7-11. Such machines can be rented. Ask the rental

Benjamin Moore and Co.

7-10. Use a power sanding machine for the main floor area. Keep the machine moving while it is turned on to avoid gouging the floor.

7-11. With an edging machine you can sand the floor up to the baseboard molding.

Benjamin Moore and Co.

agent how to use the machines. Follow the instructions carefully to avoid gouging the floor. Some corners may not be accessible even with the edging machine. These will have to be done with a hand scraper or by hand sanding. Fig. 7-12.

The floor will need a complete sanding with progressively finer grades of abrasive paper. Start out with coarse abrasive belts and follow them with medium-grade and then fine-grade belts.

On floors made up of long planks, only the coarse sanding can be done against the grain. The sandings with medium- and fine-grade belts must be done with the grain to remove any scratches made by the sander during coarse sanding.

7-12. Some corners may not be accessible even with an edging machine. These will have to be done with a hand scraper.
Benjamin Moore and Co.

On parquet floors, which are made up of many blocks of wood, you cannot sand with the grain because the blocks are set at different angles. Use only the medium and fine abrasive belts to sand the floor.

On any floor the sanding machine must be kept moving while it is operating or it will cut into the wood. To keep the power cable from getting tangled in the machine and being cut, drape the cable over your shoulder to keep it clear of the machine.

3. After you are finished, remove the dust from the floor with a vacuum cleaner and then a damp cloth or a dust mop. Remove the dust from all the moldings and the window sills as well.

4. The floor can be stained a different color at this time. Apply the stain with a soft brush and work with the grain of the wood. Wipe the excess stain off, in the direction of the grain, using a soft cloth. Fig. 7-13. The longer the stain soaks in without wiping, the darker the color will be. If the color of the floor is too light, you can apply a second coat of stain after the first coat has dried thoroughly. Read the label on the can for directions as to how the stain should be applied.

5. On open-grained wood floors such as oak, a paste wood filler can be applied to give a very smooth finish. This may be done before or after the stain is applied, depending upon the type of stain you use. Read the instructions on the can.

Paste wood filler should be thinned to the consistency of heavy cream and then applied to the oak floor with a brush. Fig. 7-14. Brush it on with the grain and allow it to dry until it loses its shine and becomes dull. Wipe it off across the grain with a piece of heavy cloth. Fig. 7-15. Burlap works well.

Work on a small section of the floor at a time. Let the filler dry overnight. Then sand the floor lightly with fine sandpaper and remove all the dust with a damp cloth.

6. Apply a coat of sealer next. White shellac (4 pound cut) can be used if it is thinned with alcohol about 50 percent (1 part alcohol to 1 part shellac). Allow this to dry over-

Benjamin Moore and Co.
7-13. Wipe the stain off with the grain, using a soft cloth.

Benjamin Moore and Co.
7-14. Paste wood filler is applied to the floor with a brush in the direction of the grain.

Benjamin Moore and Co.
7-15. Wipe the paste wood filler off across the grain with a heavy cloth, such as a piece of burlap.

night. Some floor finishes may require a special sealer. Check the label on the can of floor finish before you apply any sealer.

7. The floor finish that you select can be either varnish or plastic, high luster or low luster. This material can be applied with a brush, a sponge mop, or a roller. Two coats are usually necessary because the first one is quickly absorbed by the wood. Fig. 7-16.

Benjamin Moore and Co.

7-16. Apply the floor finish last. Two coats are usually necessary.

PAINTING A CONCRETE FLOOR

Concrete floors, found mostly in basements and garages, are often painted to make them look better and to keep dust accumulation down. There are six different types of concrete paints available:

- Polyvinyl acetate—can be used on new masonry because it leaves a waterproof film.
- Silicon sealer—transparent and water repellent.
- Rubber-base emulsion type—water soluble.
- Rubber-base solution type—resistant to moisture and detergents.
- Oil-base paint—a dry surface, a primer, and two coats of paint are needed.
- Portland cement paint—the least expensive paint.

A concrete floor is prepared and painted in the following way:

1. Check the concrete for dampness and efflorescence (a powdery white material that

7-17. Check the concrete for efflorescence, a powdery white material formed by chemical changes.

forms on top of the concrete due to chemical changes). Fig. 7-17. The efflorescence can be cleaned off with a mild solution of muriatic acid and water. Follow instructions on the container. Be sure to wear rubber gloves and goggles when using this solution. Keep windows and doors open for adequate ventilation. Rinse with clear water after you are through.

The salesperson in a paint store can also advise you on what kind of solution to use for cleaning concrete.

2. Scrape off any loose paint with a putty knife and wire-brush the surface. Wash down the concrete floor to remove all dirt. Allow it to dry overnight.

3. Mix the paint according to the manufacturer's instructions. It can be applied with a brush or a roller. After painting, block off the area so that no one steps on the floor. Clean off your brushes or roller in the proper solvent and store away any unused paint in a tightly closed container. (See Chapter 5.)

PREPARING A FLOOR FOR NEW RESILIENT TILE OR LINOLEUM

The existing floor on which resilient floor tile, sheet vinyl, or linoleum is to be installed must be in good condition. It should be smooth and dry. It should be clean and have no nails or knots protruding which would later show through the new flooring.

The following sections will describe how to prepare a floor for new resilient tile, linoleum, or sheet vinyl. Later, installation of resilient tile will be discussed. Installation of linoleum and sheet vinyl is more difficult and should be done by a professional.

Preparing a Floor in Good Condition

Remove the furniture in the room. Carefully remove the baseboard molding with a hammer and a chisel. Remove metal moldings at doorways and at any other part of the floor. Molding will later be replaced in its slightly higher position on top of the new flooring.

Make the existing floor smooth by setting down any nails that stick up and by gluing down any tiles that are starting to pull up at the corners. Sand the old flooring to give it a "tooth" so that the adhesive will adhere properly. This can be done with an orbital sander and a medium-grade abrasive paper. Lightly go over the floor, section by section.

If the floor has some minor imperfections, you can cement roofing felt (building paper) over it. The sheet flooring or tiles are cemented over that.

Preparing a Floor in Poor Condition

If the existing floor is in bad condition (with cracks or loose tiles), the whole floor should be covered with an underlayment of $\frac{1}{4}''$ plywood or masonite nailed or stapled to the floor. Underlayment comes in 3′ x 4′ sheets, in 4′ x 4′ sheets, and in 4′ x 8′ sheets. It is fastened in place with $1\frac{1}{2}''$ rosin-coated nails, $1\frac{1}{2}''$ cement-coated nails, or with annular ring nails. It can also be held down with $\frac{7}{8}''$ divergent staples which are driven with a spotnailer (an underlayment tacker).

Underlayment is installed as follows:

1. The floor must be dry and clean. Set down all nails that are sticking up. Remove the baseboard molding carefully. It will be replaced after the new floor is installed.

2. The underlayment sheets should be stacked on edge in the room where they are to be installed for at least 24 hours. This will accustom them to the temperature and humidity of that room.

3. Clear the room of all furnishings so

that you can work on the floor with complete freedom. Put the pieces of underlayment down on the floor so that the joints are staggered. In other words, there should be no continuous seams. Leave a $\frac{1}{32}''$ space between panels. This space will allow for expansion and contraction of the underlayment sheets. The single thickness of a paper matchbook cover is a good gauge for the right thickness. Fig. 7-18.

7-18. Leave a $\frac{1}{32}''$ space between masonite underlayment panels. A paper matchbook cover makes a good spacer for the right thickness. Notice how the joints are staggered.
Armstrong Cork Co.

4. Nail the underlayment every 4 or 5 inches over the entire surface of the panel. Fasten one sheet in place before installing the next sheet. If you are using masonite underlayment, the rough side should be facing up. This side is usually marked. On some masonite underlayment panels, the rough face is also marked to show the location of every nailing point. On plywood underlayment the side that has fewer imperfections should be facing up. Underlayment is easily cut with a woodworking handsaw. For curves, use a saber saw.

If you are buying underlayment, take the room dimensions with you when you go to the floor covering store or the lumberyard to buy the materials. One of the salespeople will be able to estimate how much underlayment and how many nails or staples you will need. Many of these people also rent spotnailers for a nominal fee. With a spotnailer you can drive divergent staples easily through the underlayment into the floor. It might also be a good idea to rent or buy a pair of knee pads for this job. They will make you a lot more comfortable.

RESILIENT FLOOR TILES

Several types of resilient floor tiles are available for the home. Some are suitable for use in the basement or on concrete floors. Others can only be used above ground. Each type of tile has its own specific adhesive. Self-stick floor tiles come with the adhesive already applied. Fig. 7-19. Following the manufacturer's recommendations about adhesives will insure that a tile floor will last a long time. The various types of resilient tile are as follows:

- Rubber (rubber, fillers, and color pigments).
- Cork (cork and a resin binder).
- Asphalt (asphalt base and color pigments). It can be used on concrete because it is resistant to moisture.
- Vinyl (plastic resin with felt backing). It can be used on concrete floors if they are not below ground level.
- Vinyl-asbestos (vinyl resins, asbestos fiber, binders, and color pigments). This is the best for use on concrete floors below ground level.

Installing the Tile

Measure the room that you are going to tile and sketch a simple floor plan of it. If you bring these measurements and the plan to the store where you are going to buy the

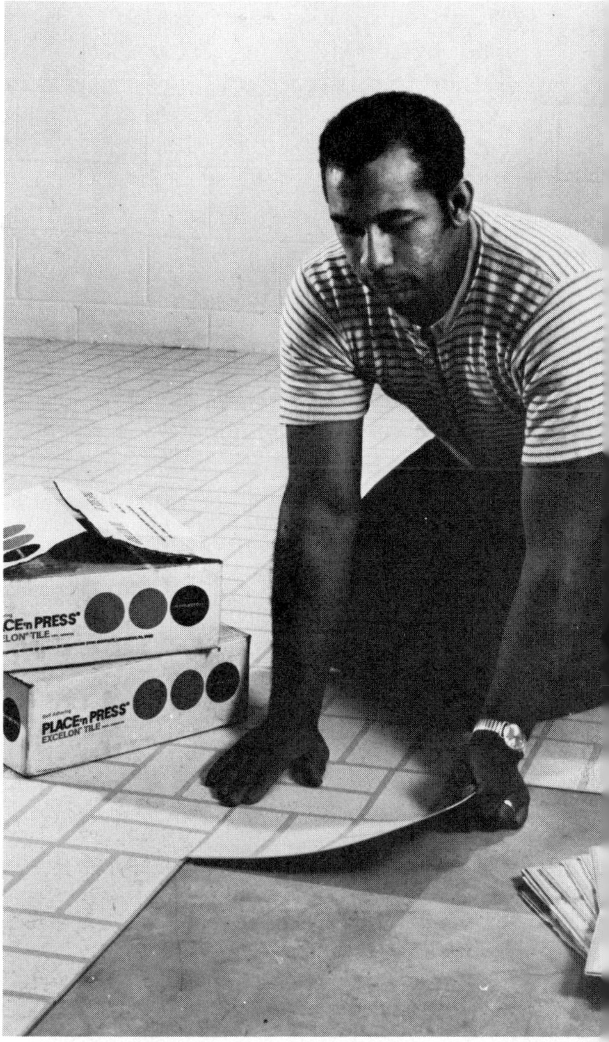

Armstrong Cork Co.

7-19. Self-stick floor tiles have adhesive on the back. They are pressed into place.

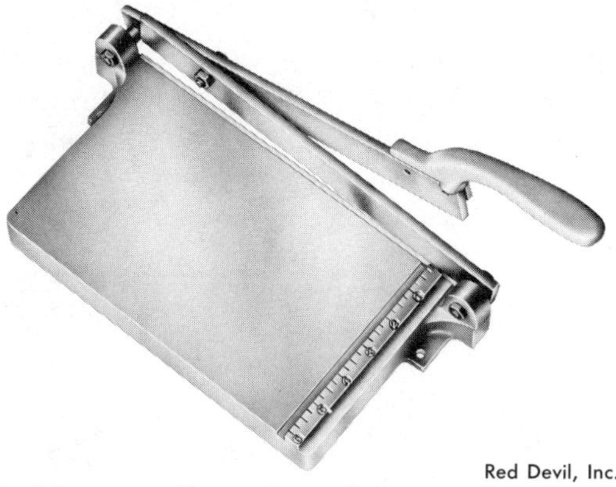

Red Devil, Inc.

7-20. A resilient tile cutter. This tool can be rented for a nominal fee.

tile, the salespeople will help you estimate how much adhesive and how many tiles you will need. They will also tell you what types of metal moldings you will need at doorways or at places where the tiles meet wall-to-wall carpeting.

The number of tiles needed depends upon the size of the room and the size of the tiles you select. Most resilient tiles are 12 inches square. Some manufacturers still have 9 inch square tiles available.

Each type of floor tile must be cut by a different technique. Some types of tile are brittle and break easily, while others are flexible. All tiles come in various thicknesses. The thicker the tile, the more difficult it is to cut. Asphalt tile must be slightly heated on the back with a propane torch. It can then be cut with a pair of tin shears or a tile cutter. Fig. 7-20. Another technique for cutting asphalt tile is to score the front with a utility knife and a straightedge. Fig. 7-21.

7-21. Score the front of the asphalt tile with a utility knife and a straightedge.

Then you can break the tile along the score mark by bending it. Fig. 7-22.

Thin vinyl-asbestos and vinyl tiles can be cut with a pair of scissors or tin shears. Fig. 7-23. Rubber and cork tiles can be cut with a tile cutter or a pair of tin shears. If they are really thick, score them with a knife and break them.

The following steps outline the procedure for installing a resilient tile floor:

1. After the floor has been cleared of furniture and made ready for the installation of the new tile, lay out the centerlines on the floor. This is done by finding the middle of the length of each side of the room. Snap chalk lines between these points to mark the floor. The two chalk lines should be perpendicular (meet at 90 degrees) to each other. Fig. 7-24.

2. Lay out one row of tiles dry (without any adhesive) to see how many tiles are needed to cross the room. Fig. 7-25. There should be one tile on each side of the centerline or else one directly in the middle. If the tiles nearest to the walls (border tiles) will be less than half a tile long, remove one tile from the row. This will increase the size of the border tiles.

Lay out a row of tiles in both directions along the chalk lines of the room. When you are satisfied that the arrangement is what you want, you will be ready to remove the test rows of tiles and start applying the adhesive. On your floor plan write down the number of tiles in each row and the widths of the border tiles so that you do not make any mistakes later.

Note: The layout described is for a rectangular room. Many rooms are not simple rectangles. For example, they may be *L*-shaped. In that case, follow Steps 1 and 2 on the larger portion of the *L* to determine the tile pattern. Then follow this tile pattern on the smaller portion of the *L*.

3. Adhesive should be sparingly applied to the floor with an old paint brush, a notched spreader, or a notched trowel. Figs. 7-26, 7-27. If too much adhesive is applied, it will

7-22. Break the tile along the score mark by bending the tile.

7-23. Thin vinyl-asbestos and vinyl tiles can be cut with a pair of tin shears.

7-24. Use a chalk line reel to snap two chalk centerlines on the floor.

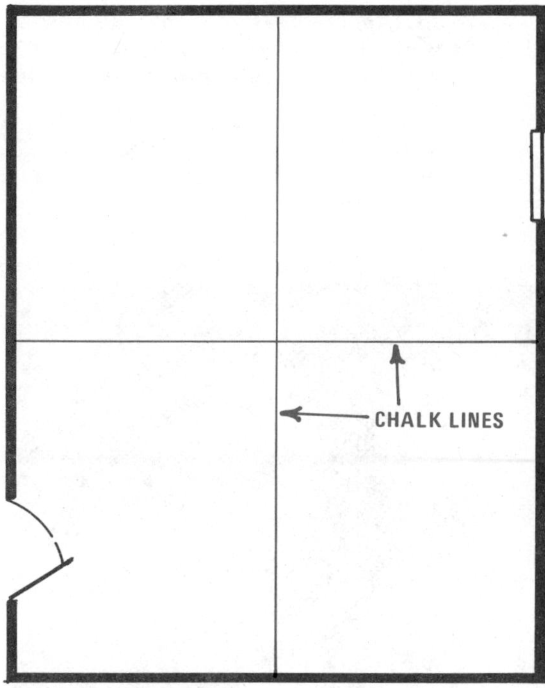

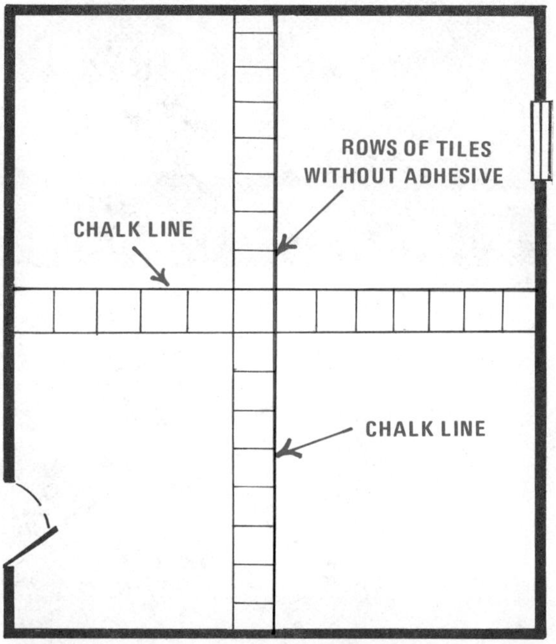

7-25. Place one row of tiles on the floor without any adhesive so that you can see how many tiles are needed from one side of the room to the other.

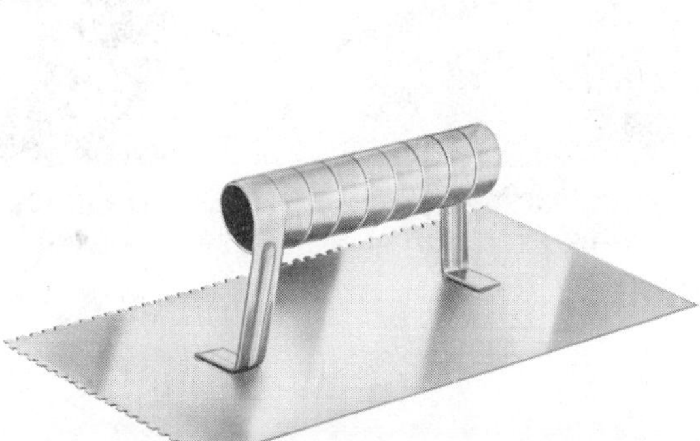

Red Devil, Inc.

7-26. A notched trowel for spreading tile adhesive.

7-27. Applying adhesive with a notched trowel.

7-28. Apply adhesive to one quarter of the floor at a time. Work carefully near the baseboards to avoid getting adhesive on them.

7-29. The tiles are put down on the adhesive, starting at the middle of the room and working toward the walls.

7-30. Put the border tile on the last full tile on the floor so that their edges are even.

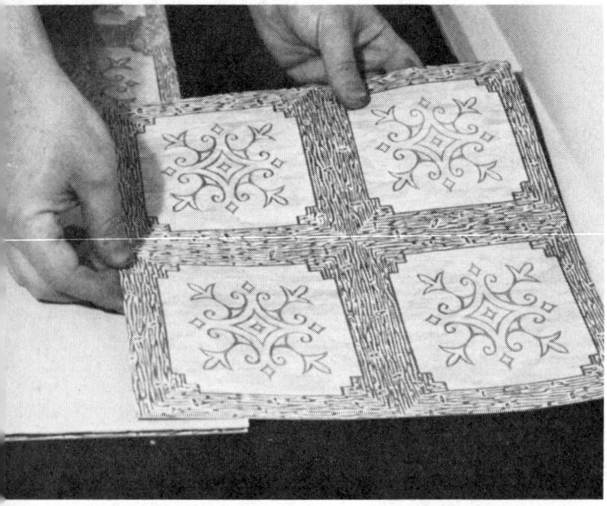

7-31. Place another full tile on top of the other two so that it touches the wall.

be squeezed up between the tiles. Follow the manufacturer's instructions on drying time, cleaning up, application, and the tools used. Apply adhesive to one quadrant (one quarter) of the floor at a time, starting at the middle of the room. Fig. 7-28. As the adhesive dries you should be able to see the chalk line through it. When the adhesive is tacky (almost dry), the tiles are placed on it.

4. Place the tiles on the adhesive and press them into place. Start at the middle of the room and work your way toward the walls. Fig. 7-29. Leave the border tiles for last. You will be kneeling on the tiles you have just put down as you work toward the wall. This will help press the tiles down firmly. Care must be taken not to slide the tiles out of position as you move over them.

5. To measure and cut the border tiles, use this technique: Put the tile that you will use for the border face down on the last full tile on the floor so that their edges are even. Fig. 7-30. Put another full tile on top of these. This tile should touch the wall as shown in Fig. 7-31. Using the edge of this tile as a guide, mark the cutting line on the border tile with a pencil. Fig. 7-32. Remove the border tile and cut it by one of the methods described earlier in this section. If a pencil mark will not show up on the tile, you may have to mark it with a utility knife. Fig. 7-33. After the border tile has been cut to size, place it on the adhesive.

7-32. Use the edge of the tile as a guide to mark the cutting line on the border tile with a pencil.

7-33. You may need a utility knife to mark the cutting line on the border tile.

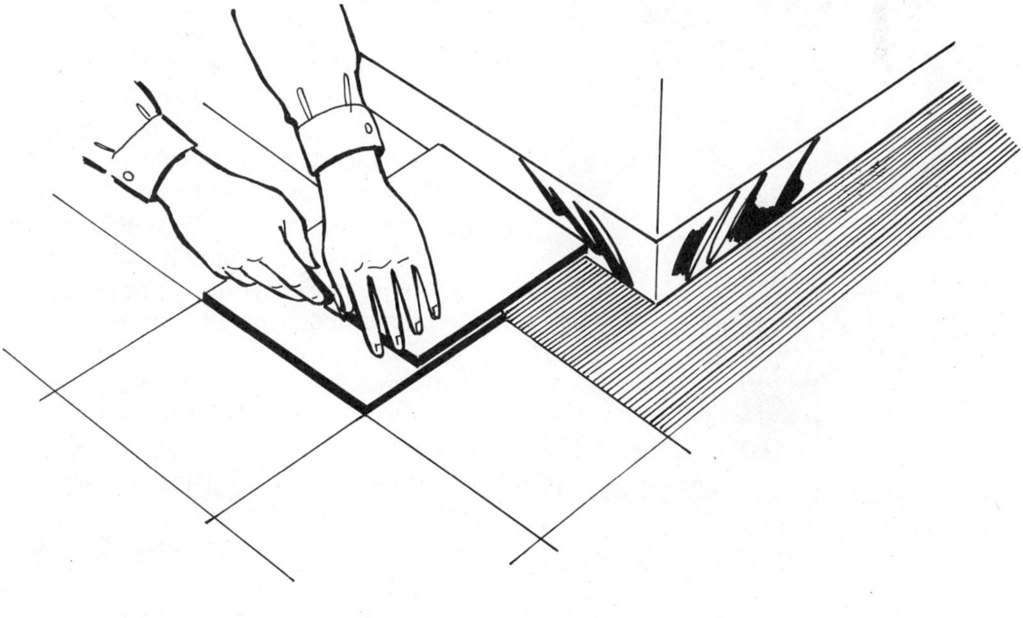

7-34. For cutting a circle or an arc, a tin can may be used to guide the knife.

7-35. After all the tiles are in place, you can go over them with a lawn roller or a special flooring roller, but this step is not absolutely necessary.

Congoleum Industries, Inc.

6. In some areas of the room you may have to make cutouts around such things as a radiator or a pipe. Make a pattern using a piece of cardboard, a pencil, a ruler, and a pair of scissors. Transfer the pattern to the tile with a pencil, and cut the tile. To cut a circle or an arc, use a tin can to guide the knife. Fig. 7-34. Cut the circle or arc before making any of the straight cuts. If the tile is too thick to cut with a knife or tin shears, a fine-toothed blade on a saber saw works well. Be sure to cut slowly.

7. After all the tiles are in place, walk on them to press them down. You might cover the floor with a couple of layers of newspaper and go over the entire floor with a lawn roller to firmly set the tiles. You may also use a flooring roller. However, this step is not absolutely necessary. Fig. 7-35.

8. Vinyl, rubber, or composition cove molding may be applied to the baseboard area after the floor is installed. The molding is bent to go around inside and outside corners. Some types of cove molding must be warmed slightly with a torch before bending. On inside corners the bottom must be notched with a knife or a pair of scissors so that the edges meet when the material is folded. Fig. 7-36. The molding is fastened to the wall with a special cove cement which is applied with a notched trowel. Do not apply the cove cement any closer than $\frac{1}{4}''$ from the top of the molding or it may squeeze up over the top. Follow the manufacturer's instructions about installation. Fig. 7-37.

9. After all the tiles are in place, install metal moldings in doorways or where the tiles meet carpeting. These moldings are cut to length with a hacksaw and a pair of aviation shears. Fig. 7-38. They are nailed down with spiral-grooved nails that are driven through the predrilled holes in the molding. Fig. 7-39.

7-36. On inside corners the bottom of the cove molding must be notched with a sharp knife so that the edges meet when the material is folded.

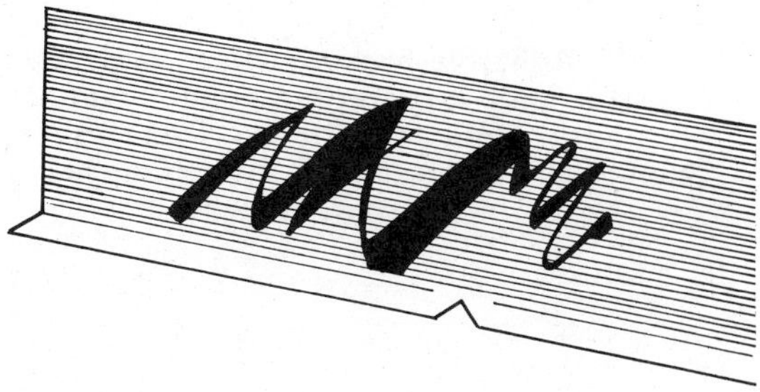

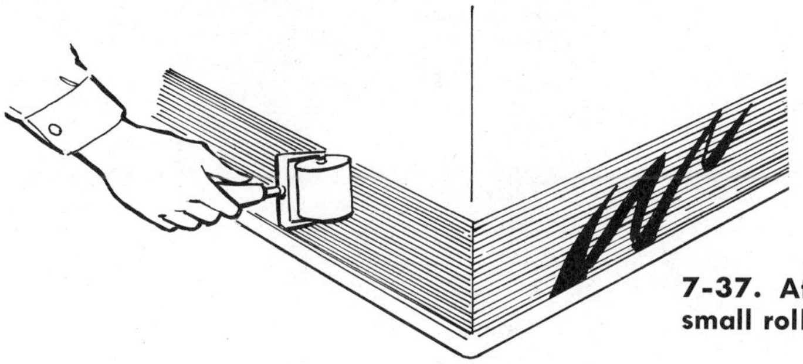

7-37. After the cement is applied, use a small roller to press the cove molding to the wall.

7-38. Metal moldings are cut with a pair of aviation shears.

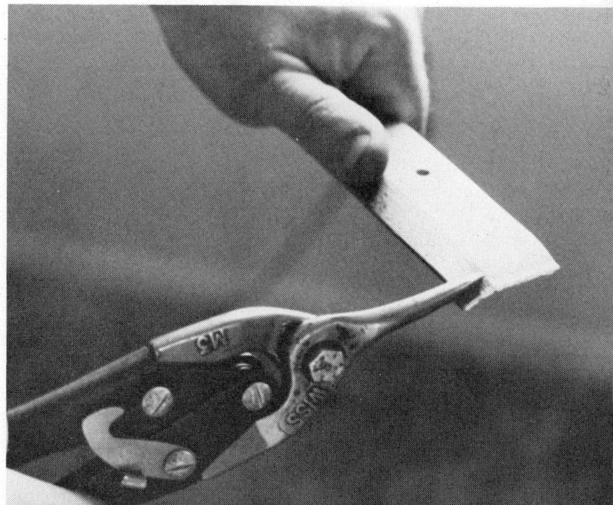

7-39. The metal moldings are nailed down with spiral-grooved nails.

Armstrong Cork Co.

7-40. Adhesive-backed tiles and carpet squares have a protective paper covering on the back. Note the arrows. Carpet squares should all be placed with the arrows pointing in the same direction.

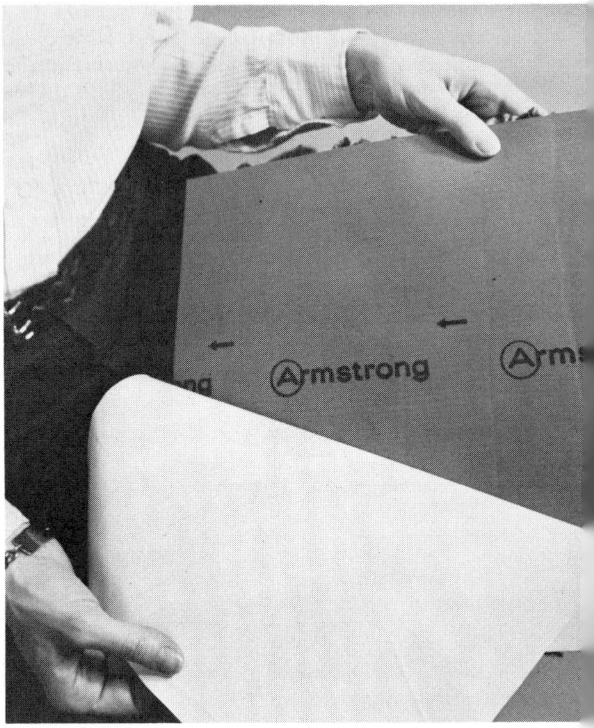

Installing Self-Stick Tile or Carpet Squares

Self-stick tiles and carpet squares have become very popular. These come with adhesive on the back. You simply peel off the protective paper and apply the tiles or carpet squares to the floor. Fig. 7-40.

Prepare the floor and lay out the centerlines as you would for ordinary tile. Fig. 7-41. Start at the middle of the room and work toward the walls. Figs. 7-42, 7-43. The border tiles or squares can be cut with scissors or a utility knife. Fig. 7-44.

7-41. You may use a carpenter's square to help you lay out the centerlines.
Armstrong Cork Co.

7-42. Start at the middle of the room and work toward the walls. Do the border tiles last.
Armstrong Cork Co.

Armstrong Cork Co.

7-43. It is best to finish one section of the floor at a time.

7.44. Border tiles can be cut with ordinary scissors.

Armstrong Cork Co.

—REPAIRING RESILIENT TILE OR LINOLEUM FLOORS—

Patching Linoleum or Vinyl Sheet Flooring

If there is a damaged part of the floor that you wish to repair, you must have a scrap piece of the same flooring to serve as a patch. You will also need the following:

- Stiff putty knife.
- Notched trowel for adhesive.
- Claw hammer.
- Masking tape.
- 1″ brads.
- Sharp knife.
- Straightedge.
- Adhesive made for the type of flooring you are working on.

1. Position the scrap piece over the damaged part of the floor. This must be done so that the pattern on both pieces matches exactly. Nail the scrap piece of flooring in place with the brads or tape it down.

2. Cut through the scrap piece and the original floor with a sharp utility or floor covering knife using the straightedge as a guide. Fig. 7-45. Cut a patch that is rectangular unless it is possible to cut the patch to match an irregular pattern on the floor. Fig. 7-46. Curves are hard to cut and should be avoided if possible.

3. Pull out the brads or remove the tape and put the patch and the excess material aside for the time being. Remove the damaged area of the original floor with a putty knife. Fig. 7-47. You may have to cut into the middle of the area to get the putty knife in under the material so that you can pry it up. Do not damage the edges that you cut into the flooring. Scrape off any dried adhesive or dirt from the floor in the area where the patch will be placed.

4. Apply adhesive to the area with a notched trowel. Allow it to dry until it is tacky or according to the manufacturer's instructions. Carefully fit the patch in place and press it into the adhesive. Walk on it to set it down. Fig. 7-48. Clean off any adhesive that has been squeezed out with whatever solvent is recommended by the manufacturer.

Replacing Damaged Resilient Tiles

Asphalt and vinyl-asbestos tiles are removed in the following ways. Use a propane torch on the damaged tile to soften the adhesive. At the same time use a stiff putty knife to pry up the tile. You can also use an electric clothes iron with a cloth under it to warm the tile until the adhesive softens. As an alternative, you can use a solvent to dissolve the adhesive under the tile. If the tile has lifted slightly, you can brush some solvent under the edge of the tile until all of it is dissolved.

Congoleum Industries, Inc.

7-45. Position the scrap piece of flooring over the damaged area. Use brads, or as in this case masking tape, to hold the piece in place. Cut through the new piece and the original flooring with a utility knife and a straightedge.

Vinyl, rubber, and cork tiles can be broken and chipped off the floor with an old chisel or a sharp putty knife. Crack the tile and then use the tool to pry and scrape it up. Clean off the area thoroughly so that no adhesive or dirt remains.

To install a new tile, use a notched trowel to apply the adhesive. Let it dry until tacky. Wipe off any adhesive that gets on nearby tiles. Set the new tile in place and press it down. Let the adhesive dry overnight.

Congoleum Industries, Inc.

7-46. Cutting the patch and the original flooring to match the flooring pattern.

7-47. Remove the damaged part of the floor. Use a putty knife if it won't come up.

Congoleum Industries, Inc.

7-48. Carefully fit the patch in place and press it into the adhesive. Walk on it to set it down or use a small roller as shown here.

Congoleum Industries, Inc.

CHECKUP

1. Are there any wood floors in your home which need work? If so, would it be better to renew the existing finish or to refinish the floor completely?
2. What is efflorescence? How can it be removed from concrete?
3. When is it necessary to install underlayment before installing new resilient tile, sheet vinyl, or linoleum?

CHAPTER 8

Fasteners and Other Hardware

Hardware is a term used to describe metal and plastic fittings and fasteners such as nails, screws, bolts, doorknobs, hinges, and closing devices. Types of hardware likely to be most useful to you for home care will be discussed on the following pages. Knowledge of the varieties of hardware will enable you to select the proper piece of hardware for each repair job.

NAILS AND SCREWS

Nails

You will no doubt use many kinds of nails for doing repair work. Nails for a specific purpose are made of special materials to suit that purpose. For example, nails used outside must be either coated or made of some material other than iron or steel, which would rust. Exterior nails are coated with zinc (galvanized), with cement, or with resin (which improves their holding power). Some exterior nails are made of aluminum, a metal especially suitable for holding siding materials such as cedar shakes or asbestos shingles.

Nails are sized by inches and also by the penny system. For example, a 6d (sixpenny) nail is 2 inches long. (Originally, the cost was 6 cents per one hundred nails.) Penny sizes are $\frac{1}{4}''$ longer for each larger size: an 8d nail is $2\frac{1}{2}''$ long, for example. Consult the chart, Fig. 8-1, for sizes of nails in both inch and penny sizes. Most boxes of nails list both sizes. Nails are usually bought by the pound.

Common nails and finishing nails are used for most home repairs. Fig. 8-2. You will probably find the following types of nails useful:

- Common—for framing and rough construction.
- Finishing—with small heads that can be set down.

8-1. This chart shows the sizes of nails in both the inch and penny systems.
United States Steel Corp.

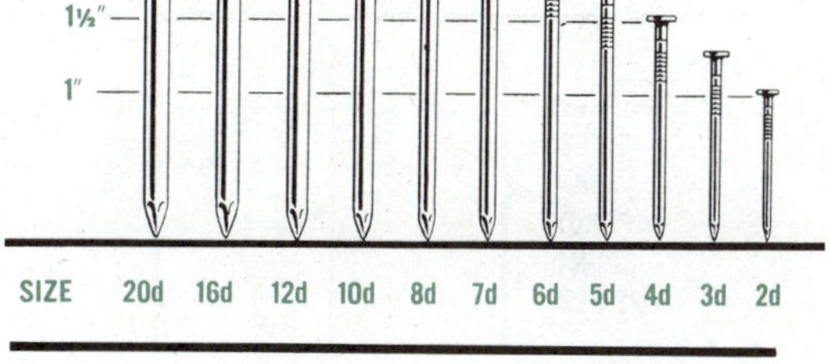

• Brads—finishing nails less than 1″ in length.

• Casing—heavier than finishing nails; used to assemble door and window casings.

• Cut—square-cut, hardened steel nails used for flooring and concrete.

• Annular ring—for wallboard, roofing, and underlayment.

• Spiral—for metal floor molding.

• Concrete—with a round and fluted shank and a wide head.

• Roofing—galvanized, with a wide head.

• Box—smaller in diameter than common nails.

Wood Screws

You will probably need wood screws for many repair jobs. It is recommended, therefore, that you know the various types of wood screws and how to install them in wood. Screws have much more holding power than nails.

Wood screws are made of mild (soft) steel, brass, or aluminum. They may have a blued or bright finish or be coated with zinc chromate, brass, cadmium, or copper. They are made in various thicknesses (gauges) from 0, the thinnest, to 24, the thickest. Fig. 8-3. They are available in lengths from $\frac{1}{4}$″ to 6″.

TYPES OF WOOD SCREWS

The following wood screws are available at hardware stores or lumberyards:

• Flathead—head is countersunk and fits flush with the surface of wood.

• Ovalhead—partly recessed in the wood.

• Roundheaded—fits on top of the wood.

These screws may have either slotted or recessed (Phillips) heads. Fig. 8-4. A fourth type of screw is the *one-way* screw. It is used on lock installations because it cannot be removed with a screwdriver. Fig. 8-5.

FASTENING TWO PIECES OF WOOD WITH SCREWS

To install wood screws you need a hand or electric drill, two twist drills of the proper size, a screwdriver, and a countersink. In addition, an awl (a sharp, pointed instrument) is useful for marking the locations of the holes. Fig. 8-6.

1. Using a combination square, locate and mark with a cross the top (shank) hole

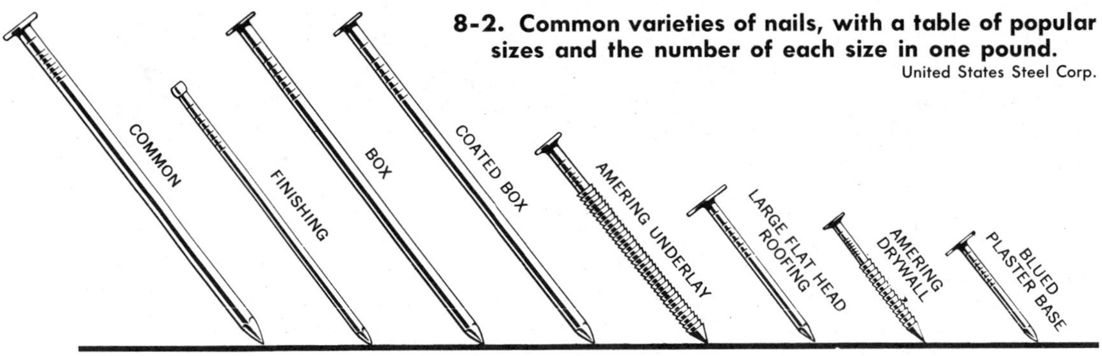

8-2. Common varieties of nails, with a table of popular sizes and the number of each size in one pound.
United States Steel Corp.

POPULAR SIZES and APPROX. COUNT PER LB.	Common		Finishing		Box		Coated Box		Amering Underlay		Large Flat Head Roofing		Amering Drywall		Blued Plaster Base	
									LENGTH		LENGTH		LENGTH		LENGTH	
	4d	294	4d	630	6d	225	6d	315	$1\frac{1}{4}$″	537	1″	390	$1\frac{1}{4}$″	361	$1\frac{1}{8}$″	473
	6d	167	6d	288	7d	200	7d	280			$1\frac{1}{4}$″	314				
	8d	101	8d	196	8d	136	8d	190			$1\frac{1}{2}$″	263				
	10d	66	10d	124	10d	90	10d	119			$1\frac{3}{4}$″	226				
	16d	47														
	20d	29														

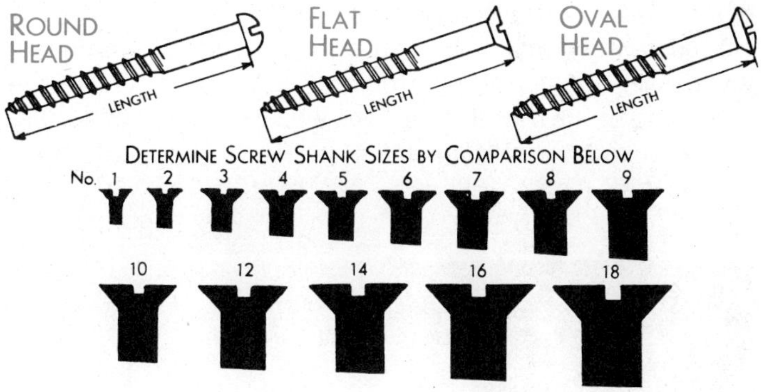

Stanley Tools

8-3. Three types of wood screws and a comparison chart of screw shank sizes in various gauges.

a b

8-4. Two types of screw heads: (a) Phillips. (b) Slotted.

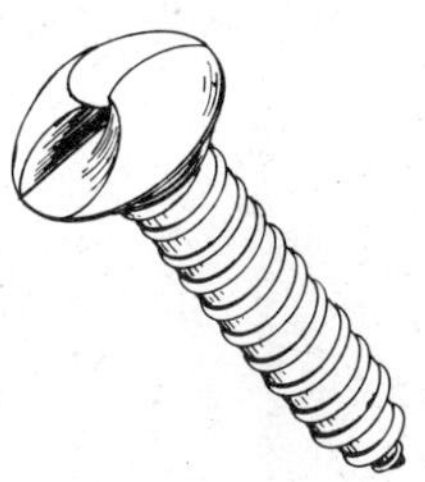

Ideal Security Hardware Corp.

8-5. A one-way screw. It is used in door hardware installation because it cannot be removed.

8-6. An awl for marking hole locations and starting small screws.

Stanley Tools

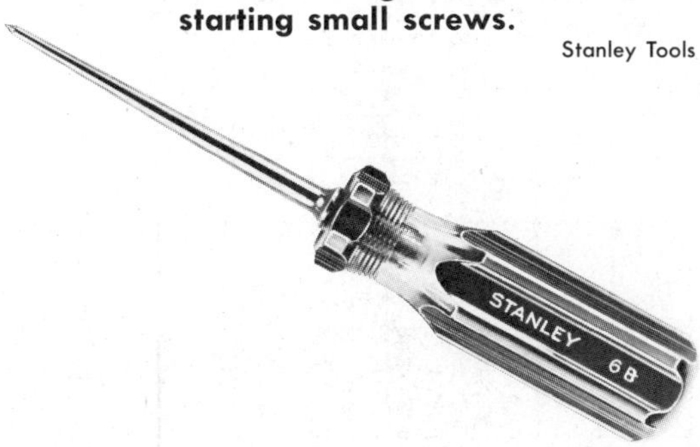

for each screw. Fig. 8-7. Do not put the screw hole closer than $\frac{3}{8}$″ from the edge of a piece of wood.

2. Bore the shank hole for the screw through the top piece of wood. Fig. 8-8. Use the drill size chart, Fig. 8-9a, to determine which size of twist drill to use. The screw should pass through the hole easily. *Note:*

8-7. Use a combination square to mark the location of the shank hole for each wood screw.

When metric wood screws become available, customary-inch drills can still be used for making shank and pilot holes. Fig. 8-9b lists some of the metric hole sizes which can be bored with customary drills.

3. If the screw is a flathead or an ovalhead, use a countersink in your drill to make the proper-sized recess for the screw head. Fig. 8-10. Test the amount of recess with the screw head to see that it is the right

8-8. With a hand drill or electric drill, make the shank hole for each screw through the top piece of wood.

DRILL CHART

mm	Customary Drill Size
1.60	1/16
2.40	3/32
3.20	1/8
3.60	9/64
4.80	3/16
5.20	13/64
5.60	7/32
6.00	15/64
6.40	1/4
7.20	9/32
7.80	5/16
8.40	21/64
9.20	23/64
10.00	25/64
10.80	27/64
11.00	7/16
11.50	29/64
11.80	15/32
12.20	31/64
12.80	1/2

Reprinted from *Metrics in Career Education* by permission of author, John R. Lindbeck

8-9b. Boring approximate metric holes with customary drills.

8-9a. Use this table to find the correct twist drill sizes to use for the shank and pilot holes when drilling into soft wood.

DRILL SIZES FOR DRIVING SCREWS INTO SOFT WOOD

GAUGE NO. OF SCREW	0	1	2	3	4	5	6	7	8	9	10	12	14	16	18	20
Shank Hole	1/16	5/64	3/32	7/64	7/64	1/8	9/64	5/32	11/64	3/16	3/16	7/32	1/4	17/64	19/64	21/64
Pilot Hole	1/64	1/32	1/32	3/64	3/64	1/16	1/16	1/16	5/64	5/64	3/32	7/64	7/64	9/64	11/64	11/64

size. If it is too shallow, use the countersink to make it a little deeper.

4. Put the top piece of wood in position over the bottom piece. Whenever possible, to keep the pieces from moving, clamp them in place with a C-clamp. Mark the position of the hole in the bottom piece of wood with an awl, through the shank hole, so that the mark is exactly in the center of that hole. Fig. 8-11.

5. Remove the top piece of wood and bore the pilot hole with the proper size drill bit. Fig. 8-12. The depth of the hole should be

8-10. Use a countersink to make the proper-sized recess for a flathead or ovalhead wood screw.

8-11. Position the top piece of wood over the bottom piece. Hold it in place with a C-clamp or in a vise. With the awl, mark the position of each pilot hole through the shank hole.

8-12. Bore the pilot hole in the bottom piece after you remove the top piece.

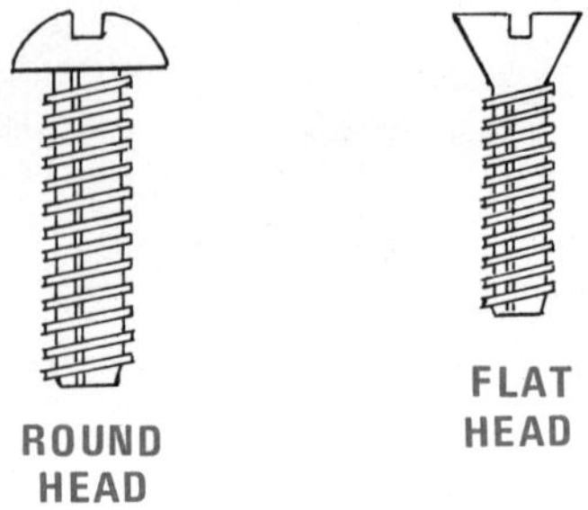

8-13a. Two common types of machine screws, one with a round head, the other with a flat head.

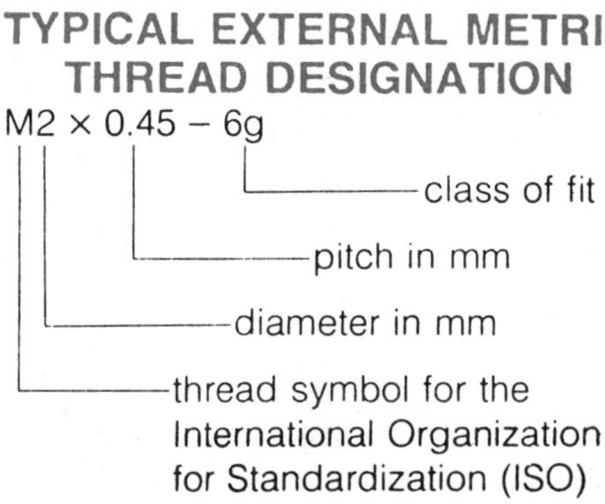

Reprinted from *Metrics in Career Education* by permission of author, John R. Lindbeck

8-13b. An example of metric thread designation.

half the length of the screw. For example, if the screw is $1\frac{1}{2}''$ long, the bottom hole would be $\frac{3}{4}''$ deep.

6. Put the two pieces of wood in position and drive the screws into the holes until the pieces are fastened tightly together. Be sure to use a screwdriver that fits the slot in the screw. For a Phillips-head screw, use a Phillips-head screwdriver of the correct size.

Machine Screws

Machine screws are used mostly for fastening two pieces of metal together. These screws come in flathead and roundheaded styles and are made in $\frac{1}{4}''$ to 4″ lengths. Fig. 8-13a. They are made in various thread sizes, such as 6-32, 10-32, and $\frac{1}{4}$-20.

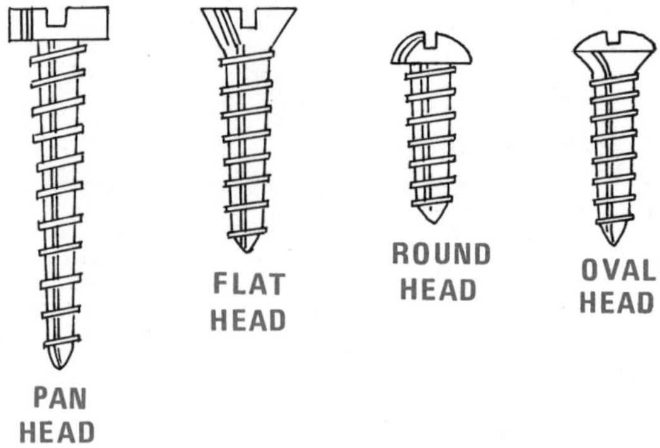

8-14. Typical sheet metal screws for home use. Note the various head styles.

The first number refers to the diameter of the screw. The second number refers to the number of threads per linear inch. For example, on a $\frac{1}{4}$-20 machine screw, the diameter of the screw is $\frac{1}{4}''$. The number of threads per inch is 20. Below $\frac{1}{4}''$, threads are measured by the gauge of wire they are made from and the number of threads per inch. For example, on a 6-32 machine screw, the 6 stands for #6-gauge wire. The 32 means that there are 32 threads per inch.

Machine-screw nuts are made to fit all these screws and are either hexagonal or square in shape.

METRIC SCREW THREADS

Metric thread designation is quite different from the customary designation just discussed. Metric threads are identified by their diameter (in millimeters), their pitch (also in millimeters), and their class of fit or tightness. A capital *M*, the ISO thread symbol, precedes the diameter. Fig. 8-13b shows a typical metric thread designation.

Sheet Metal Screws

Sheet metal screws vary in length, thickness (gauge), and head shape. Common head shapes, as shown in Fig. 8-14, are:

- Flathead—head is flush with surface of material.
- Panhead—most common shape.
- Ovalhead—partially recessed into surface.

- Roundhead.

There are several styles of threads available on sheet metal screws. Most of them are *self-tapping.* That is, as they are driven into a previously drilled hole in a piece of metal, they cut a thread.

WALL FASTENERS

There are two types of wall fasteners. One is for use on hollow walls, such as plaster, wallboard, or plywood. Hollow-wall fasteners available include:

- Collapsible hollow-wall screw anchors, which are tightened by a screw to expand the anchor. Fig. 8-15.
- Toggle bolts, either spring or solid toggle, which are pushed, with the wing attached, through a hole in the wall. Fig. 8-16.

The Rawlplug Co., Inc.

8-15. A collapsible hollow-wall screw anchor.

8-16. Toggle bolt with a spring toggle.

The Rawlplug Co., Inc.

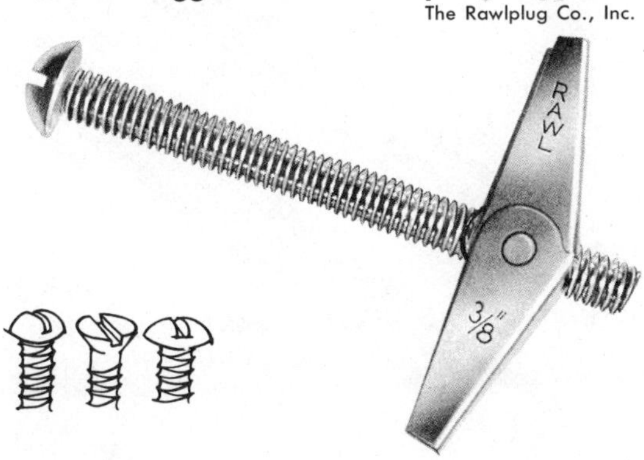

- Plastic anchors or plugs, which expand within the wall when the screw is tightened. Fig. 8-17.

The other type of wall fastener is used on masonry walls (cement, concrete block, or brick). Masonry wall fasteners include:

- Machine-screw expansion lead anchors, which require a special tool to tap them into the hole. Fig. 8-18.
- Fiber anchors with lead centers. They expand against the sides of a hole when the screw is driven in. Fig. 8-19.
- Lead lag-screw expansion plugs which expand within a hole when the screw is driven in. Fig. 8-20.

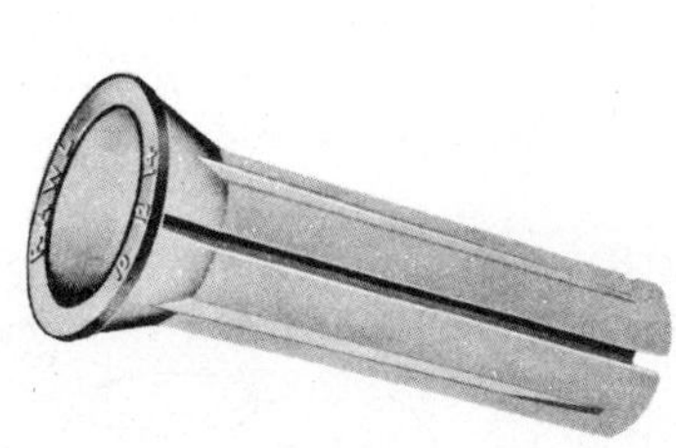

The Rawlplug Co., Inc.

8-17. Plastic anchor or plug that expands within the wall when the screw is tightened.

8-18. Machine-screw expansion lead anchor.

The Rawlplug Co., Inc.

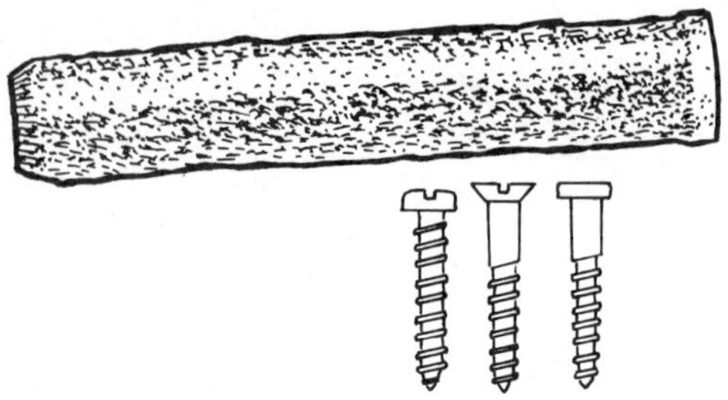

8-19. A fiber anchor with a lead center into which wood screws, lag screws, or sheet metal screws can be driven.

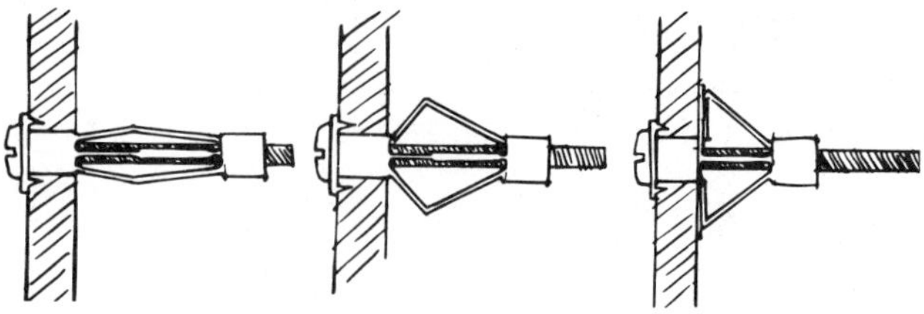

The Rawlplug Co., Inc.

8-22. Tighten the machine screw in the anchor until you can feel the pressure of the grippers against the inside of the wall. Here, the grippers are shown tightening against the wall.

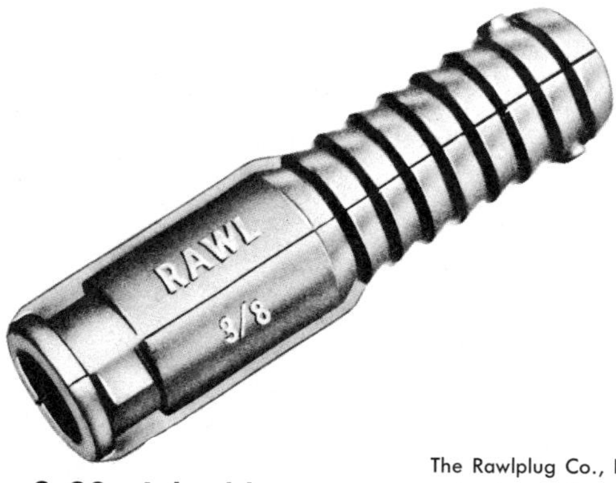

The Rawlplug Co., Inc.

8-20. A lead lag-screw expansion plug.

8-21. A concrete nail and a steel cut nail.

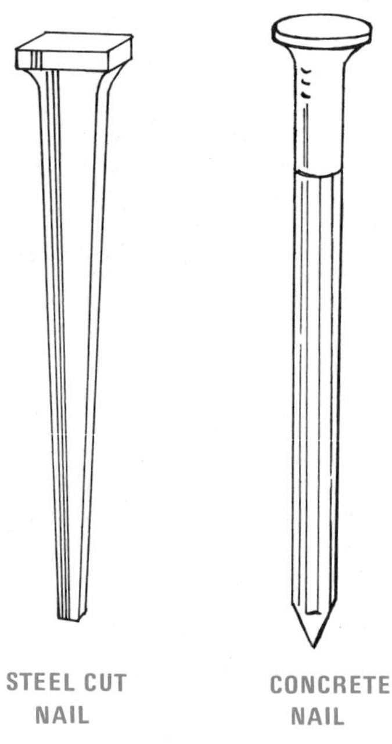

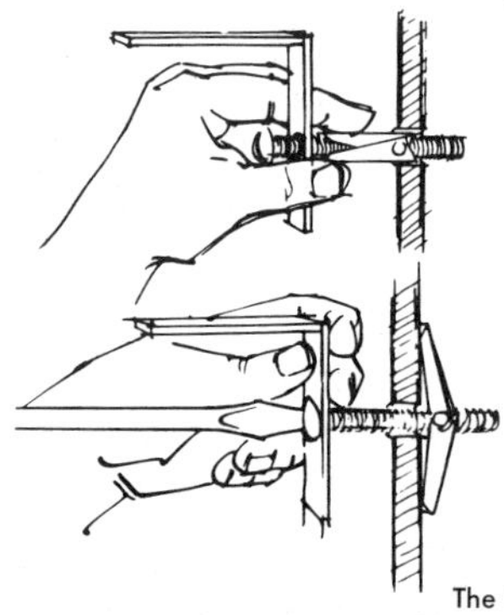

The Rawlplug Co., Inc.

8-23. Push the end of the bolt and the toggle through the hole in the wall. The spring toggle opens up once it is past the material that makes up the face of the wall. While tightening the bolt, pull on it to keep the toggle from turning.

8-24. Two types of carbide-tipped masonry drills.

The Rawlplug Co., Inc.

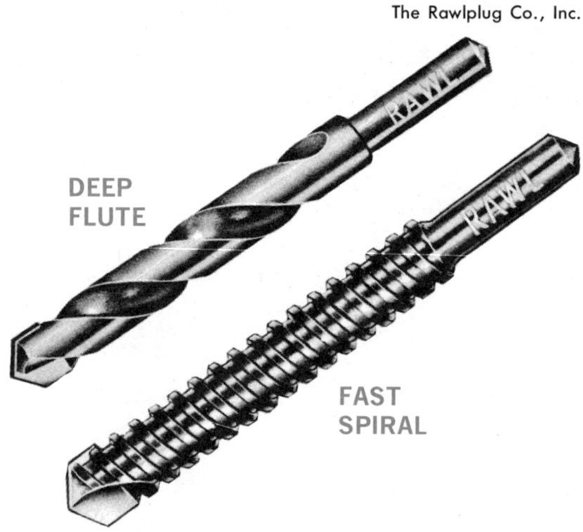

• Steel cut nails. These are square, hardened-steel nails that are driven with a heavy hammer.

• Concrete nails, usually driven with a heavy hammer after a hole is started with a drill. Fig. 8-21.

Installing Wall Fasteners

A collapsible hollow-wall screw anchor is installed with a drill and a screwdriver in the following way.

1. Drill a hole in the wall for the anchor. Manufacturer's instructions will tell you which size drill to use, or you can measure the outside diameter of the anchor with a ruler. Put the anchor into the hole and tap it into the wall until the metal teeth on the anchor head are imbedded in the wall surface. (This will keep it from turning.) Some anchors come with a small wrench which is used to keep the anchor head from turning.
2. Tighten the machine screw in the anchor until you can feel the pressure of the grippers against the inside of the wall. Fig. 8-22. The anchor is now firmly in place and will not move.
3. Remove the screw from the anchor with a screwdriver and put it through the object to be fastened to the wall. Drive the screw back into the anchor until it is tight.

A toggle bolt with either a spring or a solid (gravity) toggle, is available in lengths up to 4″. Diameters of the bolts vary from $\frac{1}{8}$″ to $\frac{1}{2}$″, and the sizes of the toggles get bigger as the diameter of the bolt increases. Toggle bolts are installed in the following way.

1. Drill a hole in the wall large enough to accommodate the toggle. Use either an electric drill or a hand drill.
2. Remove the toggle from the bolt and pass the bolt through the object being fastened to the wall. Thread the toggle back onto the bolt.
3. Push the end of the bolt and the toggle through the hole in the wall. Fig. 8-23. A solid, or gravity, toggle will drop into position inside the wall. A spring toggle will open up once it is past the material that makes up the face of the wall. Pull the bolt back so that the toggle is against the inside surface of the wall.
4. Tighten the bolt with a screwdriver while pulling on the bolt to keep the toggle from turning. Keep turning until the bolt is tight.

The holding power of the toggle bolt increases as the diameter of the bolt increases. For example, a $\frac{3}{8}$″ toggle bolt will support more weight than a $\frac{1}{8}$″ bolt. When a bolt is removed from the wall, the toggle will drop off and be lost inside the wall.

Plastic anchors are commonly used in the home to hold up racks, shelves, and other items that do not have much weight. They are installed in the following way.

1. Drill a hole in the wall, using a twist drill of the size recommended by the anchor manufacturer. (This drill-size information is usually found on the anchor package.)
2. Push the anchor into the hole flush with the wall surface. Start the screw in the anchor to expand it. Then remove the screw from the anchor, put it through the item being attached to the wall, and drive the screw in tightly.

A masonry wall fastener is installed in a hole previously drilled into the masonry. A carbide-tipped masonry drill or a star drill can be used to make the hole.

The carbide-tipped drill bit fits into a portable electric drill. Fig. 8-24. Use either a $\frac{1}{2}$″ electric drill, which runs slow, or a variable speed $\frac{1}{4}$″ drill. For safety, you should wear goggles when using an electric drill. Use an in-and-out motion when you are drilling. Fig. 8-25. Do not push the drill. Let

8-25. Drill a hole in masonry with an electric drill. Use an in-and-out motion.

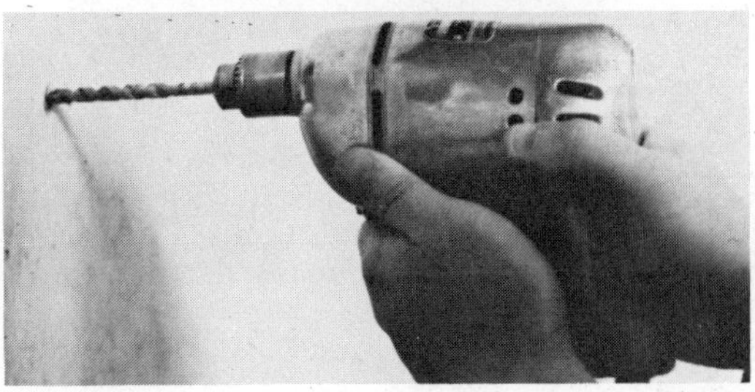

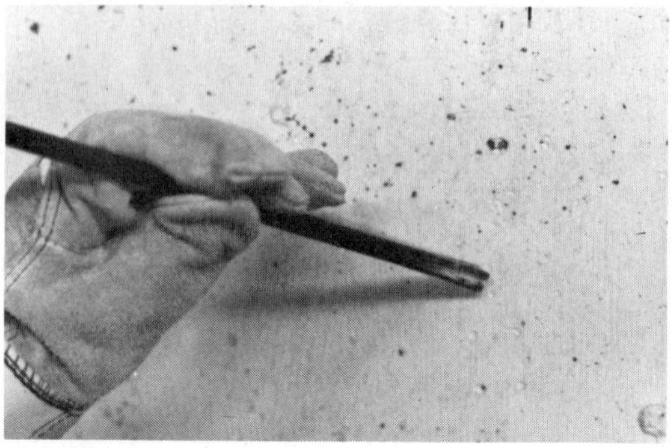

8-26. Place the star drill on the spot where you want to make a hole and strike it with a heavy hammer. Wear heavy work gloves and safety glasses when using this tool.

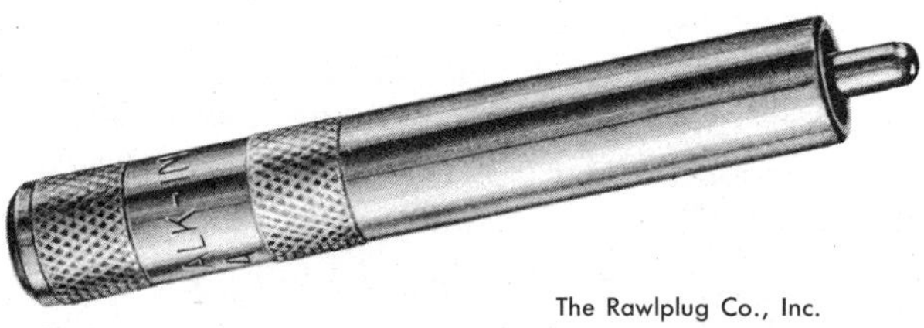

The Rawlplug Co., Inc.

8-27. A special tool used to tap machine-screw anchors into drilled holes.

8-28. Fastening a machine-screw expansion lead anchor into a masonry wall.

The Rawlplug Co., Inc.

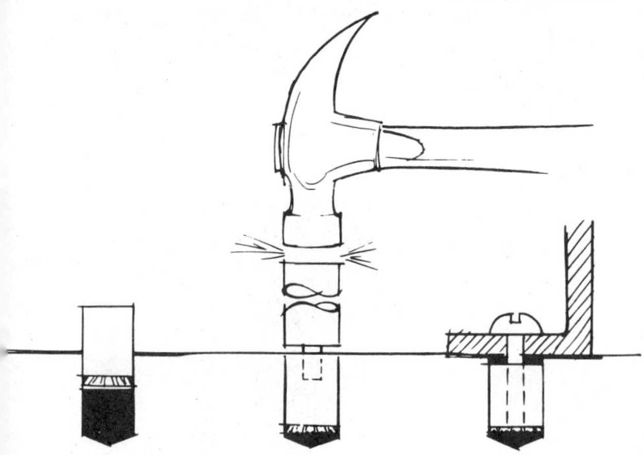

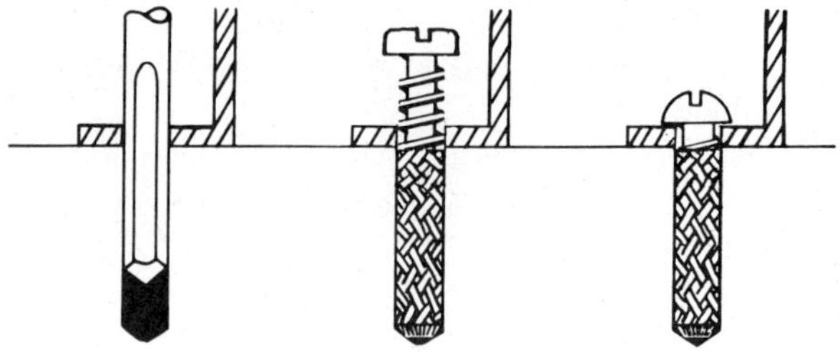

The Rawlplug Co., Inc.

8-29. Installing a fiber anchor.

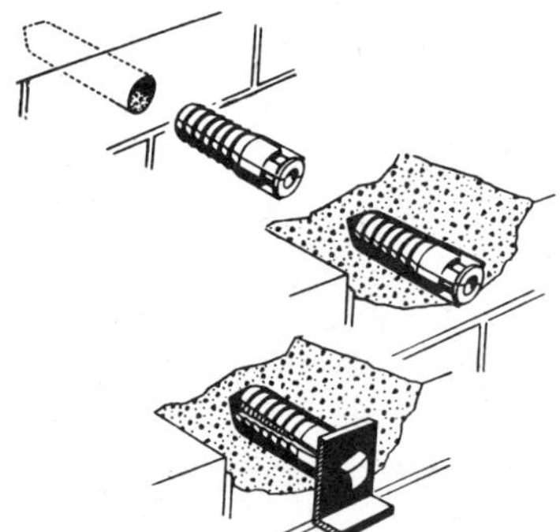

The Rawlplug Co., Inc.

8-30. Put the lead lag-screw expansion plug into the hole drilled for it. Place the lag screw into the plug and tighten it with a wrench.

8-31. A screw hook (heavy duty).

Stanley Tools

it do the work at its own speed. If you must drill a large hole, $\frac{1}{2}''$ for example, start with a smaller masonry drill and gradually work your way up to the larger size.

The star drill is used with a heavy hammer. Wear heavy work gloves and safety glasses or goggles when using this type of tool. Fig. 8-26. Place the star drill on the spot where you want to make a hole. Hold it by the shank and strike it with the heavy hammer, then rotate it a little in a clockwise motion. Strike it again and rotate it. Continue this technique until you have a hole drilled to the depth you need. Occasionally, blow or brush the concrete dust out of the hole.

The procedure for installing a machine-screw expansion lead anchor is as follows.

1. Drill a hole in the masonry wall equal to the outside diameter of the lead anchor. (Some lead anchors have the hole size marked on them.) Use a carbide-tipped drill or a star drill as explained previously. Blow all the chips and dust from the hole. Push the anchor into the hole. (Some anchors are packaged with a special tool for tapping them into holes. (Fig. 8-27.)

2. Slip the machine screw through the hole in the object being fastened and thread the screw into the anchor. Tighten the screw with a screwdriver. The anchor will expand as the screw goes in. Fig. 8-28.

A fiber anchor with a lead center is installed the same way as the screw expansion lead anchor. With an awl, slightly open the exposed end of the lead center so that the screw will go in more easily. Use a sheet metal screw. The fiber anchor is intended to hold up lightweight items only. Do not overtighten the screw, or you may draw the anchor right out of the hole. Fig. 8-29.

A lead lag-screw expansion plug is installed in the same way as the machine-screw expansion lead anchor. Fig. 8-30. The only difference between these two fasteners is that one is made to hold a tapered lag screw and the other is threaded for a machine screw.

Steel-cut nails and concrete nails are driven into masonry with a heavy hammer. Start a hole for the concrete nails with a masonry drill. Then drive the nail through the item to be attached to the wall and into the concrete, block, or brick. Steel-cut nails, in contrast to concrete nails, are driven in without a drilled starting hole. Both these types of nails are made of hardened steel. Therefore they must be hit squarely, or they will break off. Wear safety glasses or goggles when driving these nails to prevent eye injury from such an occurrence, or from masonry chips, which sometimes break off.

—BOLTS, HOOKS, AND OTHER USEFUL HARDWARE—

You will probably find several kinds of hardware useful for home maintenance. Here, the most common types of screw hooks, bolts, washers, nuts, hinges, and door hardware will be listed and illustrated. *Note:* When metric hardware replaces the hardware now used, hinges and locks will require metric screws.

Screw Hooks

Screw hooks are installed by first making starting holes with an awl or a small drill. A pair of pliers may then be used to turn the hooks into a piece of wood. Some useful types of screw hooks are:

- Cup hook—for light duty.
- Screw hook—for heavy duty. Fig. 8-31.
- Screw eye—comes in many sizes, from light to very heavy duty. Fig. 8-32.
- Hook and eye—doors, storm windows, and cabinets. Fig. 8-33.
- Square-bend screw hook, or *L* hook—for hanging tools and utensils. Fig. 8-34.

Stanley Tools

8-32. Screw eyes, such as this one, are available in many sizes.

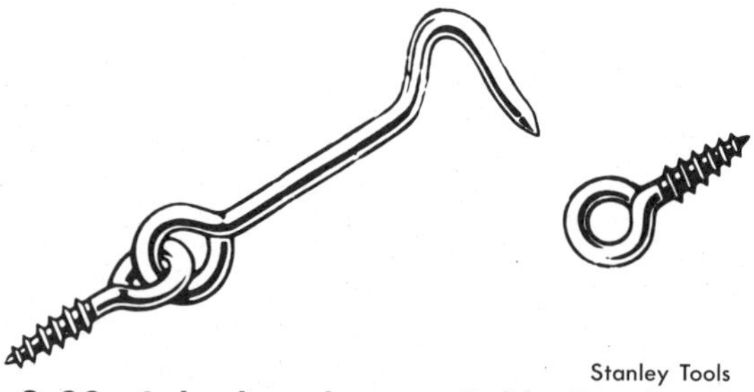

Stanley Tools

8-33. A hook and eye suitable for doors, storm windows, and cabinets.

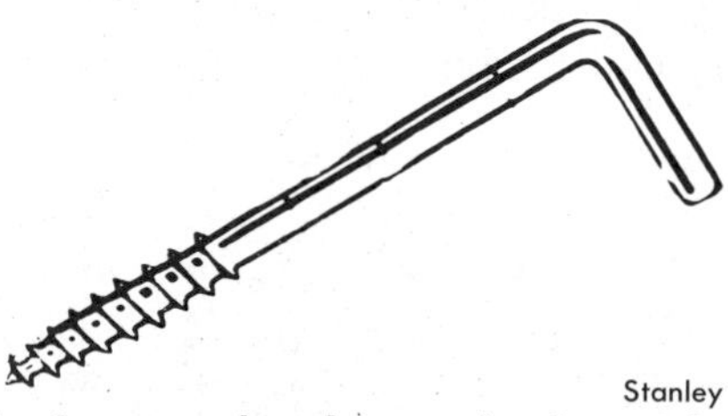

Stanley Tools

8-34. A square-bend screw hook, or *L* hook.

8-35. A square-headed machine bolt.

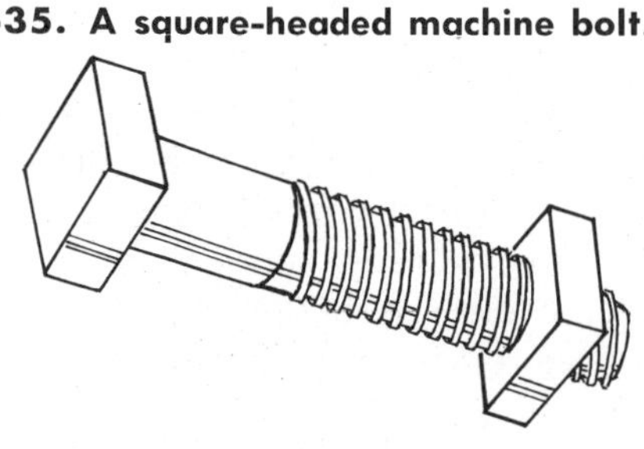

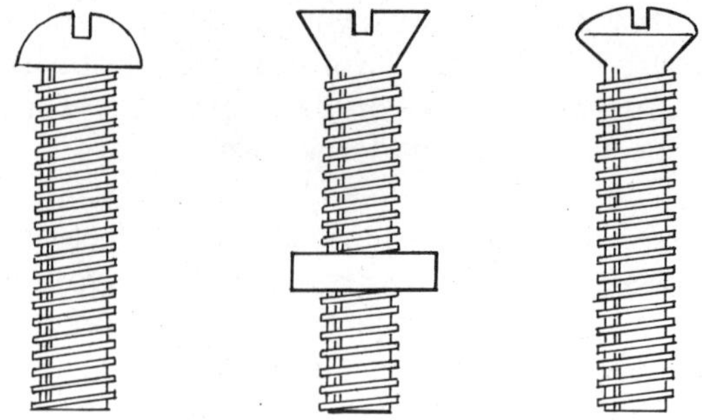

STOVE BOLTS

8-36. Three types of stove bolts (left to right): roundheaded, flathead, and ovalhead.

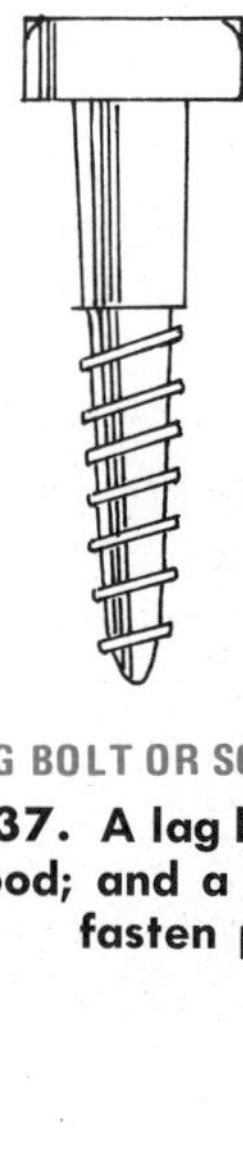

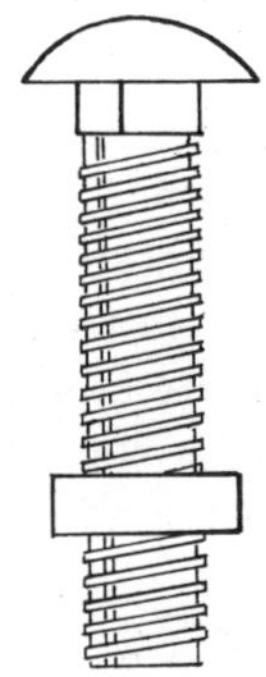

CARRIAGE BOLT

LAG BOLT OR SCREW

8-37. A lag bolt, which can be threaded into wood; and a carriage bolt, which is used to fasten pieces of wood together.

8-38. A flat metal washer.

Stanley Tools

Bolts

Bolts are used to fasten two heavy pieces of wood together or to fasten pieces of metal together in such a way that they can be taken apart if necessary. Bolts are used with nuts, and sometimes with washers. Common bolts include:

- Machine bolts—square and hexagonal heads. Fig. 8-35.
- Stove bolts—flat, oval, and round heads. Fig. 8-36.
- Lag bolts, or screws—threaded into wood or lead anchors.
- Carriage bolts—for fastening heavy pieces of wood together. Fig. 8-37.

Washers and Nuts

Washers are made of steel, aluminum, or other metals. The most commonly used washer is a flat steel one. Fig. 8-38. Washer sizes are based on the inside hole diameter, such as $\frac{1}{4}''$, $\frac{5}{16}''$, or $\frac{3}{8}''$. Another commonly used washer is the spring-lock washer, which presses against the nut and prevents it from coming loose.

Machine-screw nuts, as well as nuts for other types of threaded fasteners, are made of steel, aluminum, or brass. Fig. 8-39. They can also be plated with other metals (such as cadmium) to match the bolts and screws with which they are used. Nuts are made in various thread sizes. Common varieties are:

- Hexagonal nut—probably the most-used variety.
- Square nut.
- Wing nut—used when you want to disassemble the object easily.
- Locknut—sometimes made of fiber.
- Castle nut—made to hold a cotter pin.

Hinges

Hinges hold doors and windows in place, yet make it possible to swing them in and out. Differences between one hinge and another may be found in the shape of the *leaves* (the parts of the hinge that are flat and have screw holes in them) and in the arrangement of the *knuckle* (the part containing a pin on which the two leaves move).

Some hinges open partially; others open all the way. On some hinges the leaves are completely hidden. Some have them partially concealed, and others are meant to be mounted on the surface, where their appearance is either decorative or is not important. Butt hinges are mounted in *mortises* (portions in a doorjamb or the door itself cut out to accommodate the hinge leaf). Some of the hinges available for home use include:

- Butt hinge—with loose pin or fast pin. Fig. 8-40.
- Spring loaded—for automatic closing of a cabinet or screen door.
- Semiconcealed—for cabinet doors. Figs. 8-41.
- *H* hinge—for surface mounting. Fig. 8-42.
- *HL* hinge—for surface mounting. Fig. 8-42.

8-39. Four types of machine-screw nuts useful in home repair work. They are made in thread sizes to fit any machine screw or bolt.

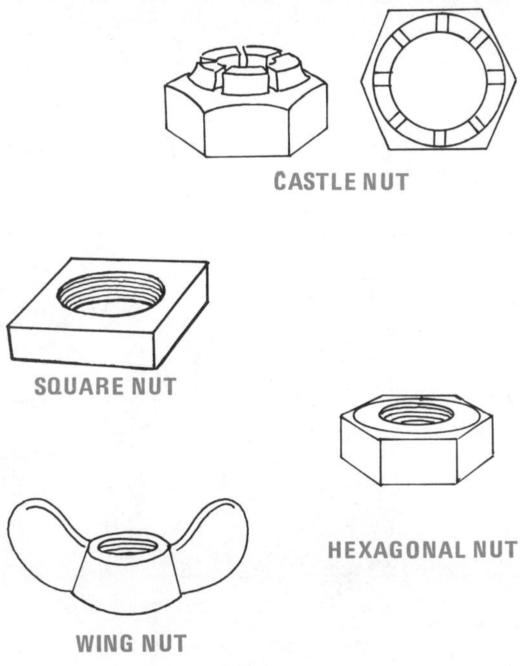

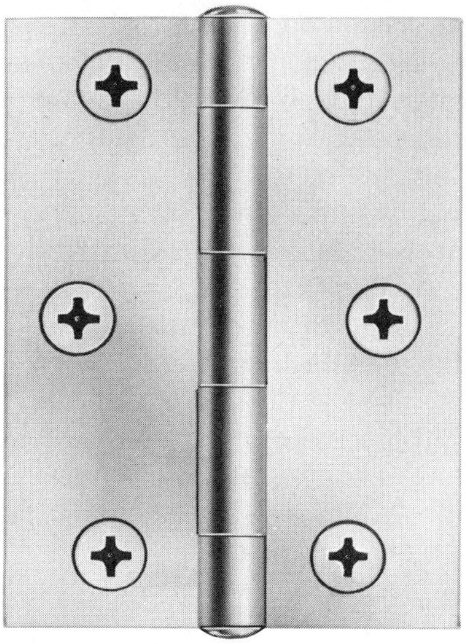

Stanley Tools
8-40. A butt hinge with a fast pin, which cannot be removed.

Stanley Tools
8-41a. One type of semiconcealed hinge.

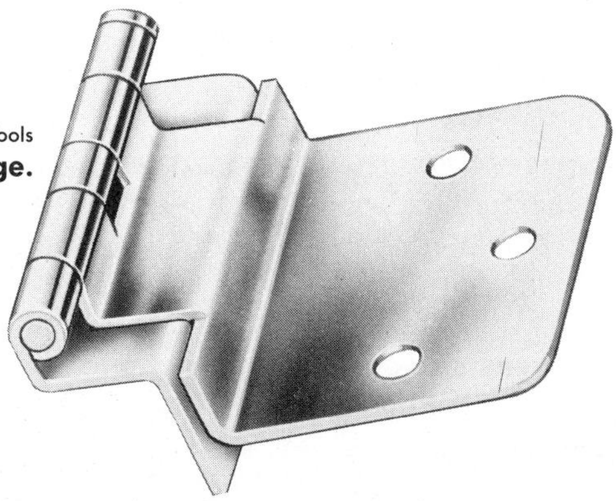

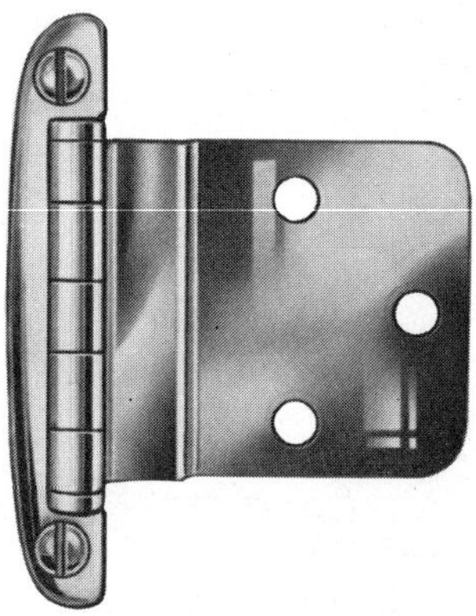

Stanley Tools
8-41b. A semiconcealed hinge used for cabinet doors.

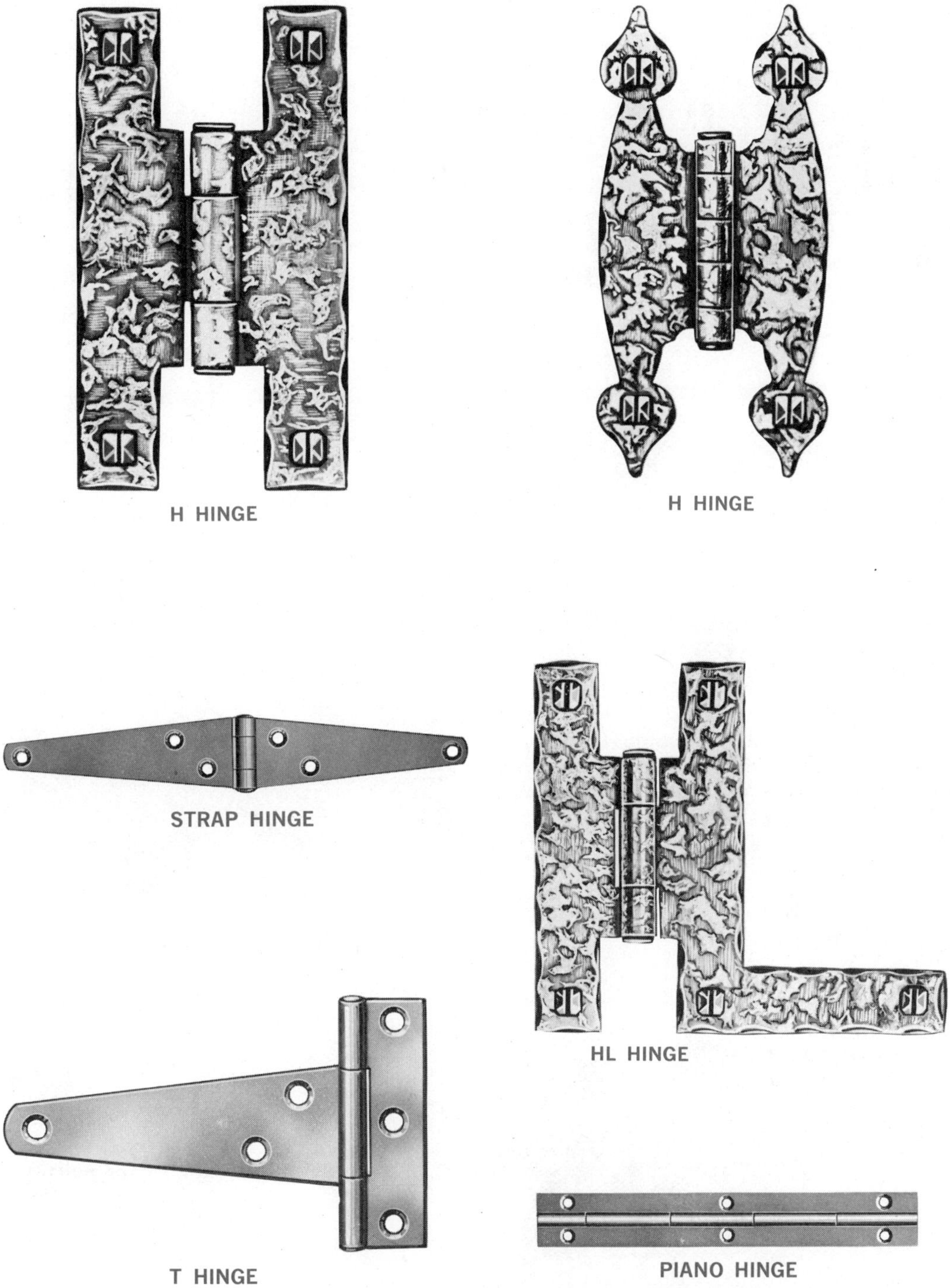

Stanley Tools

8-42. Various types of hinges.

Stanley Tools

8-43. One type of cabinet latch.

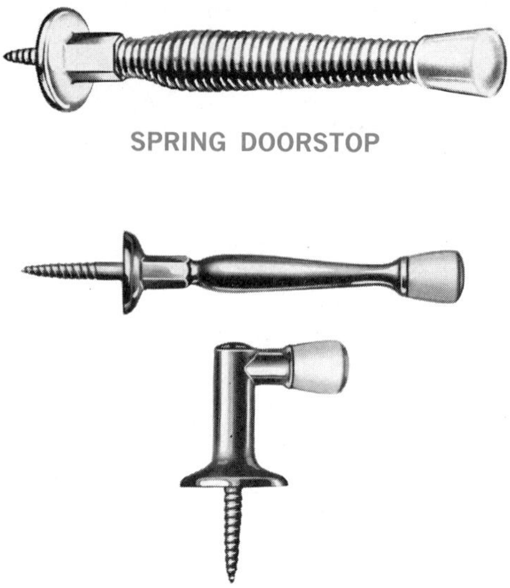

Stanley Tools

8-46. Doorstops.

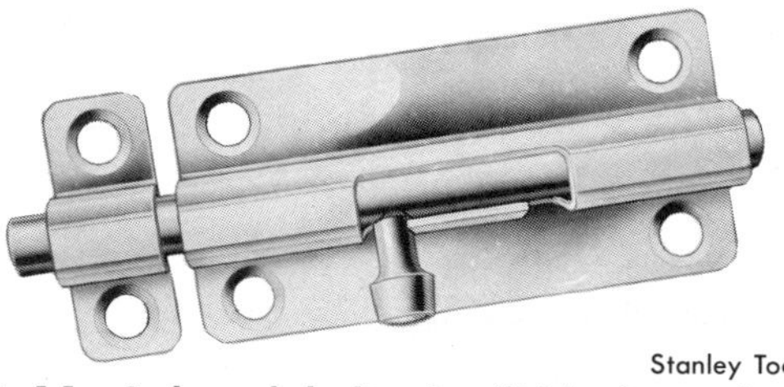

Stanley Tools

8-44. A barrel bolt. Available in various sizes, barrel bolts are suitable for closing small cabinet doors or large entrance doors.

Stanley Tools

8-47. A decorative knob, used for drawers or cabinet doors.

8-45. A chain door fastener.

Stanley Tools

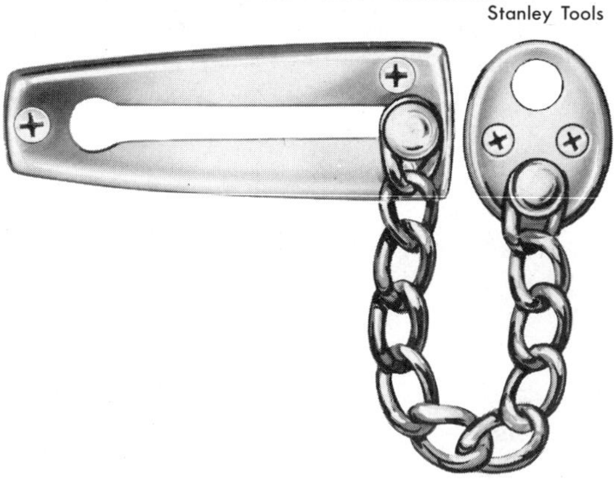

8-48. Two cabinet-door pulls.

Stanley Tools

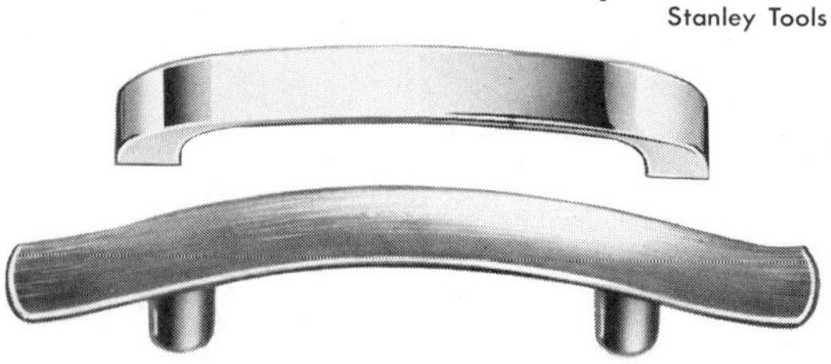

Stanley Tools

8-49. A magnet catch (top) and a friction catch for cabinet doors.

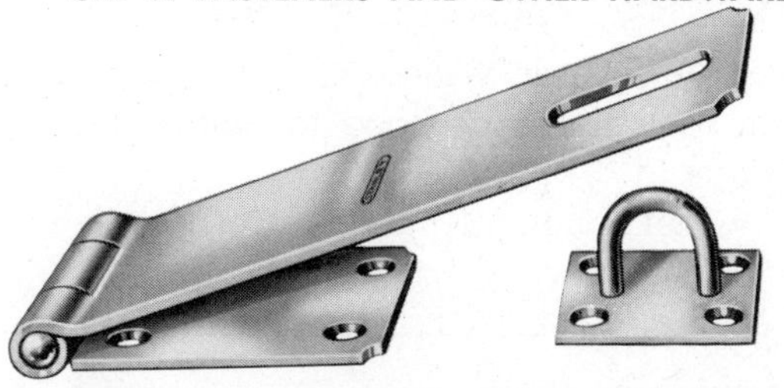

Stanley Tools

8-50. A hasp and staple are fastened to both the door and doorframe so that a padlock may be used.

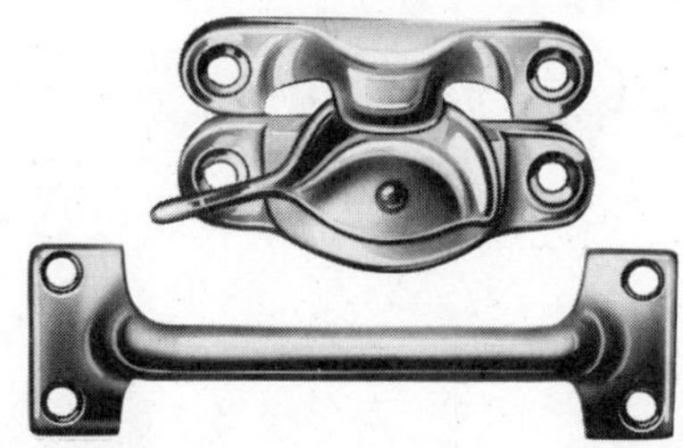

Stanley Tools

8-51. Sash lock (top) for a double-hung window, and one type of sash lift.

- Strap hinge—for surface mounting on doors and gates. Fig. 8-42.
- *T* hinge—surface mounted on doors and gates. Fig. 8-42.
- Continuous hinge—for cabinets. Also called a piano hinge. It is available in various lengths. Fig. 8-42.

Door Hardware

This type of hardware includes an assortment of items used to lock, close, or to stop a door from opening too far. These items may be found in the home on cabinet doors as well as on interior and exterior doors.

- Latch. Fig. 8-43.
- Barrel bolt. Fig. 8-44.
- Chain door fastener. Fig. 8-45.
- Spring doorstop. Fig. 8-46.
- Rigid doorstop. Fig. 8-46.
- Knobs—for drawers and cabinet doors. Fig. 8-47.
- Door pulls. Fig. 8-48.
- Friction catch—for cabinets. Fig. 8-49.
- Single-roller catch—for cabinets.
- Magnet catch—commonly used on kitchen cabinets. Fig. 8-49.
- Hasp and staple—for locking doors with a padlock. Fig. 8-50.

Miscellaneous Hardware

This section shows other types of hardware which are often useful to anyone doing home repairs.

- Sash lock—for double-hung windows. Fig. 8-51.
- Sash lift—for windows. Fig. 8-51.

• Corrugated fasteners. These are driven into two pieces of wood to hold them together.

• Metal-mending plates. Corner plates, flat corner, straight, and *T*-plates are available. Fig. 8-52.

• Staples—in various lengths, driven in with a gun or a hammer. Fig. 8-53.

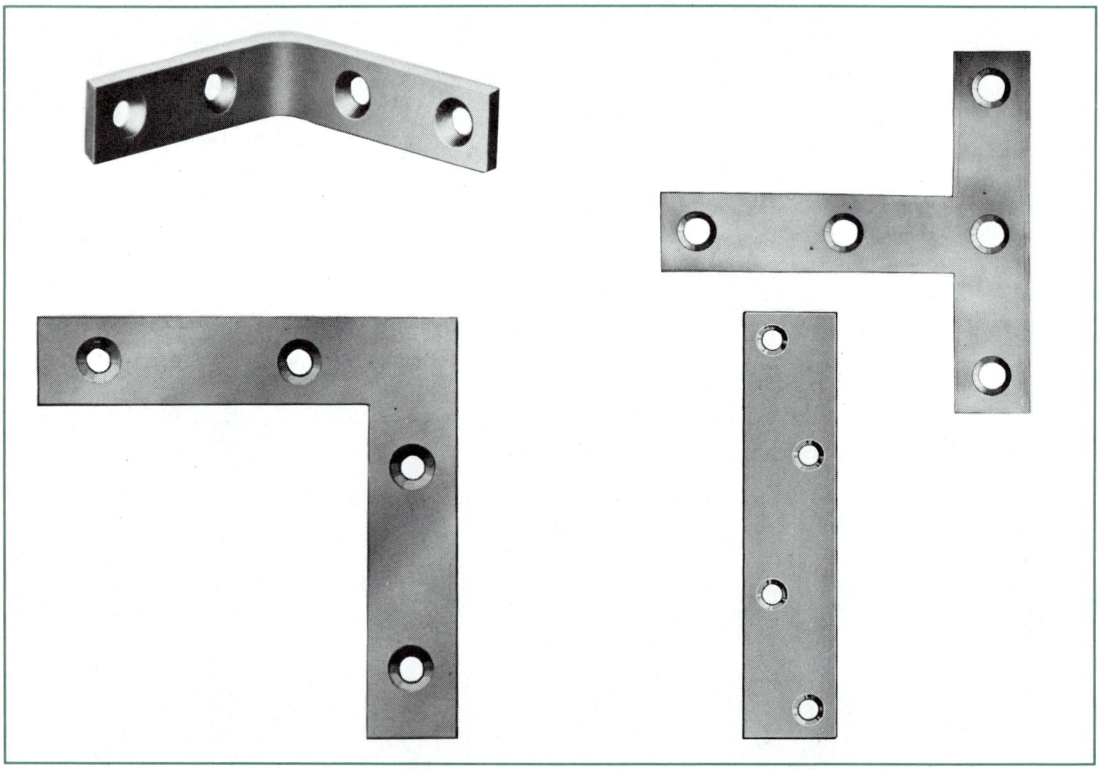

Stanley Tools

8-52. Shown here are four shapes of metal-mending plates. They are used to reinforce or repair structures such as screen doors.

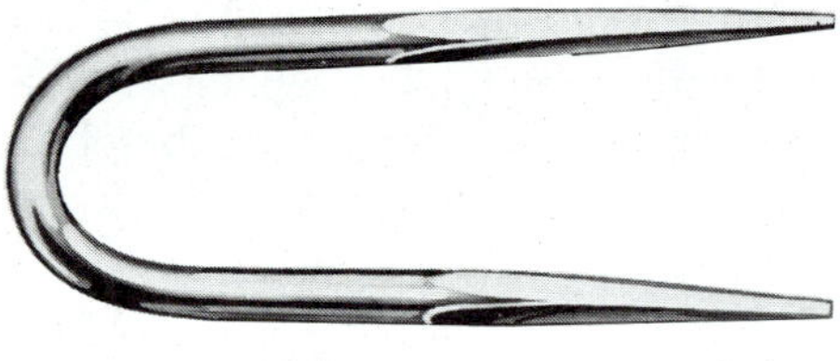

Stanley Tools

8-53. One type of staple which is driven with a hammer. Staples come in many sizes and are made for such purposes as holding up fencing, screening, and electrical cable.

CHECKUP

1. What are some common types of nails and how are they used?
2. Do wood screws have more holding power than nails?
3. What types of wall fasteners might you use for plaster, wallboard, or plywood walls?

CHAPTER 9

Door Repairs

TYPES OF DOORS

Several types of doors are found in the average house. They can be grouped into interior doors (within the building for room entrances and closets) and exterior doors (entrances to the house).

Interior doors are thinner and lighter in weight than exterior doors. They may be bought in these styles: hollow core flush doors, French doors, panel doors, or louvered doors. Fig. 9-1. They are made of wood, molded plastic, or aluminum. Interior doors are hung in both wooden frames and steel frames.

Exterior doors are usually $1\frac{3}{4}''$ thick and solid in construction. They are weather-stripped to keep out drafts and moisture. Exterior doors come in many styles, such as solid flush doors, panel doors, and Dutch doors. Figs. 9-2, 9-3. Some doors come with one or more windows in them. Exterior doors may be made of wood, metal, or a combination of wood and molded plastic decorations. The building codes of many localities require that a wooden door used between a house and an attached garage have a metal sheet fastened to the garage side of the door to make it fire resistant.

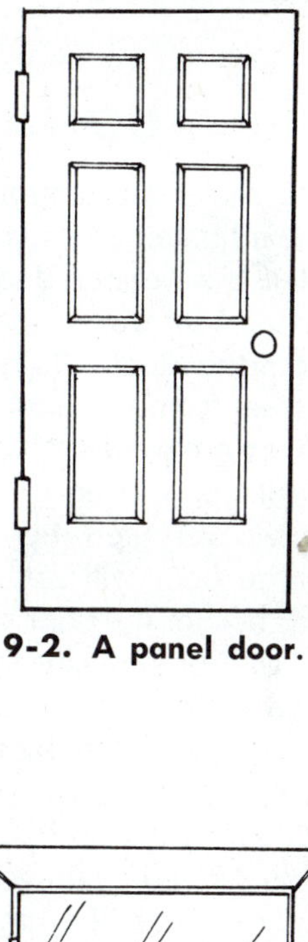

9-2. A panel door.

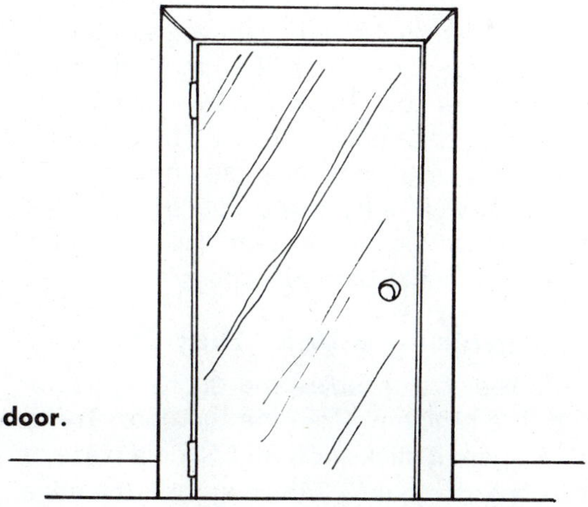

9-1. A flush door.

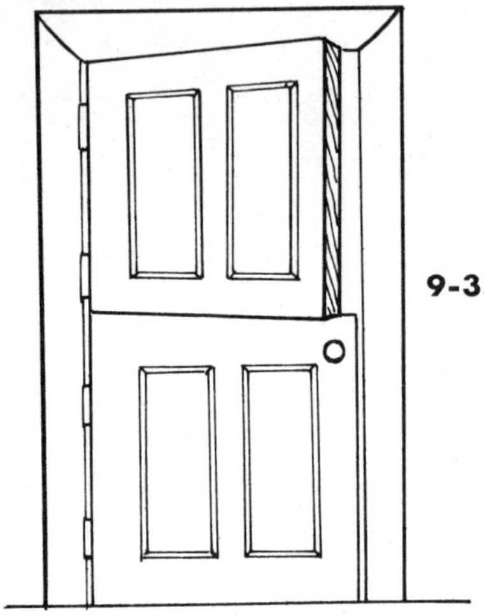

9-3. A Dutch door. The top and bottom open separately or as one unit.

COMMON DOOR PROBLEMS

Wooden doors and doors hung in wooden frames can be adjusted and repaired by the do-it-yourselfer. If a wooden door is hung in a metal frame, however, repairs can be made only on the door. Nothing can be done to the steel frame to alter it. In many cases the hinges are welded to the frame so that they cannot be moved.

There are two very common door problems. Either the door will not open easily and seems to stick, or the door springs open by itself and will not stay closed. A sticking door is caused by loose hinges, by a doorframe that is out of square, by swelling due to moisture, or by too much paint on the edges of the door. If the door springs open, that problem is caused by hinge mortises (a mortise is a recess that the hinge fits into) that are set too deeply, or by a latch that does not engage the strike. These conditions may result from the use and abuse of a door as well as from improper installation. A badly warped door that will not close properly should be replaced.

Repairing a Door That Sticks

To repair a troublesome door, first analyze the problem. Examine the door. Try to find where it sticks or binds. Slide a piece of cardboard about $\frac{1}{16}''$ thick around the edge of the door when it is closed. There should be at least that much clearance on all sides for the door to fit properly.

Check the hinges to see if they are loose. Pull on the door. It will jiggle if the screws holding the hinges are loose. To tighten the hinges try to tighten the screws with a screwdriver. If the holes are too large, you can replace the old screws with longer wood screws. You can also put a sliver of wood or a wooden match in each hole and then drive the old screw back into the hole until it is tight. Fig. 9-4.

If the door still sticks, try shimming the upper or lower hinge. This is done by cutting a $\frac{1}{16}''$-thick piece of cardboard to fit under the hinge leaf. Fig. 9-5. The cardboard pushes the opposite edge of the door closer to the doorjamb. The rules for shimming a door are:

1. If the top of the door hits against the jamb, shim the bottom hinge.
2. If the bottom of the door hits the jamb, shim the top hinge.

For example, if the lower hinge is shimmed out, the lower corner of the door will be out further and the upper corner will be lifted slightly. Remove the screws from the hinge leaf. Place the cardboard shim behind it. Put the screws back in place.

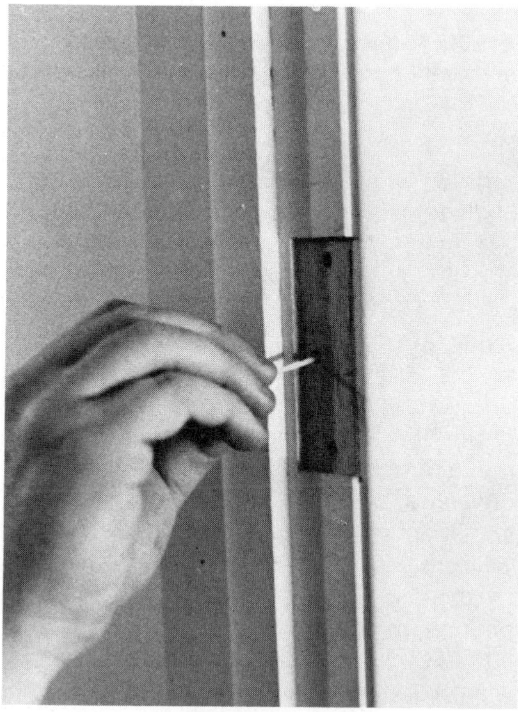

9-4. Put a sliver of wood or a wooden match in each screw hole and then drive the old screw back into the hole.

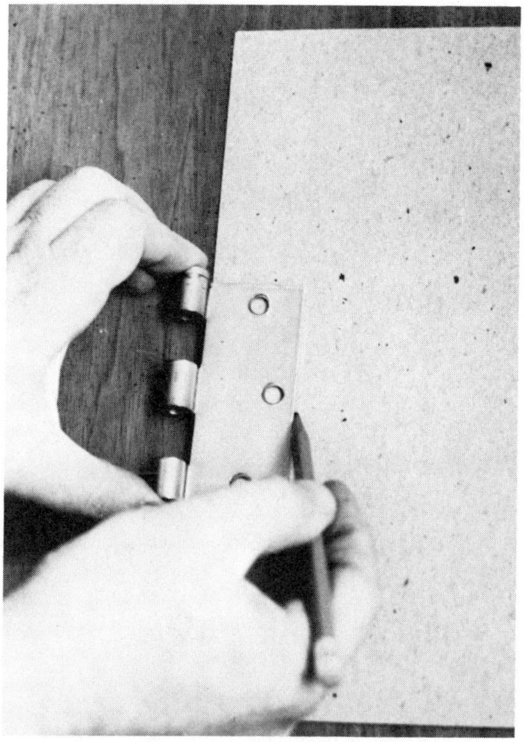

9-5. Cut a piece of cardboard to fit under the hinge leaf.

More than one piece of cardboard may be needed to correct the door binding.

If this technique does not work or if you think that there is not enough space to allow the door to be aligned properly, then the edges of the door will have to be shaved to fit the doorframe. This will have to be done, for example, if there is too much paint on the edge of the door. The tool used to shave the edge of a door is a plane. Fig. 9-6. It is not necessary to remove the door to plane it. Be sure that the plane blade is sharp and that you do not hit any metal with the blade. If the edge of the door that is near the lock is to be planed, remove the lock so that the latch plate on the edge of the door does not interfere with the plane. Close the door to test it after planing the edge $1/16''$. Do not take off too much wood, just enough so that the door opens easily.

9-6. Shave the edge of the door with a plane. Be careful not to take off too much wood.

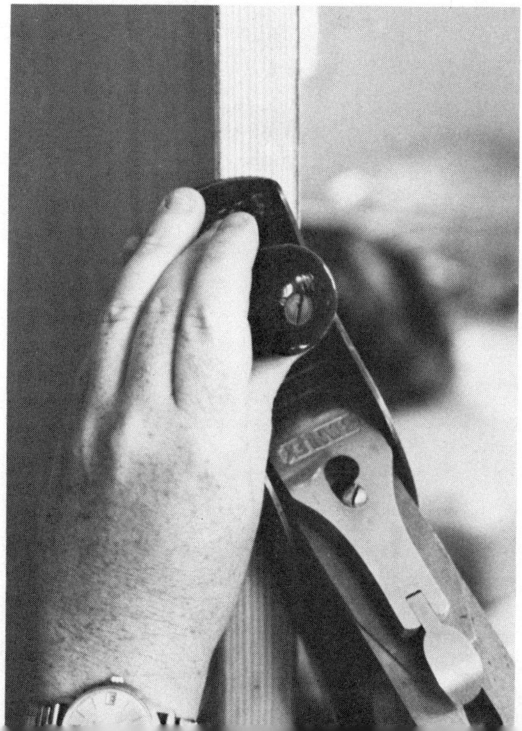

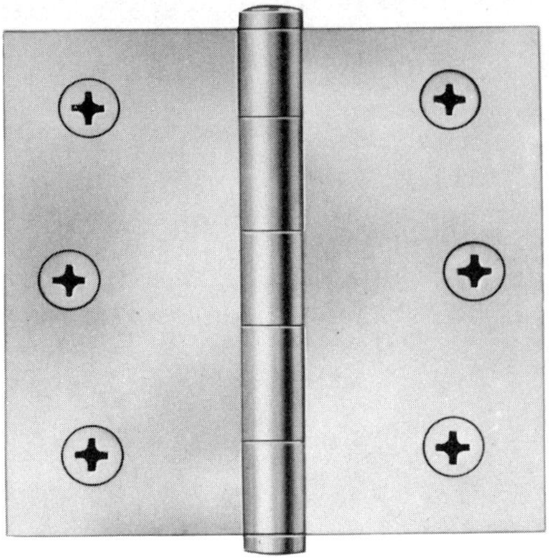

Stanley Tools

9-7. A butt hinge, the most common type used on interior and exterior doors in a house.

If you would find it more comfortable to plane horizontally, you can take the door off its hinges. Fig. 9-7. You will need a hammer and an old screwdriver to take the hinge pins out. The pins, on which the hinges swing, are driven up and out of the knuckles on the hinges. Fig. 9-8. Put the tip of the screwdriver under the little knob on the top of the pin. Tap the screwdriver handle with the hammer. Fig. 9-9. Slowly the pin will be driven up. When the first pin is loose, do not take it out of the knuckle because the hinge will come apart and the door will be hanging by the remaining hinge(s). Loosen all the pins; then, holding the door with one hand, lift out each pin and pull the hinges apart. It is a good idea to have a helper hold the door while you pull the hinge pins out.

To check if the doorframe (the jambs and the header) is square, use a combination square. Test the corners of the door opening. A house settles after some years, and this may put enough stress on the frame to shift it. If planing the door or shimming a hinge does not help the door to close properly, you may need a carpenter to rebuild the doorframe and rehang the door.

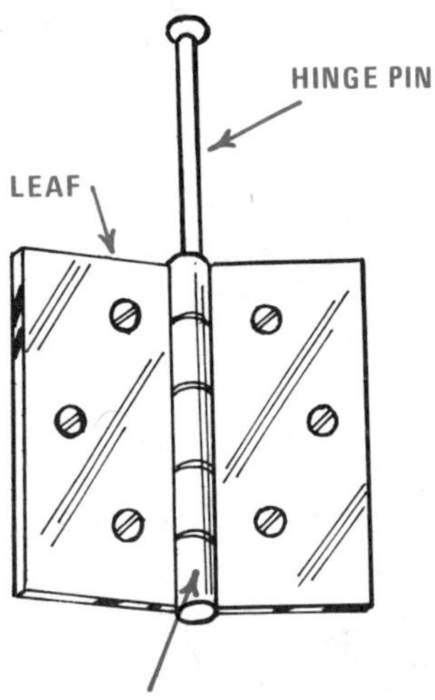

9-8. The pin on which the butt hinge swings is driven up and out of the knuckles on the hinge.

Repairing a Door That Will Not Close Properly

If the door will not stay closed, examine it to find the problem area. If the latch does not hold the door closed, you can make a cardboard shim to put behind the strike plate on the doorjamb. Take the two screws out of the strike plate. Fig. 9-10. Put the plate on a piece of cardboard and trace around it. Fig. 9-11. Cut the shape out

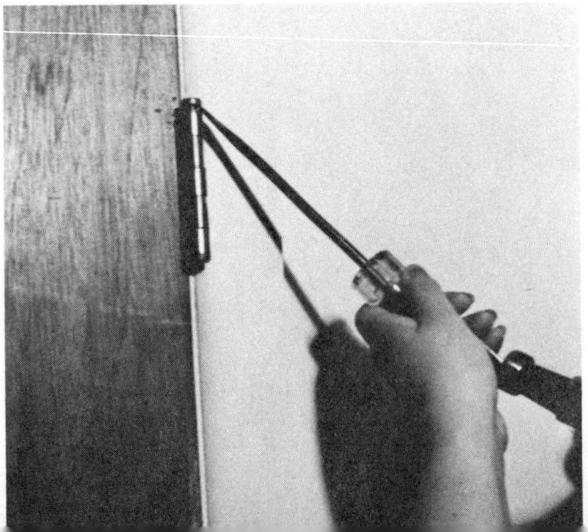

9-9. To loosen the hinge pin, put the tip of the screwdriver under the little knob on the top of the pin. Tap the screwdriver handle with the hammer. The pin will be driven up.

slightly smaller than the plate. Put it in place on the jamb under the plate and replace the two screws. More than one shim may be necessary to bring the strike out enough to catch the spring latch.

Sometimes the strike plate is not in the correct position. You may have to move the strike plate slightly to catch the spring latch. This can be done if the doorframe is made of wood. Put the plate in the new position and drive one wood screw to hold it. Try the door to see if it stays closed. If not, move the strike and try it again. If the door stays closed, drive in the second wood screw. Trace around the strike on the jamb to mark the new recess. Remove the screws and the plate. Use a sharp wood chisel to enlarge the recess (mortise) for the plate. The plate should fit into the jamb so that it is flush with the surface of the wood. Drive the screws back through the plate again. You can fill the exposed part of the old mortise with wood filler or spackling compound. After it is painted, it will not be noticeable.

If these remedies are not enough to allow the latch to enter the strike, perhaps the mortises for the hinges are set too deeply. This problem can be solved by shimming out the hinges so that the door shifts closer to the strike. When the door was originally installed, the hinges may have been recessed too deeply. They should be flush with the surface of the doorframe. You can shim both hinges equally with one or two pieces of cardboard behind each hinge. Remove the door by driving out the hinge pins as previously explained. Remove the hinge leaves from the doorjamb. Put the leaves on a piece of cardboard and trace around them. Cut out the necessary shims and install them under the hinges. Then replace the screws and rehang the door.

You may need more than one shim under each hinge to get the door to stay closed. You may also have to take off all the doorstop molding and, after closing the door, reposition it. Fig. 9-12. To do this use a piece of thin cardboard as a spacer between the door and the stop molding. The molding is nailed in position with $1\frac{1}{2}''$ finishing nails. Fig. 9-13. Set the nails down and fill the holes with spackling compound or wood filler.

9-10. Take the two screws out of the strike on the doorjamb.

9-11. On a piece of cardboard, trace around the strike plate.

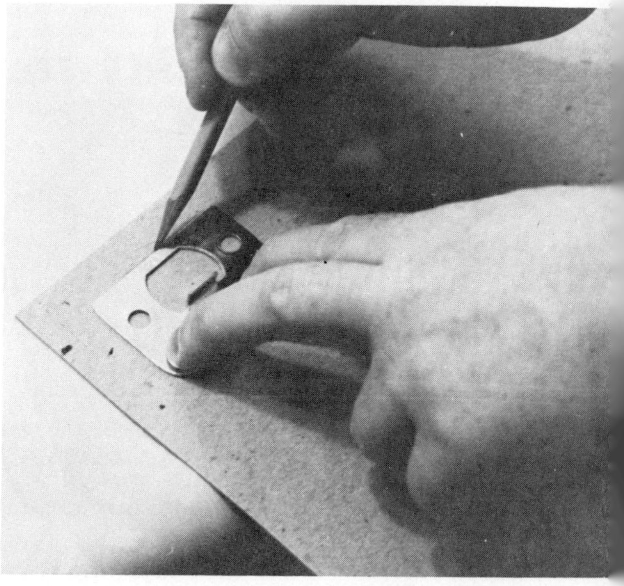

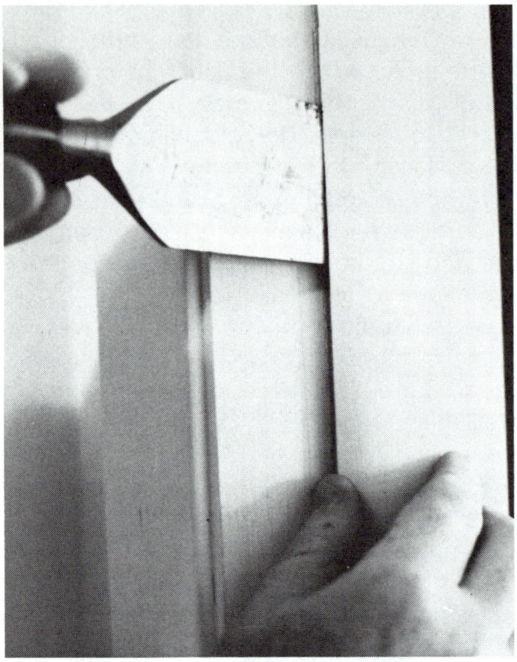

9-12. Take off the doorstop molding with a wide chisel.

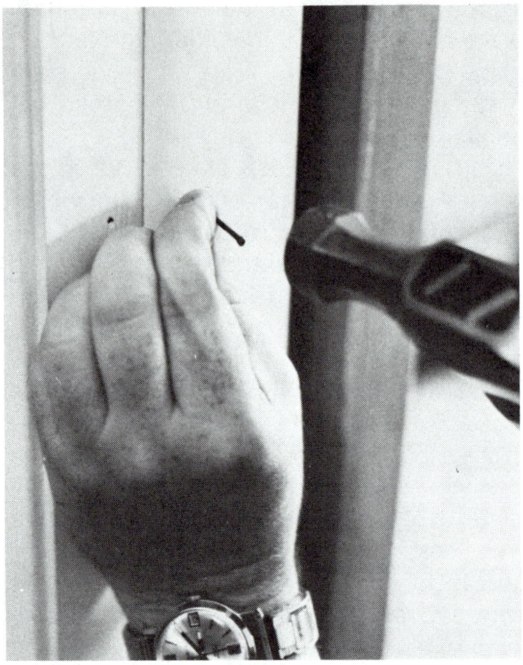

9-13. Nail the molding in position with 1½" finishing nails.

While you are adjusting the door, it is a good idea to lubricate the hinges so that they do not squeak. Squirt a few drops of oil on the hinge pins. Open and close the door a few times to let the oil spread out around the pin and the knuckles. In place of oil you can use graphite in oil or a silicon lubricant. Wipe off any excess lubricant with a cloth.

WEATHER-STRIPPING A DOOR

Weather stripping is designed to keep out drafts and moisture. There are several different types of weather stripping available. They each come with installation instructions. The varieties of door weather stripping are:

- Sweeps and threshold strips—installed on the bottom of the door and as a doorsill.
- Foam attached to doorstop molding—replaces the old doorstop. Fig. 9-14.
- Felt stripping—attaches to the door-

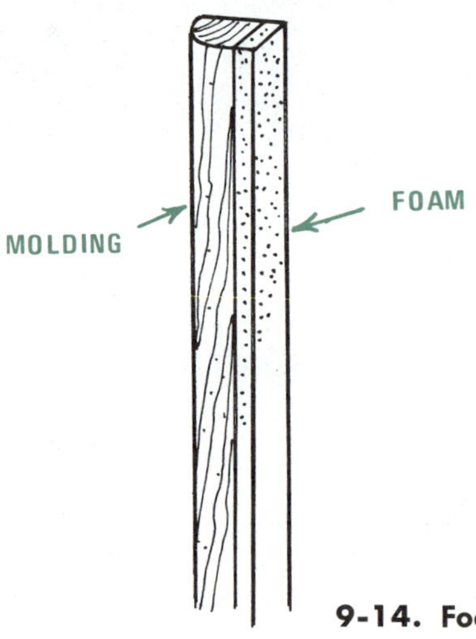

9-14. Foam attached to doorstop molding.

9-15. Flexible rubber weather strip attached to the edge of the door with tacks.

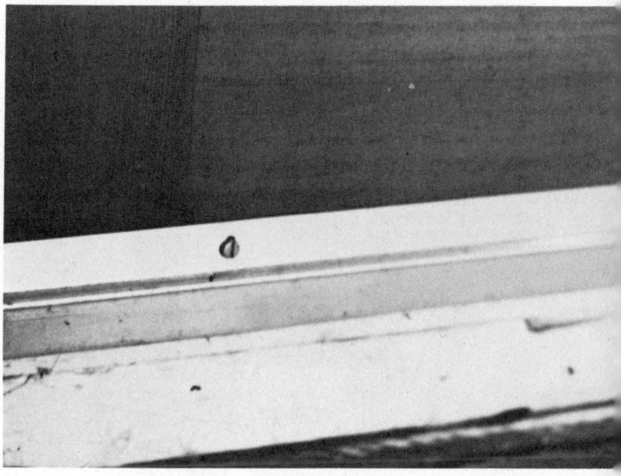

9-16. A sweep attached to the bottom of an exterior door with screws.

stop or jamb and compresses when the door is closed.

• Flexible rubber or vinyl strips—attached to the edge of the door or frame with nails or tacks. Fig. 9-15.

These materials can be purchased at hardware stores and lumberyards. Measure the edges and top of the door that you want to weather-strip and buy a slightly longer piece of stripping than that measurement. Sweeps and threshold strips come in lengths to accommodate standard doors (30″, 36″, etc.). Fig. 9-16. Measure the width of the door so that you know what size piece to buy. If the original weather stripping on the front or backdoor is the interlock type, replacing it is a job for a professional. (Interlocking weather stripping has a bend along its edge which catches a bend on a similar piece along door edges.)

ADJUSTING SLIDING DOORS

Sliding doors consist of two or three doors supported by a top track and a bottom guide or track. Lightweight interior doors such as those used for a closet are top-hung. Heavy exterior doors such as glass patio doors rest on rollers or guides on the bottom track.

Sliding doors may not operate properly due to any of the following:

- An obstruction in the track.
- Dirty or bent tracks or guides.
- One wheel out of adjustment.

Move the doors back and forth to detect the cause of the problem. You may be able to locate the obstruction or the area where the track is bent. If you cannot spot the difficulty, then you will have to remove the doors. You will probably have to remove them later anyway to make repairs. The procedure for removing and adjusting a sliding door is as follows:

1. On top-hung doors lift the door up and swing the bottom out. The bottom edge of the door should clear the track or guide.

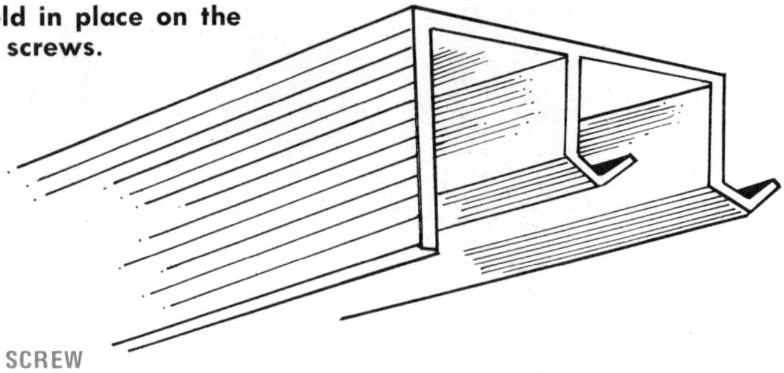

9-17. The top track is held in place on the doorframe with screws.

9-18. Top-hung doors usually have an adjustment screw to raise or lower each wheel so that the door hangs level.

Some types of sliding door hardware have keys, or spaces, in the top track. Move the door along until the wheels line up with these keys; then lift the door off.

On heavy sliding doors such as patio doors, the door is lifted up and swung out into the room. These doors are very heavy, and you may need help in removing them from the doorframe. Be careful of the glass in the doors.

2. Check the bottom track or guide to see that it is clean and has no obstructions in it. Make sure that it is straight. You should tighten any loose screws because the track will shift if any screws are loose. Brush or vacuum out the dirt and remove any obstacles in the track. If the track is bent in one place, use a block of wood and a hammer to straighten the bend. Tap the metal lightly, moving the block along on the other side of the track to back the hammer blows. Working slowly and carefully, you should be able to straighten the track.

3. Inspect the top track. If it is bent, you can straighten it with a wooden block and a hammer. If necessary, remove the track. It is held in place with screws. Fig. 9-17. Straighten it and clean it before you replace it on the doorframe.

4. If one or more wheels are out of adjustment, causing the doors to drag, readjust the wheels while the doors are hanging. On a top-hung door there is usually an adjustment screw to raise or lower a wheel so that the door hangs level. Fig. 9-18. Be sure to tighten the adjustment screw after you are finished. Level the doors so that they do not lean on the bottom guide, but instead just ride on it.

5. If the wheels or any of the other parts are broken, replacements can be bought at a hardware store, providing that the sliding door hardware was made by a large manufacturer and that the hardware is not very old. Take the broken piece with you to the store. If the same brand is not available, perhaps the salesperson can find a similar piece made by another manufacturer.

ADJUSTING BIFOLD DOORS

Bifold doors are any two- or four-panel set of doors hinged together along their edges. Fig. 9-19. The upper edges have a pivot and a guide which slide in a metal track. The doors or panels swing open and closed on a top and a bottom pivot. The top guide keeps the doors from getting out of alignment.

The top and bottom pivots may get out of alignment vertically because the locking screws that hold the pivot sockets in place have loosened. Fig. 9-20. These can be tightened with a special wrench that is supplied with the bifold hardware. If you no longer have this wrench, a small open-end wrench or a screwdriver can be used to tighten the locking screws. Align the top or bottom pivot or both so that the space around the doors is even and the doors open easily without rubbing against the doorjambs or the other panels on the doorway. Fig. 9-21.

9-20. The pivot sockets are held in place with locking screws.

9-19. A two-panel bifold door.

9-21. Loosen and move the bottom pivot socket so that the door opens easily.

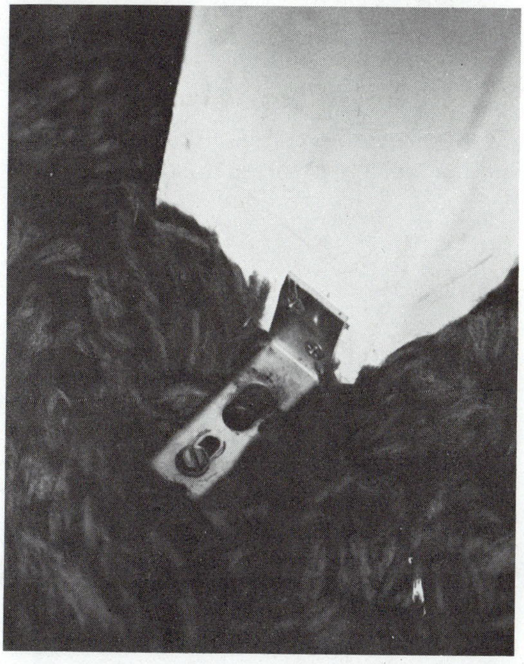

9-22. The bottom pivot on the door can be raised or lowered with a special wrench by turning the hexagonal-shaped pivot.

If the panels are too low—for example, if they don't clear the carpeting in a room—the doors can be raised or lowered by adjusting the bottom pivot. Use the special wrench or a small open-end wrench to turn the hexagonal-shaped pivot, which is threaded into the plate that fastens it to the door. Fig. 9-22. The doors can be adjusted in either the open or closed position.

DOOR LOCKS AND KNOBS

One of the big problem areas with doors involves locks. All exterior doors have entry locks, and some interior doors, such as bathroom doors, have privacy locks built into the knob sets. Locks wear out in time and it is easier to replace them than to repair them. Replacements can be bought at a locksmith shop, hardware store, or a lumberyard.

Common Lock Problems

- The key does not go into the lock easily. This problem is solved by squirting some powdered graphite or graphite in oil into the keyway. These lock lubricants come in a container that is designed to allow you to squirt the contents into the lock. Fig. 9-23. Work the key back and forth a few times to spread the graphite within the lock.
- A frozen lock. Heat the key with a match and then work it slowly into the lock. You may have to repeat this activity two or three times to thaw the lock enough to turn the key. Do not force the key or you will break it. Do not attempt to heat the lock itself!
- A broken key left in the lock. Use a hairpin or a thin coping saw or jeweler's saw blade to remove the broken key. If enough

9-23. Squirt some powdered graphite or graphite in oil into the keyway.

of the key is sticking out past the cylinder, try to grab it with a pair of pliers and pull it out. A locksmith can remove the cylinder and push the key out if you cannot dislodge it.

• The key turns in the lock without opening it. This is a problem for a locksmith because the locking mechanism is broken. As an alternative, you could replace the entire lock yourself.

Types of Locks

There are three major types of locks found on doors in a house. The old type of locking device is called a mortise lock. It is set into a rectangular hollow in the edge of the door. It usually has a cover plate on the housing that can be removed so that the workings of the lock can be seen.

Within the last twenty-five years a lock that is installed in a hole bored through the door has come into wide use. Fig. 9-24.

Ideal Security Hardware Corp.

9-24. This type of lock is installed in a hole bored through the door.

9-25. A door chain.

Ideal Security Hardware Corp.

There are two varieties of this lock: the cylindrical lock and the tubular lock.

On the doors in your house there may be auxiliary locks that are used in addition to the regular locks. These are surface mounted. Examples are chains, sliding bolts, night latches, and dead-bolt locks. Fig. 9-25, 9-26.

Removing a Mortise Lock

If you have an old mortise lock that has to be repaired or replaced, it must be removed from the door first. Since there are many different makes of mortise locks, these are only general steps in removing the lock.

1. Remove one knob by loosening the setscrew on the shank of the knob with a small screwdriver. Pull or unscrew the knob off the square spindle that goes through the lock.

2. Pull the square spindle out of the lock by the other knob attached to it.

3. On the door edge there are two screws that hold the lock in place. Unscrew them and slide the lock out of the mortise. Fig. 9-27.

9-26. A dead-bolt lock.

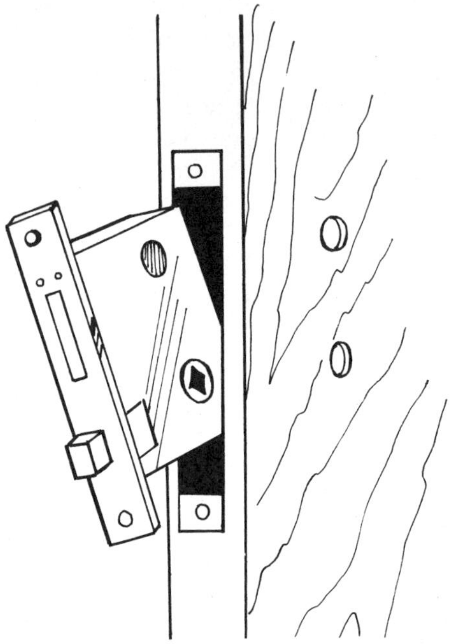

9-27. Slide the lock out of the mortise after you have removed the knobs and the spindle.

9-28. Push in the catch on the shank of the inner knob with a screwdriver.

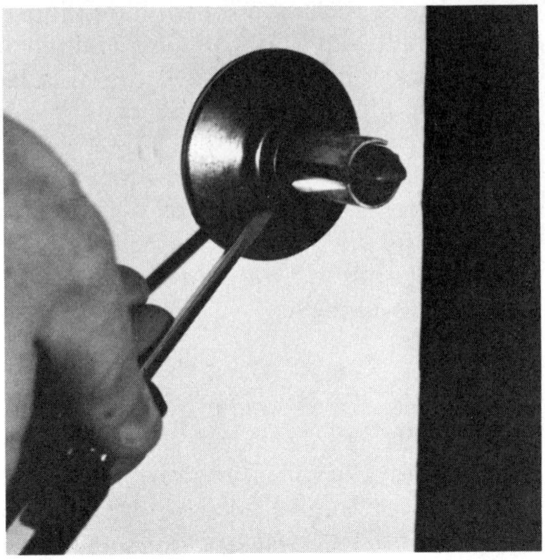

9-29. Take off the rosette that fits over the spindle.

9-30. Unscrew the two machine screws that hold the knob mechanism to the mounting plate.

Removing a Cylindrical Lock

If you have to replace a cylindrical lock, removing it from a door is done as follows:

1. Push in the catch on the shank of the inner knob with a screwdriver blade to remove it from the spindle. Fig. 9-28. Take off the rosette (the round metal cover) that fits over the spindle and covers the lock. Fig. 9-29. It usually snaps off the spindle when a small spring is pressed.

2. Remove the two machine screws that hold the knob mechanism to the mounting plate. Fig. 9-30. The mechanism can now be pulled out of the face of the door. Fig. 9-31.

3. The spring latch is held in a mortise on the edge of the door with two screws. Remove the screws and pull the mechanism out of the door. Fig. 9-32.

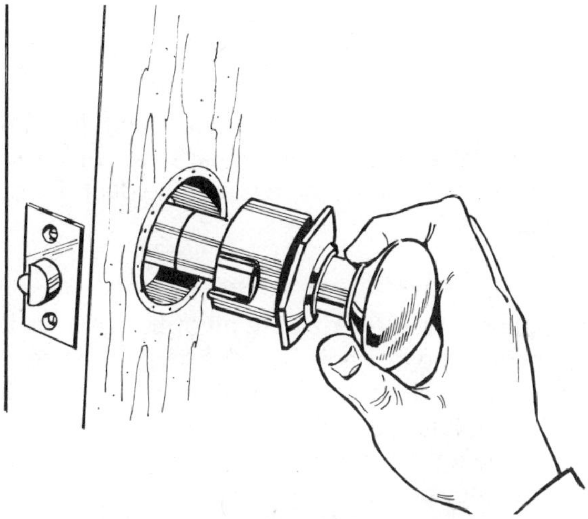

9-31. The knob mechanism can be pulled out of the face of the door.

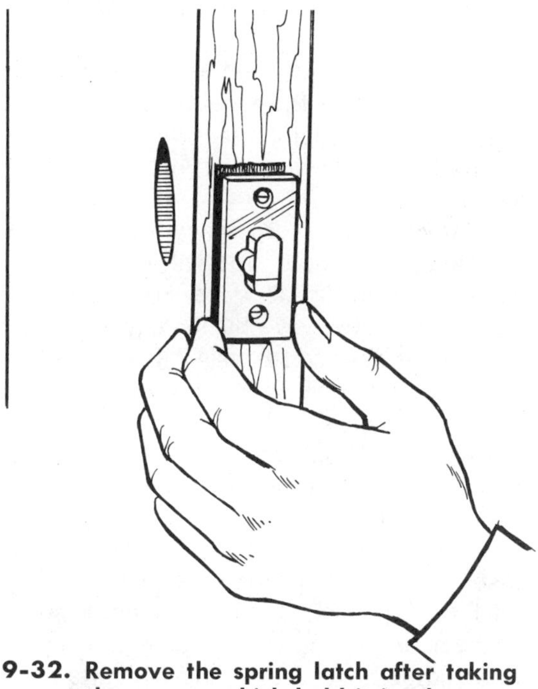

9-32. Remove the spring latch after taking out the screws which hold it in place.

9-33. Unscrew the two machine screws on the rosette on the interior side of the door.

9-34. Pull the interior knob mechanism out of the door.

Removing a Tubular Lock

The procedure for removing a tubular lock is similar to that used to remove a cylindrical lock. The steps in removing the tubular lock set are:

1. Unscrew the two machine screws on the rosette on the door's interior side. Fig. 9-33. The knob mechanism will then pull apart into two separate sections. Figs. 9-34, 9-35.

9-35. Pull out the exterior knob.

2. The spring latch is attached to the door edge with two wood screws. Unscrew them and pull the latch out of the door. Figs. 9-36, 9-37.

Installing a New Lock

Locks made today are all of the type that is installed in a hole bored through the door. All new lock sets come with instructions and a template; so drilling the proper holes and installing the lock are a matter of following the instructions. General instructions for installing a new lock are given here.

1. Remove the old lock. Also remove the old strike from the doorjamb. If the previous lock was installed in a hole bored through the door, then you can probably install the new tubular or cylindrical lock in the same hole. Measure the diameters of the two holes (the one in the face of the door and the one in the edge). Take these measurements with you when you look for a new lock set.

2. If you have to drill a new hole through the face of the door, you will need an expansive bit and a bit brace. Fig. 9-38. You can set the expansive bit for any diameter hole that is needed (usually $2\frac{1}{8}''$). Mark the location of the hole with the cardboard template supplied with the lock set. Fig. 9-39. Try to drill the hole from both faces of the door to avoid splitting the wood as you come through it. Fig. 9-40.

3. Also use the template as shown in the instructions to mark the hole for the spring latch. This hole is drilled at the center point of the door edge and must be perpendicular to the knob hole. Use an auger bit and a bit brace to drill the $\frac{7}{8}''$ hole usually required for the latch. Fig. 9-41. Place the latch in the hole and mark the outline of the plate with a pencil. Use a sharp wood chisel to make a cut on the outline. Then remove $\frac{1}{8}''$ of wood

9-36. Remove the wood screws that hold the spring latch to the door edge.

9-37. Pull the latch out of the door.

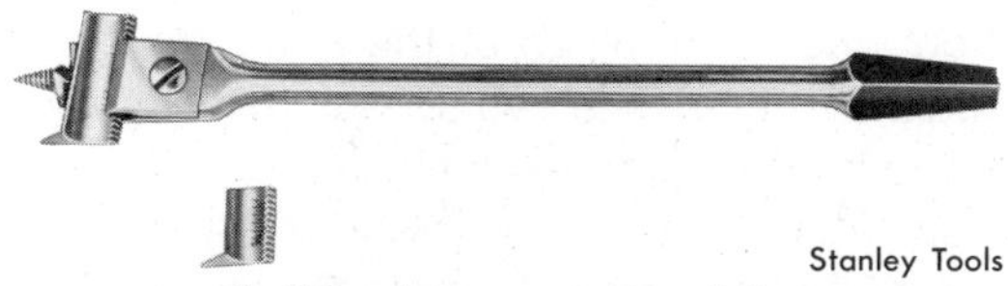

Stanley Tools

9-38. An expansive bit.

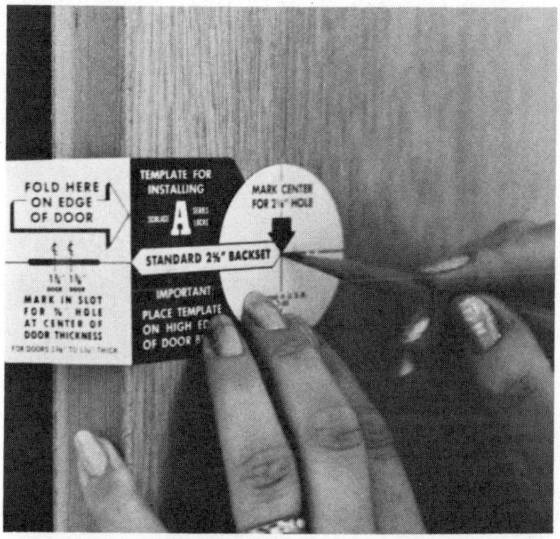

9-39. To mark the location of the hole, use the cardboard template supplied with the lock.

so that the plate fits flush with the surface of the door's edge. Fig. 9-42. Install the latch once more and drive the two wood screws that hold it in place.

4. To install a new strike, mark a horizontal line on the jamb that is exactly opposite the latch centerline on the door edge. On some instructions the template is used to locate this line. Mark a vertical centerline opposite the center of the latch hole. Drill a $\frac{7}{8}''$ hole where the lines meet as shown in the instructions. Put the strike in place on the jamb and match the vertical centerline with the two screw holes. Trace around the outside of the strike plate. This area must be chiseled out to a depth of $\frac{1}{16}''$ so that the

9-40. Drill the new hole through the face of the door with an expansive bit and a bit brace.

9-41. Use an auger bit and a bit brace to drill the hole for the latch.

9-42. Use a sharp wood chisel to remove ⅛" of wood so that the latch plate fits into the edge of the door.

strike fits flush with the jamb. Fit the strike in place and drive in the two wood screws that hold it.

5. Install the knob mechanism following the steps in the manufacturer's instructions. Then test the lock by turning the knob a few times. Close the door to test whether the latch engages the strike properly. If the latch does not spring back to its outer position when you let go of the knob, you may have tightened the two screws that hold the knob mechanism too much. Loosen them a quarter turn and test the lock again. Perhaps they will need to be loosened another quarter turn before the lock works smoothly. Do not lubricate the lock set. The knob assembly has already been lubricated at the factory.

CUTTING A DOOR TO CLEAR CARPETING

In a newly carpeted room, the existing doors may not close properly because the carpet is in the way. The doors may rub the carpet or jam on the raised height of the floor due to the height of the carpeting and the padding underneath. To cut an interior door to clear the carpeting, do the following:

1. With the door still on the hinges, measure up from the bottom of the door to mark the height of the carpeting. Fig. 9-43. A high pile carpet or a shag rug might require more space than a low pile rug.

9-43. Measure up from the bottom of the door to mark the height of the carpeting.

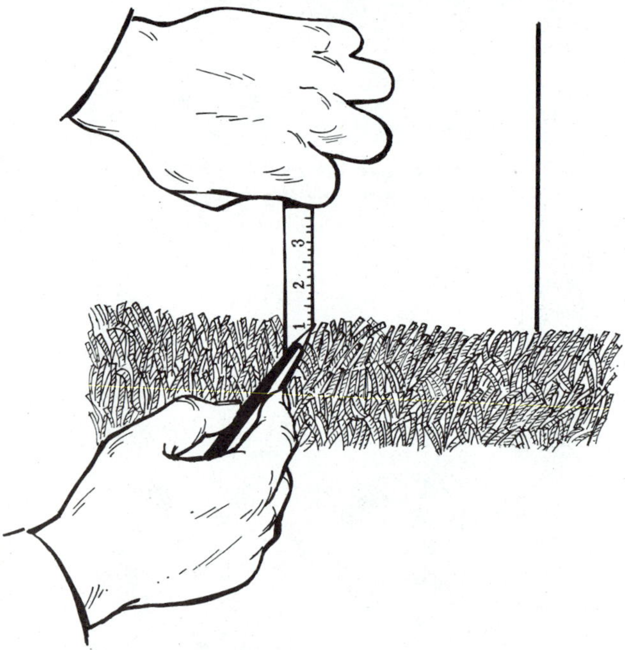

2. Take the door off its hinges by knocking out the hinge pins with an old screwdriver and a hammer. Do not remove the pins completely until you have loosened each of them. Hold the door up with one hand while you pull the pins out with the other hand, or get someone to help you. Remove the door.

3. Mark a line across the door with a combination square and a pencil. Use the hinge edge of the door as the straight edge against which to hold the square. Fig. 9-44. If you are going to cut off the door with a portable circular saw, score the line on the door with a utility knife two or three times.

9-44. Mark the cutting line on the door with a combination square and a pencil.

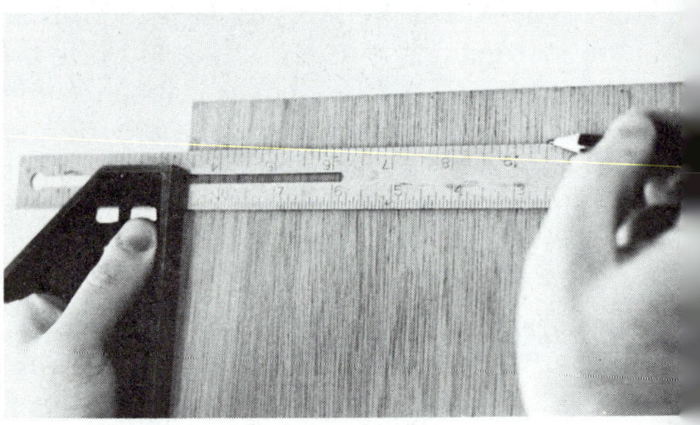

Fig. 9-45. This will prevent the outside wood covering on the door from splitting (the saw blade on the circular saw spins up towards the operator).

4. Use a fine toothed blade to cut the door. You can use either a portable circular saw or a hand crosscut saw. Smooth the edges of the newly cut section with abrasive paper. Replace the door on the hinges. Do not drive the hinge pins in yet. Just put them in the hinges to hold the door while you test the door for clearance. If you are satisfied with the result, you can drive the pins down with a hammer.

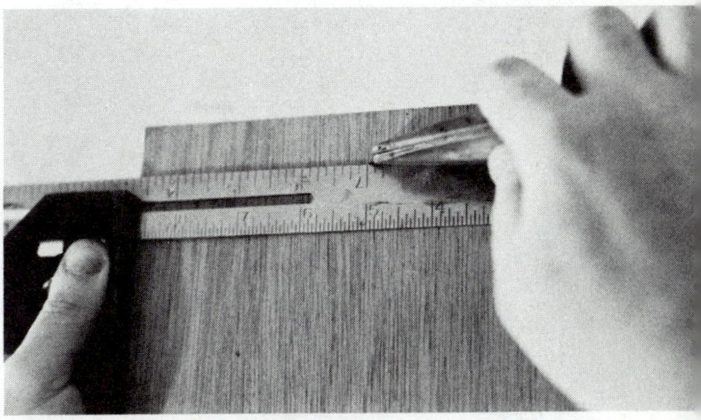

9-45. If you are going to cut the door with a portable circular saw, score a line on the door with a utility knife.

CHECKUP

1. What causes a sticking door?
2. What causes a door to spring open by itself?
3. How can weather-stripping a door save energy?

CHAPTER 10

Window Repairs

TYPES OF WINDOWS

There are several types of windows found in homes. The frames may be made of wood, wood covered with vinyl, aluminum, or steel. Windows can be arranged singly, in pairs, in a bow window, or in a bay window. The various types of windows are:

- Double-hung—these consist of an upper and a lower sash which are balanced by sash weights on chains or cords. (The sash is the window glass and the frame around it.) Some types work on a spring balance. Fig. 10-1.
- Casement—the sashes swing on hinges attached to one side. Some models are operated with a crank handle attached to the sill. Fig. 10-2.
- Awning—these are hinged on top and swing out from the bottom. They are operated with a locking handle. Fig. 10-3.
- Jalousie—they are similar to awning windows except that they have a pivot pin on which each piece of glass moves. The glass forms louvers which are opened and closed with a crank handle.
- Sliding—they slide from side to side on rollers or a track. Fig. 10-4.
- Picture—the glass is set in a frame that does not move. Picture windows offer a large viewing area.

Many window problems can be corrected by the do-it-yourselfer. The types of windows that can be repaired easily are double-hung, casement, and sliding windows.

Andersen Corp.

10-1. A double-hung window.

Andersen Corp.

10-2. A casement window with a crank handle to open and close it.

Andersen Corp.

10-3. An awning window.

Andersen Corp.

10-4. A sliding window.

REPAIRING DOUBLE-HUNG WINDOWS

A double-hung window can become difficult to open and close if too many coats of paint have built up on it. To correct this problem, do the following:

1. Use a putty knife around the sash and stop molding to loosen a stuck sash. Fig. 10-5. (The stop molding holds the sash in place.) A wide chisel can be used to pry the window open at the sill and break the paint seal. Put a piece of scrap wood under the chisel to avoid damaging the windowsill.
2. Sand the paint off the stop molding. Use a sharp chisel to remove lumps of paint or to scrape off thickly painted areas.
3. If the sash is stuck in an open position, drive it down until it closes. Use a block of wood and a hammer. Be careful not to damage the sash.
4. Rub on some paraffin or spray some silicone on the metal or plastic tracks in the window frame. Work the window up and down a few times to distribute the lubricant.

Moisture can make a window sash swell and stick. It can be eased in the following way:

1. Remove the stop molding with a wide chisel and a hammer. Be careful not to break the molding.
2. Sand the sides of the sash about $\frac{1}{16}''$. This can be done without pulling the sash out of the window frame. Use medium-grade abrasive paper and a sanding block.
3. Put the stop molding back in place and nail it in one or two spots. Test the window. It should slide. If it works well, finish nailing the stop molding. If the window is still tight, remove the two nails holding the molding and sand the sides of the sash again.

The most common malfunction of double-hung windows is a broken sash cord or chain. The sashes are balanced by weights attached to the cords or chains. Without the cords or chains the sashes cannot open or close properly. Sash chain lasts longer than cord. If you have to replace the sash cord, replace it with chain. Sash chain can be bought by the foot at hardware stores or lumberyards. These are the steps in replacing a broken sash cord or chain:

1. If the lower sash does not operate because the chain or cord is broken, carefully take off the first stop molding with a hammer and a chisel. If the upper sash does not operate properly, you must first remove the stop molding for the lower sash. Pull out the lower sash. Then remove the stop molding on the side of the upper sash where the cord or chain is broken. Always remove the molding on the side where the broken chain or cord is located.
2. Pull the sash out on the side where you have removed the stop molding so that you can see the sash pocket cover in the side of the window frame. This pocket gives you access to the sash weight which is attached to the cord or chain. Fig. 10-6. Two wood screws usually hold the pocket cover in place. Remove them and the cover to see the weight inside the frame.

10-5. Run a putty knife between the sash and the stop molding to loosen a stuck sash.

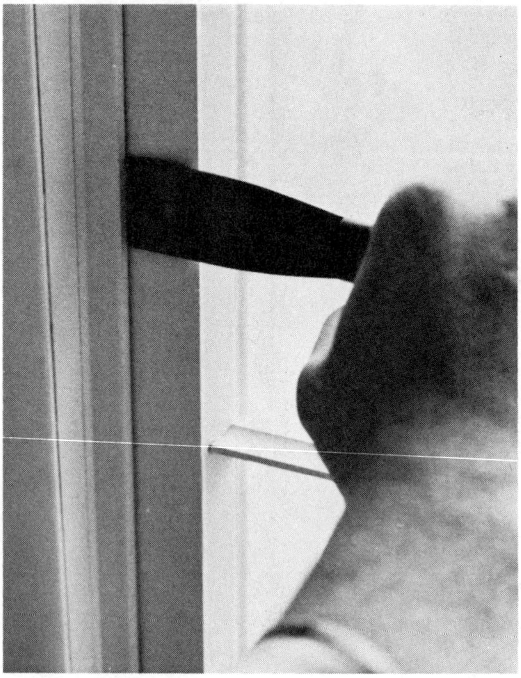

3. Remove the old cord or chain from the weight and from the side of the sash. A knot in the cord holds it in a knot pocket on the side of the sash. A chain is held in place on the sash with a snap link. Save the old snap links.

4. Cut a new length of sash chain. If possible, use the old piece to measure the new one. The chain can be cut with a pair of pliers.

5. Loop the chain over the pulley on the window frame. Drop one end of the chain down the channel so that it comes out through the sash pocket. You may have to tie a few washers on that end to give it added weight so that it goes through the channel. When the end of the chain is visible in the sash pocket, remove the washers and put a snap link on the chain. Attach it to the sash weight.

6. Rest the sash on the windowsill. Slip the chain through the groove on the side of the sash and out through the knot pocket. Fig. 10-7. Put a snap ring through the last link on the chain. Push the ring into the knot pocket.

7. Put the sash back in place in the window frame and raise it to the top of the frame. If the sash chain is the right length, the weight should now hang down inside the sash pocket to within 3″ of the windowsill. If the chain hangs down any lower, disconnect it from the side of the sash again, cut it shorter with a pair of pliers, and re-install it.

8. Make sure that the sash is back in its proper position in the window frame. Fasten the cover back on the sash pocket with the two wood screws. Replace the stop molding in its original position and nail it in place. Move the sash up and down two or three times to make sure that it operates correctly.

Sometimes the sashes do not go up and down because the cord or chain cannot travel over the pulley in the window frame. The pulley may be jammed with dirt or rust, or it may be broken. To gain access to the pulley so that you can clean or replace it, do the following:

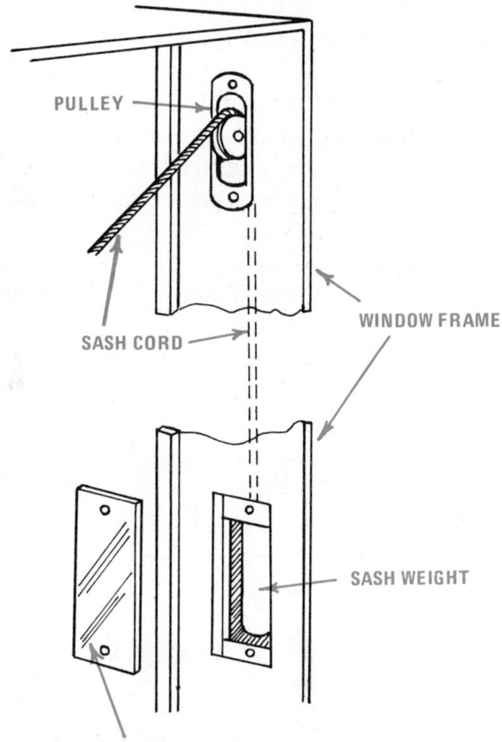

10-6. The sashes of a double-hung window are balanced by weights on chains or cords.

10-7. The groove on the side of the sash. The knot on the sash cord fits into the knot pocket. On a sash chain, a snap ring fits into the knot pocket.

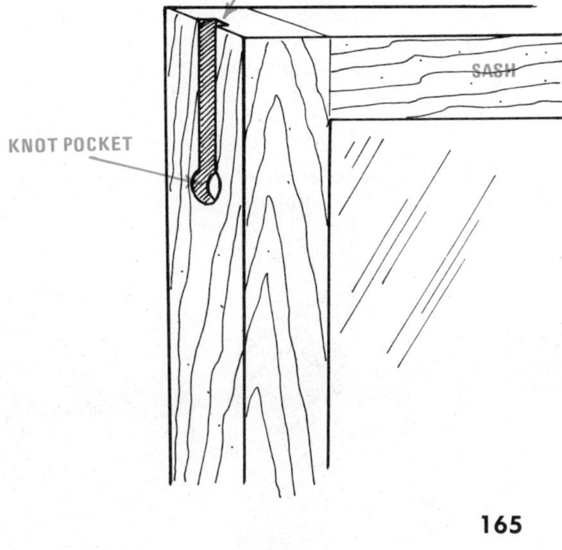

1. Lift the lower sash so that you can see the sash pocket cover. Remove the screws holding it and take the cover off. Prop up the sash with a piece of wood.

2. Detach the weight from the chain or cord. Pull the chain or cord out of the pulley so that it is hanging outside the window frame.

3. The pulley is held to the frame with two screws. Remove them and take the pulley out. If it is dirty or rusty, clean it off with emery cloth or steel wool. Put a few drops of light machine oil on it so that it moves easily. Replace it in the frame.

If the pulley is broken, replace it with a new one. Put the pulley in position in the frame. Make sure that it fits properly.

4. Loop the cord or chain back over the pulley and guide it down the channel inside the window frame until it appears inside the sash pocket. You may have to tie a weight to the end of the chain or cord to move it down the channel. A few washers will serve as a weight. When the cord is down in the proper position, you can replace the screws used to hold the pulley in place.

5. Pull the end of the chain or cord out of the pocket and attach it to the sash weight again. The chain is held to the weight with a snap ring. The cord is tied to the weight. Put the weight back into the pocket and install the pocket cover. Tighten the two screws that hold it.

REPAIRING CASEMENT WINDOWS

Wooden casement windows sometimes do not close properly because the hinges are loose and the window is sagging. Tighten the screws that hold the hinges. If they do not tighten because the holes are too large, put slivers of wood or wooden matches in the holes. Then drive the screws in again. If a hinge pin is loose, you will have to install a new hinge. Replacing a hinge is not possible on a steel casement window because the hinges are welded in place.

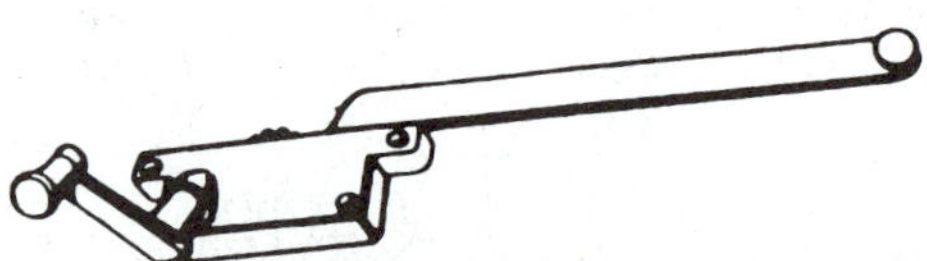

Ideal Security Hardware Corp.

10-8. The opening mechanism for a casement window. It consists of a crank and a worm gear.

10-9. The handle on the opening mechanism.

Ideal Security Hardware Corp.

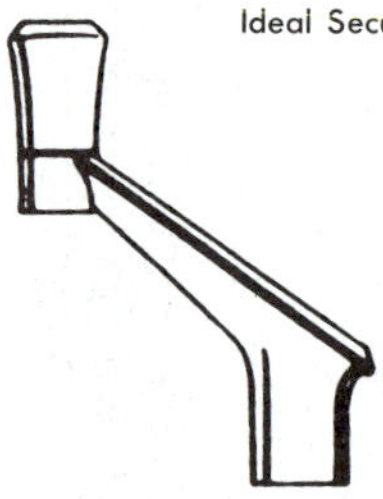

If a wooden casement window does not close properly because it is swollen or has too much paint on it, you can sand off the excess paint or $\frac{1}{16}''$ of the wood. Do not take off too much wood because the wooden sash will contract in dry weather and during the winter heating season.

Some casement windows have an opening mechanism which consists of a crank and a worm gear. Fig. 10-8. These get dirty and need cleaning from time to time. They should be lubricated with a silicone spray or some light oil. If the sliding rod that moves the sash gets dirty or has paint on it and does not move easiy, clean it with paint thinner. Then lubricate it with silicone or paraffin. Brush out the track that it slides in and rub some paraffin in the track.

If the opening mechanism does not work, the gear inside is probably dirty or broken. Repairing this mechanism on a casement window is done as follows:

1. The opening mechanism is on the inside window frame. To open it up so that you can gain access to the gear, you have to remove the handle first. Fig. 10-9. Loosen the setscrew and pull the handle off. Then remove the screws that hold the gear housing to the window frame.

2. With the housing free you can slide the lever arm along the track until it reaches the track end. Remove it from the track.

3. Turn the housing over and look at the gear inside. If it is dirty you can clean it with a thin piece of wood. Work the handle so that you clean all sides of the gear. Lubricate the gear with a silicone spray or some light machine oil. Replace it on the window.

4. If the gear is broken you will have to obtain a replacement. When buying a new unit, take the entire gear housing to the store. If you cannot get a unit made by the same manufacturer, the replacement should have a lever arm of the same length. The space between the mounting screw holes should also be the same as on the old unit.

Install the new unit. Be sure to replace the lever arm in the track before you fasten the gear housing onto the window frame.

REPAIRING SLIDING WINDOWS

This type of window sometimes sticks because there is too much paint on the sashes. Excess paint can be removed by sanding the sashes.

Dust and dirt in the tracks can also keep the window from sliding properly. Clean out the tracks with an old paint brush. Fig. 10-10. Lubricate them with paraffin or silicone spray. You may have to remove the sashes before you can do any work on the tracks. They lift up and are swung out into the room. Fig. 10-11.

If the sash sticks because the track is bent, you can straighten it out. You will need a block of wood and a hammer. Fig. 10-12. Place the wood block behind the metal track and tap the metal back into shape little by little. Keep the wood behind the area you are tapping.

10-10. Clean out dust and dirt from the tracks with an old paint brush.

10-11. Lift up the sash to remove it from the track.

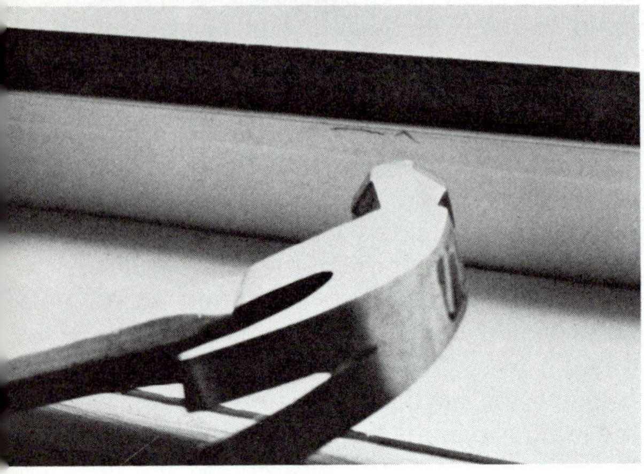

10-12. Straighten the track with a block of wood and a hammer.

WEATHER-STRIPPING A WINDOW

When you find that a window is leaking cold air into a room, there are several types of weather stripping you can use to seal out drafts. Weather stripping usually comes in kits which include instructions for installation.

The stop molding on a window can be replaced with a new type of stop molding that has foam glued to it. Fig. 10-13. This foam presses against the sash lightly and seals out drafts while still allowing the sash to move easily. Flat felt stripping which

10-13. Stop molding with foam attached to it can be used on a casement window.

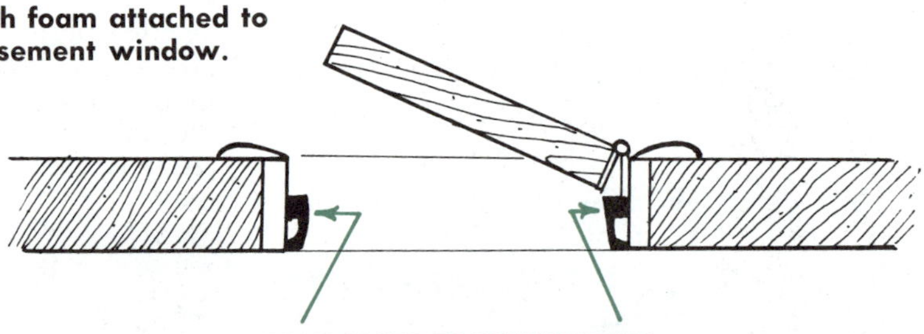

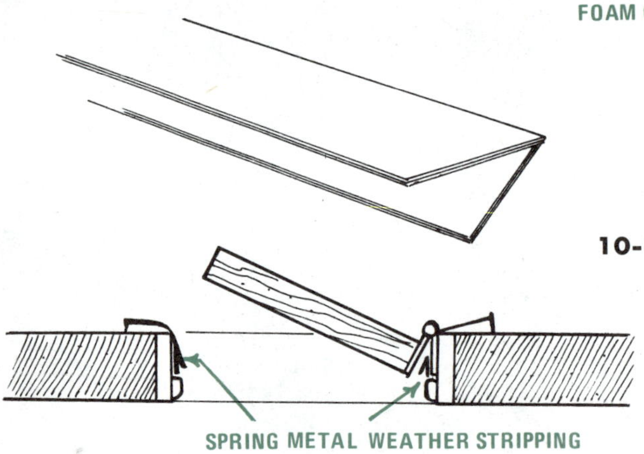

10-14. Spring metal weather stripping used on a casement window.

comes in rolls can be attached to casement stops on the sash or double-hung stop molding. Glue or tacks hold this material in place.

Double-hung windows and casement windows can be weather-stripped with spring metal. Fig. 10-14. These V-shaped strips are nailed to the upper and lower sashes according to the manufacturer's instructions. When the window is closed, the metal pushes against the sash and seals out drafts.

A window can be temporarily sealed with a rope-type caulking that is pressed into place with the fingers. These ropes of pliable material can be removed at the end of the cold season and reused the next year.

REPLACING A BROKEN WINDOW PANE

Several kinds of glass are used in windows. Some of these cannot be replaced by the do-it-yourselfer. One example is insulated glass, which is actually two sheets of glass with an air space between them. The ends are sealed so that the sheets cannot be separated. Only a professional can make this glass to the correct size for the window. Safety glass and tempered glass must also be cut to size by a professional glazier.

Single- and double-strength sheet glass can be cut and installed by the do-it-yourselfer. Plastic substitutes for glass can also be cut and installed without professional help. However, metal windows in which neoprene gaskets are used to hold the glass in place should be repaired by a glazier.

In many windows the glass is held in place with glazing compound. To replace a broken or cracked pane of glass in such a window, you will need the following tools and materials:

- Putty knife.
- Chisel.
- Pliers.
- Propane torch.
- Ruler.
- Hammer.
- Linseed oil putty or glazing compound.
- Glazier's points.
- New pane of glass.

You will also need some trim paint and a small brush.

These are the steps in removing a window pane and installing a new one.

1. You do not have to remove the sash. If you can reach the window with a ladder, you can work from the outside. However, if the sash is easy to remove (as for example, a sliding window sash), then take it out and put it on a flat work surface such as a workbench.

2. From the outside of the sash, chip out the old putty with a chisel. If the putty is very hard, use a propane torch to heat it slightly until it softens. Pry the putty out with the chisel or a putty knife. Wear heavy gloves or use some rags to hold the pieces of glass as you pull them out.

3. Use a pair of pliers to pull out all the glazier's points or clips (on a metal sash). Scrape all the old putty out of the channels with a chisel. Fig. 10-15. If the channels are

10-15. Use a chisel to scrape the old putty out of the channels.

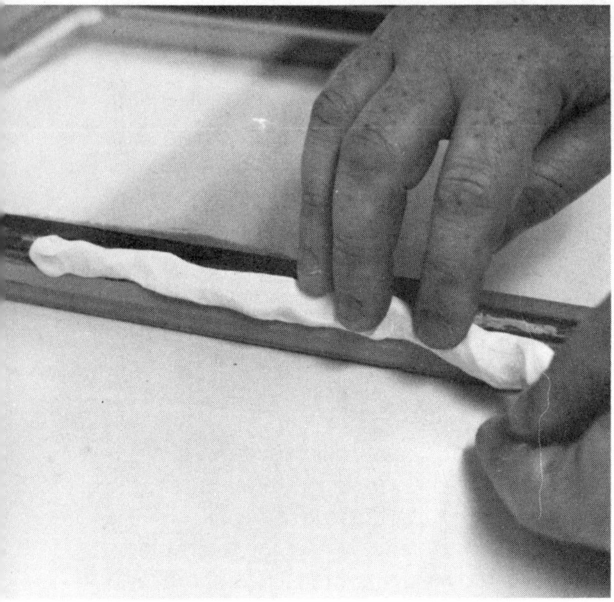

10-16. Press the glazing compound or putty into the channels on all four sides.

10-17. Press the piece of glass firmly into the glazing compound or putty.

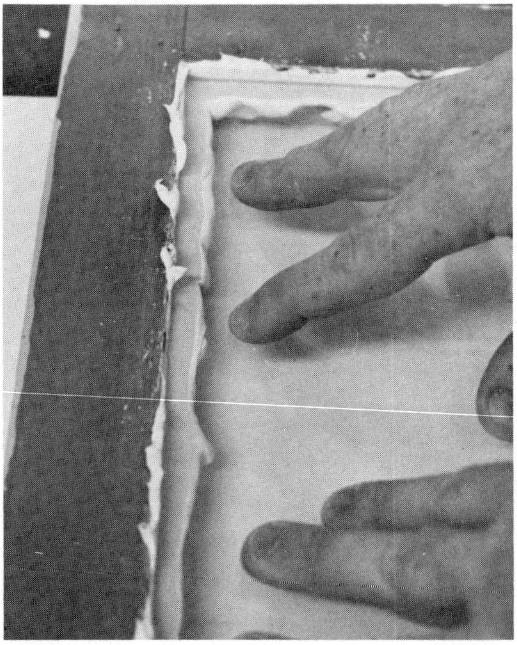

10-18. Put the glazier's points into the wood to hold the glass in place. You can use a special tool and a hammer to push the points in.

10-19. Press the bead into place with a putty knife.

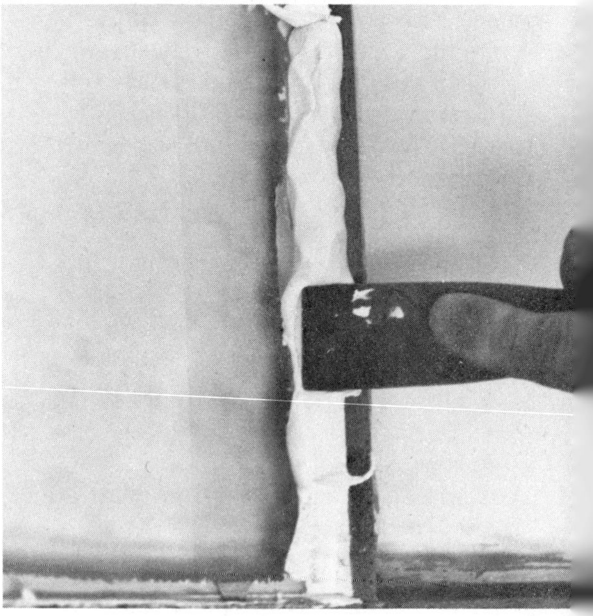

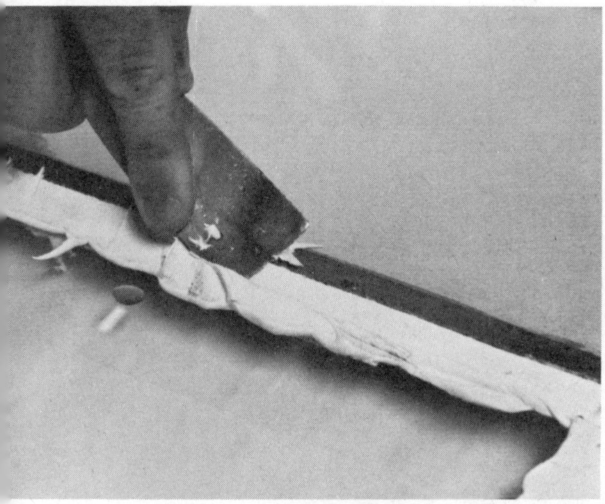

10-20. Use a putty knife to trim off the extra compound.

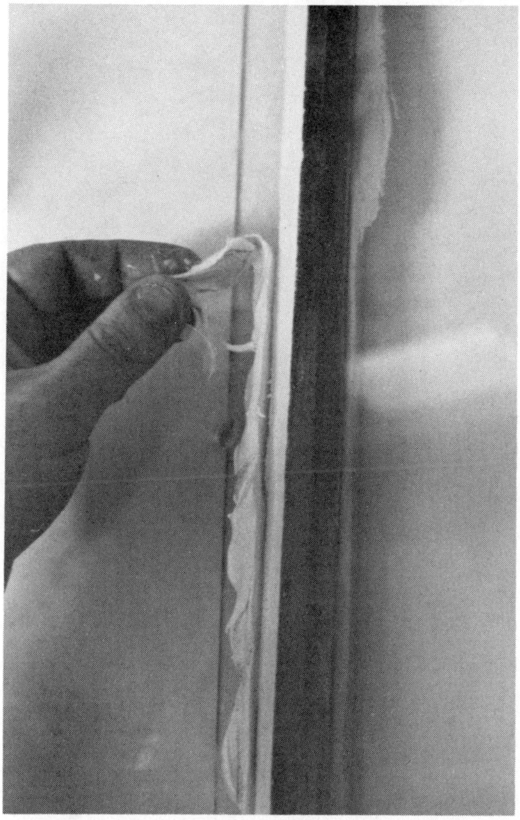

10-21. Pick up the excess glazing compound from the glass.

raw wood, prime them with some trim paint. Priming will seal the wood so that it does not absorb oil from the new glazing compound or putty. The paint does not have to dry before you put the glass in.

4. Measure the opening for the glass *accurately*. Subtract $\frac{1}{8}''$ from the width and from the length. That is the size of the piece of glass you need. You can buy a piece of glass cut to size at a hardware store or a lumberyard. If you want to cut the glass yourself, follow the instructions given immediately after this section.

5. Make sure that the channels into which the glass will fit are clean. Use an old paint brush to remove any dust and dirt. The putty will not stick if the channels are dirty.

6. Roll out a $\frac{1}{8}''$-wide bead of putty or glazing compound long enough to fill each of the four channels. Press the beads into the channels on all four sides. Fig. 10-16. Press the piece of glass firmly into the beads. Fig. 10-17. Put the glazier's points into the wood to hold the glass in place. One point every 5 or 6 inches will hold even a large piece of glass. You can use a pair of pliers to push the points in, or you can use a hammer and the special tool that comes with a box of glazier's points. Fig. 10-18. The tool fits over the end of a point. Tap it carefully with a hammer. Drive the points halfway into the wooden channel.

7. Roll out a bead of putty or glazing compound big enough to cover the frame up to the top edge of the outer frame molding. Press it into place with a putty knife. Fig. 10-19. Trim off the extra compound with the edge of the putty knife. Fig. 10-20. *Note:* Wet the blade of the knife with water to keep the putty from sticking to it as you remove the excess. Figs. 10-21, 10-22.

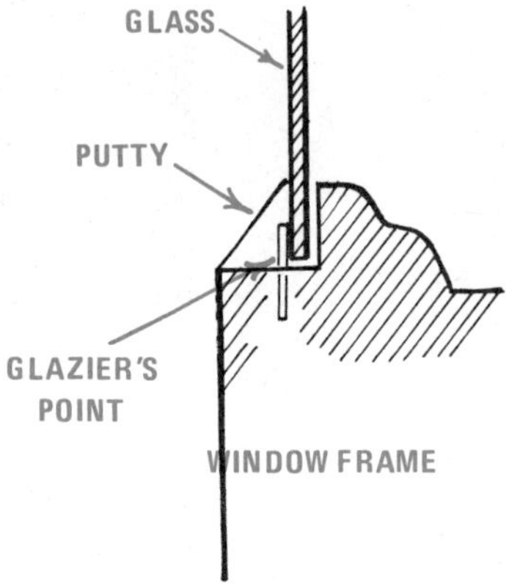

10-22. A sectional view of a window frame showing the glass, the glazier's point and the putty on the outside of the frame.

Red Devil, Inc.

10-23. A glass cutter with a metal ball end.

10-24. Mark the location of the cuts on the glass. Here you can see the piece of old carpeting under the glass.

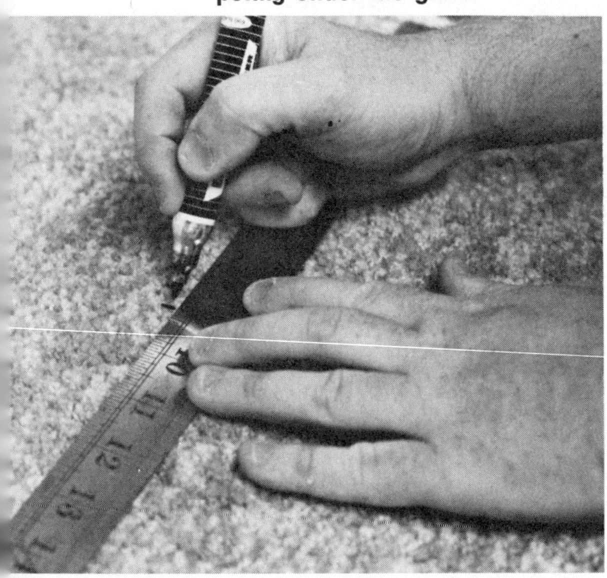

10-25. Put a few drops of oil on the wheel of the glass cutter so that it moves easily.

10-26. Place the straightedge on the glass about 1/16″ from the marks you made. Hold the glass cutter between your index finger and your middle finger.

8. The manufacturer's directions will tell you how soon you may paint the putty or compound. Paint it to match the rest of the window. Allow the paint to overlap the glass by $\frac{1}{16}''$ so that the paint seals the putty against water.

Cutting a Piece of Glass

You will need these items to cut glass:

- Glass cutter. Fig. 10-23.
- Straightedge.
- Ruler.
- Grease pencil or china marker.
- Piece of old carpet or a newspaper.
- Light machine oil.

These are the steps in cutting glass:

1. Obtain a piece of single-strength window glass. Be sure that it is clean. Mark the location of the cuts on the glass with a grease pencil or a china marker. You can also use a crayon or a felt-tip marker. Fig. 10-24.

2. Put the piece to be cut on several thicknesses of newspaper or a piece of old carpeting. Put a couple of drops of oil on the wheel of the glass cutter. Fig. 10-25. You can also dip the cutter in kerosene as another way of lubricating the wheel so that it moves easily.

3. Put the straightedge on the glass about $\frac{1}{16}''$ from the marks that you made. Fig. 10-26. Hold it down securely. Hold the glass cutter between your index finger and middle finger. Your fingertips rest on the flat part of the handle. The cutter is slanted towards you with the cutting wheel away from you. Fig. 10-27.

Press down firmly on the cutter and move it along the straightedge on the cutting line. You will hear the sound of the glass being scored as you move the cutter from the far edge of the glass to the edge nearest you. You must score the glass in one stroke.

4. Take the straightedge off the glass and put it under the score mark. (One edge of the straightedge should line up with the score mark.) Press on both sides of the piece of glass until it snaps apart. Fig. 10-28. It should snap off cleanly if you scored

10-27. The correct way to hold a glass cutter.

10-28. Put the straightedge under the score mark on the glass. Press on both sides of the piece of glass until it snaps apart.

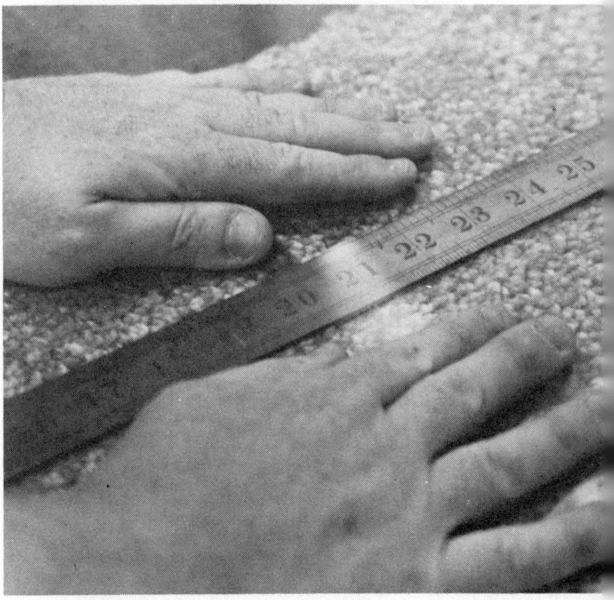

10-29. Move the glass over to the edge of the worktable. Tap the glass under the score mark with the end of the cutter.

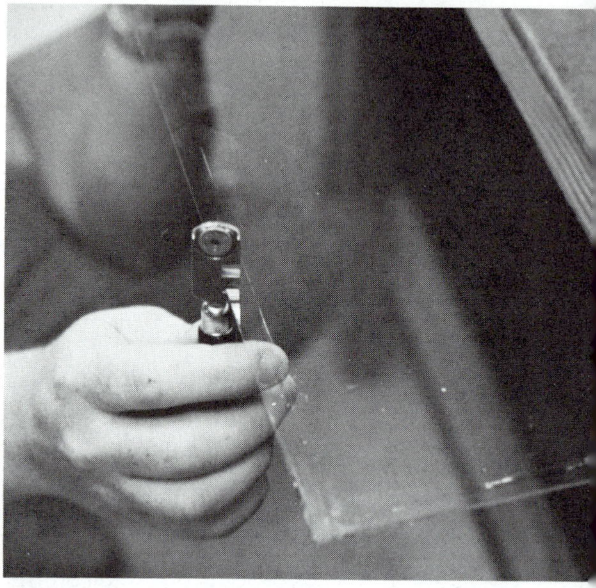

10-30. A narrow piece of glass is scored and then snapped off by holding it with the notches on the glass cutter.

the glass properly. As an alternate method for snapping the glass, you can remove the straightedge and move the glass over to the edge of the worktable. Tap the glass under the score mark with the end of the cutter (some cutters have a special metal ball end on them). Fig. 10-29. Then press down on the waste piece of glass and snap it off cleanly.

5. Narrow pieces of glass are scored and then snapped off by holding them with the notches on the glass cutter. Fig. 10-30. These notches act as a wrench or pliers to grip the narrow glass.

REPLACING A WINDOW SCREEN

Window screens have either wooden or aluminum frames. Replacing a screen in one is quite a different task from replacing a screen in the other.

Most screening used today is made of aluminum. Screening may be bought in standard widths to fit different sized screens. It can be purchased in rolls or by the foot.

Screens in Wooden Frames

The tools and materials you will need to replace a screen in a wooden frame are:

- $\frac{3}{4}$'' brads.
- Claw hammer.
- Two C-clamps.
- Two pieces of scrap wood.
- Tin snips or scissors.
- Pliers.

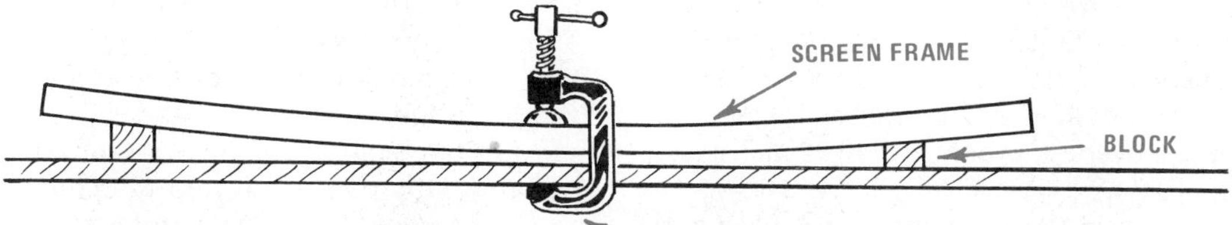

10-31. Preparing a frame for screen installation.

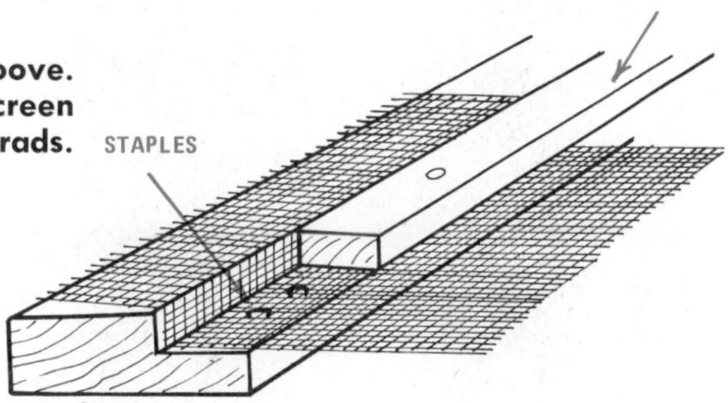

10-32. Staple the screening into the groove. The screening will be covered by screen molding which is held in place with brads.

- Screwdriver.
- Staple gun with $\frac{1}{4}''$ staples.
- New screening.

These are the steps in replacing the screen:

1. The screen molding on the frame is held in place with brads. Pry up the molding and pull all the old brads out with a screwdriver and a hammer. Try not to break the molding so that you can use it again.

2. Remove the old screening by pulling the staples out with a pair of pliers. The new piece of screening that you will use should be 3 or 4 inches larger than the frame. Cut it with scissors or tin snips.

3. Place the frame on your workbench. Put a block of wood under each end of the frame. A piece of $\frac{3}{4}''$-thick lumber will be sufficient. Place a C-clamp in the middle of each side. Tighten the clamps until the frame bows about $\frac{1}{2}''$, but not enough to crack the frame. Fig. 10-31.

4. Place the screening over the opening so that there is an even amount overlapping the frame all around. The mesh in the screen should be parallel to the sides of the frame. Staple the top and bottom edges to the groove in the frame where the old screening was attached (usually a rabbet around the inner edge). Start at the center of each edge and work out from there.

5. When you have finished stapling both edges, loosen both clamps slowly and remove them. The frame will straighten out and pull the screening tight.

6. Staple both long sides to the groove. Start at the center and work out toward the corners of the frame. Be careful to avoid wrinkles in the screening. Fig. 10-32.

7. Cut off the excess screening with scissors or tin snips. You can also trim the screening with a sharp utility knife. The screening should not extend past the area that will be covered by the molding.

8. Replace the screen molding. Nail it in place with the $\frac{3}{4}''$ brads.

Screens in Aluminum Frames

These are the tools and materials you will need to replace a screen in a metal frame:

- Neoprene spline.
- Screening.
- Screening tool.
- Tin snips.
- Sharp utility knife.

The procedure is as follows:

1. Remove the neoprene spline. Fig. 10-33. Pry one end of it out of the channel and pull it all out. Remove the old screening.

2. Cut a new piece of screening that is 3 or 4 inches larger all around. Put the new screening in place so that the mesh is parallel to the sides of the frame. The screen should overlap evenly on all four sides. Fig. 10-34.

3. Inspect the old spline. If it is dried out, measure it and obtain a new piece that is somewhat longer. Neoprene splines come in different diameters. If you buy a new spline, take the old one to the hardware store with you for comparison.

Start the spline at one corner. Use a screening tool to push it into the channel. Fig. 10-35. Do one side first and then bend

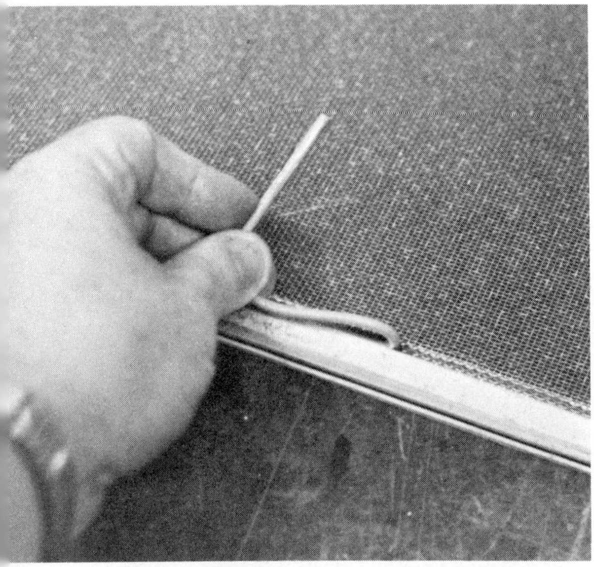

10-33. To remove the neoprene spline, pry one end of it out of the channel and pull it all out.

10-34. Cut a new piece of screening that is 3 or 4 inches larger all around. It should overlap the frame evenly on the four sides.

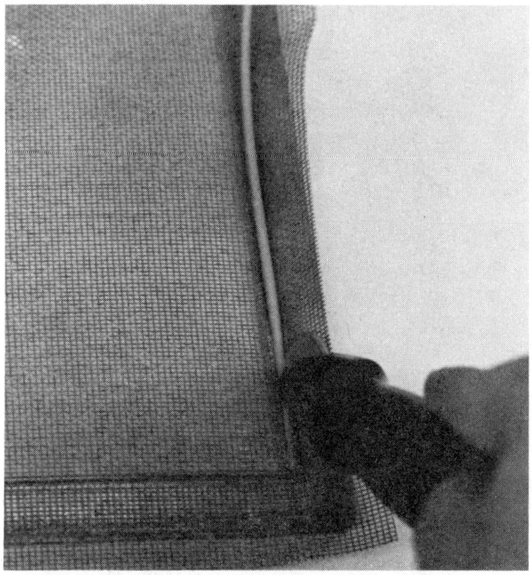

10-35. Starting at one corner, push the spline into the channel with a screening tool.

10-36. As you work around the frame pushing the spline into the channels, you will stretch the screen tight.

the spline around the corner of the channel. Stretch the screen out so that there will be no wrinkles in it. As you work around the four sides of the frame pushing the spline into the channels, you will stretch the screen so that it is tight. Figs. 10-36, 10-37.

4. Use a utility knife to trim off the excess spline. Also trim the screening that is sticking out of the channel with the knife.

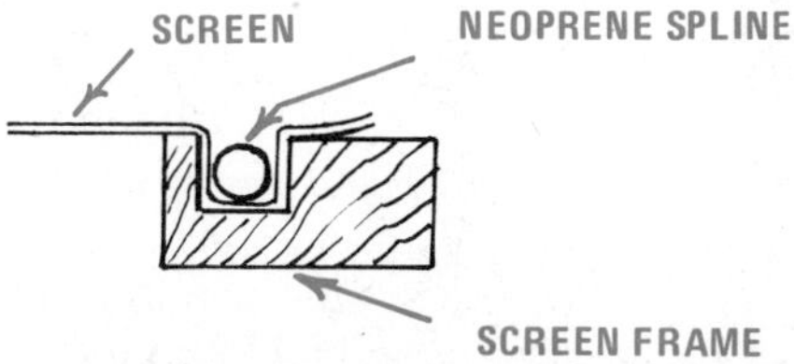

10-37. A sectional view of a metal screen frame showing the screening in the channel held in place by the neoprene spline.

PATCHING A SCREEN

If a screen has a small hole in it, it is not necessary to replace it. You can patch the hole with a scrap piece of the same type of screening. It is a good idea to save scrap pieces of screening to use as patches, although you can buy patches at the hardware store. To patch a piece of metal screening do the following:

1. Cut a scrap piece of screening 2″ wider and longer than the hole in the screen. Use scissors or tin snips to do the cutting.

2. Unravel the edges. Remove two or three strands of wire on each side. Fig. 10-38. Use a piece of wood as a form over which to bend the strands 90 degrees. Bend all the strands on one side first. The strands on all sides should be bent in the same direction.

3. Insert the strands through the holes in the existing screen as you place the patch over the repair area. Bend the strands of wire over the screening. Fig. 10-39. Use a piece of wood to push the strands down so that the patch is tight.

10-39. Insert the strands through the screen as you place the patch over the hole. Bend the wire strands over the screening.

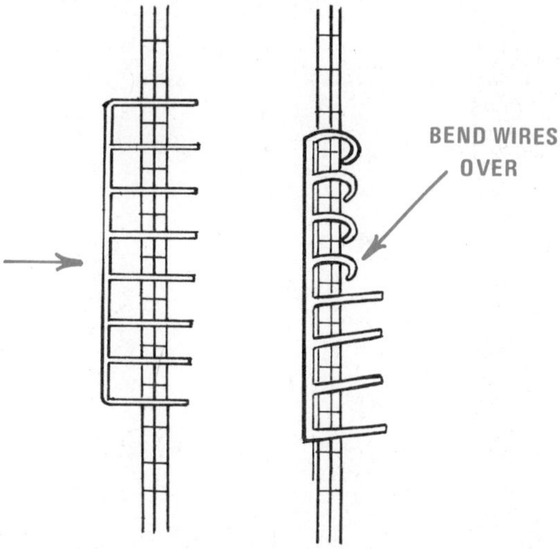

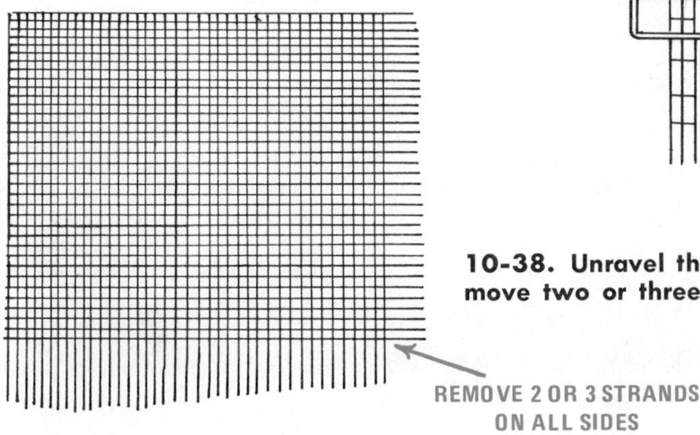

10-38. Unravel the edges of the patch. Remove two or three strands of wire on each side.

CHECKUP

1. What are some common window problems? Do you have any of these problems with the windows in your home?
2. What kinds of weather stripping are available for windows? Do the windows in your home have adequate weather stripping?
3. Should you replace insulated glass yourself or have a professional do it? Why?

CHAPTER 11

Exterior Carpentry Repairs

ROOF REPAIRS

Roof repairs are difficult to make because of the location of the repair and because the damaged part may be hidden. Weather conditions can also make repair work difficult. All repairs should be made in good weather. There should be no rain (roofs are very slippery in wet weather). Ideally the weather should be warm because asphalt shingles get brittle in cold weather and will break when you walk on them. In addition, there should be little or no wind because you will be climbing a ladder and standing on a sloping roof.

There are four types of materials used for the majority of roofs on private homes. They are:

- Clay tiles—ceramic tiles which are either curved or flat. Figs. 11-1, 11-2.

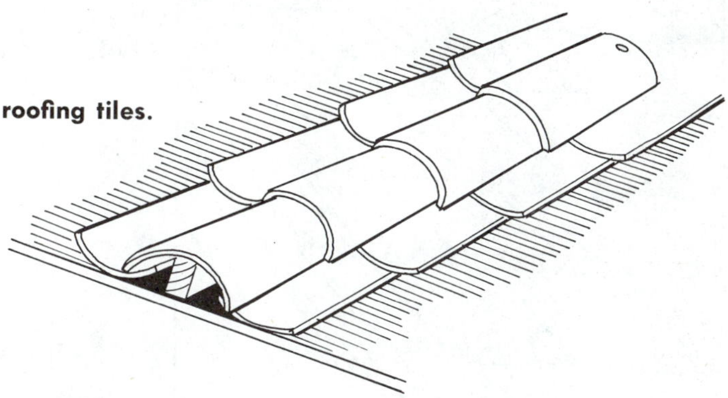

11-1. Curved ceramic roofing tiles.

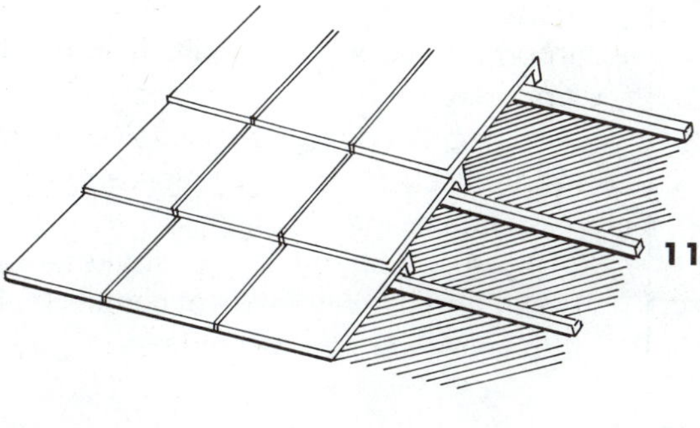

11-2. Flat ceramic roofing tiles.

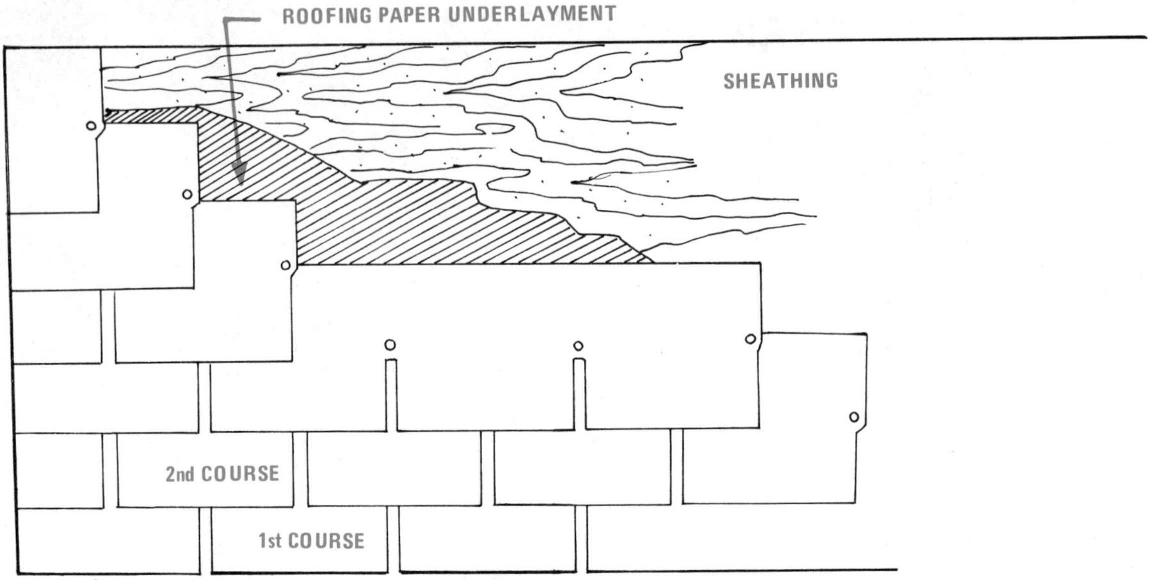

11-3. An asphalt shingle roof. This drawing shows the sheathing, the roofing paper, and the courses of shingles.

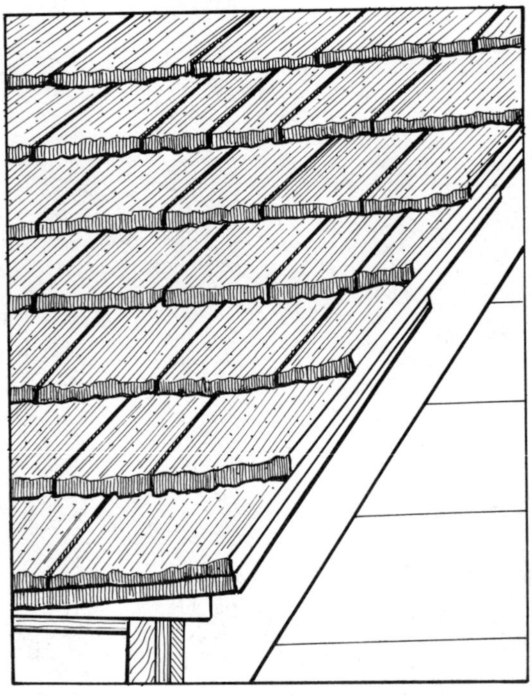

11-4. A wood shake roof.

• Rolled roofing felt—also called roofing paper. It is made up of paper or wood fibers impregnated with asphalt. It is used as an underlayment or on flat roofs.

• Asphalt shingles—usually covered with mineral chips to add color and some fire resistance. Fig. 11-3.

• Wood shingles or shakes—split or sawn and usually made of cedar. Shakes are a heavier version of shingles. Fig. 11-4.

REPAIRING A LEAKY ROOF

Inspecting the outer surface of the roof will not always help you to find the location of the leak. If you can get into the attic of the house, inspect the roof sheathing for stains and the attic floor for puddles. You will find in most cases that the water has run a distance from the leak to the place where it made a puddle. Water runs along the rafters and roof sheathing on a sloping roof.

Most leaks occur around plumbing vent pipes, chimneys, at valleys in the roof (a valley is the low point where two surfaces of the roof meet), and at the peak or ridge of the roof. Most of these places have metal flashing which can corrode or pull away from the roof. Fig. 11-5. The ridge has shingles bent over it as a cap, but the underlayment or sheathing may not quite meet at that spot.

Go into the attic during the daytime. You may be able to spot sunlight coming through the holes in the roof. If you find a hole, push a long nail through it to mark it from the outside. If there is a leak in the flashing at a valley or around the chimney, measure that distance from the ridge so that you can find it when you are outside.

Once you are on the roof, look for broken or loose shingles, missing shingles, or loose flashing near the spot where you have located the leak. That is the trouble area and the place where repairs must be made.

Repairing a Leak in an Asphalt Shingle Roof

After you have chosen the best possible weather conditions to do the actual roof repair, assemble your equipment and materials. You will need an extension ladder that is long enough for you to reach the roof easily. It must extend at least 3 feet above the roof so that you can climb off it safely. Place the base of the ladder a distance equal to one quarter of its vertical height away from the house wall. This will keep the ladder from falling over when you are on it. Make sure the ladder stands on a nonskid footing, such as wide wooden boards, if the ground is soft underneath. See Chapter 5 for more tips on ladder use.

11-5. A roof valley with flashing.

11-6. Pull out the old nails with the curved end of a pry bar if you can get in close to the nails.

11-7. Courses of asphalt shingles. The ends of the shingles are staggered so that the edges of the tabs line up on alternate courses.

You will need some shingles to make the repair. Try to get shingles that match the existing roof. In addition you will need the proper nails; $1\frac{1}{2}''$ galvanized roofing nails are used for asphalt shingles. You will also need the following:

- Hammer.
- Utility knife.
- Pry bar.
- Ruler.
- Hacksaw blade.
- Plastic roofing cement. Roofing cement is sold in lumberyards as plastic asphalt cement or vinyl ashalt cement.

The steps in making the repair are:

1. Remove the broken shingles. Lift the shingles in the course, or row, above the broken ones to get to the nails. Be careful not to break any additional shingles. Cut the nails with a hacksaw blade so that you can pull the damaged shingle out. You can also pull the old nails out with a piece of steel with a slot cut in it or with the curved end of a pry bar if you can get it in close to the nails. Fig. 11-6.

2. Use roofing cement to repair any holes in the roofing paper underneath the shingles or in the sheathing. Replace the lowest course of shingles first. Be sure to stagger the ends of the shingles so that they match the pattern of the existing roof. Fig. 11-7. Four nails are driven into each shingle as shown in Fig. 11-8. The nails are placed so that the row above covers them. Be sure to

11-8. Four nails are driven into each shingle. This is a self-sealing shingle which has adhesive strips on it that will adhere to the tabs of the shingles above it.

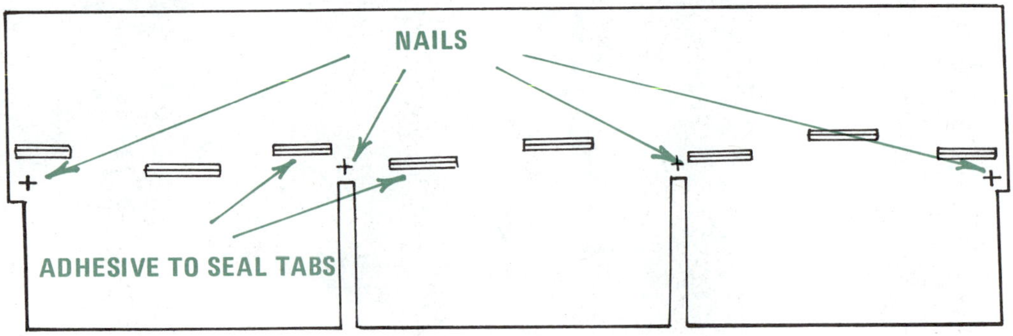

11-9. Nail the shingles in place with galvanized roofing nails.

use galvanized roofing nails. (Galvanized nails have been coated with zinc to prevent rust.) Fig. 11-9.

3. Lift the ends of the shingles in the course above to nail the last row of shingles. Fig. 11-10. In warm weather the shingles will lift without cracking unless they are very old and dried out. If the new shingles are not self-sealing, apply a spot of roofing cement under each of the tabs on the shingle. Fig. 11-11. This will keep them from lifting in a high wind or a driving rainstorm. Self-sealing shingles have a strip of heat-activated adhesive on them so that the tabs of the shingle just above adhere to them.

Repairing a Leak in a Wood Shingle Roof

The repairs on a wood shingle or shake roof are similar to those on an asphalt roof. You will need the following:

- Claw hammer.

11-10. Lift the ends of the shingles above to slide the last row of new shingles into place.

11-11. If the new shingles are not self-sealing, applying a spot of roofing cement under each of the tabs will keep them from being lifted by wind or rain.

- Hacksaw blade.
- Wood chisel.
- Handsaw.
- Roofing cement.

The repair procedure after you locate the leak is:

1. Remove the broken, warped, loose, or cracked shingles with a claw hammer and a wood chisel. Break the wood if necessary. Slip a hacksaw blade under the shingles to cut through the nails that you cannot reach.

2. Start replacing the lowest course of shingles first. Fit them into place so that they match the pattern of the other shingles on the roof. On some roofs the shingles or shakes are placed in a rustic pattern with the edges of the shingles on several different levels.

Shakes or shingles that do not fit may be cut to size with a handsaw. They are then driven into place under the upper row with a hammer and a block of wood.

3. Wood shakes and shingles are nailed at sections that will be covered by the next course. The last course of shingles, however, must be nailed in place through the sections exposed to the weather. Fig. 11-12.

Use either aluminum nails or galvanized steel nails. Do not set the nails down into the wood, as this crushes the fibers. Put a

Red Cedar Shingle and Handsplit Shake Bureau

11-12. A wood shake roof showing the placement of the nails. The last course must be nailed through sections of the shake exposed to the weather.

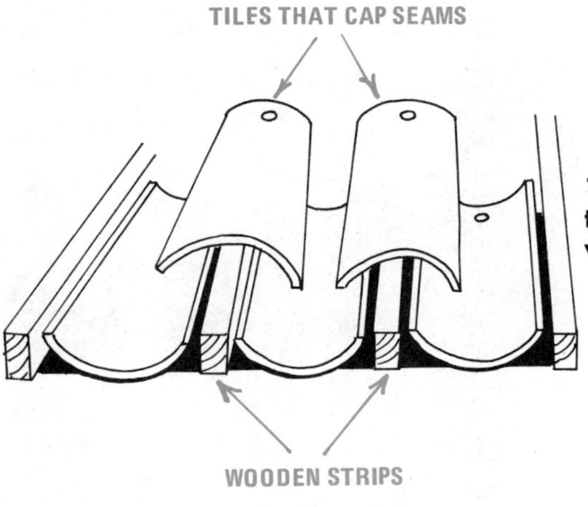

11-13. Installation of curved tiles. Here the tiles with the concave portion up are capped with other curved tiles with the concave portion down.

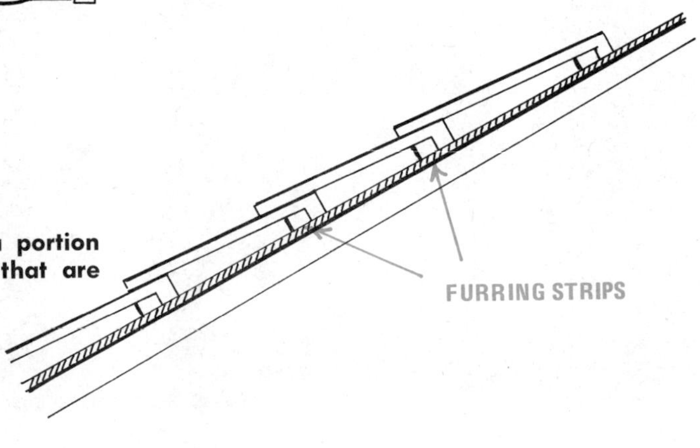

11-14. Flat tiles are made with a portion that hooks over the furring strips that are nailed to the roof.

little roofing cement on each exposed nailhead to make a waterproof joint.

Repairing a Ceramic Tile Roof

A leak in a ceramic tile roof is caused by one or two tiles breaking or shifting out of position. The roofing felt under the tiles may be damaged by the shifting tiles. The felt can be repaired with roofing cement after the broken tiles are removed.

Ceramic roof tiles come in two styles, *U*-shaped (curved) and flat. The *U*-shaped tiles are installed as shown in Fig. 11-13. The roof is first covered with rows of tiles fastened with the concave portion up, like a *U*. Over the upraised sides of two rows of curved tiles, another row of curved tiles is fastened with the concave side down. This second row of tiles is fastened in place with wires or nails. It acts as a cap over the seam between the rows of tiles underneath.

Flat tiles have a part which hooks over furring strips that are nailed to the roof. Fig. 11-14. Furring strips are pieces of 1″ x 2″ lumber.

Both the curved and the flat tiles are replaced by simply removing the broken tiles and placing new ones on the roof. Both types of tiles are nailed in place through the predrilled holes in them. Do not try to nail through any other part because the tiles will crack. When walking on the roof, try to step on at least two tiles with each foot to distribute your weight. The tiles are brittle, and too much weight will cause them to crack.

Repairing a Roof Covered with Rolled Roofing Felt

Leaks in roofing felt usually occur near a seam or at a blister. They can be fixed with roofing cement, some roofing felt, and nails. You will need a putty knife, a hammer, and a utility knife.

1. Cut away any loose felt so that the damaged area is neat, with no roofing felt sticking up. The trimming can be done with a sharp utility knife. Slit a blister so that you can get roofing cement inside it. Fig. 11-15.
2. Apply roofing cement under the loose edges of the felt with a putty knife. Press the roofing felt down tightly so that it adheres. Nail it around the edges with galvanized roofing nails.
3. Spread roofing cement over the cracked area and all the nailheads to waterproof the repair.
4. If there is a large cracked area, apply a patch over it. Cut a piece of roofing felt that is at least 6 to 8 inches bigger all around than the section to be covered. Nail it all around the edges with roofing nails. Fig. 11-16. Be

11-15. Slit a blister with a sharp utility knife. Use a putty knife to apply roofing cement under the felt.

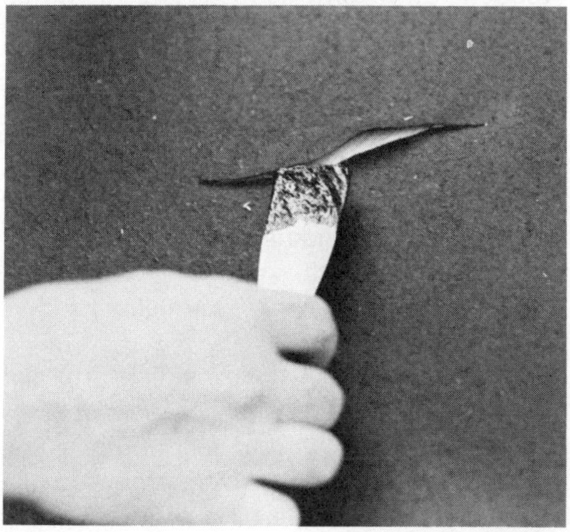

11-16. Nail the patch all around the edges with roofing nails.

sure to cover the nailheads with roofing cement when you seal the edges. Fig. 11-17. You may find it easier to use an old paint brush to apply the cement to the edges.

Repairing Flashing

Metal strips that are installed to allow water to run off a roof are called flashing. Flashing is placed around vent pipes, chimneys, roof vents, and at valleys where two roof surfaces meet. For example, flashing is installed under the closest row of shingles near the joint where a vent meets the roof. Flashing is usually made of sheet metal such as copper or aluminum. Some of the newer vent flashing is made of plastic.

If the flashing is corroded or torn, replacement is a job for a professional roofer. Usually the flashing leaks because the adhesive around the edges of the metal has dried up and cracked. You can repair the leak by cleaning off the cracked sealant and spreading new roofing cement over the edges. Work some of the cement under the edges of the flashing where the old cement has cracked. Here an old paint brush works well. Roof caulking and roofing cement also come in cartridges which fit a caulking gun. This is a handier way to seal the edges and fill the spaces in the flashing.

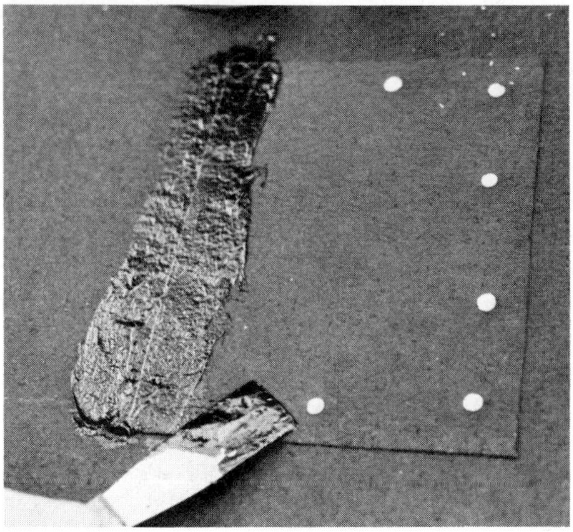

11-17. When you seal the edges of the patch with roofing cement, be sure to cover the nailheads also.

REPAIRING OR REPLACING DAMAGED SIDING

Weyerhaeuser Co.

11-18. Beveled siding.

Siding can be divided into two kinds: wooden and nonwooden. The common types of wooden board siding are: beveled siding, (Fig. 11-18), tongue-and-groove siding, (Fig. 11-19), vertical board-and-batten siding, (Fig. 11-20), drop siding, (Fig. 11-21), and rustic (novelty) siding, (Fig. 11-22). In addition to these there are varieties of exterior plywood siding and hardboard siding materials which come in large sheets. Cedar shakes and shingles are also used as siding.

The types of nonwooden siding are: aluminum siding, vinyl siding, and asbestos shingle siding. Vinyl and aluminum siding rarely need repair, but when they do the repair should be done by a professional.

11-19. Tongue-and-groove siding.

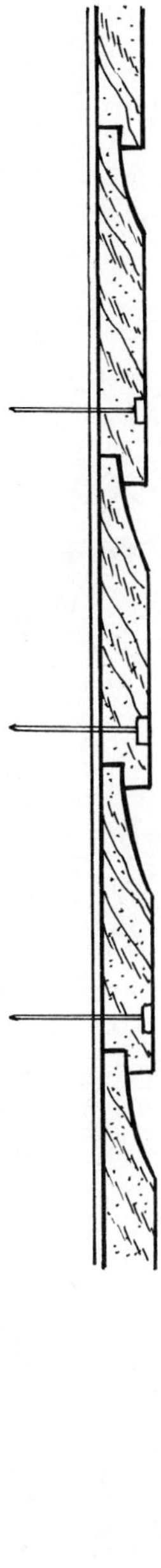

11-21. Drop siding.

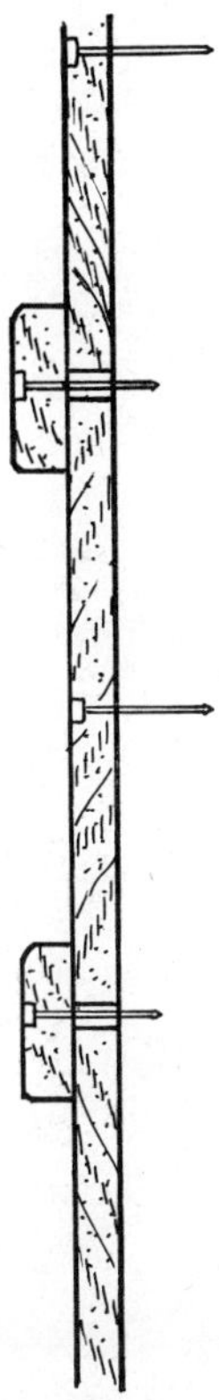

11-20. Vertical board-and-batten siding, viewed from above.

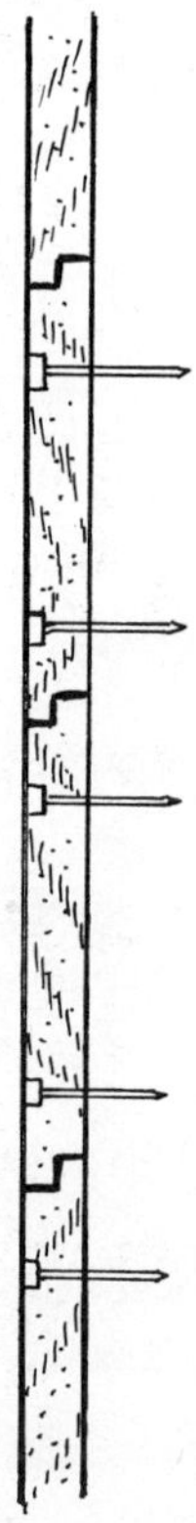

11-22. Novelty or rustic siding.

Repairing Wooden Siding

A piece of cracked, warped, or broken siding can be repaired by nailing it back in place on the studs. Use caulking to fill the nail holes and the cracks after the repair is completed. If a piece of siding is badly warped, use long screws to pull it back into position. Drive the screws through the siding into the wall studs. This should straighten the piece of siding. If it splits or

11-23. Mark off the area to be removed on the existing siding. Use a square and a pencil.

11-24. Set your circular saw so that the blade sticks out slightly less than the thickness of the siding you are going to cut.

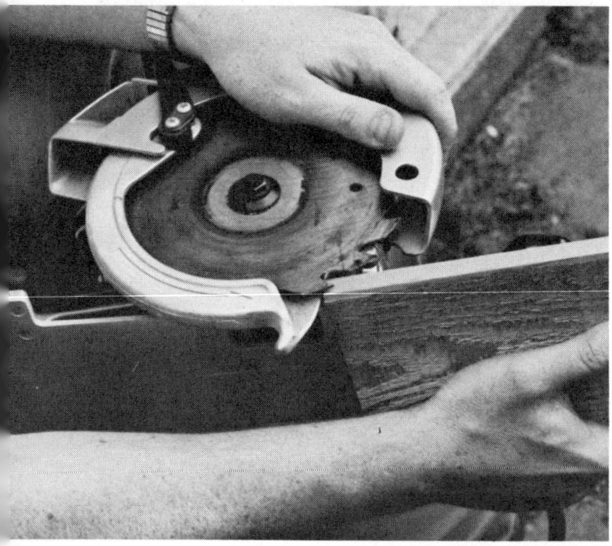

11-25. Cut the damaged siding on the pencil lines.

11-26. After the cuts are made, pry out the board with a wrecking bar.

refuses to straighten, the best thing to do is to replace that section of siding.

Replacing Wooden Siding

If one or two boards have to be replaced because they cannot be repaired, you will need the following:

- Replacement siding of the same size as the old siding.
- Aluminum or galvanized nails.
- Combination square.
- Ruler.
- Portable circular saw.
- Wrecking bar.
- Chisel.
- Claw hammer.

The procedure for making the repair follows.

1. Mark off the area to be removed on the existing siding with a square and a pencil. Fig. 11-23. Later you will make saw cuts along these marks to remove the damaged siding. On drop siding, beveled siding and rustic siding, use the wrecking bar to pry up the board that you want to remove. Drive a wedge under the board to keep it up and away from the sheathing on the house.

2. Set the portable circular saw so that the blade sticks out slightly less than the thickness of the siding to be cut. Fig. 11-24. This is done to avoid damaging the sheathing and the black roofing paper underneath the siding. Cut the damaged siding along the pencil lines. Fig. 11-25. Tongue-and-groove siding needs to be cut horizontally as well as vertically so that you can pry the piece off the wall. Otherwise the piece would be held in place by the tongue and the groove on the top and bottom.

3. After the cuts have been made, pry out the boards. Use a chisel or the wrecking bar to get the piece out. Fig. 11-26. Pull out any nails that remain. If the roofing paper underneath is damaged, cover it with a new piece of tar paper. Hold the patch in place with galvanized roofing nails.

4. Cut a new piece of siding to length. Measure carefully so that it will fit tightly. Fig. 11-27. Use a block of scrap wood and a hammer to drive the new piece into the opening. Then use the block and the hammer on the lower edge of the piece to drive it under the piece of siding just above it, as in the case of beveled siding or drop siding. Fig. 11-28. You will have to cut off one lip of the groove on the inside of new tongue-

11-27. Cut the new piece of siding to length after carefully measuring so that it fits tightly.

11-28. Use a block of scrap wood and a hammer on the lower edge of the piece of siding to drive it under the piece of siding above it.

11-29. Face-nail the new piece in place. Use galvanized or aluminum nails, which will not rust.

11-30. Cedar shingles and the smooth undercourse shingles beneath them.

and-groove siding so that you can slip the new piece into place.

5. Nail the new piece into place from the outside. (This is called face nailing.) Fig. 11-29. Use galvanized nails or aluminum nails to avoid rust spots. Caulk the end seams and the nail holes. Prime the new wood with paint. When that is dry, paint the new wood to match the rest of the siding.

Replacing Siding of Cedar Shingles or Shakes

Cedar shingles or the somewhat thicker cedar shakes have to be replaced when they crack, warp, or loosen. They are replaced in the same manner as wooden roof shingles.

1. Remove the broken shingles or shakes, using a claw hammer. Break them if necessary in order to remove them. A hacksaw blade slipped underneath can be used to cut any remaining nails without damaging the nearby shingles or shakes. Try not to damage the undercourse shingles, which are directly beneath the outer ones. Fig. 11-30.

11-31. An asbestos shingle cutter.

2. Fit the new shingles (or shakes) into place so that they match the placement of the other shingles in that course. Slip the shingle into place and nail it with a minimum of two nails about 2″ up from the lower end. Use aluminum or galvanized shingle nails. If the shake or shingle is too wide, cut it to size with a hand saw. It should fit tightly. Paint or stain all the replacement shingles to match the rest of the house.

Replacing Asbestos Shingles

One type of nonwooden siding that can be replaced by the do-it-yourselfer is asbestos shingle. This type of shingle is very brittle and cracks easily. Asbestos shingles are sold individually or by the bundle at lumberyards. These shingles are usually colored white or gray but may sometimes be found in a few other shades. The aluminum shingle nails and the roofing paper tabs that go behind each seam can also be bought at the lumberyard. You can also rent a shingle cutter at the lumberyard or at a tool rental agency. Fig. 11-31. The only other tools that you will need to replace these shingles are a hammer, a ruler, and a wide chisel. The steps in replacing a shingle are:

1. Remove the old broken or cracked shingle. It cannot be repaired. If it will not come off easily, strike it a sharp blow with a hammer. It will crack and you can then break off the pieces. Pull out the nails. If there are roofing paper tabs between the shingles, inspect these. They may need to be replaced when you put up the new shingle. The tabs slip behind the two butted edges of the shingles and are held in place with the same nails that hold the shingles. Put the tabs in before you replace the shingle.

2. Fit the new shingle in place. Part of the shingle goes under the shingle above. Fig. 11-32. If you cannot get the top edge under the upper shingle, use a wide chisel to carefully pry the edge out a little. Be very careful. As said before, asbestos shingles are brittle and will break very easily. Slip the new shingle in place and make sure that the edges are even with the other shingles in that course. Nail the lower edge of the shingle through the holes with the aluminum shingle nails. Be careful not to drive the nails in too deeply or you will crack the asbestos.

3. If the shingle that you are replacing is not rectangular or is shorter than the size of a full shingle, it will have to be cut. Use a shingle cutter for this job. A shingle cutter looks very much like a paper cutter or a resilient flooring tile cutter, and it works the same way. It also has a section that punches nail holes and another section that works as a nibbler. Fig. 11-33. With the nibbler you can cut any shape out of the shingle to fit around a window or a doorway. Fig. 11-34.

Ask the person from whom you rent the cutter to show you how it works. Before you start cutting the good shingles, practice on a scrap piece so that you will be familiar with the workings of the machine.

4. To cut a shingle to a particular shape, take accurate measurements and transfer these to the shingle. It may be possible to use the old shingle as a pattern. Draw the

11-32. Fit the new shingle in place. Part of it goes under the shingle above.

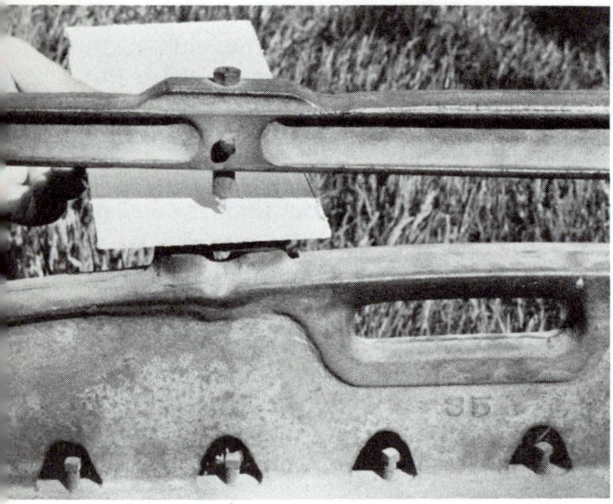

11-33. Use the shingle cutter to punch a new nail hole in an asbestos shingle.

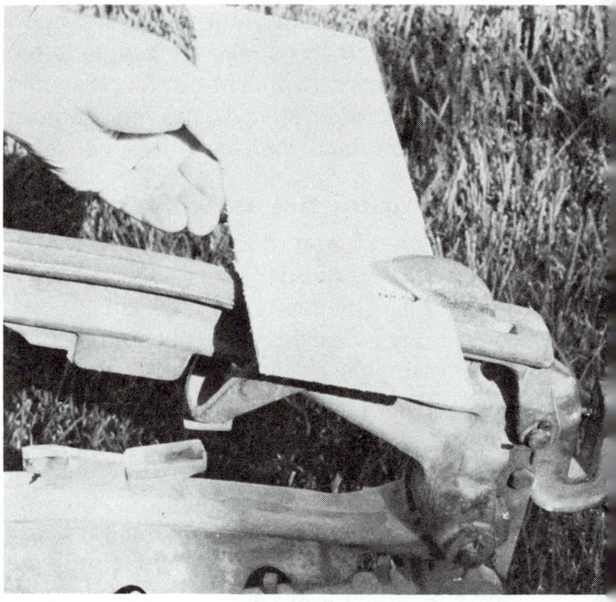

11-34. Nibble a section out of the shingle with the shingle cutter.

cutting lines on the shingle with a pencil. Cut all the straight lines first. Punch a couple of holes in the corners of each interior cut before you start to nibble along the lines. Asbestos shingles are easier to work with in warm weather. They are very brittle in cold weather and break easily.

REPLACING EXTERIOR TRIM

A piece of trim (door casing, window sill, fascia, etc.) that is rotting, broken, or badly cracked should be replaced. It is probably easier to replace it than to try fixing it. The new piece of trim must be exactly the right size; so measure carefully. Unless your house is very old, a lumberyard should have the material that you need. Replace the trim as follows:

1. Remove the old trim with a wrecking bar and a claw hammer. A chisel may be useful to pry out small pieces of trim and also to scrape out the old paint and caulking around the edges of the place where the trim was fastened.

2. Measure and cut the new piece of trim to size with a crosscut saw. Fit it into place but do not nail it. Take it off and back-prime the wood. Painting the back of the trim with primer will help it last longer by keeping moisture and insects out.

3. When the primer is dry, inspect the area where the trim is to be placed. If the area is wet, let it dry out for a few warm days. Putting the trim over moisture will encourage rot and insect problems later.

Nail the trim in place using galvanized finishing nails. Set the nails down below the surface of the wood.

4. Prime the face of the wood. When it is dry, caulk the nail holes and caulk around the trim where it meets the siding. Paint the new piece to match the existing trim.

CAULKING THE OUTSIDE OF THE HOUSE

Caulking is needed anywhere on the outside of a house where water might collect. Such places are usually found where two different materials meet. Examples are the areas where the wooden doorframe meets the siding, where the chimney meets the siding, and where an outside hose connection comes through the siding. On every home there are dozens of places where caulking is necessary. Fig. 11-35.

In time, caulking dries up, cracks, and may fall out. When this happens, it should be replaced. Caulking is best done in warm weather. Instructions on a caulking container will tell you the lowest temperature at which you can use that particular brand.

To replace caulking, carefully scrape out the old material. Use a putty knife or an old chisel and perhaps a wire brush. Then either brush out all the dust with an old paint brush or use a vacuum cleaner to get the area clean. The joint to be caulked must be clean and dry, or the caulking will come loose in a short time.

Squeeze the new caulking into the area with a caulking gun; or, if it is rope-type caulking, push it into place with your fingers. The caulking should fill the cavity completely with an even bead showing on the surface. The most common form of caulking sold comes in a cartridge which fits into a metal gun. Fig. 11-36. These guns are inexpensive and can be used with any replaceable caulking cartridge. You merely place the cartridge in the gun, cut the tip off the nozzle, and puncture the seal in the nozzle. Fig. 11-37. Press the trigger, and the

11-35. Caulk around an outside electrical outlet.

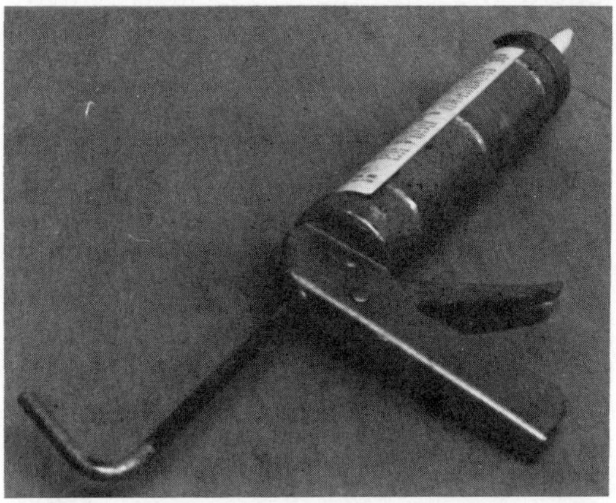

11-36. A metal caulking gun with a cartridge in it.

11-37. Place the cartridge in the caulking gun. Notice that the tip of the nozzle has been cut off.

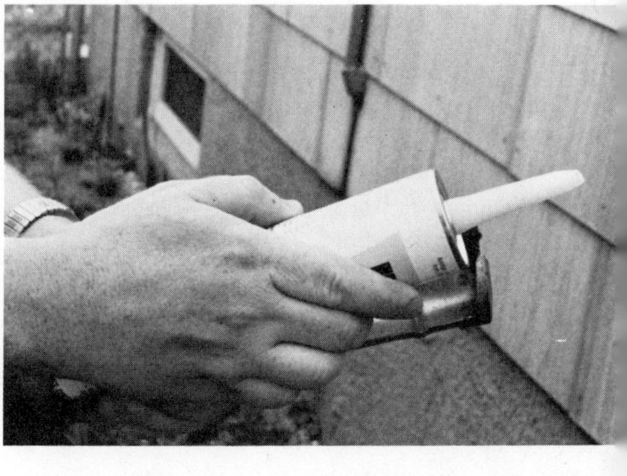

plunger will work its way forward to squeeze out the caulking compound.

There are three common types of caulking: architectural grade caulk (oil base), latex caulk (plastic), and butyl caulk (rubberized). The latex and the butyl varieties last a long time and can be painted with any type of paint. Caulking usually comes in white or gray and is sold in hardware stores and lumberyards.

CLEANING AND REPAIRING GUTTERS

Gutters and downspouts are troughs that carry rainwater and melted snow away from the house. The water rolls off the edge of the roof into the gutters, which are pitched toward the downspout openings. Gutters are made of copper, galvanized iron, wood, aluminum, or vinyl.

Cleaning Gutters

The most common problem with gutters is blockage caused by leaves and other debris. When gutters are close to tall trees, they should be covered wth screening or hardware cloth. Downspout openings should have a special strainer over them to keep debris from clogging up the downspout. Both the downspout strainers and the rolls of screening for the gutters can be purchased at hardware stores.

Once a year the gutters should be cleaned out by pouring water through them to flush out any debris and also to check for blockage. This can be done with either a bucket of water or by pulling the garden hose up the ladder with you and directing the spray into the gutters.

Repairing Gutters and Downspouts

If the gutters are sagging or if they are not pitched enough toward the downspouts to allow for proper drainage, the hanging devices that hold them up need to be adjusted. Spikes and ferrules, roof hangers, and wrap-around hangers are some of the devices used to support gutters. If a hanger is loose, causing the gutter to sag, put up a new hanger near the location of the old one. You can tighten spikes and ferrules or straps by driving the nails in tight. The nails may have been pulled out somewhat by the weight of rain and snow over the years.

If galvanized iron gutters are starting to rust inside because the galvanizing (zinc coating) has worn off, you can coat the gutters to prevent further corrosion. Clean off the rust with a wire brush. Prime the metal with a metal primer and paint it with a special rustproof paint. Ask the paint store salesperson for a paint made for this purpose. You could also paint a cold tar on the inside of the gutter to protect the metal. This tar can be applied with an old paint brush.

A hole in a metal gutter can be repaired if it is not too large. If there is more than one large hole, it may be easier to replace the gutter. Small holes, if there are not too many, can be filled with epoxy cement or tar.

Clean the area around the hole with a wire brush and emery cloth. Be sure to remove all the corrosion before you apply the epoxy. If the hole is too large to be filled with epoxy or tar, it has to be patched with a piece of metal. A piece of galvanized sheet metal can be soldered in place over the hole in a galvanized gutter or cemented in place with epoxy. Be sure to tar or epoxy the edges of any patch so that it will not leak. After a gutter is repaired, pour a bucket of water into it to test the patch for leaks.

Downspouts usually leak at the joints where the elbows meet the downspouts. The leak can be repaired with some gutter seal or mastic. Squeeze the mastic into the joints all around the elbow.

If the bands or straps which hold the downspouts in place on the side of the house have loosened, you can pull out the old nails and move the straps so that they hold the downspout more tightly. Renail them to the wall using galvanized roofing nails (with large heads). If the straps are damaged, they can be replaced with new ones.

REPLACING GUTTERS AND DOWNSPOUTS

Sometimes it is necessary to replace gutters and/or downspouts. Aluminum gutters are one type that is easy for the do-it-yourselfer to install. Fig. 11-38. Just a few tools are needed. You may also need another person to help you hold the gutters up when you are fastening them to the fascia (the front of the overhang) on the house. The following tools are necessary for the installation of new aluminum gutters and downspouts:

- Hammer.

11-38. An aluminum rain-carrying system with all the accessories for the system.
Alcan Aluminum Corp.

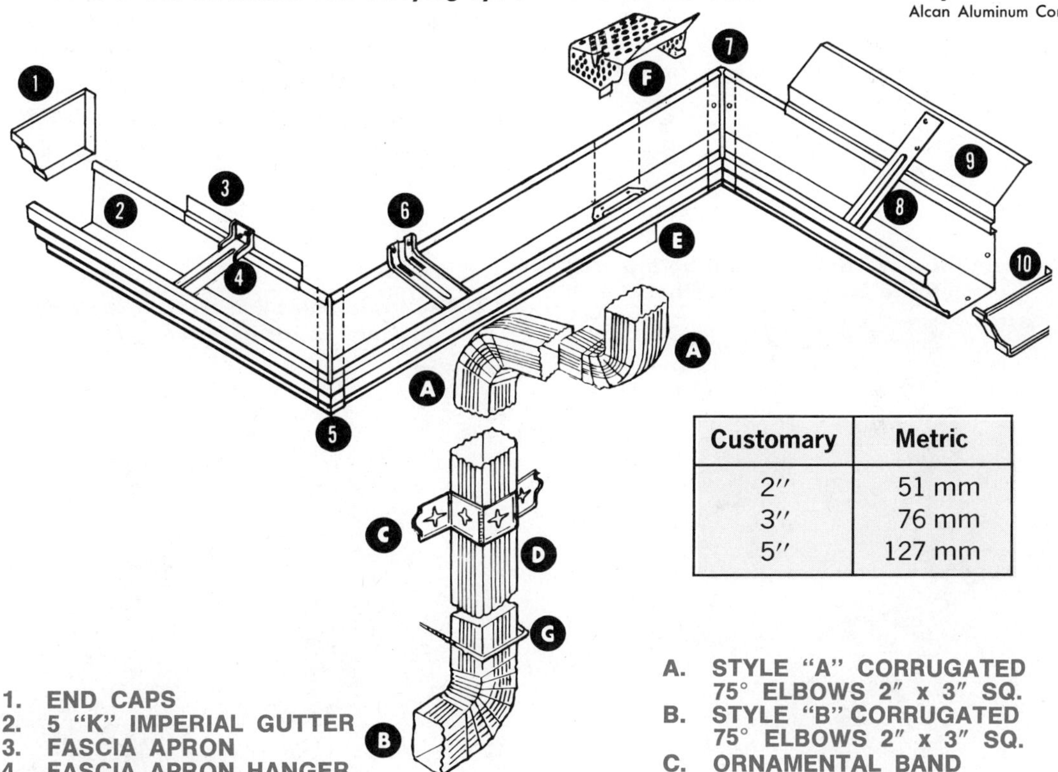

Customary	Metric
2″	51 mm
3″	76 mm
5″	127 mm

1. END CAPS
2. 5 "K" IMPERIAL GUTTER
3. FASCIA APRON
4. FASCIA APRON HANGER
5. STRIP MITRE - OUTSIDE
6. COMBINATION HANGER
7. STRIP MITRE INSIDE
8. ROOF APRON
9. ROOF APRON HANGER
10. END CAPS

A. STYLE "A" CORRUGATED 75° ELBOWS 2″ x 3″ SQ.
B. STYLE "B" CORRUGATED 75° ELBOWS 2″ x 3″ SQ.
C. ORNAMENTAL BAND
D. 2″ x 3″ SQ. CORRUGATED DOWNSPOUT
E. DROP OUTLET TUBE
F. 5″ PERFORATED ALUMINUM STRAINER
G. WHITE WOOD SICKLE HOOKS

11-39. One type of blind riveting tool that will hold 1/8″ diameter rivets.

Stanley Tools

11-40. A pair of aviation shears for cutting aluminum gutters.

- Blind riveting tool. Fig. 11-39.
- Long measuring tape.
- String.
- Hacksaw with a fine-tooth blade.
- Combination square.
- Aviation shears. Fig. 11-40.
- Electric drill with a set of twist drills.
- Ladder.

The steps in the installation of aluminum gutters are:

1. Take down the old gutters and downspouts. If it comes down in one piece, the old gutter can be measured to obtain the length of the new one. If not, measure the fascia.

2. Use the old gutters as a guide when making a list of the new pieces needed. For example, any length of gutter needs two end caps, at least one outlet tube for the downspout, and a tube of gutter seal (caulking) to apply to all seams. Ask the salesperson at the lumberyard or building supply store where you will buy the materials to check your list. You can also get some

11-41. Drill a 1/8″ hole through both pieces of metal to be riveted together.

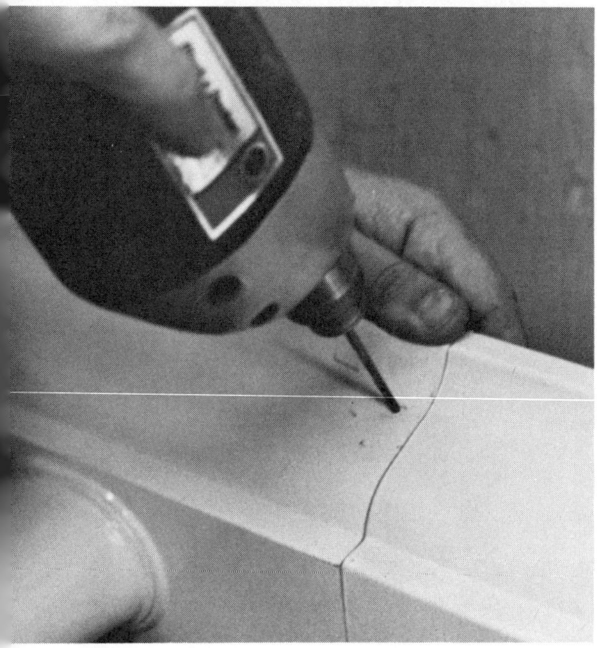

11-42. Insert the blind rivet in the riveting tool as far as it will go.

literature and advice on how to install the gutters and downspouts at the same store.

3. The entire length of gutter with all its components is assembled on the ground before it is installed. On some gutter systems all the components slip together. On others you will have to blind-rivet some of the parts to the gutter. Purchase some $\frac{1}{8}''$ diameter blind rivets when you buy the gutters. The rivets are put into the metal by first drilling a hole with a $\frac{1}{8}''$ twist drill through both pieces of metal. Fig. 11-41. Insert the rivet in the riveting tool. Fig. 11-42. Push the rivet through the hole and squeeze the tool. Fig. 11-43. The rivet will be fastened permanently in place.

Assemble the gutter sections to make up the proper length for your house. Put the end caps in place and rivet them if necessary. Figs. 11-44, 11-45. Make an opening for the outlet tube by drilling an entry hole and then cutting out the opening with aviation shears. Blind-rivet it in place so that it is tight. If the outlet tube is already included in a short section of gutter, fasten it to the end of the gutter with blind rivets and gut-

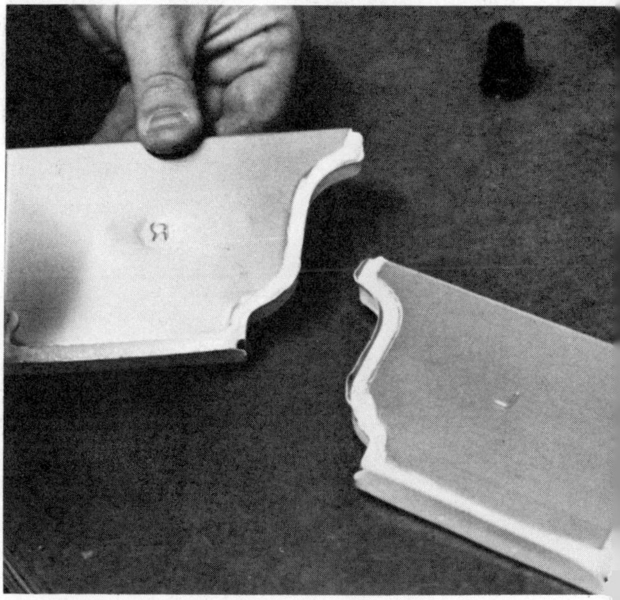

11-44. Put some gutter seal on the end caps before you place them on the gutter.

11-43. Push the rivet through the hole in the metal. Squeeze the tool and the rivet will be fastened permanently in place.

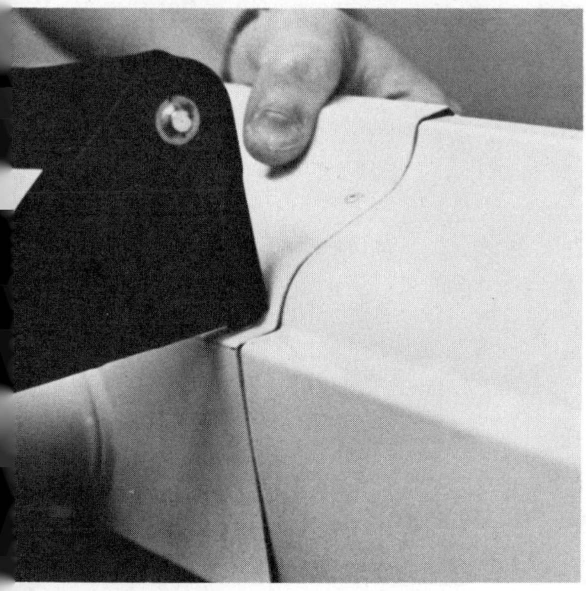

11-45. Tap the end cap into position so that it is on securely.

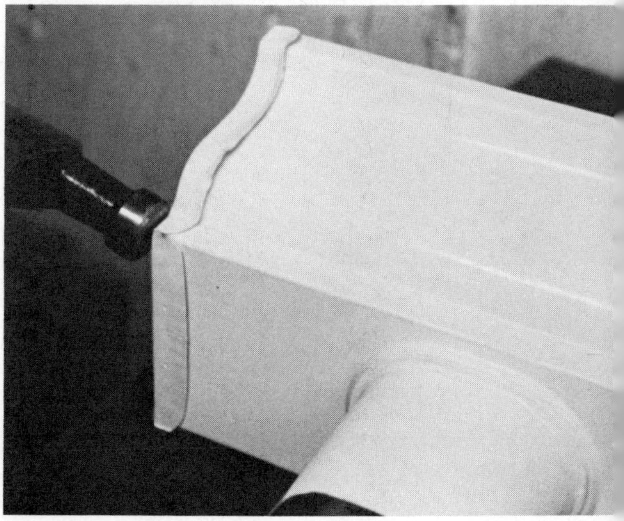

ter seal to make sure that the joint is waterproof. Fig. 11-46.

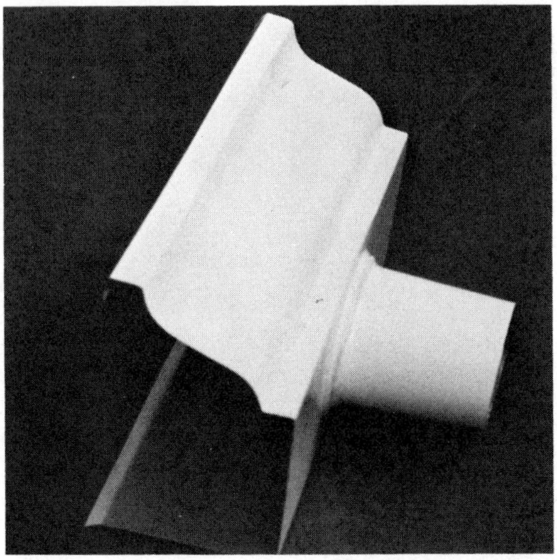

11-46. An outlet tube included in a short length of gutter as a one-piece unit.

11-47a. A diagram showing the cutting necessary to join one length of gutter to another.

Alcan Aluminum Corp.

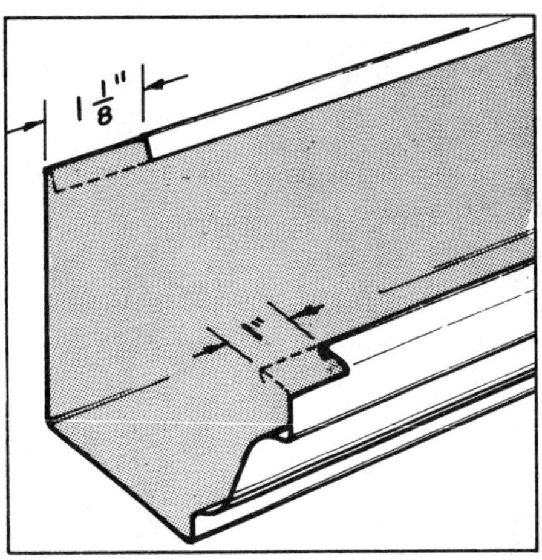

Customary	Metric
1″	25.4 mm
1⅛″	28.6 mm

Use gutter seal on all seams to make them waterproof. Fig. 11-47. Drill ¼″ holes for the spikes and ferrules if that is the hanging system you are going to use. The spikes are driven every 30″. Drill the first hole 30″ in from one end of the gutter.

4. After assembling the gutter completely, you will be ready to put it up on the fascia. To guide you in pitching the gutter toward the downspout so that the gutter will drain, fasten a string along the length of the fascia. The string should be attached to the fascia with two nails, one driven at each end of the fascia. Since the string will mark the top of the gutter, it should be lower on the downspout end. The correct pitch is approximately one inch every sixteen feet.

If the gutter is to have a downspout at each end because it is very long, then the middle should be high and the two ends should be pitched as previously mentioned.

5. Have someone help you put the gutter into position on the fascia. You will need two ladders, one at each end of the gutter. Attach a gutter hanger to one end to hold the piece in place. If you are using a spike and a

11-47b. Rivet two lengths of guttering together and seal the seam with gutter seal to make the joint waterproof.

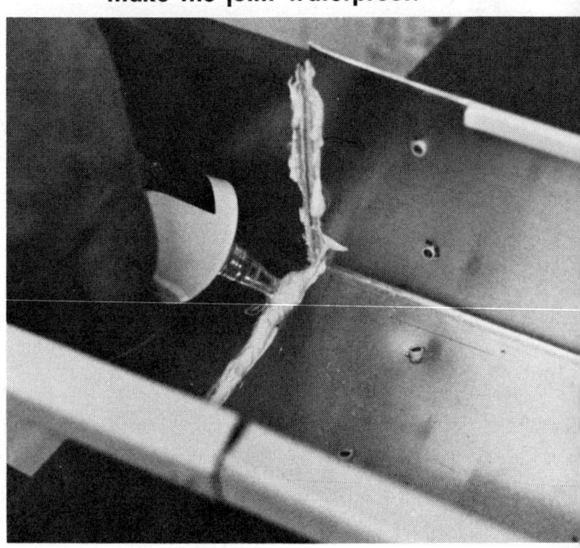

ferrule, drive the spike through the nearest predrilled hole into the fascia. Fig. 11-48. Do the same at the other end. Be sure that the gutter lines up with the string that you put up on the fascia. Look at the gutter from a distance to see that it is pitched properly.

6. If the gutter is pitched properly toward the downspout, then you can attach the other hangers. Make sure that all the hangers are tight.

7. Assemble the downspout sections. The downspout pieces come in lengths of 10′. Any cutting to length can be done with a hacksaw that has a fine-tooth blade or with aviaton shears. Fig. 11-49. The assembled downspout should have an elbow on the top and on the bottom. Fig. 11-50. Rivet all the components together with blind rivets.

Sometimes the overhang of the house is quite large. To make the downspout connect to the outlet tube on the gutter and yet lie flat against the house wall, you will need two elbows and a short section of downspout between them. Fig. 11-51.

To prevent leaks, the upper section always slips inside the lower section of the

11-48. Drive a spike and ferrule through the nearest predrilled hole in the gutter and into the fascia.

11-49. To cut a downspout section to length, use a hacksaw with a fine-tooth blade.

11-50. The downspout should have an elbow on the bottom to carry rainwater away from the house. The crimped end of the downspout goes inside the elbow.

11-51. If the overhang on the house is large, you will need two elbows and a short section of downspout between them. Drill 1/8″ holes and blind-rivet all the components together.

11-52. The assembled elbows and downspout in position. The downspout is held in place with bands or straps, one of which is nailed to the siding just below the elbow.

downspout. For example, the end of the upper elbow slips inside the downspout. The lower end of the downspout slips inside the lower elbow. For appearances sake the downspouts should all be the same length on the house.

8. Each downspout requires two bands or straps to hold it in place on the house. These are nailed to the siding with wide-head roofing nails. Put the downspout in place on the outlet tube. Hold the downspout against the siding so that it is vertical. Nail one end of a band in place on the siding. Bend it around the downspout and nail the other end to the siding so that the band holds the downspout tightly. Do the same with the other band. Put the first band on the downspout near the place where it meets the upper elbow. Nail the second band about 2′ up from the lower end of the downspout. Fig. 11-52.

9. To check if the system works properly and has no leaks, pour a pail or two of water into the gutter. The water should drain through the downspout quickly. Check for leaks at the elbows, where lengths of gutter are joined, and at any other seams. Any leaks can be repaired by applying more gutter seal to the joint.

CHECKUP

1. What are the most common roofing materials for homes? Which type is used on your home?
2. Why is it often difficult to find the exact location of a leak in the roof?
3. Where is caulking necessary?

CHAPTER 12

Ordering Lumber and Other Building Materials

Occasionally you may have to do some work around the house that requires the use of lumber or other building materials. If these materials are not on hand, they must be bought from the local lumberyard. In this chapter, you will be given a basic understanding of lumber and other wood products. You will learn how lumber is graded, the types of wood materials available, and their sizes.

LUMBER

There are two types of wood: *hardwood* and *softwood*. Softwood is lumber that comes from conifers, or evergreen trees. Hardwood is lumber that comes from broad-leafed deciduous trees (they shed their leaves every year). This hardwood and softwood classification has nothing to do with the actual hardness of each kind of wood. For example, spruce (a softwood) is harder than basswood (a hardwood) as far as workability is concerned. Listed in Fig. 12-1 are some of the common varieties of wood that you may be using.

Softwoods are the most commonly used lumber in home repair work. All building lumber, such as 2 x 4s and 2 x 3s, is made from fir trees. Fig. 12-2. Shelving is usually made from pine. Plywood commonly used

12-1. This table lists some common varieties of hardwoods and softwoods. You will problably use some of these in home maintenance.

COMMON HARDWOODS AND SOFTWOODS

HARDWOODS (Deciduous)	SOFTWOODS (Conifers)
White Ash	White Fir
Black Cherry	Douglas Fir
Lauan (Philippine Mahogany)	Ponderosa Pine
Sugar Maple	White Pine
White Oak	Red Cedar
Red Oak	Redwood
	Sitka Spruce

Weyerhaeuser Co.

12-2. A section of a house frame constructed of 2 x 4s made of fir.

by the do-it-yourselfer is fir plywood. Lumber used for fences and decks is usually cedar, redwood, or spruce. Flush doors used in the home may be faced with lauan mahogany. Doorsills and finish flooring are made of oak. Except for those limited uses, hardwoods are not usually found in the structure of a house.

Grades of Lumber

Lumber is graded by quality. The clearest and straightest lumber is graded the highest. The price of lumber also depends upon the grade. The use for the lumber depends upon its grade. Wood that has many defects (such as loose knots and splits) or is warped, is not suitable for use in house construction and is usually reserved for packaging heavy machinery and for making skids or pallets. Some of the common defects found in a piece of lumber are:

- Knots—the place where the branch of the tree was. Fig. 12-3.
- Splits or checks—cracks along the grain. Fig. 12-4.
- Pitch pockets—cavities that contain resin.
- Wane—bark on the edge of the board.
- Warp—a cup, bow, hook, or twist in the board. Fig. 12-5.

12-3. A knot in a piece of pine.

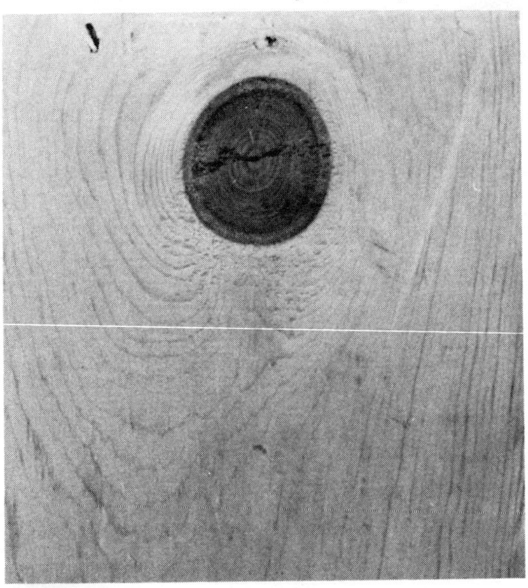

12-4. Splits in the end of a board.

Some of these defects are acceptable if they are not severe. Warped wood, however, is difficult to work with, and splits or checks in a board mean that the split section of the wood must be cut off as waste. Loose knots can fall out of the wood, but knots that are tight and stay in place do not affect the use of the wood.

The standard grading system used by lumberyards is divided into two separate sets of grades, one for softwoods and one for hardwoods. The softwood classifications, which are stamped on one face of the board, are as follows:

- A Select (clear).
- B Select.
- C Select.
- D Select (small defects).

- #1 Common—best in this classification but does contain some faults.
- #2 Common.
- #3 Common—Contains the most objectionable defects. Fig. 12-6.
- #4 Common } not available in lumberyards because
- #5 Common } of poor quality.

The hardwood classifications are as follows:

- Firsts and Seconds—FAS is stamped on the boards. This is the best grade of hardwood.
- Selects—These are a slightly lower grade and not as clear as FAS.
- #1, #2, and #3 Common—These are lesser grades with many objectionable defects. #1 is best in this category.

Before lumber is sold, some of the moisture in it must be removed. Lumber can be air dried or kiln dried. If the lumber has been air dried, about 12 to 18 percent of the moisture or sap remains in the wood. Lumber dried in a kiln or oven has 7 to 10 percent of the moisture remaining in it and usually has fewer defects. Most construction grade lumber is kiln dried.

Common Sizes of Lumber

After lumber has been cut into boards or beams at the lumber mill, it is surfaced (dressed) by a planing machine until it is smooth. Softwood is surfaced on four faces and edges and is therefore marked S4S (surfaced four sides) or D4S (dressed four sides). Hardwood is surfaced on four sides (S4S) or it comes rough and is marked RGH.

Some wood is lost in the surfacing. Therefore the actual piece of wood that you

12-5. A warped board.

12-6. A softwood classification stamped on the face of a board. This is #3 Common pine.

COMMON SIZES OF LUMBER

HARDWOOD THICKNESSES (inches)	
Rough	Surfaced
3/8	3/16
1/2	5/16
5/8	7/16
3/4	9/16
1	25/32
1 1/4	1 1/16
1 1/2	1 5/16
SOFTWOOD SIZES (inches)	
Rough	Surfaced
1 x 2	3/4 x 1 1/2
1 x 3	3/4 x 2 1/2
1 x 4	3/4 x 3 1/2
1 x 6	3/4 x 5 1/2
1 x 8	3/4 x 7 1/4
1 x 10	3/4 x 9 1/4
1 x 12	3/4 x 11 1/4
2 x 2	1 1/2 x 1 1/2
2 x 3	1 1/2 x 2 1/2
2 x 4	1 1/2 x 3 1/2
2 x 6	1 1/2 x 5 1/2
2 x 8	1 1/2 x 7 1/4
2 x 10	1 1/2 x 9 1/4

12-7a. Common sizes of hardwood and softwood lumber. Both nominal (rough) and surfaced (dressed) sizes are shown.

buy is not the size that was originally cut. A rough 2″ x 4″ beam (which is called a 2 by 4) actually measures 1 1/2″ x 3 1/2″ after it is surfaced.

The common sizes of lumber that would be useful to the do-it-yourselfer are listed in Fig. 12-7a.

METRIC LUMBER SIZES

No metric standards for lumber have yet been established in the United States. When they are, the new sizes will probably be very close to present sizes of lumber. A 2 x 4, for example, is actually 1 1/2″ x 3 1/2″. The exact metric equivalent of 1 1/2″ x 3 1/2″ is 38.1 mm x 88.9 mm. Since this would be an awkward size to work with, the metric replacement for a 2 x 4 will probably measure 40 x 90 millimeters. Fig. 12-7b lists common softwood lumber sizes and their possible metric replacements.

12-7b. This table shows the metric lumber sizes which may replace the present customary standards.

Reprinted from *Metrics in Career Education* by permission of author, John R. Lindbeck

SOFTWOOD LUMBER POSSIBLE METRIC REPLACEMENT SIZES

Nominal (inch)	Actual (inch)	Replacement (mm)
1 x 4	3/4 x 3 1/2	20 x 90
1 x 6	3/4 x 5 1/2	20 x 140
1 x 8	3/4 x 7 1/4	20 x 180
1 x 10	3/4 x 9 1/4	20 x 230
1 x 12	3/4 x 11 1/4	20 x 280
2 x 4	1 1/2 x 3 1/2	40 x 90
2 x 6	1 1/2 x 5 1/2	40 x 140
2 x 8	1 1/2 x 7 1/4	40 x 180
2 x 10	1 1/2 x 9 1/4	40 x 230
2 x 12	1 1/2 x 11 1/4	40 x 280

Sheet materials: 4′ x 8′ replaced by 1200 mm (47.24″ x 94.48″ or approximately 3/4″ narrower and 1 1/2″ shorter)
Metric lumber lengths in meters: 2, 2.4, 3, 3.5, 4, 5, 5.5 and 6

GRADES AND TYPES OF PLYWOOD, PARTICLE BOARD, AND HARDBOARD

Plywood

Plywood is made of layers of wood which are glued together. These layers are called *plies*. The grain of each layer runs at right angles to the grains of adjoining layers. The front and back faces always have their grains running in the same direction. Most plywood is made of Douglas fir, a softwood. There are two kinds of plywood: exterior plywood (made with waterproof glue) and interior plywood (for use inside where there is little moisture).

Plywood can be purchased in common thicknesses of 1/8″, 1/4″, 3/8″, 1/2″, 5/8″, and 3/4″. Plywood is usually sold in sheets measuring 4′ x 8′. You will also find half sheets (4′ x 4′) available at most lumberyards. *Note:* Standard 4′ x 8′ sheets will probably be replaced by 1200 x 2400 mm sheets in metric conversion.

Plywood sheets are graded by the quality of the face and back plies, or veneers. Plywood is made with either softwood or hardwood faces. Therefore there are two systems of grading. Softwood plywood (also known as construction and industrial plywood) is graded as follows:

- N is the best veneer and is used for natural finishes.
- A, B, C, and D grades are next. (D is the poorest.)

A sheet of plywood gets two letters as a grade, one for the back and one for the front. For example, a sheet can be marked A-D (the first letter is the face and the second letter is the back). This panel is good on one side, but the back has knots and other defects. Figs. 12-8, 12-9.

Hardwood plywood is graded somewhat the same way, but numbers are used instead of letters. The grades are 1, 2, 3, and 4. Number 1 has the clearest, most carefully matched grain. Numbers 3 and 4 have knots, patches, and other defects. With this grading system, a sheet of hardwood plywood marked 1-3 has a good front face with a patched, knotty back veneer.

The most commonly used plywood has a veneer core. This plywood is made of several plies glued together. Fig. 12-10. There is another type of plywood available called lumber core. Lumber-core plywood is used for cabinetwork and furniture. It consists of a core of solid wood with hardwood face and

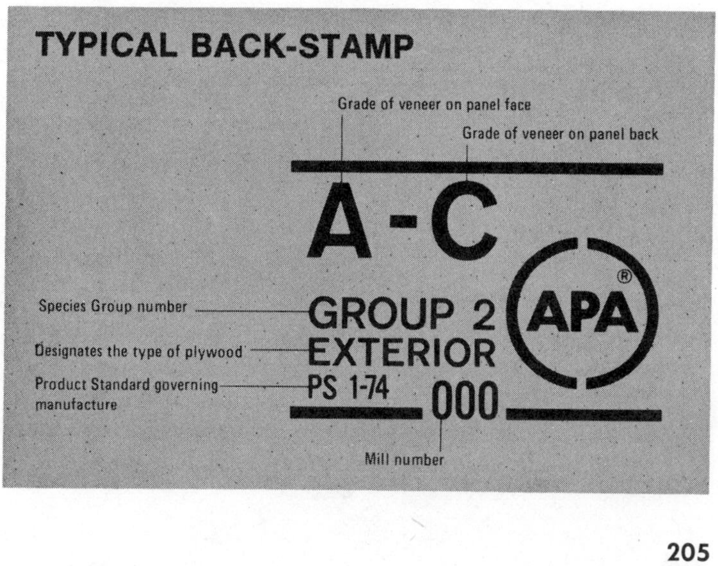

American Plywood Association

12-8. The meaning of the various symbols used in a typical back-stamp on a sheet of softwood plywood. The grades of veneer on the front and back are important to the do-it-yourselfer.

VENEER GRADES

A	Smooth and paintable. Neatly made repairs permissible. Also used for natural finish in less demanding applications.
B	Solid surface veneer. Circular repair plugs and tight knots permitted.
C	Knotholes to 1". Occasional knotholes 1/2" larger permitted providing total width of all knots and knotholes within a specified section does not exceed certain limits. Limited splits permitted. Minimum veneer permitted in Exterior-type plywood.
C Plgd	Improved C veneer with splits limited to 1/8" in width and knotholes and borer holes limited to 1/4" by 1/2".
D	Permits knots and knotholes to 2-1/2" in width and 1/2" larger under certain specified limits. Limited splits permitted.

American Plywood Association

12-9. An explanation of veneer grades A through D on softwood plywood.

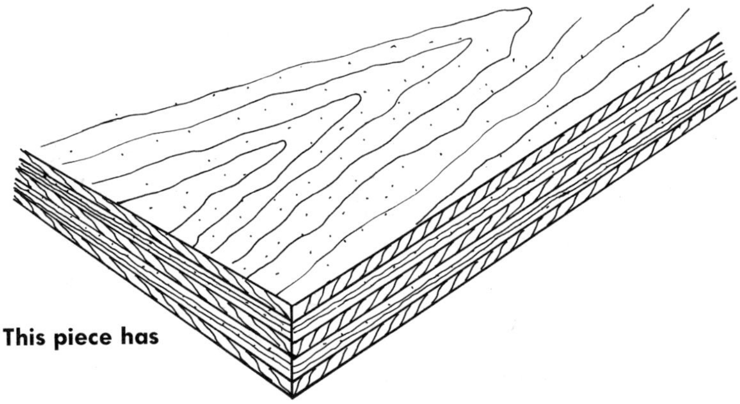

12-10. Veneer-core plywood. This piece has five plies.

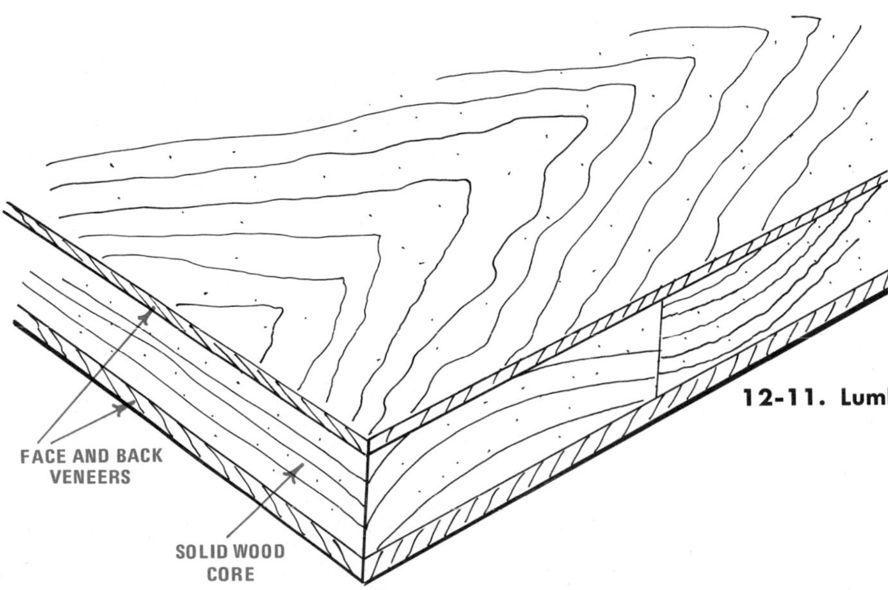

12-11. Lumber-core plywood.

12-12. A piece of particle board.

12-13. A piece of plastic laminate on particle board.

back veneers glued to it. Fig. 12-11. Particle board is also used as a solid core for some hardwood plywood. This is called chip-core plywood.

Particle Board

This wood product is made of wood chips and shavings which are bonded together with adhesives under pressure. Fig. 12-12. It is also called "chip board" and "flake board." It is available in sheets of various sizes with thicknesses from $\frac{1}{8}''$ to more than 1″. Particle board is used mainly as a base for plastic laminates in the making of counter tops, bathroom vanities, and kitchen cabinets. Fig. 12-13. It is also used as a base for hardwood veneers in the making of furniture.

Hardboard

Hardboard is made of wood fibers which are pressed together to form a dense sheet of material. The two types of hardboard are standard and tempered. Tempered hardboard is impregnated with oil and resins to form a harder, heavier, and water-resistant sheet. Hardboard sheets may be smooth on two sides or smooth on only one side. The sheets are 4 feet wide and come in standard lengths of 8, 10, 12, and 16 feet.

Hardboard is manufactured in many forms. It comes as pegboard (perforated), in filigree patterns, textured, and coated. It is made into wall paneling with embossed wood grains, painted surfaces, plastic coatings, or metallic speckles to create many attractive effects.

TYPES OF MOLDINGS AND THEIR USES

Moldings serve to cover joints or protect walls as well as to beautify parts of the home such as walls, doors, doorways, and windows. They are installed vertically or horizontally and are held in place with finishing nails or brads. Moldings may be made of pine or a hardwood (Fig. 12-14), or they may be made of plastic which is molded to resemble wooden molding. They are installed flat and are mitered at outside corners and either mitered or coped at inside corners. Two or more moldings can be combined, one over the other, to give a totally different appearance than any single piece of molding.

Certain moldings have special functions, and you should understand the uses of these moldings. Each of these moldings comes in several different styles. Some of these special moldings are as follows:

Western Wood Moulding and Millwork Producers

12-14. Wooden blanks being fed through a "molder" machine which carves them into their final shapes.

12-15. Casing is used around doors and windows. Here are four varieties of casing molding.

Western Wood Moulding and Millwork Producers

Western Wood Moulding and Millwork Producers

12-16. Stop molding is used to hold windows and doors in place. These are six of the shapes available.

• Baseboard—installed where the floor and walls meet.

• Casing—for door and window trim. Fig. 12-15.

• Stop—for door and window stops, to keep them in place. Fig. 12-16.

• Chair rail—as a railing on a wall to keep furniture from hitting the wall or as a decorative piece.

• Corner guard—used to cover outside corners on walls and over paneling.

• Round—used for clothes poles in closets. Fig. 12-17.

• Quarter-round—used in corners or where two surfaces meet. Fig. 12-17.

• Screen—used to trim wooden screen doors and window screens. Fig. 12-18.

• Cove—used to cover an inside corner where two surfaces meet, such as two walls or a wall and a ceiling. Fig. 12-19.

• Window stool—this is the inside window sill. It makes a tight joint with the bottom of the window.

Western Wood Moulding and Millwork Producers

12-17. Three types of round moldings, which come in many sizes. From left to right they are half-round, quarter-round, and full round.

Many types of moldings are available at lumberyards. They come in various colors to match the many prefinished panels available. Some moldings are covered with a colored vinyl and others are painted or stained.

Western Wood Moulding and Millwork Producers
12-18. These three types of screen molding may also be used where a thin molding is needed as a decoration.

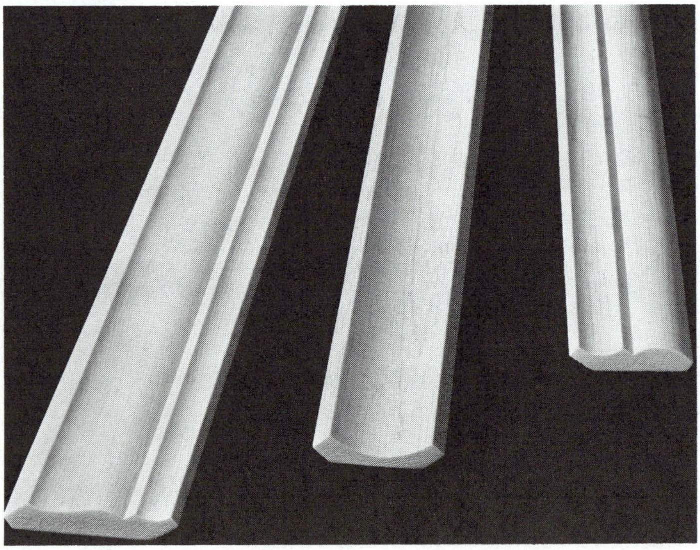

Western Wood Moulding and Millwork Producers
12-19. From left to right: crown molding, cove molding, and bed molding. They are used primarily for wall to ceiling joints.

CHECKUP

1. What is the difference between hardwood and softwood?
2. Under what conditions are defects in wood acceptable?
3. What are some common uses for particle board?

CHAPTER 13

Cement and Tile Work

RESETTING CERAMIC TILE

Ceramic tiles sometimes fall off the wall because the adhesive or cement holding them to the wall dries out. Ceramic tiles also crack easily because they are brittle. Any pressure or a sharp blow can cause them to crack, and these broken tiles must be replaced. It is often difficult to obtain tiles that match exactly. Colors in the ceramic glazes on tiles vary from one batch to another. If you cannot buy a tile that exactly matches or at least comes close in color to the existing tiles on the wall or floor, try a contrasting tile or decorative tile.

If the tile is loose or has fallen off the wall and is still in one piece, you can scrape off all the old adhesive and reglue the tile. Soak the old tile in a pail of water for an hour or two and then scrape off the adhesive with a putty knife. If the tile is cracked, however, and still adheres to the wall, it must be removed and a new tile put in its place. Replacing a tile is done this way:

1. Scrape the grout from around the tile or tiles that are to be replaced. Fig. 13-1. Use an old screwdriver or an old pointed can opener as a scraping tool.

2. Pry the cracked tile off the wall with a thin putty knife. If that does not work, use a cold chisel and a hammer to further crack and loosen the tile. Fig. 13-2. Then pry the pieces of tile off. Try not to damage the wall underneath.

13-1. Scrape the old grout from around the tile with a pointed can opener.

13-2. A cold chisel and a hammer can be used to crack and loosen a tile.

3. After the tile is removed, scrape off the remaining cement or tile adhesive from the wall. If necessary, repair the surface of the wall with spackling compound so that it is level with the rest of the wall. Allow the repairs to dry.

4. Spread the ceramic tile adhesive on the back of the new tile if you are just replacing one tile. If you are replacing several tiles next to each other, spread the tile cement on the wall. Use a notched trowel and spread the adhesive evenly. Fig. 13-3.

5. Place the new tiles firmly in position on the wall. Try not to slide them into the adhesive. Fig. 13-4. Leave an even spacing around the tiles for the grout. Fig. 13-5. Some tiles have little spacers on them. If you place them on the wall so that the spacers on two tiles touch, there will be an even grout area all around the tile.

If you have to cut straight lines on any of the tiles, use a ceramic tile cutter. Fig. 13-6. (These cutters can be rented. The person who rents it to you will show you how to use it). Score the glazed side of the tile with the cutter as you pull it over the tile and apply pressure. Then press down on the cutter handle to break the tile evenly. The tile cutter has a guide to help you make 90-degree cuts as well as 45-degree cuts. Practice using this tool on an old tile before you try cutting a good tile.

Irregular shapes are cut with a tile nipper (pliers-type cutter). Fig. 13-7. The desired shape is drawn on the tile with a pencil. The tile is then nibbled at with the cutter until the proper shape is obtained. Any rough edges can be filled with grout after the tile is on the wall.

Red Devil, Inc.

13-3. A notched trowel used to spread tile adhesive.

13-4. Place the new tiles firmly in position on the wall, being careful not to slide them into the adhesive.

13-5. Leave an even spacing around each tile for the grout.

6. After the tiles have set, you can grout them. The purpose of grouting is to fill in spaces between the tiles. Check the directions on the can of tile adhesive to find out whether you can grout immediately or have to wait a period of time. Grout can be purchased ready-mixed or in powdered form. The powdered tile grout is mixed with water to make a thick paste. Directions for mixing are given on the package. Use a disposable container, such as an aluminum foil pie plate, for the mixing so that you can throw the container away when you are finished.

7. You can use a rubber-covered grout float to apply the grout. Fig. 13-8. You could also press the grout into the spaces around the tiles with your fingers or a sponge. Wipe the grout on so that all the spaces are completely filled. Wipe off any excess with a damp sponge. Keep a pail of water nearby to rinse the sponge.

Let the grout dry for an hour and then wipe away the remaining film with a damp sponge and clear water. The next day, when the grout is completely dry, there may still be some film. Wipe this off with a damp sponge. Do not let that area of the tile wall or floor get wet for at least 24 hours.

13-6. A ceramic tile cutter.
Red Devil, Inc.

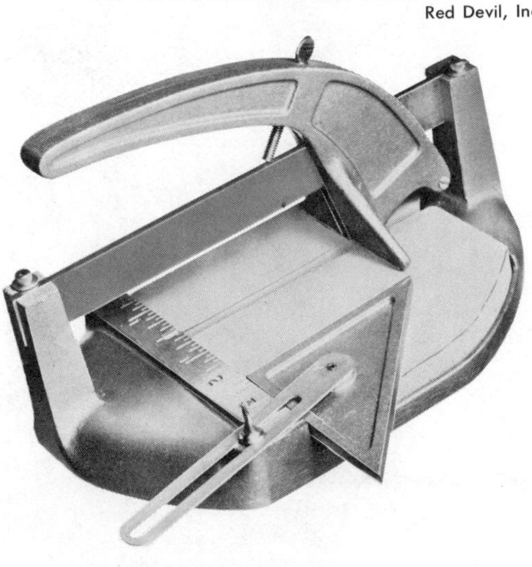

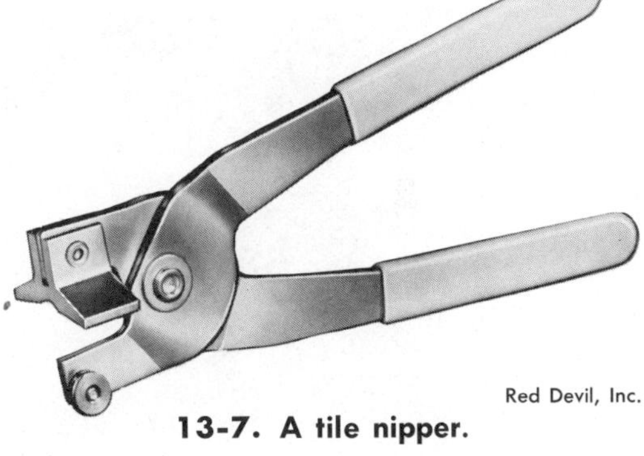

Red Devil, Inc.
13-7. A tile nipper.

13-8. A rubber-covered grout float.
Red Devil, Inc.

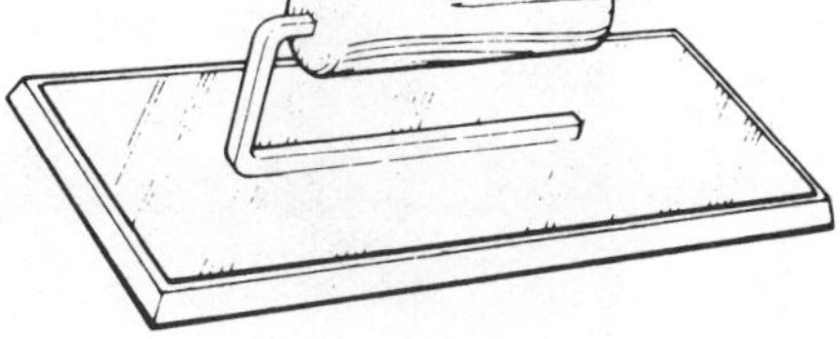

REGROUTING A CERAMIC TILE WALL

The grout between ceramic tiles often cracks or falls out of the spaces. Periodically the wall needs to be regrouted. Choose either ready-mixed or powdered tile grout in a color to match the existing grout. Most grout is either white or gray. You will also need the following:

- Disposable container for mixing the powdered grout.
- Sponge.
- Water pail.
- Old paint brush.
- Rubber-covered grout float (if you want to use one).
- Old pointed can opener to scrape out the old grout.

1. Scrape out all the loose grout with the pointed can opener. Brush or vacuum out all the old grout particles and dust. Fig. 13-9. Wet all the spaces to be regrouted with a sponge and some clear water. Fig. 13-10. This will prevent the existing grout and the edges of the tiles from absorbing water from the new grout too fast. Rapid absorption of water from new grout could cause it to crack as it dries.

2. If you are using powdered grout, mix up a batch of it to make a thick paste. Fig. 13-11. Apply the mixture to the spaces between the tiles with a grout float or a sponge. Fig. 13-12. Wipe away the excess grout with a damp sponge. Keep rinsing the sponge in a pail of water. As you are wiping off the excess grout, be careful not to remove the grout from the spaces between the tiles.

3. Let the grout dry for an hour and then wipe off the film of grout on the tiles with a sponge and clear water. Allow the grout to dry overnight. Wipe off any slight film of grout that remains with a damp sponge and clear water.

13-9. You can use an old paint brush to sweep out grout particles and dust.

13-10. Moisten all the spaces to be regrouted with a wet sponge.

13-11. Pour the powdered grout into a disposable container and add water to make a thick paste.

13-12. Apply the grout to the spaces between the tiles.

—CAULKING AROUND A BATHTUB OR SHOWER—

The rigid grout mentioned in the previous section sometimes cracks and falls out of the space where ceramic tiles meet a bathtub or shower base. The main reason it cracks is that the tub or shower base shifts slightly due to the weight of gallons of water (in a tub) and the person in the tub or shower. The rigid grout should be replaced with flexible caulking or grout (also called tub caulking). This is a silicon rubber or latex compound which cures (dries) and yet always remains flexible.

The procedure for regrouting around a bathtub or shower base is as follows:

1. Scrape out all the old grout along the shower base or bathtub. Use an old screwdriver or a pointed can opener to scrape all the cracked grout out of the space. Clean all the dust and chips of grout out of the area with an old paint brush, or vacuum them out. Make sure that the crevice to be filled is clean and dry before you fill it with caulking.

2. Tub caulking comes in tubes. It is made in white and various colors to correspond to bathtub or tile colors. Read the instructions on the tube before using the caulking. The instructions will tell you how fast the material will set and how soon it is safe to get it wet. Some tubes have a nozzle that screws on. The tip of the nozzle is cut off at an angle with a sharp knife. Fig. 13-13.

3. Put the tip of the nozzle against the space you are trying to fill. Squeeze the tube slowly so that an even, smooth bead of caulking fills the crevice and forms a tight

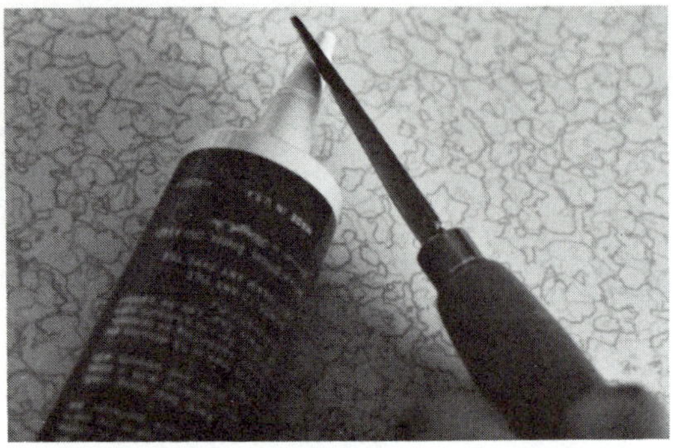

13-13. The tip of the nozzle is cut off at an angle.

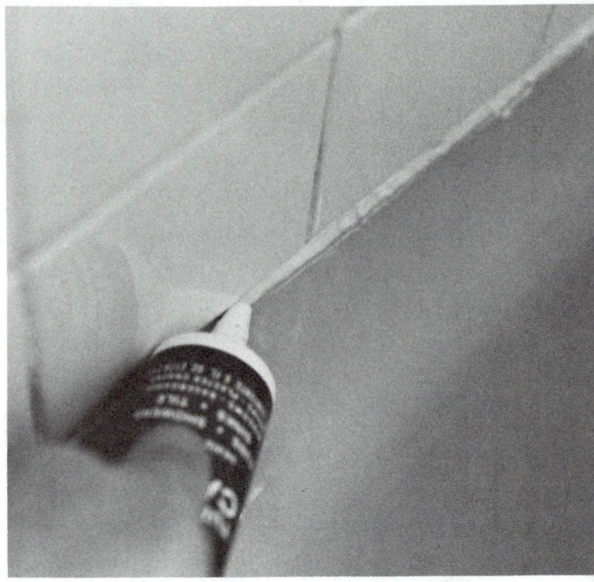

13-14. Squeeze the tube slowly so that an even, smooth bead of tub caulking fills the crevice.

seal between the tub and the bottom of the ceramic tile. Fig. 13-14. Clean off any excess caulking immediately with a wet cloth. Fig. 13-15. Allow the caulking to set for the proper length of time before getting it wet.

—REPAIRING CRACKS AND HOLES IN CONCRETE—

You can repair holes and cracks in basement walls and floors, sidewalks, patios, and steps using only a few tools. Making these repairs requires only small amounts of cement which are mixed by hand rather than with a cement mixer.

For small repairs, prepared patching cement mixes in either dry or liquid form can be used. There are three types of special patching cements: latex cement (mixed with its own liquid), vinyl cement (the powder is mixed with water), and epoxy cement (the hardener is mixed with the emulsion). These patching cements are prepared for use by following the manufacturer's directions.

Cement mixes can be purchased by the bag under various brand names. If a large amount of cement is needed, however, these prepared mixes are not economical. It is less expensive to buy the ingredients, such as portland cement and sand, and mix them yourself.

Mixing Cement

To mix your own cement for patching cracks and holes, you will need a square-point shovel, a pail, a hoe, and either a wooden platform or a mixing tub (metal or plastic). Fig. 13-16. You could use a wheelbarrow instead of a tub in which to do the mixing. A good mixture for patching is one unit of sand to three units of portland cement. Mix the cement as follows:

1. Put the sand on the mixing platform or tub. Spread the portland cement over the sand. Use a pail to measure the ingredients. For example, if you use one pail of sand, then you would add three pails of cement to it.

To mix these two dry ingredients evenly, turn them over with the shovel until there are no gray streaks of cement showing.

2. Form a mound of the dry mixture as shown in Fig. 13-17. Use a hose or the pail to add a little cold water at a time to the

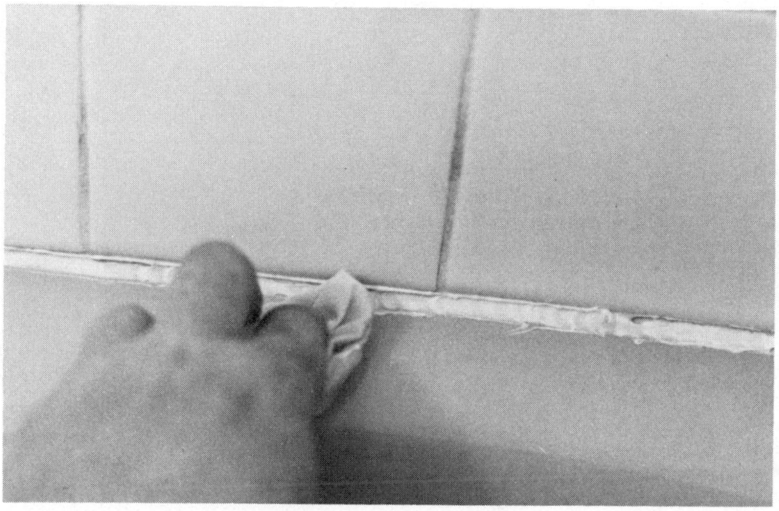

13-15. Wipe off any excess caulking immediately with a damp cloth.

center of the mound. Turn in the edges of the mound toward the center with the shovel or the hoe. When the water is mixed into the dry ingredients, reform the mound with the hollow in the middle. Add a little more water and mix again. Repeat until there are no dry parts and the mixture is fairly stiff. Fig. 13-18. Shovel the mix from the bottom of the mound over itself. The cement must be used within half an hour after it is mixed.

Filling Small Cracks and Holes

You will need the following tools for this repair:

- Whisk broom or old paint brush.
- Cold chisel.
- Hammer.
- Trowel. Figs. 13-19, 13-20.
- Hose.
- Tamp (a tool to press down the cement). Fig. 13-21.

These are the steps in making the repair:

1. Clean out the cracks with a cold chisel and a hammer. Fig. 13-22. The cracks should be about 1″ deep and wider on the inside than on the outside. Fig. 13-23. This shape holds the cement in place. Use a

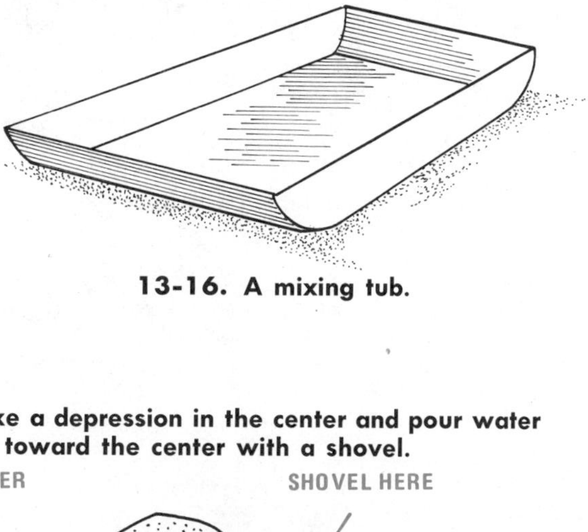

13-16. A mixing tub.

13-17. Form a mound of the dry ingredients. Make a depression in the center and pour water into it. Turn in the edges of the mound toward the center with a shovel.

13-18. Mixing cement on a wooden platform with a square-point shovel.

Red Devil, Inc.

13-19. A pointed trowel.

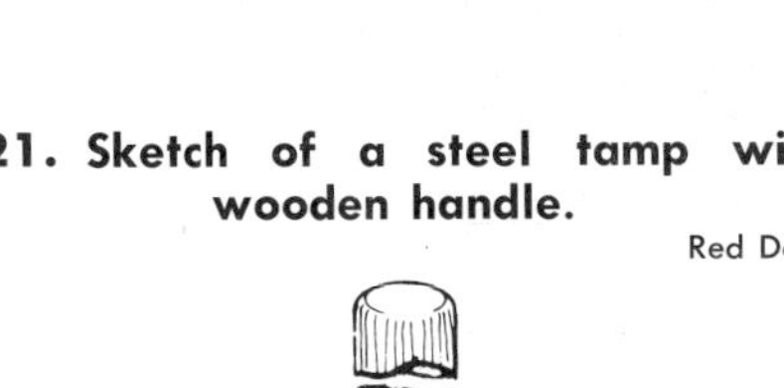

Red Devil, Inc.

13-20. A cement finishing trowel.

13-21. Sketch of a steel tamp with a wooden handle.

Red Devil, Inc.

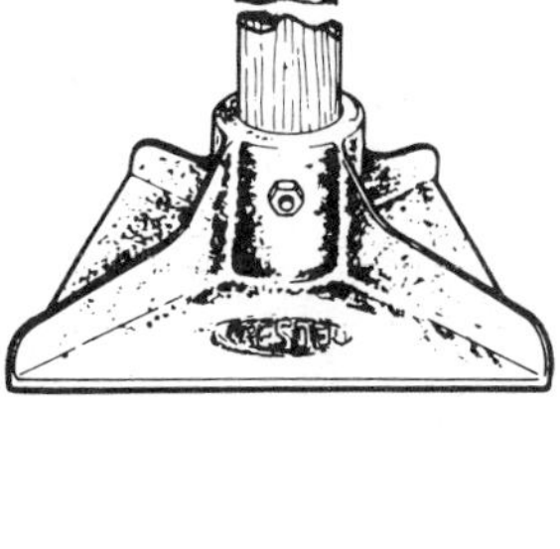

13-22. Use a cold chisel and a hammer to clean out the cracks.

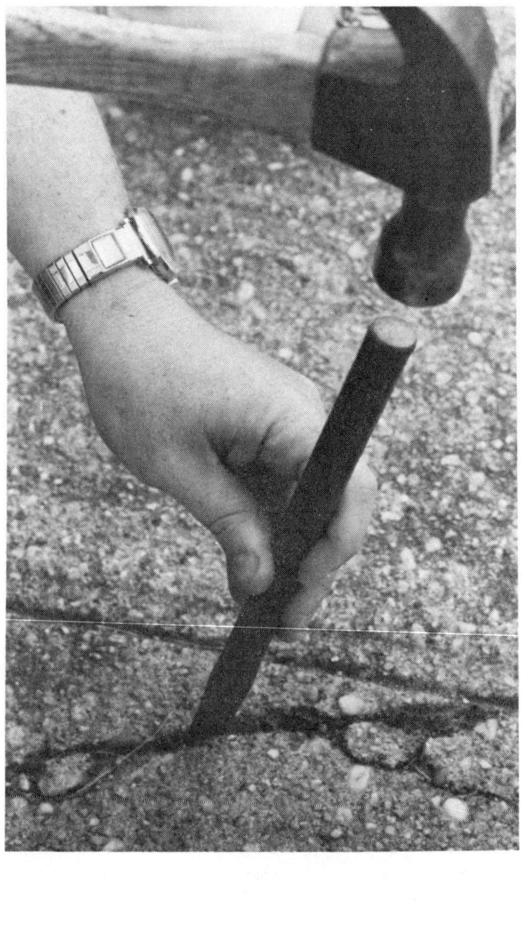

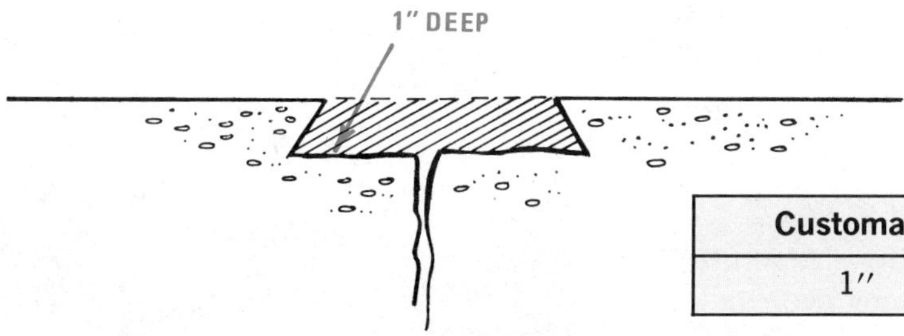

Customary	Metric
1″	25 mm

13-23. The cracks should be made wider on the inside than on the outside.

whisk broom or an old paint brush to clean out all the cement chips and dust from the area.

2. Wet the area with a hose before filling with cement. Be sure to wet the edges of the old concrete too. Fill the area with fresh cement (one part sand to three parts portland cement). Force it into the crack or the hole with either a steel tamp or a wooden tamp that you can make yourself. Fig. 13-24. If the opening is too small for a tamp, use a trowel to push the cement in tightly. Fill the area with cement so that it is slightly above surface level. It will shrink a little when it dries.

3. Two or three hours later, level the surface with a trowel. You can use a broom to give the surface a roughened finish or you can use the trowel to make a smooth finish. Fig. 13-25. The rough surface is safer for areas that are to be walked on.

4. The repaired area will take three or four days to cure. Each day spray the area lightly with a hose. This will keep it from drying out too quickly. Sprinkling is particularly important if the weather is hot. An alternative is to cover the area with wet burlap sacking for three days.

5. After you finish the work, thoroughly clean off all tools with water. Be sure to clean off the mixing platform or the tub that you used.

Repairing Large Cracks and Holes

The procedure for repairing large cracks and holes is similar to that discussed in the previous section. However, there is a pre-

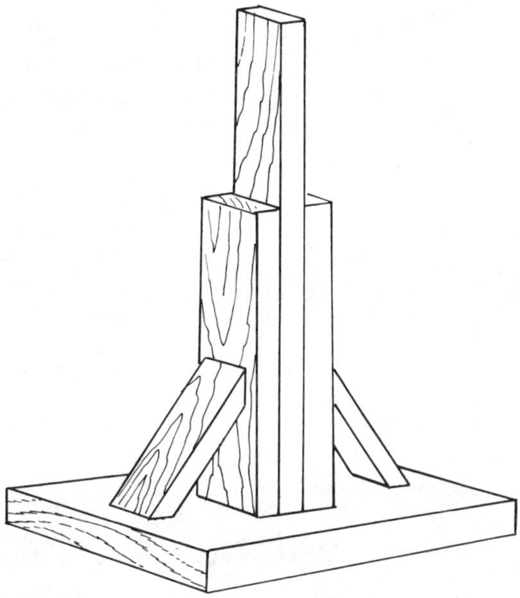

13-24. A wooden tamp that you can construct.

13-25. Use a trowel to make a smooth finish.

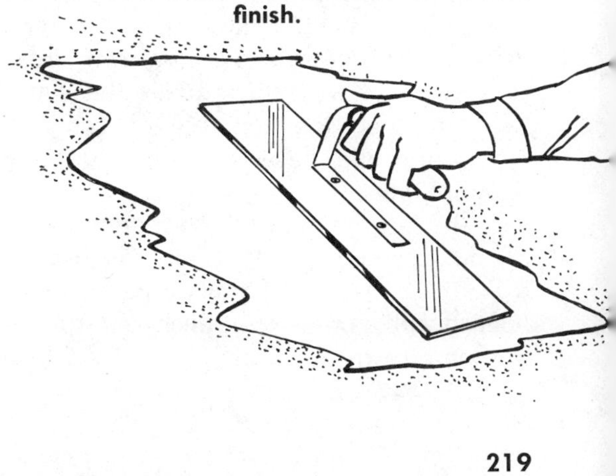

13-26. The patching mixture is packed into the cavity with a pointed trowel.

liminary step in fixing a large area. A grout or bonding agent is spread thinly over the existing concrete. This grout is made of portland cement and water and has the consistency of heavy cream. No sand is used in the mixture.

Moisten the existing concrete with a hose or with a brush dipped in water. Spread the grout on the concrete where it will touch the new cement. Then pack the patching mixture of sand and portland cement into the cavity with a trowel. Fig. 13-26. Tamp the cement down firmly right over the moist grout. The remainder of the repair procedure is the same as for small cracks and holes. Remember, the area takes three or four days to cure and must be kept damp during that time. Be sure to clean off all your tools with water as soon as you finish working with them.

WATERPROOFING BASEMENT WALLS

Leaks and wet spots on basement walls have two causes. The first is a crack or cracks in the foundation wall when the house settles. The second cause is gutters and leaders that may be blocked and do not carry water away from the house. There may be no splash blocks or runoffs to keep the rainwater and melted snow away from the basement walls. Eventually the water soaks through the concrete or concrete block, and the basement walls become damp or wet.

There are commercially made waterproofing compounds that you can use on the outside basement walls. They may be applied with a brush or a roller. Waterproofing compounds are made with polyvinyl acetate or silicone resin which seals the concrete.

Before any waterproofing compounds can be applied to the walls, all cracks must be repaired as described earlier. Be sure to use the grout mixture first and then a mixture of one part portland cement to two parts mortar sand. Any cracks below ground level must be dug out first. Pack the mixture in well because this repair has to withstand a great deal of pressure from water and soil on the outside of the foundation. The mixture should be very stiff to keep it from falling out of the cavity in the wall as you tamp it in. Allow the cement to harden for three or four days before you re-cover the area with soil.

PATCHING STUCCO

Stucco is a special cement mixture spread on the outside of a wooden frame house or over a concrete block wall. It usually contains portland cement, sand, and lime. It has a textured surface which can be painted. Repairing stucco applied over a wooden frame involves putting on three coats of cement. The procedure for this repair is as follows:

1. Break off the loose pieces of stucco. Repair the roofing paper underneath the stucco. Roofing cement can be used to fix small holes, or a new piece of roofing paper can be put over the damaged area if there are large holes.

2. Wire lath is put over the wooden frame to hold the stucco onto the house. If you find the wire lath torn when you remove the broken stucco, you must patch it. Interlace wire into the lath to form a patch or to hold a torn piece in position. Fig. 13-27.

3. Wet the edges of the area to be repaired. The first coat is made up of one part portland cement to three parts coarse sand. Make a stiff mixture so that it will stay on the wall. Apply the first coat of patching stucco with a trowel to within $1/4''$ of the surface level of the wall. When this first coat starts to set, scratch it with a nail to make it rough (give it tooth) so that the next coat will adhere to it. Keep it damp for three days until it cures.

4. The second coat is applied with a trowel to within $1/16''$ of the wall surface. Leave this coat smooth. Keep it damp for two or three days until it hardens. The cement for this coat is made up of one part portland cement to three parts coarse sand, just as the first coat was.

5. The cement for the third coat (finish coat) has the following ingredients: three parts sand, one-quarter part lime, and one part portland cement. This coat is troweled level with the outside wall. Level it with a straightedge, such as a piece of wood. After the stucco is leveled off, you can give the surface a texture in one of the following ways. A sandy finish is achieved by troweling the surface with a wooden float at the time that the stucco begins to set. Figs. 13-28, 13-29. A rough texture can be achieved by scrubbing the cement when it is nearly set, with an old brush or broom. Keep the cement damp and allow it to cure for three days.

The procedure for repairing stucco that has been applied over concrete block is

13-27. Torn wire lath. Patch the wire lath by interlacing wire through it over the hole. This must be done to hold the new stucco in place.

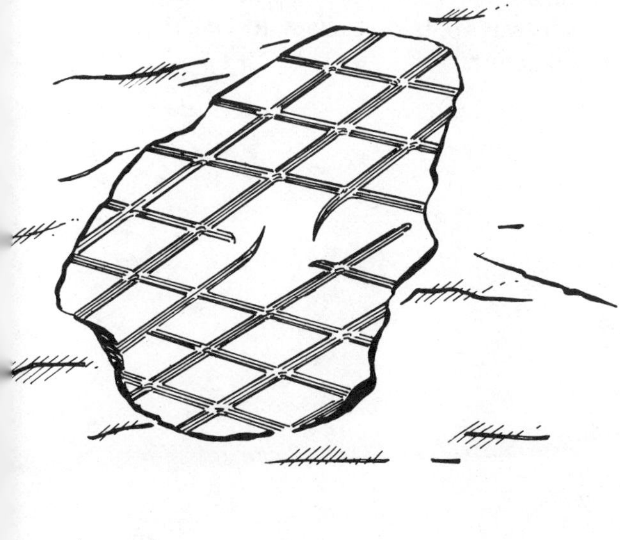

13-28. A wooden float.

Red Devil, Inc.

13-29. Troweling the surface with a wooden float when the cement begins to set produces a sandy finish.

13-30. Stucco applied over a concrete block foundation wall.

similar. Fig. 13-30. There is no roofing paper or wire lath to be concerned with. The stucco is applied directly to the block. Before applying the first coat of cement, wet the existing stucco and the concrete blocks with a hose. Trowel the first coat right on the concrete blocks. The other two coats are applied as previously discussed.

CHECKUP

1. Why is flexible grout better than rigid grout for caulking the area where ceramic tiles meet a bathtub or shower base?
2. When is it more economical to mix cement yourself rather than to buy a prepared mix?
3.. What causes leaks and wet spots on basement walls? How can this condition be remedied?

CHAPTER 14

Basic Electrical Repairs

You can do many basic electrical repairs at home without professional help. These repairs involve the visible parts of the electrical system, such as the switches, the outlets, electrical cords, plugs, and light fixtures. You can also change fuses or reset circuit breakers if a branch circuit becomes overloaded. Materials for any of these repairs can be bought at most hardware stores or electrical supply houses. The following basic home repair tools are all that are needed for most repairs:

- Pair of long-nose pliers with a cutter. Fig. 14-1.
- Standard tip screwdriver.
- Screwdriver with a cabinet tip.

A pair of lineman's pliers with a cutter and a wire stripper would also be helpful in making these repairs. Figs. 14-2, 14-3.

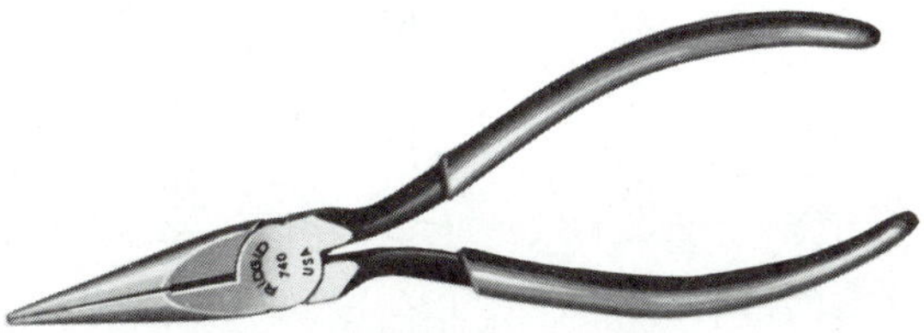

Ridge Tool Company

14-1. Long-nose pliers with a cutter.

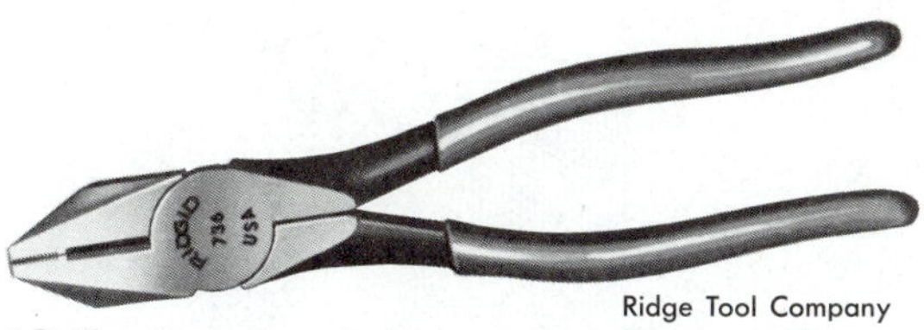

Ridge Tool Company

14-2. A pair of lineman's pliers with a cutter.

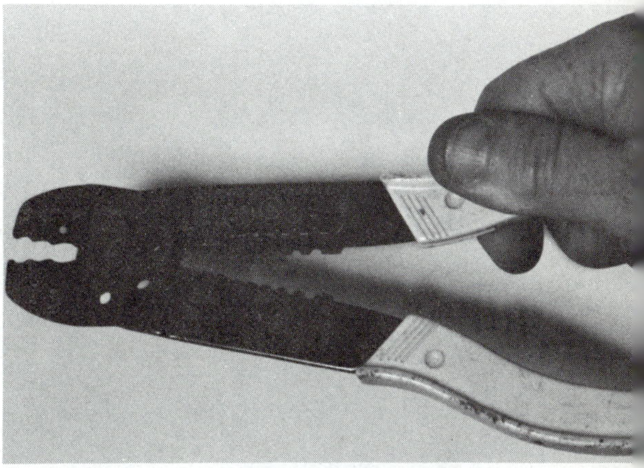

14-3. One type of wire stripper.

HOW ELECTRICITY COMES INTO YOUR HOME

In order to work safely with the electricity in your home, you should understand some basic facts about a house wiring system. The following is a simplified explanation of the path that electricity takes to enter a house and travel to the various switches, receptacles, and appliances within the house.

14-4. The power cable runs down to the meter socket, which contains the electric meter.

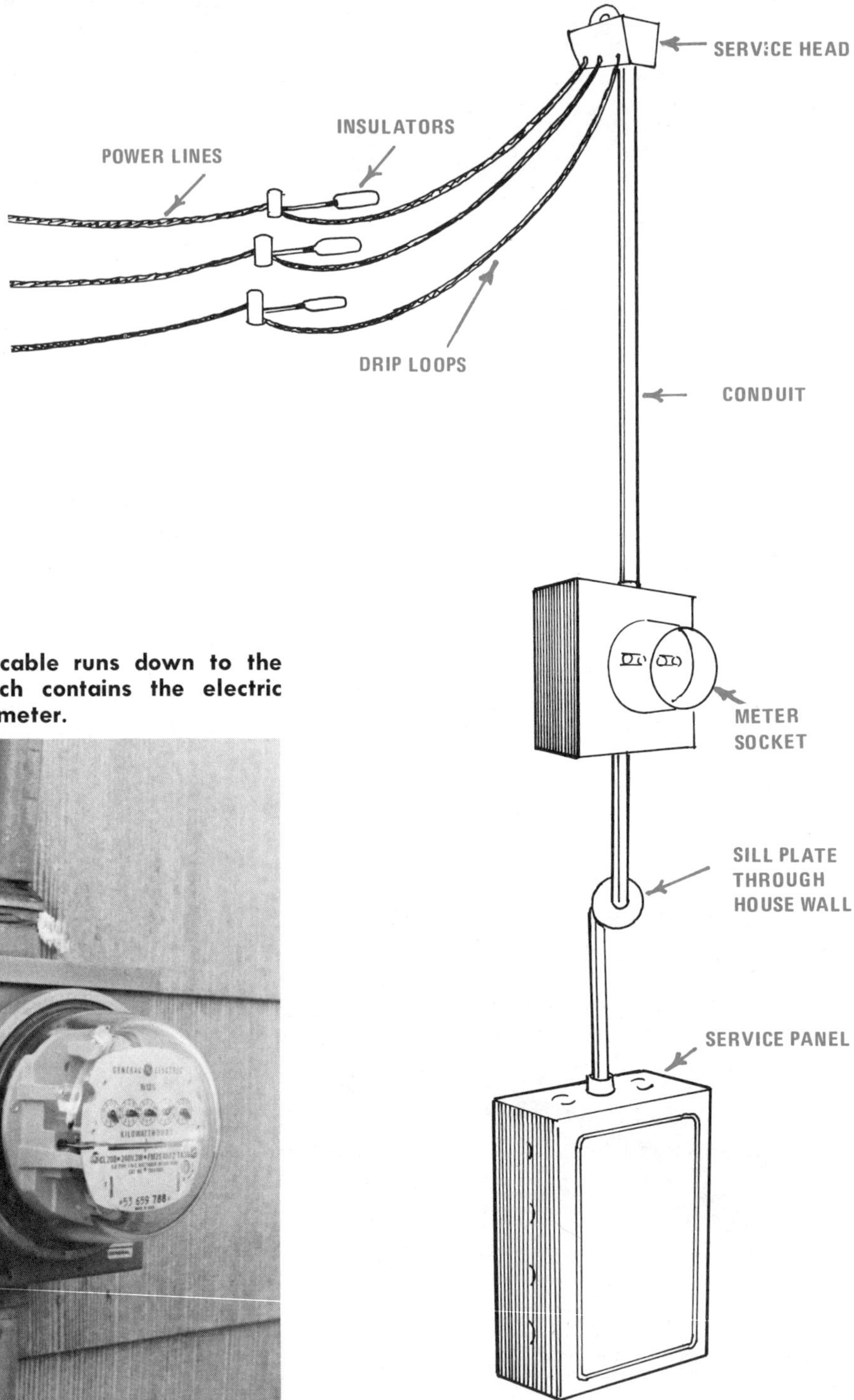

14-5. How electricity comes into your home.

Electricity enters the house through power lines from nearby utility poles. (In some localities the wiring is underground.) The overhead power lines are attached to the outside of the house at the service head (connection where cables meet house). The lines run down to the meter socket (a metal box with the electric meter in it). Fig. 14-4. On newer homes the meter socket is installed outside. Older homes have the meter socket indoors. The lines run through the meter socket into a service panel. The service panel is either a circuit breaker or fuse box. (Fig. 14-5.)

The electrical cable running down the side of the house is protected from mechanical damage by a piece of heavy conduit (pipe) which surrounds the cable and is 10 or 12 feet long. Fig. 14-6. The voltage (or force) of electricity let into the house is 220. The electrical lines are split so that one 110-volt line goes to each side of the fuse panel or the circuit breaker panel. Figs. 14-7, 14-8.

14-6. The electric cable running down the side of the house is protected by heavy conduit (pipe). The cable enters the house through a waterproof connection called a sill plate.

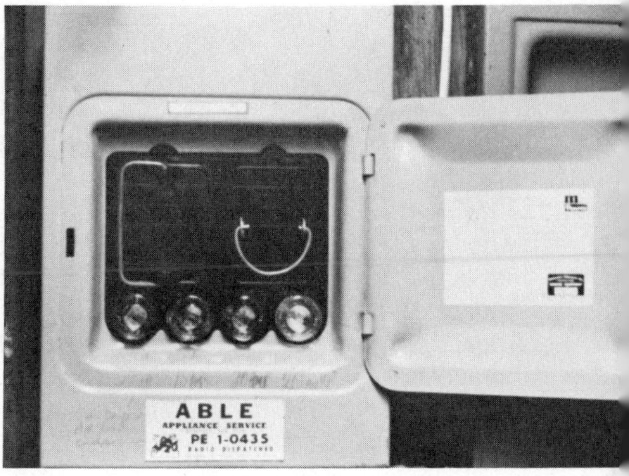

14-7. A fuse box.

14-8. A circuit breaker panel with push-type switches. Note the directory inside the door. It will be used to list the rooms or appliances that are on each circuit.

Oklahoma Industrial Arts News Photograph by Emmett Osgood

ELECTRICAL DEVICES WITHIN THE HOUSE

Fuses or circuit breakers are safety devices which prevent the overloading of a particular circuit. Sometimes there are too many appliances or there is a defective appliance on a circuit. The wires carrying the electricity would become overheated and possibly start a fire if there were no fuse or breaker guarding that line. For example, when the limit of 15 or 20 amperes (amperes are the amount of flow of electricity) is reached on a circuit, the 15- or 20-ampere fuse burns out or the circuit breaker switches off. This shuts off the current in that line. A fuse must be replaced. A circuit breaker can be turned on again after the amperage is reduced by turning off some of the appliances or removing and repairing a faulty appliance that is causing a short circuit.

14-9. Outlet receptacles and switches are housed in metal boxes attached to 2 x 4s within the wall.

The electricity runs from the service panel (fuse box or circuit breaker box) to the various outlets and switches in the house through electrical cable. The cable is run through the ceiling or floor beams and then out between the wall studding (2 x 4s) to the outlet or switch. Each outlet receptacle or switch is housed in a metal outlet box attached to a nearby 2 x 4. Fig. 14-9. All you see is the cover plate on the outside of the box. All connections are made within the metal box. Connections between two or more pieces of cable are made within the walls in a metal junction box with a cover plate on it. Fig. 14-10. This prevents mechanical damage to the wires. Outlet boxes and junction boxes are made in different sizes and shapes to suit any type of house wiring situation. Fig. 14-11.

The type of cable used in wiring a particular house depends upon the local laws governing electrical installations (the electrical code). Some electrical cable, called BX cable, is covered with an armored shield. Fig. 14-12. Another type is non-metallic shielded. Its cover is heavy plastic, and it is waterproof. One variety of this cable can be used for underground wiring or in damp places. Another type of non-metallic shielded cable is suitable for indoor wiring. It is commonly referred to as Romex cable. Conduit is another type of metal covering for electrical wiring. It is a metal tube which may be flexible or rigid. There are three varieties of conduit: thin-wall (rigid), thick-wall (rigid), and Greenfield (a flexible con-

14-10. Any electrical connections between two or more pieces of cable are made within the walls in a metal junction box that has a cover plate. This is BX cable (armor shielded) connected inside a square junction box.

14-11. An octagonal junction box without the cover plate. This is non-metallic shielded cable (Romex) connected with solderless connectors.

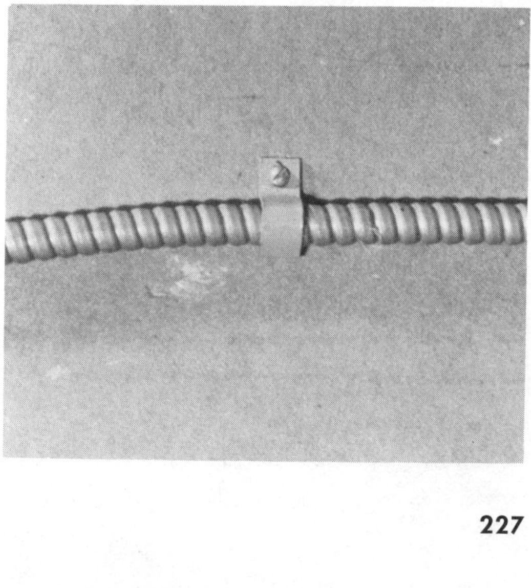

14-12. BX cable held in place on a wall with a strap.

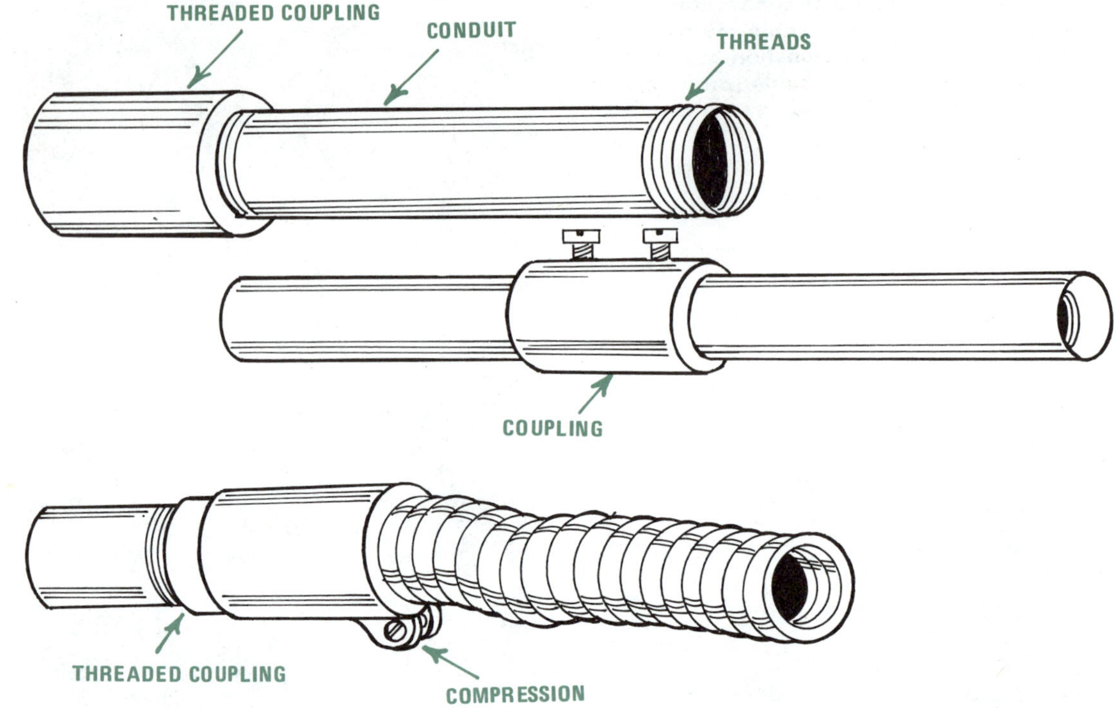

14-13. The three types of conduit (top to bottom): thick-wall conduit with a threaded coupling device, thin-wall conduit, and Greenfield (or flexible) conduit shown with a device that connects it to thick-wall conduit.

duit). Fig. 14-13. Wires are pulled through the conduit after it is fastened in place.

A piece of electrical cable used in a 110-volt circuit has two or three wires. One wire is the live wire, one is the neutral wire, and the third is the ground wire. The black wire is live; the white wire is neutral. In three-wire cable the third, colored wire is the ground wire. In cable that is two-wire with ground, the ground wire is a bare copper wire. These wires are connected to other wires in an outlet box or a switch box with plastic electrical tape or solderless connectors (wire nuts). The wires may also be connected to the terminal screws on a switch or an outlet receptacle.

ELECTRICAL WIRING REGULATIONS

To insure that electrical wiring is done properly in homes and industrial buildings throughout the country, the National Board of Fire Underwriters publishes a detailed book of electrical specifications called the *National Electrical Code.* This code describes the materials and methods of installation for all types of wiring. Each locality usually has a code of its own that is based on the *National Electrical Code.* A large city or a county may have its own code, while a small town may use the NEC directly. Each locality also has electrical inspectors who check new wiring jobs in any building.

In addition, many localities allow only licensed electricians to do new house wiring. The locality in which they work licenses the electricians after they take a qualifying exam. In some places homeowners can do their own new wiring if the work meets the standards of the electrical code. An electrical inspector checks all the wiring and makes recommendations for changes so that the jobs will meet the standards set by the local code.

SAFETY IN WORKING WITH ELECTRICITY

One of the most common causes of fires in the home is electricity. Electrical devices in poor condition and faulty wiring are the major causes of electrical fires. Electricity is a form of energy which is dangerous and must be handled with care.

If you are to keep electrical equipment in good working order, you must use the right materials for repairs. Always replace switches and receptacles with like materials. You should not improvise with inferior materials or with wire which is not the proper thickness (gauge) for the electrical load it must carry.

When working with electricity, remember that water on the floor can create a shock hazard. Do not touch appliances with wet hands or stand on a damp surface when using electrical equipment. Doing so will ground you. That is, it will complete an electrical circuit so that the electricity flows through you instead of the wiring.

Do not do electrical work while standing on a metal ladder. This also creates a shock hazard. Your tools for electrical work should be equipped with insulated handles. Screwdrivers and pliers should have plastic or rubber handles. You may find it useful to buy a small test light or a neon tester so that you can check an outlet or switch to determine if it is live (has current going to it) before starting to work on it. Fig. 14-14.

On all electrical repair jobs remember to remove the fuse or turn off the circuit breaker that controls the current to that piece of equipment before starting repairs. If you cannot find the correct fuse or breaker, turn off the main fuse or circuit breaker to completely shut off power to the entire house.

14-14. A test light (left) and a neon tester (right) for testing an outlet or a switch to determine if it is live.

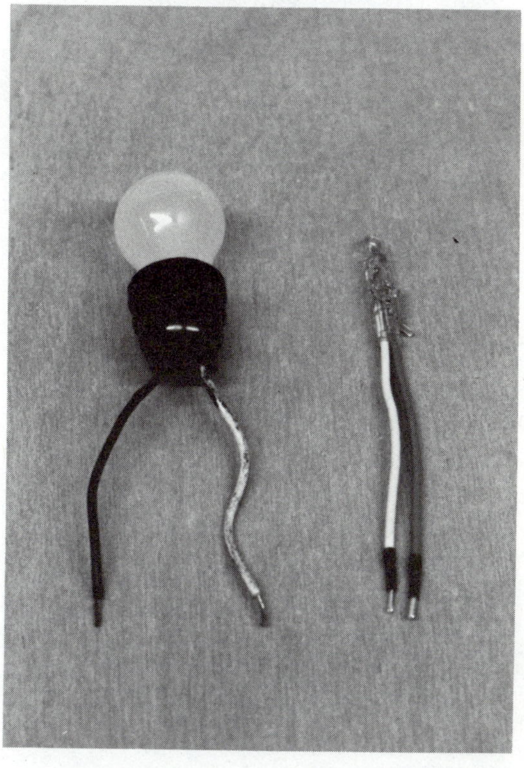

REPLACING A PLUG FUSE

Whenever there are too many appliances on one branch circuit in your home or one of the electrical devices is causing a short circuit (a path of low resistance across an electric circuit), the fuse for that circuit will blow out. As a result, the electricity to all those appliances will stop. The fuse must be replaced to restore electrical service. It is a good idea to keep a supply of spare plug fuses of the correct type and size near the fuse box so that they can be found easily when they are needed. Fig. 14-15. Replacing a blown fuse is done as follows:

1. Go to the fuse box with a flashlight so that you can see what you are doing. Look at all the plug fuses to see which one is blown out. The burned-out metal strip will be visible through the window in the fuse. Fig. 14-16. It will be easier to know which fuse is out if you have a chart on the fuse box door listing each fuse and the appliances and lights it controls. The lights or appliances that do not operate in the house will guide you to the fuse needing replacement.

2. When you have located the troublesome fuse, turn off the main power supply. On some service panels this is done by throwing a switch on the box. Fig. 14-17. On other panels the main fuse or fuses (cartridge fuses) are contained in blocks which must be pulled out of the panel box by their handles. Figs. 14-18, 14-19. This will turn off all the power in the house. Now it is safe to remove the faulty fuse.

3. Now that you have turned off all the electricity in the house, you will probably need the flashlight to help you see. Unscrew the burned-out fuse and remove it from the box. To replace it now without finding out what caused it to fail will result in the same fuse blowing again.

4. Trace along the circuit to see where the faulty electrical device is. This is done by putting the power back on again. Go through the house to see what equipment does not work without the fuse. Check the plug on each item for a blackened or burned surface. A short-circuited appliance will flash when plugged in, causing a blackened surface.

Try to remember what was turned on just before the fuse blew out. If necessary, unplug everything controlled by that fuse, replace the fuse, and turn the power back on. One by one, plug in each piece of equipment until the fuse blows. The last item plugged in is the one that is overloading the circuit or has a short circuit in it. This method will cost you another fuse, but it will help you to locate the troublesome appliance. After the appliance at fault has been found, plug it into another electrical circuit.

14-15. One type of plug fuse.
General Electric Company

14-16. The windows in plug fuses let you see whether the fuse is good (a) or blown (b).

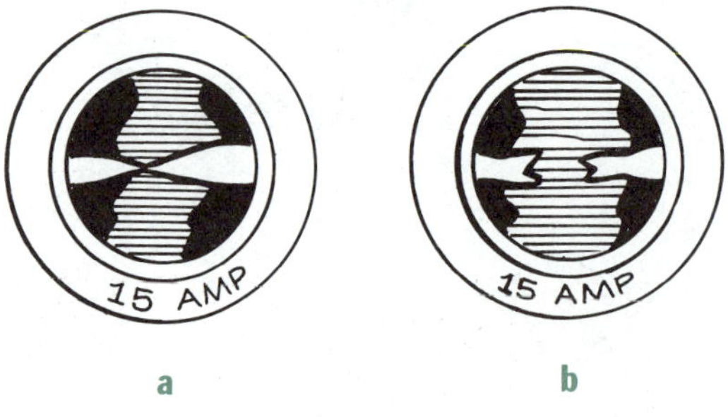

If it has a short circuit, however, it will have to be repaired by a professional.

5. Turn off the power and install the new fuse. Be sure the new fuse is the same size and type as the old fuse. At no time should other objects (such as pennies) be placed in the fuse socket behind the fuse, even temporarily. Doing so will cause the wires to become overloaded, and excess heat will be produced. A fire could result. Turn on the power again after you have replaced the fuse. Be sure to buy more fuses of that size so that you always have a supply on hand.

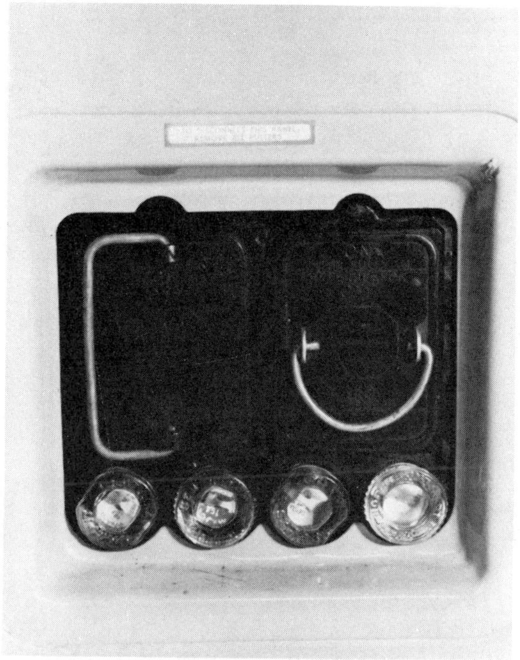

14-18. A fuse box with the main fuses contained in blocks above the fuse panel.

14-17. A fuse box where the main power supply is turned off by throwing the switch on the box.

14-19. One of the main fuse blocks has been removed from the box. It contains two cartridge fuses. To shut off all power to the house, the other block must also be removed.

RESETTING A CIRCUIT BREAKER

There are several types of circuit breakers found in private homes. Some breakers are reset by throwing the breaker switch from the "off" position to the "on" position. Others have a push-button arrangement which automatically shows an "on" or an "off" signal.

It is not necessary to turn off all the power to reset a breaker. When a breaker goes off, it is a good idea to trace the source of trouble as explained in the section on fuses. Otherwise the circuit breaker will continue to shut off. After you have found out which appliance caused the breaker to cut off, plug it into another circuit. If you spot any indication of a short circuit, have the item repaired before you plug it in again.

REPLACING AN OUTLET RECEPTACLE OR A SWITCH

The outlet receptacles and switches in a house are constantly being used, and they wear out after a time. Neither of these electrical devices can be repaired; so they have to be replaced. A wall receptacle must be replaced with the same type. For example, a two-wire outlet receptacle must be replaced with another two-wire outlet receptacle. You cannot use a three-wire outlet receptacle (grounded) in place of a two-wire one. Fig. 14-20. Several varieties of switches can be used to replace any broken wall switch. Some of these are single-pole switches, mercury switches, quiet switches, dimmers, and push-button switches. Fig. 14-21.

Replacing an Outlet Receptacle

Obtain a replacement 110-volt outlet receptacle of the same type as the existing one. You need a screwdriver and a pair of long-nose pliers to complete the repair. The steps are as follows:

1. Turn off the current. Either remove the fuse that controls the circuit for that outlet or turn off all the current in the house. The outlet can be tested to see whether it is live with a neon tester or a test light. To use a tester, put one of the test leads in each opening of either the upper or lower section of the receptacle. The bulb will light if the outlet has current going to it. Fig. 14-22.

If you can get a plug to work in the outlet, there is another way to test it. Plug in a lamp and turn it on. Have someone watch the lamp while you go to turn off the break-

14-20. A three-wire outlet receptacle (grounded).
General Electric Company

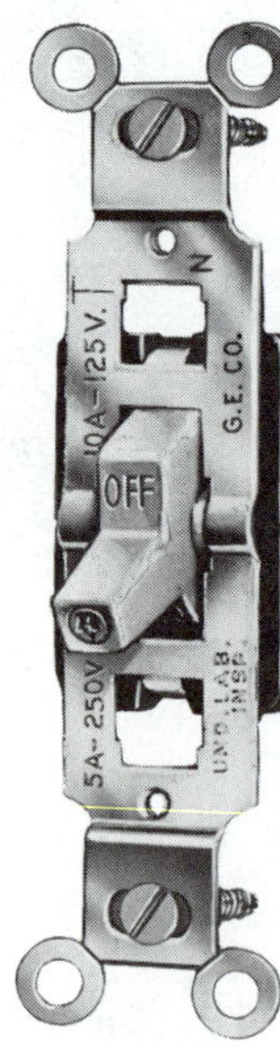

General Electric Company
14-21. A single-pole switch.

ers or remove fuses one by one. Have that person signal you when you have turned off the current to the outlet.

2. Remove the faceplate on the outlet. One or two ovalhead screws hold it in place. Fig. 14-23. Put the plate and the screws aside so that you can replace them later.

3. Unscrew the top and bottom mounting screws holding the old receptacle in place. Fig. 14-24. Pull it out of the box. Fig. 14-25.

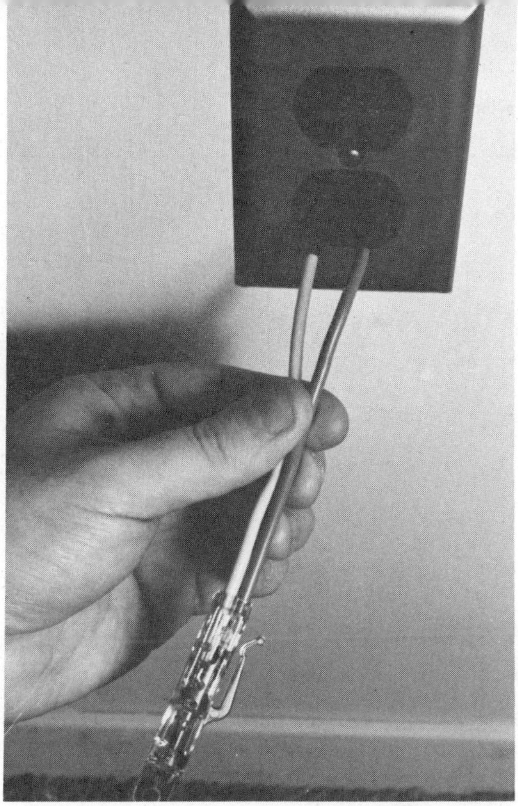

14-22. Testing an outlet with a neon tester to see if it is live.

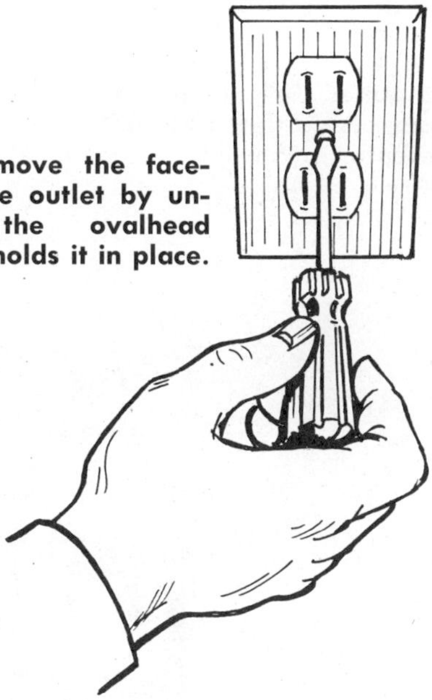

14-23. Remove the faceplate on the outlet by unscrewing the ovalhead screw that holds it in place.

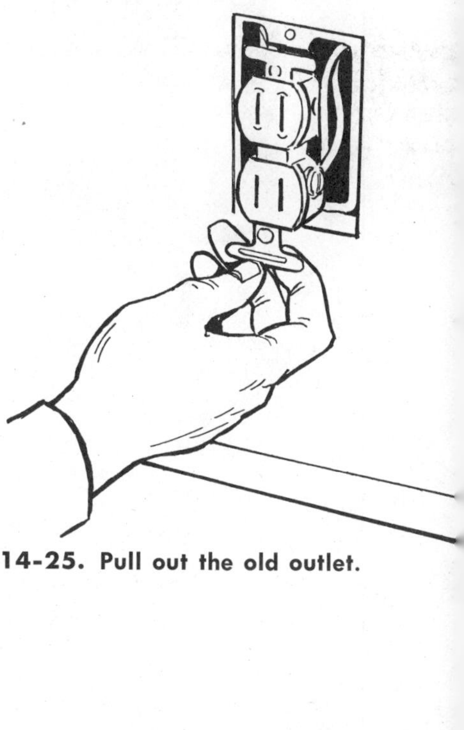

14-25. Pull out the old outlet.

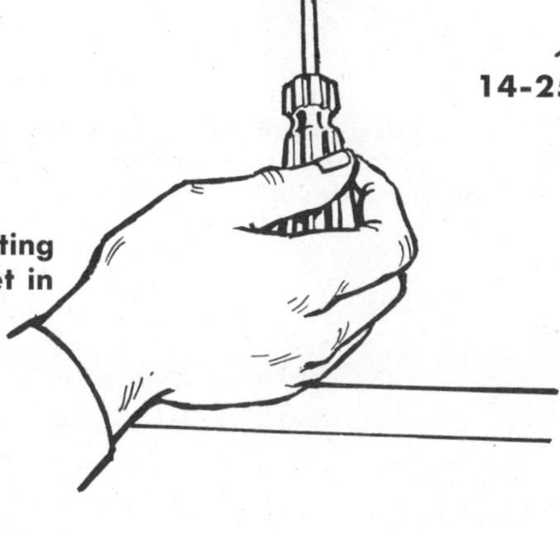

14-24. Unscrew the mounting screws that hold the old outlet in place.

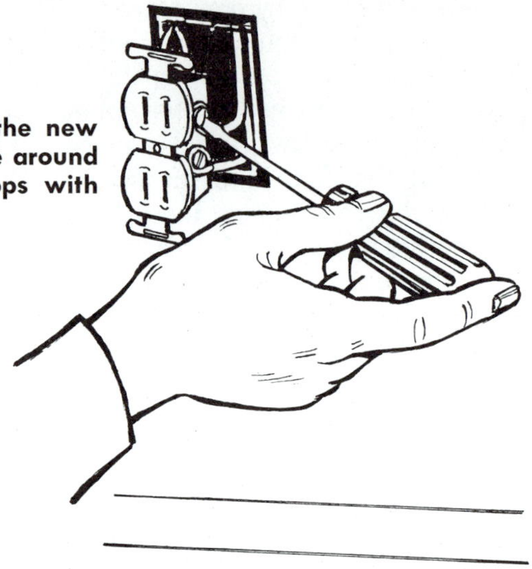

14-26. Put the wires in place on the new receptacle. They should go clockwise around the terminals. Tighten the wire loops with pliers.

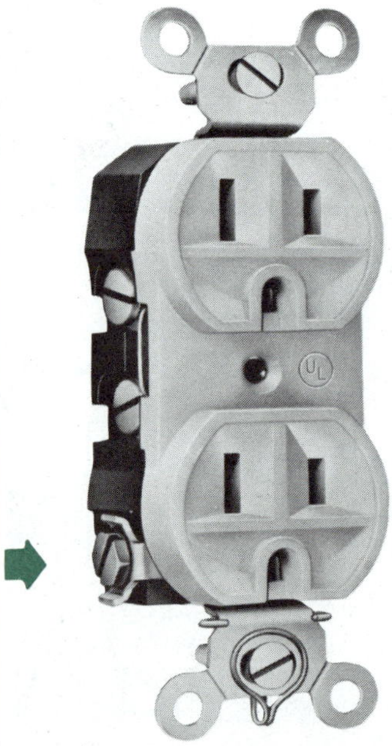

General Electric Company

14-27. A grounded outlet. The green hexagonal grounding screw is on the lower left side of the receptacle (arrow).

General Electric Company

14-28. The ears on the switch (arrows) and the mounting screws. The terminal screws are on the sides of this switch.

Loosen the terminal screws and remove the wires. Notice the placement of the wires on the outlet. You may have to unbend the loops of wire around the terminal screws with pliers.

4. Put the wires in place on the new receptacle so that they go clockwise around the terminals. Tighten the wire loops around the screws with pliers. Fig. 14-26. The black (hot) wire should go to the brass screw; the white (neutral) wire to the chrome screw; and, in the case of a grounded outlet, the green or bare ground wire goes around the green screw. Fig. 14-27. Tighten all the screws so that the wires are held down securely.

5. Fold the wires and push them back into the box. Push the receptacle back into the box. Line up the screws with the mounting holes on the electrical box. Tighten the screws so that the outlet is back in place and straight up and down. Put the faceplate back and tighten the screws that hold it in place. Be sure that the plate and the outlet are lined up so that the receptacle openings appear through the plate openings and are tight against the faceplate.

Replacing a Wall Switch

You will need a pair of long-nose pliers and a screwdriver to replace a wall switch. Obtain a replacement for the broken switch.

1. Turn off the current going to that switch by removing the fuse or by turning off the proper circuit breaker. When in doubt about whether or not the switch is live, turn off all the power in the house. You can test the switch after you remove the faceplate by touching each of the terminals with a lead from a neon tester or test light.

2. Remove the faceplate and put it aside.

3. Unscrew the top and bottom mounting screws that go through the ears on the switch and pull it out of the box. Fig. 14-28. Loosen the terminal screws and remove the wires. Fig. 14-29. Unbend the loops with a pair of long-nose pliers if necessary. Fig. 14-30. Dispose of the old switch.

14-29. Loosen the terminal screws and remove the wires.

14-30. You can unbend the wire loops with a pair of long-nose pliers.

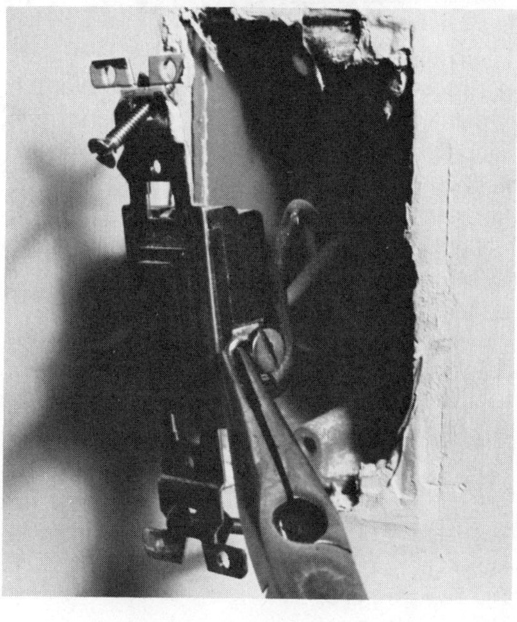

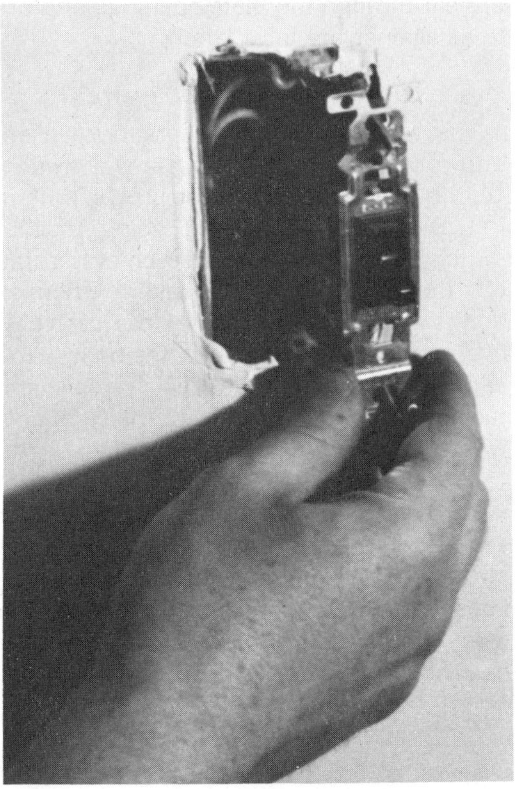

4. Fasten the wires to the terminal screws on the new switch. The wires should go around clockwise, and the loops should be closed around each screw before the screw is tightened. The black (hot) wire goes to the brass screw and the white (neutral) wire goes to the chrome screw. If the old switch had a different wire arrangement (as in the case of a two-way switch), make a note of it and follow that arrangement on the replacement switch.

5. Fold the wires back into the box and replace the switch, making sure that the screw holes line up. Fig. 14-31. Tighten the mounting screws so that the switch is placed vertically in the middle of the electrical box. Replace the faceplate so that the switch protrudes through the opening in the plate.

14-31. Fold the wires back into the box and replace the switch so that the mounting screw holes line up.

REPLACING A CEILING LIGHT FIXTURE

A ceiling light fixture needs to be replaced if it does not work. You may also want to replace it with a fixture of a different style. When you unpack the new fixture, you will usually find assembly and hanging instructions in the box. The fixture wires are connected to the wires in the electrical box by twisting them together and putting a solderless connector on each of them or by wrapping them with plastic electrical tape. Fig. 14-32. The steps in replacing the fixture are:

1. Shut off the power on that circuit. Have someone watch the fixture when it is on while you remove individual fuses or push circuit breakers to the "off" position. Have that person call you when the lights in the fixture go off.

2. To remove the old light fixture, stand on a stepladder below the fixture. If possible, remove all the glass parts and light

14-32. Solderless connectors (wire nuts).

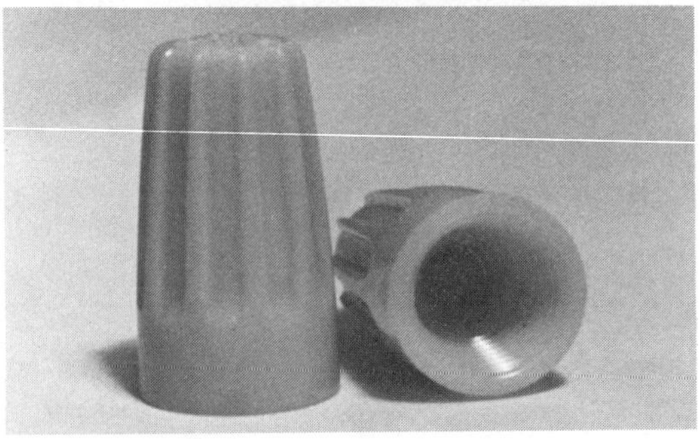

14-33. Nick the insulation carefully all around. Use the cutter on the long-nose pliers.

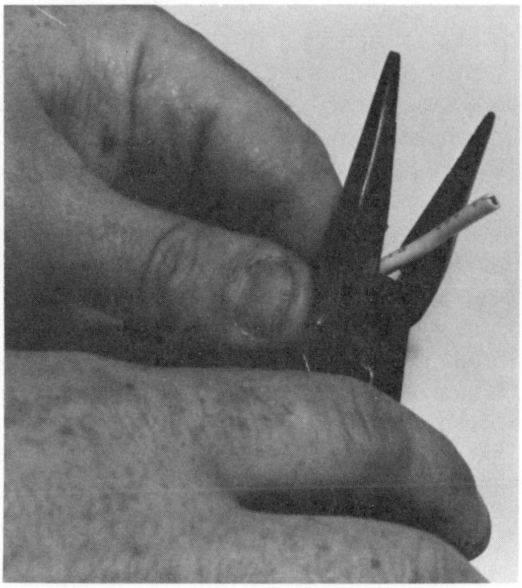

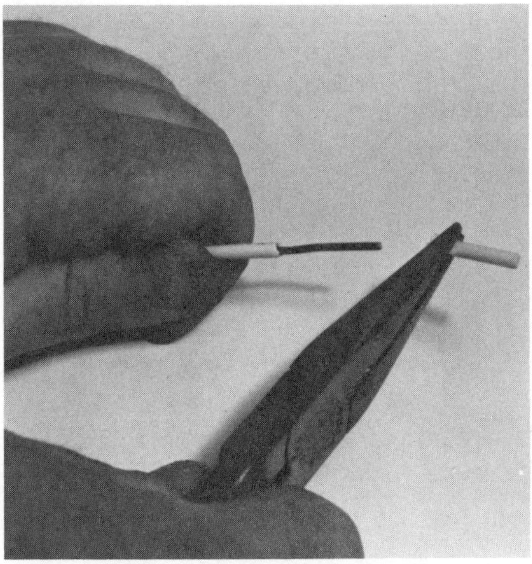

14-34. Holding the cut piece of insulation with the plier jaws, pull the piece off to expose the bare wire.

bulbs before you unfasten the fixture canopy (the metal bowl that covers the electrical box). Unscrew the nuts holding the canopy and lower it so that you can get to the wires inside. You may need help to hold it up if it is a large, heavy ceiling light, since only the wires are holding it up now.

3. Unwrap the tape or unscrew the solderless connectors that hold the fixture wires to the wires in the box. If you cannot undo the connections, cut a little off the wires coming from the box with a pair of pliers. Keep all the wires in the box in the same place they were before. All the black wires go together, as do all the white wires.

4. If you had to cut the wires coming out of the ceiling box, strip $\frac{1}{2}''$ of insulation off each one for the new connections. Strip $\frac{1}{2}''$ of insulation off each wire on the new fixture with your pliers, being careful not to nick the metal wires. Nick the insulation carefully all around with the cutter on the pliers. Fig. 14-33. Grab the insulation with the plier jaws and pull the piece of cut insulation off to expose the bare wire. Fig. 14-34.

Connect the two sets of wires according to the instructions that came with the new light or as described previously. Twist the wires together (black to black, etc.) and thread a solderless connector on each one. Figs. 14-35, 14-36. Be sure that no bare wire is exposed. Wrap some plastic electrical tape around any bare wire.

5. Position the canopy of the new fixture over the electrical box. If the mounting screws that held up the old fixture fit through the holes in the new one, put them through the canopy and thread the nuts on them to hold the canopy in place. Be sure that the canopy is fastened securely and is tight against the ceiling.

If the screws do not line up with the holes in the new fixture or if there are no screws, use the hanging device that comes with the fixture. Usually this is a crossbar that goes across the electrical box and is held in place with two screws to that box. Fig. 14-37. Through slots in the crossbar, a screw on each end comes through with a decorative nut on it. After fastening the crossbar in place, test the canopy to see if the screws are long enough to thread the nuts on. Make sure that the screws are in the right places. When everything is set up properly, fasten the fixture in place. Make sure that the nuts are tight so that the fixture will not work loose and come down.

6. Some ceiling fixtures are hung from a central threaded nipple (hollow threaded pipe) which is connected to a threaded stud in the center of the electrical box by an adapter. Fig. 14-38. The nipple fits through the middle of the fixture. A decorative nut fits on the end of the nipple to hold the fixture against the ceiling. This threaded nipple may be removed if the new ceiling light cannot be hung in this manner.

14-35. Twist the wires together. A pair of pliers makes the job easier with solid wire.

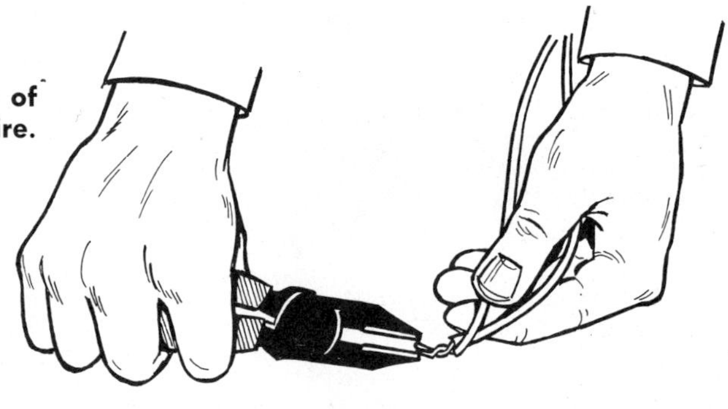

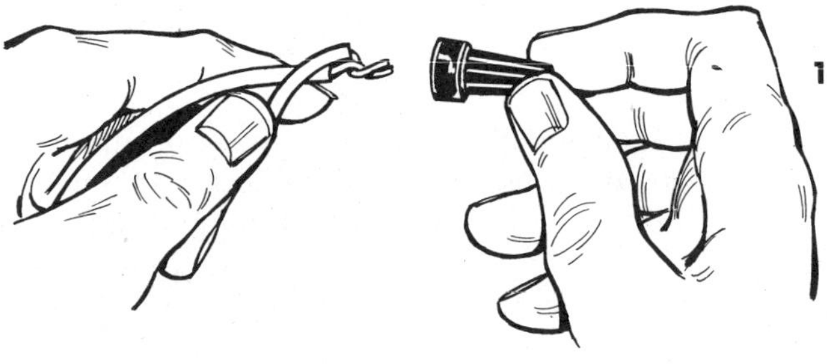

14-36. Thread a solderless connector on the wires. Turn the connector until it is tight.

Threaded nipples can be bought in various lengths to accommodate any type of light. You can also cut one to length with a hacksaw if necessary.

7. Install any glass parts on the fixture. Put in the light bulbs. Turn on the power and test the fixture to see if it works properly.

14-37. A crossbar that goes across the ceiling electrical box and is held in place with two screws. Note the slots for the screws.

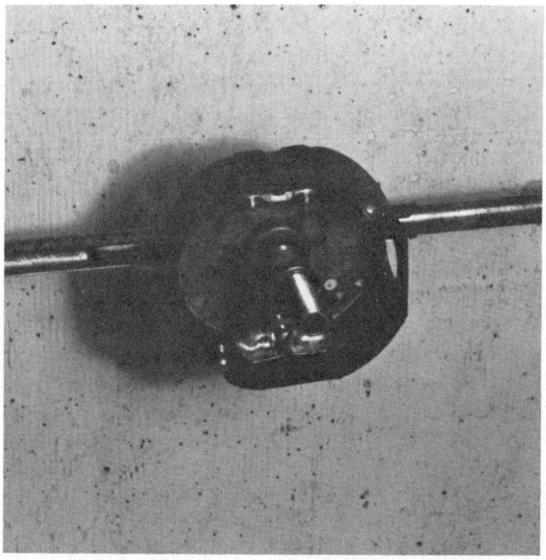

14-38. Some ceiling fixtures are hung from a central threaded nipple which is connected to a threaded stud in the center of the electrical box.

REPAIRING A DOORBELL CIRCUIT

The doorbell circuit in a house is a low-voltage system. The electricity does not have enough force to do any harm to a person working on the system. The transformer attached to the bell circuit changes the standard 110 volts to 12 or 16 volts.

The doorbell circuit has four components. They are the push button, the chime or bell, the transformer (12 to 16 volts), and the wiring for either a front doorbell or a front and a back doorbell. Fig. 14-39. To repair a circuit which does not work, do the following:

14-39. A transformer for a doorbell circuit.

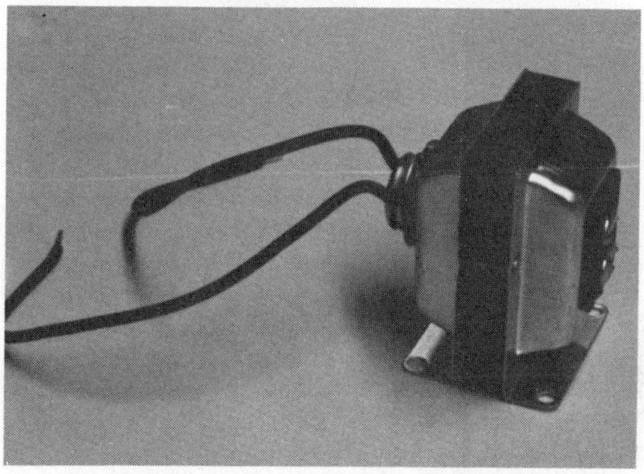

1. Check the push button first. Unscrew the faceplate and remove the button. Fig. 14-40. Disconnect the two wires and touch them together. If the doorbell or the chimes ring, then the push button needs to be repaired.

On some buttons you can clean the contacts with fine emery cloth or fine abrasive paper. Reconnect the wires to the terminal screws and test the button. If it will not work after the contacts have been cleaned, then the button must be replaced. Buy a new push button and install it like the old one.

2. If, when you touch the wires together at the button, the chime does not work, then the trouble spot is not the button. It may be in the bell or the chime itself. Fig. 14-41. Check the wires connected to the bell to make sure that they are tightly connected to the terminal screws. Fig. 14-42. If everything is all right at the bell and it still does not operate properly, the next step is to look at the transformer.

14-40. To check the push button, unscrew the faceplate and remove the button.

3. The transformer can be found on the side of the service panel box (fuse or circuit breaker box) or on a junction box near the push button. Fig. 14-43. To test the transformer, use a piece of electrical wire to short-circuit the terminals on the *low-voltage* side. This is the side that is connected to the bell wire that runs through the walls to the push button and the bell. Strip a little insulation off both ends of a piece of electrical wire and hold it so that the bare ends each touch a terminal on the transformer. If there is electricity coming through the transformer to the low-voltage side, there should be a small spark when you touch the two terminals.

If the transformer is not working, you will have to replace it. Turn off the circuit breaker or fuse that controls the current to the doorbell system. The transformer is held to a junction box or to the service panel through a knockout (a portion of the metal

14-41. A bell unit for a front and back door system.

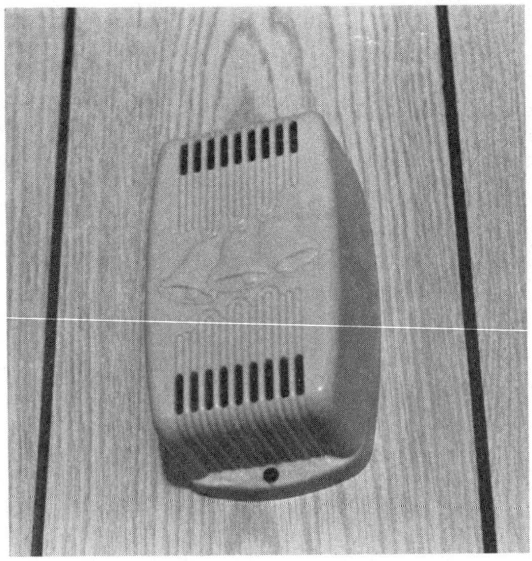

box that is removed, making a round opening). The back of the transformer has a round threaded stud and a locknut. Fig. 14-44.

To remove the transformer from the box, open the locknut, which is inside the box, with a hammer and a screwdriver. Tap the nut so that it turns and then unscrew it. Remove the transformer and disconnect the wires from the terminals.

Install another transformer of the same voltage size. Be sure to hook up the wire to the terminals on both sides in the same way that the old transformer was installed. The wires go around the terminal screws clockwise so that they are tightened as the screws are tightened.

4. If the transformer is working properly but the components refuse to work, it is possible that the fault lies in the wiring itself. This is not common; but if there is a break in the bell wire somewhere along the line, the electricity will not get to the bell or the push button.

Turn off the current. Trace the exposed bell wire to see if you can detect the break.

14-42. Check if the wires connected to the bell are securely fastened to the terminal screws.

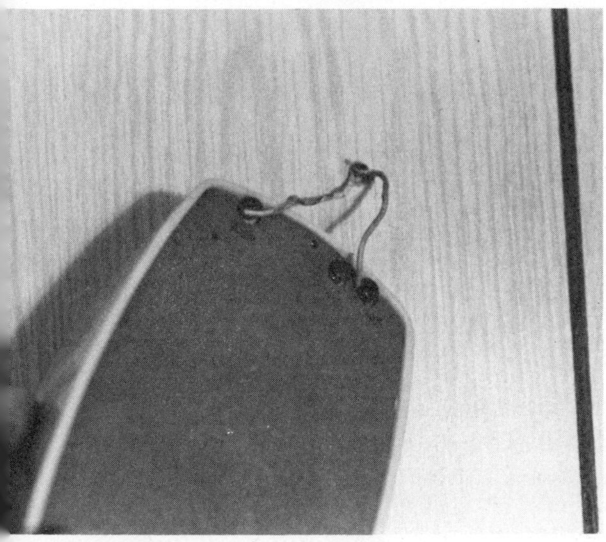

14-43. The transformer is often located on the side of the service panel box.

14-44. The back of the transformer has a round threaded stud and a locknut. The two wires are connected to live terminals in a circuit breaker or fuse box. These wires can also be attached to live wires in a junction box.

If a break in the wire can be seen, replace the entire wire between the two components (transformer and bell or bell and button). Look at the markings on the transformer to see what voltage the bell system is. Figure the amount of wire that you will need for the rewiring. Buy the proper bell wire somewhat longer than the amount you think you will need.

Disconnect the wire at the bell and at the transformer or button. Tie one end of the new wire to the existing wire by twisting the ends together securely. Wrap some electrical tape tightly around the connection to make it even more secure. Pull the old wire through the walls, using it to get the new wire into place. When the new wire is completely through, disconnect it from the old. Hook up the new wire to the terminals on the components just as they were attached before. Test the bell system.

REPLACING A LAMP SOCKET

There are several types of sockets used on lamps. Some are made of plastic, but most types are brass. There are sockets for three-way bulbs as well as sockets for standard bulbs. Basically the difference among sockets is the way they are turned on. Some of the varieties include: key sockets (Fig. 14-45), pull-chain sockets, push-button sockets (Fig. 14-46), and sockets with a turn switch.

If a lamp does not work correctly, it may have a faulty socket. However, first check the male plug and the wire to make sure they are sound and electricity is reaching the socket. If these are all right, then the socket is faulty and must be replaced.

1. Unplug the lamp or fixture. Remove any bulbs and the shade. Remove the harp that holds the shade upright. Fig. 14-47.

2. Separate the socket body and shell from the cap. On the socket shell near the cap is imprinted the word PRESS. By pressing here and pulling on the two sections at the same time, the two should come apart. If you have difficulty, slip a thin screwdriver or knife blade between the two parts and pry gently. Be careful not to bend the edges of the cap or the socket shell. Fig. 14-48.

3. The inside of the socket is now completely accessible. Check the terminal screws and the wires to see if any of the wires are loose. If a wire is loose, tighten the terminal screw, reassemble the socket, and test it with a light bulb after you plug the lamp into a live outlet. Fig. 14-49. If the socket still does not work, it must be replaced.

4. Take the socket apart and loosen the

General Electric Company

14-45. The body of a key socket.

General Electric Company

14-46. The body of a push-button socket.

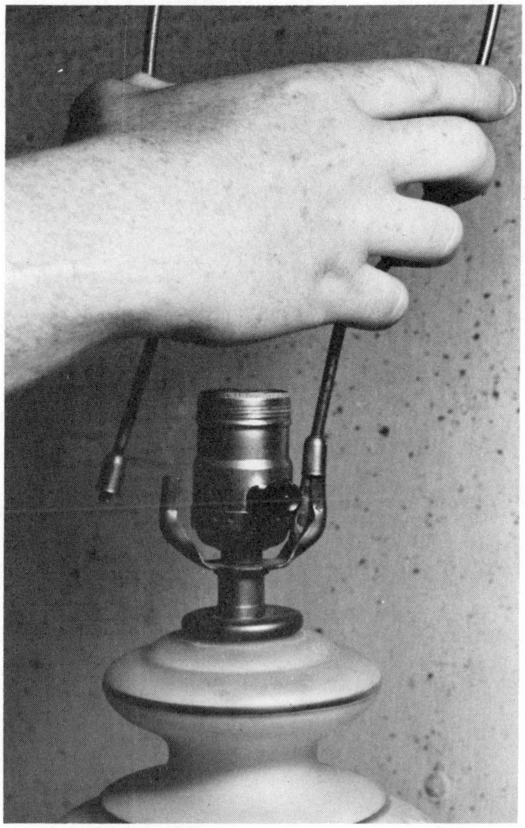

14-47. Remove the harp by lifting the sliding pieces that fit over the ends. Then squeeze the harp slightly to unhook it from the lamp.

14-48. Separate the socket body and shell from the cap. The cardboard insulator shown here should be left inside the shell.

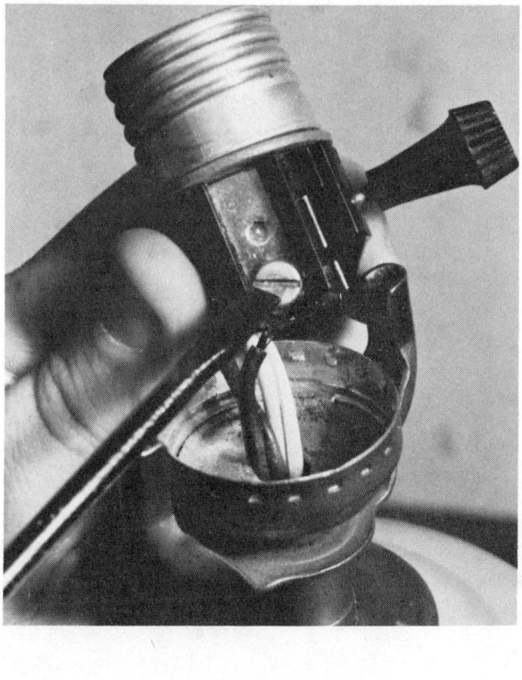

14-49. If a wire is loose, tighten the terminal screw and reassemble the socket. This is a socket with a turn switch.

General Electric Company

14-50. A lamp socket. The upper arrow points to the shell. The lower arrow points to the socket cap, which screws onto the threaded conduit coming up from the lamp body. This socket cap has a setscrew in it to keep it from turning on the conduit.

14-51. Put the shell and the cardboard insulator over the socket. Snap the shell into the socket cap.

terminal screws with a screwdriver. Remove the wires from the screws.

5. Buy a new socket of the same type. Check the shell to see whether it fits into the old cap. If it does, you can go on to install the new socket. If the new shell and the old cap do not fit together, then the old cap must be removed. It unscrews from the threaded conduit (nipple) coming up from the lamp body. Some socket caps have a setscrew in them to keep them from turning. Fig. 14-50. If the cap has a screw, loosen it first before attempting to remove the cap. After the cap is off and pulled over the wires, you are ready to put the new socket on.

6. Screw the new cap on first and tighten the setscrew, if there is one. Take the socket out of the new socket shell. Leave the cardboard insulator inside the shell. Loosen the terminal screws on the socket. Bend a loop on each wire and connect one wire to each terminal screw. The wires should go on the screws in a clockwise direction. Put the shell and cardboard insulator over the socket and snap the shell into the socket cap. Fig. 14-51. Test the lamp to see that it works.

REPLACING A PLUG

Plugs on the ends of electrical cords have to be replaced when they are cracked or broken. A plug that arcs (that is, sparks come out) when it is pushed into an outlet receptacle should be checked for loose wires at the terminals. If, after the wires are tightly fastened to the screws, the plug still arcs, replace it.

Several types of plugs are available. Most are made of plastic; some of the heavy duty ones are made of hard rubber. There are male plugs (with prongs) and female plugs (without prongs). Fig. 14-52. Some plugs are easy to install because they are the clamp-on variety. They are only good for light duty use with lamp cord. Fig. 14-53. Instructions

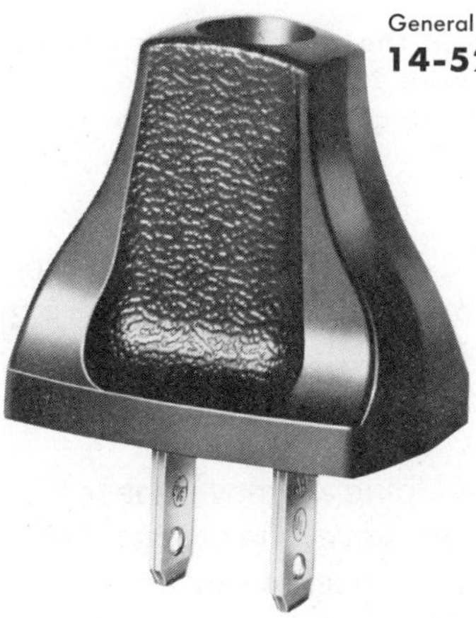

General Electric Company
14-52. A male plug made of plastic.

General Electric Company
14-53. A clamp-on female plug (left) and a clamp-on male plug (right). These are for light duty use with lamp cord.

come with the package. All the other types of plugs have terminal screws to which the wire is attached after the insulation is stripped off.

The various types of electrical cords have to be prepared differently for the installation of a plug. The rubber- or plastic-covered cords have to be split at the center where the two wires meet. Fig. 14-54. Then the insulation is removed from each wire so that ½″ of bare wire is exposed. The stranded wire must be twisted together. On sheathed wires, you have to remove the cotton or asbestos covering so that you can get to the insulation. On asbestos-covered cord, wrap some thread around the asbestos covering so that it stays out of the way when you put the plug on.

Replacing a Male Plug

To replace a male plug (a plug with prongs) other than the clamp-on type, do the following:

1. Buy a new plug of the same type as the old one. Cut off the old plug plus a little of the electrical cord using a pair of pliers with a cutter. Split the covering on the cord about 2″ up so that the two insulation-covered wires are separated. This can be done with a sharp knife.

2. Strip the insulation from the ends of the wire so that ½″ of the copper wire is showing. To strip the wire, nick the insulation with the cutter on the long-nose pliers. Then grab the loose piece of covering and pull it off the wire. If you have a wire stripper, set it for the proper thickness of wire and squeeze it on the insulation so that it is

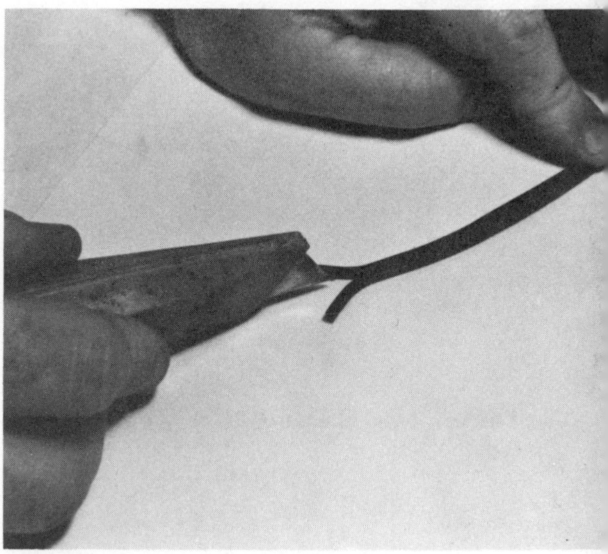

14-54. Cords covered with rubber or plastic have to be split at the center where the two wires meet.

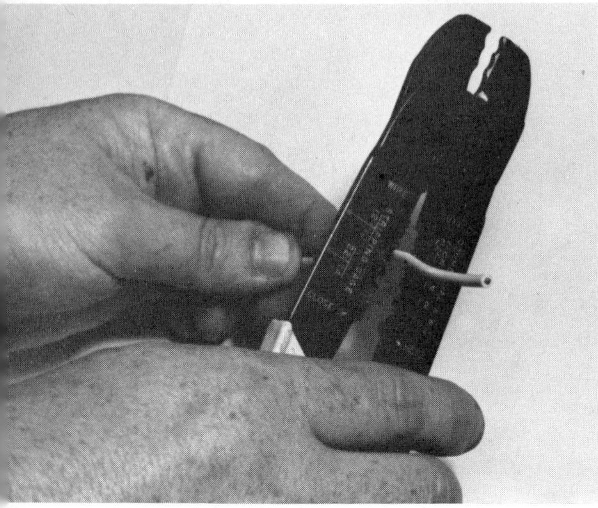

14-55. Set the wire in the proper notch on the stripper for that wire thickness. Squeeze the stripper to cut through the insulation.

cut through. Fig. 14-55. Then pull the cutter off to the side so that the piece of covering slips off the wire. Twist the strands together so that they form one compact wire. Fig. 14-56.

3. On the new plug, remove the cardboard disk that slides over the prongs. Push the wire through the opening in the top of the plug so that the split is past the end of the plug. Fig. 14-57. Tie a knot with the two lengths of insulation-covered wire so that the cord cannot be pulled through the plug again. The type of knot used is an Underwriter's knot. (See Fig. 14-58, which shows how the Underwriter's knot is tied.) Pull the knotted section of the cord back into the body of the plug.

4. Loop the wires around the prongs of the plug so that they form an S. Form a loop on the end of each wire and secure it around a terminal screw so that the wire travels around the screw in a clockwise direction. Fig. 14-59. Tighten the screw with a screwdirver to hold the wire tightly in place. Be sure that no bare metal wire touches the prongs. Replace the cardboard disk that goes over the prongs so that it covers the wires inside the plug.

14-56. Twist the strands of wire (bottom) together so that they form one compact wire (top).

Replacing a Female Plug

The most common type of female plug is used on appliances and disassembles into two parts. Heavy duty female plugs have a strain reliever, such as a coil spring, to keep the electrical cord from being pulled loose from the plug. The plugs are held together with screws or, in some cases, clamps. Figs. 14-60, 14-61. Replace a worn or broken plug in the following way:

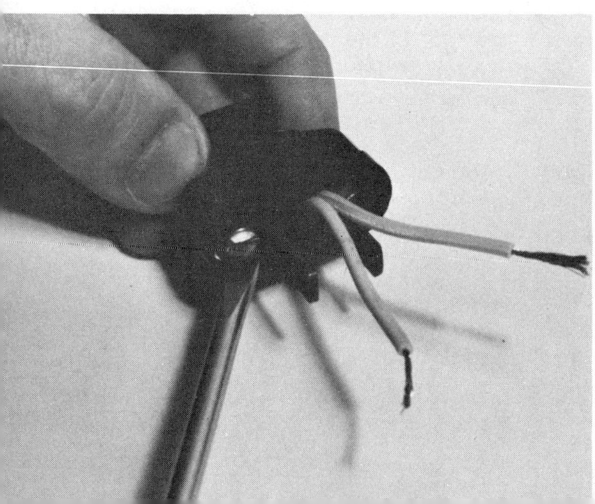

14-57. Push the wire through the opening in the top of the plug. Loosen the terminal screws with a screwdriver.

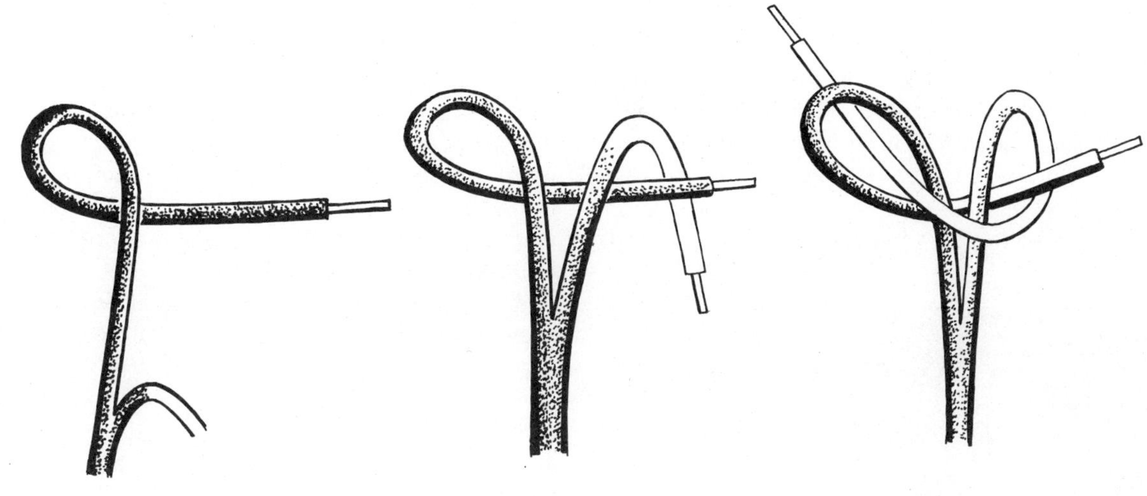

14-58. The steps in tying an Underwriter's knot.

14-59. Loop the wires around the prongs of the plug to form an *S*. Form a loop on the end of each wire.

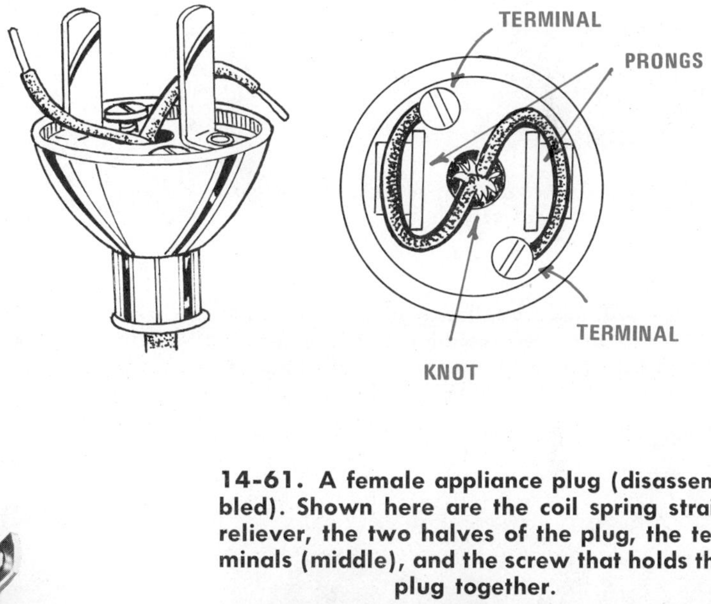

14-61. A female appliance plug (disassembled). Shown here are the coil spring strain reliever, the two halves of the plug, the terminals (middle), and the screw that holds the plug together.

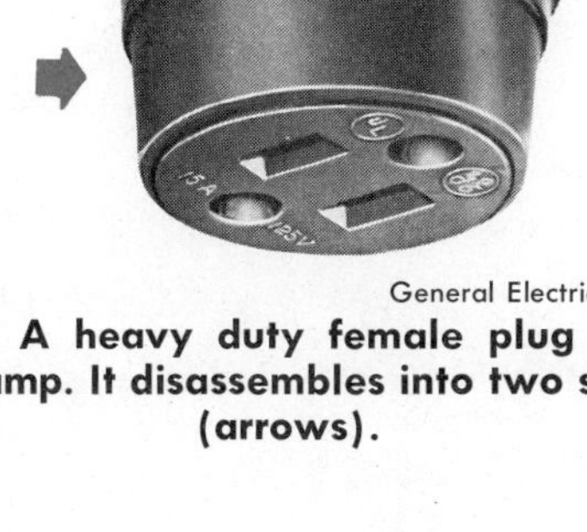

General Electric Company

14-60. A heavy duty female plug with a wire clamp. It disassembles into two sections (arrows).

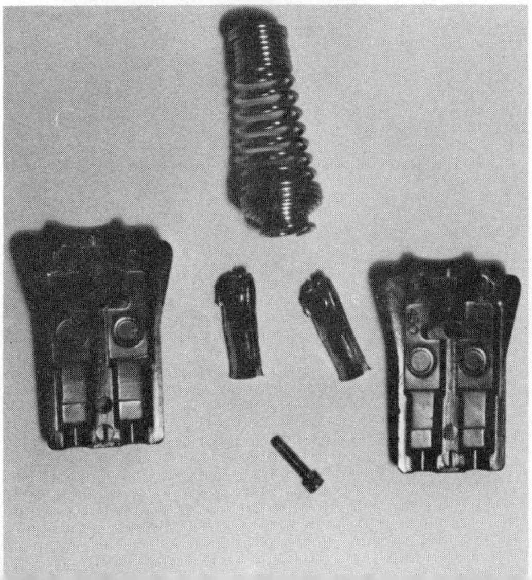

1. Obtain a new plug of the same type as the old one. Cut off the old plug with a pair of pliers. Cut off a little of the cord at the same time.

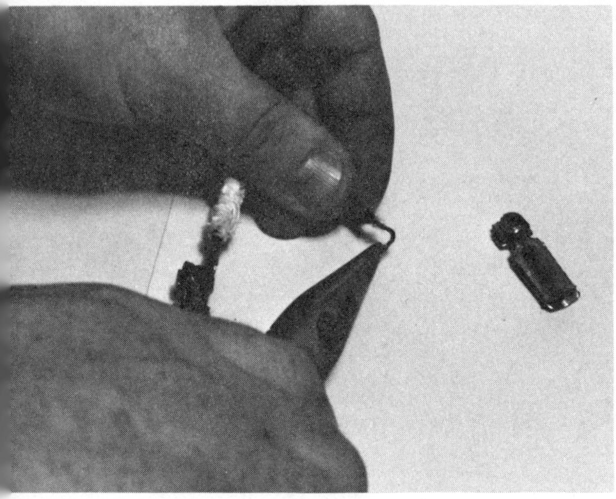

14-62. Put the wire loops around the terminal screws.

2. Split the electrical cord about 2″ up with a snarp knife. Remove the outer covering and, if the cord is asbestos covered, wrap thread around the asbestos to keep it in place. Strip the insulation off ½″ on each of the two wires so that they are exposed. Make a loop on the end of each wire.

3. Take the new plug apart by either removing the screw or screws that hold it together or by pushing the two clamps off it. Put the wire loops around the terminal screws and tighten them so that the wires are secure. Fig. 14-62. Before you reassemble the plug, make sure that the terminals are in the right places and that the strain reliever (coil spring) is in the correct position. Fig. 14-63. Put the screws in place after fitting the two sections of the plug tightly together. Tighten the screws or push the clamps into position, and the repair is complete. Fig. 14-64.

Replacing a 220-Volt Male Plug

The procedure for replacing a 220-volt male plug is almost the same as that for

14-63. A female appliance plug (disassembled) with the strain reliever and the terminals on asbestos-covered cord. Two *U*-shaped clamps hold this plug together.

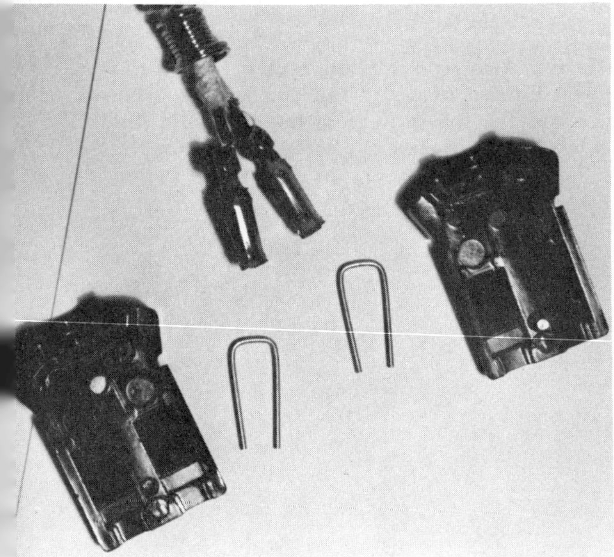

14-64. Push the clamps into position after fitting the two sections of the plug together tightly.

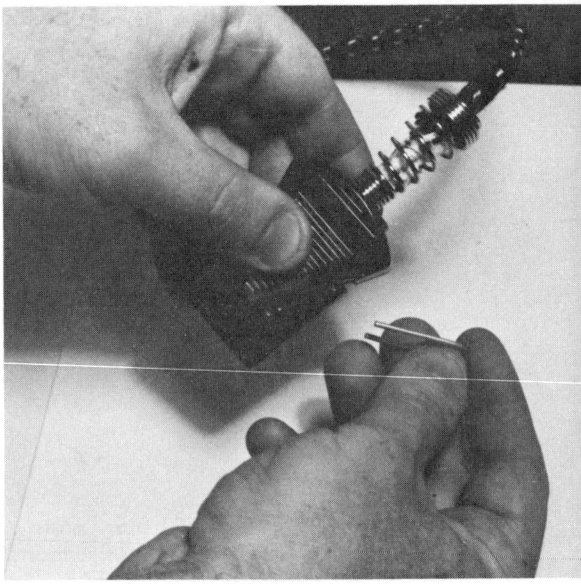

replacing any other plug. These plugs are heavy duty, and they are wired in a slightly different way. Care must be taken to wire them correctly. The black wire in the electrical cord goes to the brass terminal screw. The red wire goes to the copper screw, and the white wire (which is the ground wire) goes to the terminal screw on the grounding prong (the third prong). This screw is usually chrome colored. Be sure that the wires are looped around the screws in a clockwise direction and that they are securely fastened in place. No bare wire should touch any of the other components of the plug.

SAFE USE OF ELECTRICAL DEVICES

Each year many injuries and fires result from neglect of or improper use of electrical devices. The following is a list of safety tips to help you avoid accidents.

• Some homes, especially older ones, may not be adequately wired for all the appliances we use today. If the house wiring is inadequate, too many appliances in use at the same time will overload the electrical circuits. This will cause fuses to burn out or will shut off circuit breakers. If your television picture shrinks or lights dim when appliances are turned on, your home may have inadequate wiring. Consult a licensed electrician for additions to your electric service panel.

• Use the correct size fuses. Fifteen amperes is standard for most household circuits. Larger sizes are used for special circuits for appliances such as electric ranges and clothes dryers. A fuse is a safety device. Using a fuse that is too large or placing a penny behind a fuse defeats the purpose. Too much current will be allowed to pass through the wires. The wires could overheat and possibly start a fire.

• Replace electrical cords that have worn insulation. Pay special attention to the point where the cord enters an appliance and to the area near the plug. These areas usually show signs of wear first.

• Make sure that any electrical equipment you buy, such as cords or Christmas tree lights, has the UL seal. This means that the device has been checked for safety by Underwriters' Laboratories, Inc. The UL is an independent laboratory which tests various products for safety.

• Remove a cord from an outlet by pulling on the plug, not on the cord. This will avoid wear and tear on the cord.

• Do not run electric cords under rugs, doors, or other places where they could easily be damaged without your being able to see the damage.

• Do not let cords touch hot radiators or appliances. This could damage the insulation and expose the wires. Keep cords away from moisture. Because some household pets like to chew on electrical cords, it is wise to keep the cords out of reach of these pets. A cord punctured by a pet's tooth may expose the metal wire and present a shock hazard.

• When you buy an extension cord, check the label to make sure that it is the right type for the job. For example, power tools need special heavy-duty cords.

• Take special care when buying Christmas lights. Lights for outdoor decorating should be labeled for outdoor use. Do not string lights on aluminum Christmas trees. Aluminum conducts electricity and may cause a shock. Use only "cool lights" for plastic trees. Buy only lights with the UL seal.

• Avoid connecting too many appliances to the same circuit at one time. This will cause the circuit to overload.

• When cleaning electrical appliances, keep the electrical elements dry. Never put an electrical appliance into water unless you are specifically directed to do so by the manufacturer.

- Connect appliances to wall outlets, not to lamp sockets. Lamp sockets are designed to carry only very small electrical loads.
- Water and metal are good conductors of electricity. Do not touch appliances, lights, switches, or fuses when your hands are wet, when you are standing on a wet surface, or when you are also touching water, plumbing, or anything metal.
- Washing machines should have a grounding wire connecting the frame of the washer to a water pipe as a precaution against shock. This wire should be installed by an electrician.
- Some electric space heaters should not be placed directly on tile or carpeting because of the heat they give off. Never put a space heater next to flammable materials. Follow the manufacturer's directions for use.
- Outdoors, do not use electric tools in the rain or on wet surfaces. For example, do not use an electric lawn mower on wet grass. Make sure extension cords are designed for outdoor use. Do not leave electrical equipment unprotected outdoors.
- Rooftop antennas should be placed where they cannot touch or fall on electric lines. They should be grounded and have lightning arresters.
- Know the location of the service panel in your home. You may need to shut off the power in an emergency or when making repairs.
- If an electrical appliance or household wiring catches fire, unplug the appliance or switch off the current at the electric service panel. Call the fire department. While waiting for help, you may be able to bring the fire under control using a fire extinguisher or baking soda. *Do not use water* on live wires or on appliances that are plugged in.
- Outdoors, never touch a broken or fallen wire. Do not touch anyone or anything that is in contact with the wire. The current will pass through both of you. Call the utility company and the police.

CHECKUP

1. What is a *service panel*? Do you know its location in your home?
2. When checking the electrical devices and appliances in your home for safety, what conditions should you look for?
3. How can you test a circuit to determine whether it is live?

CHAPTER 15

Heating System Maintenance

TYPES OF HEATING SYSTEMS

Most home heating systems use one of three fuels: gas, fuel oil, or electricity. Radiators and warm air ducts with registers are the common ways of distributing heat to the rooms of a home.

One type of radiator is steam heated. The steam is carried to the radiator through a pipe. Another type of radiator has hot water circulated through it. Fig. 15-1. The hot water is carried through a pipe to the radiator and then back to the boiler. In the boiler, the water is reheated and again circulated by a pump through the radiators in the house. Fig. 15-2.

In a forced-air system the furnace creates heat (hot air). A fan blows the air through

15-1. A radiator with hot water circulating through it.

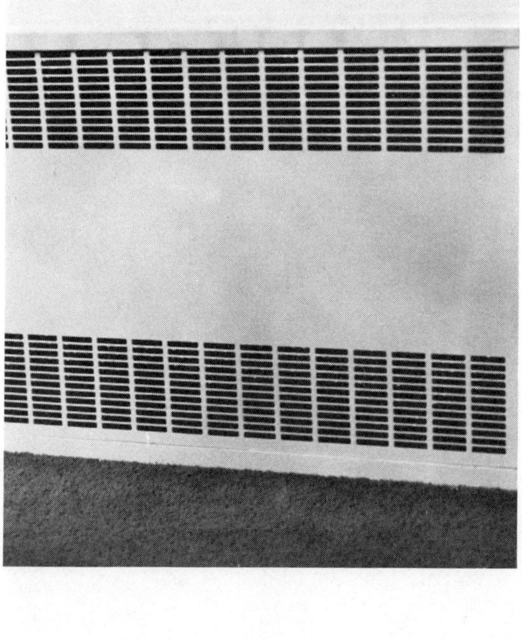

15-2. A heating system which circulates hot water through the radiators in the house.

ducts to each room of the house. In each room the duct is covered by a grill (register). Fig. 15-3. These registers are found on the wall near the baseboard, high up on the wall near the ceiling, or in the floors. The registers can be opened or closed to control the amount of heat let into the room.

Most of the maintenance work on heating systems can be done only by a professional. There are, however, a few maintenance jobs that can be done by the do-it-yourselfer, depending upon what type of heating system the home has.

15-3. A register with louvers.

RADIATOR MAINTENANCE

In a hot water system, air gets trapped in the radiators and causes loud noises when the heating system is on. The air pocket blocks the circulation of hot water in the radiator. The "bleeding" of the radiators to remove the air should be done at least once a year *when the heat is off.* The procedure is as follows:

1. Lift off the cover on the front of the radiator. Fig. 15-4.

2. Open the small tap on the valve at the end of the radiator. Fig. 15-5. Hold a container under the tap to catch any water that

15-4. Lift the cover off the radiator.

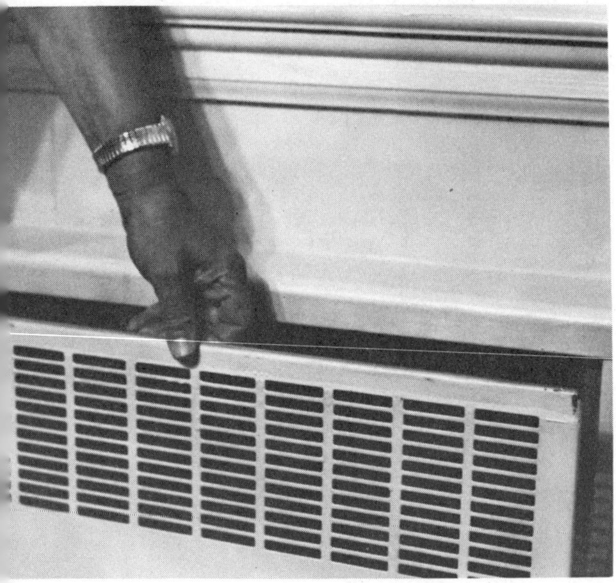

15-5. The valve on the end of the radiator.

15-6. A key for opening the valve on a radiator.

15-7. Turn the tap with a screwdriver. A hissing sound means that the trapped air is being released. As soon as water begins to flow into the container, close the tap.

comes out. The tap is opened with a screwdriver or a special key which may be bought at a hardware store. Fig. 15-6.

3. Turn the tap until there is a hissing sound of air being released. As soon as water begins to flow into the container under the valve, close the tap. Fig. 15-7.

WARM AIR SYSTEM MAINTENANCE

Gas- or oil-fired warm air heating systems should have an annual service checkup. You should request this service from the company that supplies your heating system fuel. There are also some things that you can do to keep the system working properly.

Forced-air heating systems have a blower motor and a fan motor. Fig. 15-8. At least once a year, check the oil cups on the motors to see whether they are dry. While the heat is off, squirt light machine oil into the cups until they are full.

Adjust the levers on the dampers so that the dampers are open to allow the passage of hot air through the ducts. The dampers are located on the main ducts near the furnace. Fig. 15-9. They control the heat going to branch ducts in the various sections of the house. To test if the dampers are open, check all the registers in the various rooms for even heating. If little or no heat comes out of an open register, the damper for that duct is probably closed.

The grills, or registers, covering the heat outlets in all the rooms should be vacuumed at least once a year to remove dust and dirt.

15-8. The blower motor on a forced-air furnace.

The grills are usually held in place with two sheet metal screws. Take out the screws and remove the grills. Use the vacuum cleaner to remove dust and dirt from the ducts.

Furnace Filters

If you have a forced-air system, you should periodically clean or replace the furnace filter during the heating season. If the filter is not clean, it will block the flow of warm air to the rooms. The filter is designed to trap dust carried by heated air. After a while the filter becomes partially blocked by the dust.

Many furnaces have disposable filters. Hardware stores sell all the various sizes of disposable filters. The size of the filter is marked on the edge. Fig. 15-10. You merely buy a replacement of the same size and throw away the old filter.

On some heating units, the filter is permanent. To clean a permanent filter, vacuum both sides of it or wash it under a sink faucet to remove the dust particles.

To test whether a filter needs cleaning or replacement, hold it up to the light. If you

15-9. The lever that controls the damper.

15-10. A disposable furnace filter with the size marked on the edge. Notice the arrow which indicates which way the filter should be placed in the slot.

15-11. The location of the furnace filter on the duct that returns cool air to the heating chamber (arrow).

cannot see light through it, the filter needs to be cleaned or replaced.

The furnace filter is found near the duct that returns cool air to the heating chamber of the furnace. Fig. 15-11. The filter fits into a slot in the duct. On the edge of the filter you will find its size and an arrow. The arrow indicates which way the filter should be placed in the slot. The arrow on the filter should point in the direction of the airflow. The air moves from the cool-air duct into the furnace.

AIR CONDITIONING

Many homes have window air conditioners or central air conditioning systems. For maximum efficiency, keep air conditioner filters clean. If you have central air conditioning as part of a forced-air system, change the furnace filter regularly (every 3–4 months).

Except for changing or cleaning the filter, any maintenance or repair work should be done only by a qualified professional.

HOT WATER HEATERS

Hot water heaters, whether gas or oil heated, require maintenance. Rusty hot water is a problem that can be avoided by draining the heater at least once a year to rid the tank of the rust and sludge that collect in it. This material settles to the bottom of the tank near the burner. Every hot water heater has a drain spout. Generally the procedure for draining the tank is:

1. Shut off the incoming water supply by closing the cold-water valve over the hot water heater. Fig. 15-12. If the heater does not have such a valve, shut off the main water supply to the house.

2. Open a hot water faucet somewhere in the house to release any trapped air.

3. Screw a garden hose onto the drain spout on the heater. Fig. 15-13. (The spout is threaded to take one.) Put the other end

15-12. Shut off the incoming cold-water supply valve above the hot water heater.

15-13. The drain spout on the hot water heater.

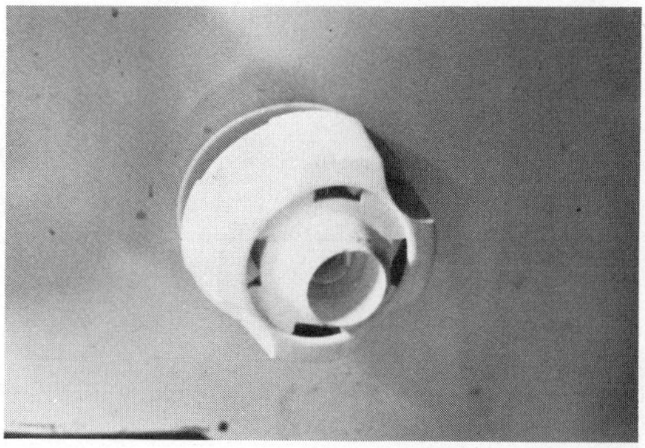

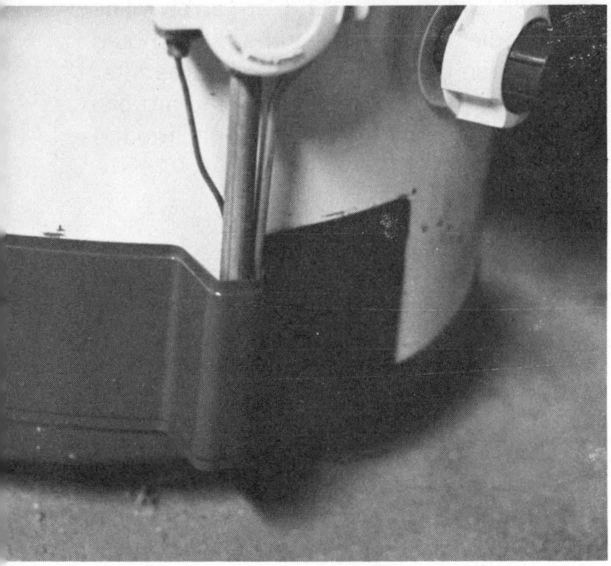

15-14. A lift-up door covers the burner under the hot water heater.

15-15. The access to the burner. Periodically check the flame to see if it is burning with a bluish light.

of the hose in an empty water pail or near the drain in the basement floor. *Caution:* The water will be scalding hot.

4. Open the drain spout by turning it until you get a steady flow of water. Dump the pails of water and keep drawing water from the tank until all the rust and sludge are gone and the water runs clear. Turn off the drain spout when you are finished, and make sure that the valve is closed tight. Remove the hose. Open the incoming water supply valve.

Periodically check the flame under the hot water heater. Poorly burning flames cause a deposit of carbon on the bottom of the tank. This carbon acts as an insulator and cuts down on the heating efficiency of the unit.

Access to the burner is usually through a small lift-up door on the front of the heater. Figs. 15-14, 15-15. The flame should be bluish in color. If it is red or orange, the flame must be adjusted. Call your local power company for service if the unit is gas heated. If it is oil fired, ask your oil supplier to send someone to adjust the flame.

CHECKUP

1. What are the most common fuels used in home heating systems? What kind of fuel does your home heating system use?
2. How often should furnace filters be cleaned or replaced?
3. How can you avoid the problem of rusty hot water?

CHAPTER 16

Insulation

In the past, many homes were built with little or no insulation. Today, fuel shortages and the high cost of energy have made good thermal insulation a necessity. Thermal insulation blocks or slows down the passage of heat. In winter, it keeps heat from passing through the house to the outside. In the summer, the insulation helps homes stay cooler by keeping heat out.

Thermal insulation is made into various forms from many different kinds of material. *Flexible* insulation, in the form of blankets or batts, is made of mineral or vegetable fibers. Fiberglass insulation is an example. *Loose fill* insulation is put in place by pouring, blowing, or by hand packing. It can be made from various materials, including wood fibers, glass wool, and vermiculite. *Foam* insulation is made from a synthetic material. It is sprayed or foamed in place. *Reflective* insulation is made from sheets of aluminum or other materials which reflect heat. *Rigid* insulation usually comes in sheets. It may be structural or nonstructural. The structural type is used for roof decking, sheathing, wallboard, and so forth. Although it does provide some resistance to heat flow, its main purpose is as a building material. Nonstructural rigid insulation is nailed to rafters to insulate the roof. The roof sheathing and shingles are applied over the insulation. Fig. 16-1.

16-1. Types of insulation: (A) Blanket. (B) Batt. (C) Loose fill. (D) Reflective (one type). (E) Rigid.

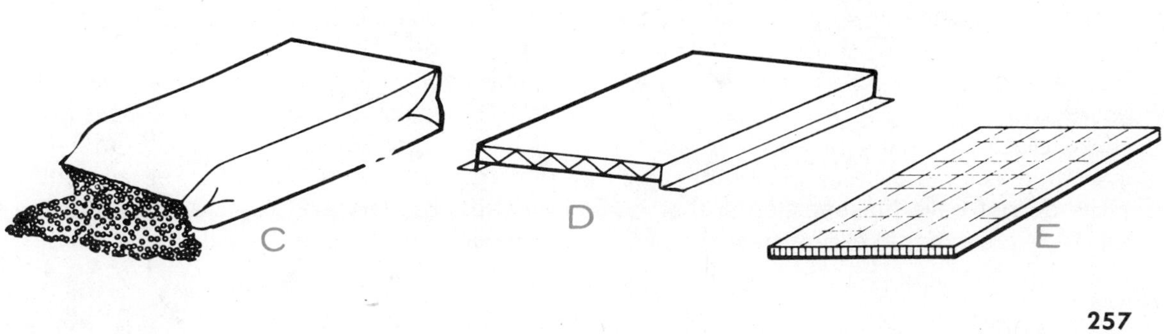

Insulation is rated on its resistance to the passage of heat. This resistance is known as the *R* value. The higher the *R* value, the greater the thermal resistance. Your utility company can advise you on the amount of insulation recommended for homes in your area.

The list below gives *R* values of fiberglass batts and blankets. When buying insulation, look for the *R* value on the package.

THICKNESS OF FIBERGLASS	*R* VALUE
3½″	R-11
6″	R-19
9½″ (6 + 3½)	R-30
12″ (6 + 6)	R-38

The following lists common types of insulation and the *R* value for one inch of that material.

TYPE OF INSULATION	*R* VALUE PER INCH OF THICKNESS
Loose fill vermiculite	2.0–2.6
Loose fill perlite	2.0–2.7
Loose fill rock wool	3.0–3.3
Loose fill fiberglass	3.1–3.3
Loose fill cellulose	3.7–4.0
Blown rock wool	2.8–3.8
Blown fiberglass	2.8–3.8
Blown cellulose	3.1–4.0
Fiberglass board	4.0–4.3
Extruded polystyrene board	4.0–5.4
Urethane board	6.7–8.0

In choosing insulation, consider *R* values, resistance to fire, vermin and decay, weight, and ease of installation, as well as cost.

INSTALLING INSULATION

Any area that separates heated from unheated spaces should be insulated. This includes walls, ceilings, roofs, and floors. Fig. 16-2. Most insulation is placed between the framing members (studs and joists) of the home. (Rigid insulation is an exception.) In new construction, the contractor installs insulation as the house is being built. However, older homes may have little or no insulation. In such cases, the homeowner must find ways to better insulate the house.

It is difficult to insulate walls, floors, or ceilings that have been closed in. One method is to make holes in the surfaces and blow in loose fill insulation. This is usually done from the outside of the house. Shingles or pieces of siding may be removed first. Insulation may also be foamed in by this method. Such jobs should be done by a reputable contractor who has the required equipment and skills.

One place the do-it-yourselfer can install insulation is in the attic. Most unheated attics do not have finished floors; that is, the joists are exposed except near the center where there is usually a catwalk made of a few boards. There should be at least 6″ of insulation between these joists. Installing flexible or loose fill insulation in an attic floor is fairly simple.

Attic Insulation—Flexible

As stated before, flexible insulation comes in the form of blankets (in a large roll) or batts (in a large package). Both types are made in widths for 16″ or 24″ joist spacing. Both forms of insulation are made in 3½″, 4″, and 6″ thicknesses, with or without a vapor barrier attached to one side. If there is no insulation in the attic, install batts or blankets with a vapor barrier. If there is insulation already in the attic, but you want to make it thicker, use the material that has no vapor barrier.

The vapor barrier is usually aluminum foil. This vapor barrier resists the passage of water vapor. To keep moisture from getting trapped next to the floor, always put the vapor barrier next to the warm side, that is, against the back of the ceiling. Fig. 16-3.

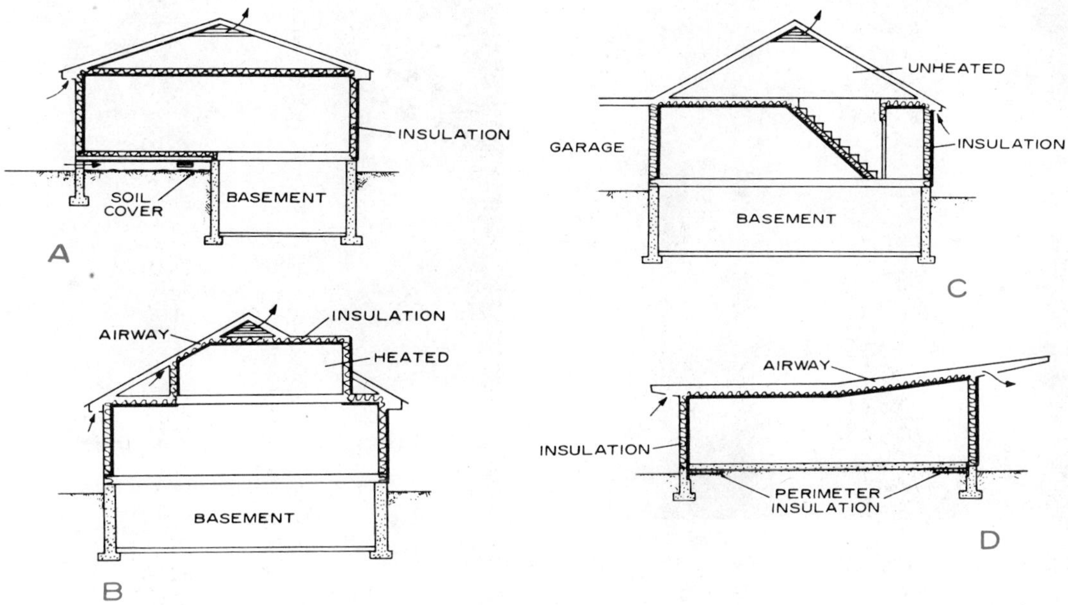

16-2. Placement of insulation: (A) In walls, floor, and ceiling. (B) In 1½-story house. (C) At attic door. (D) In flat roof.

To determine the size of the batts or blankets and the amount of insulation needed, follow this procedure:

- Measure the depth of the existing insulation, if there is any, by pushing a ruler down between the attic joist and the insulation until the ruler hits the ceiling below. This will help you determine what thickness of insulation you should buy.
- Measure the space between the joists (attic beams). The space will be either 15″ or 23″ in most homes. Buy insulation wide enough to fill this space.
- Measure the length and width of the attic. Multiply the length by the width to get the total square feet of attic space. To account for the space taken up by the joists, multiply the total square feet by .94 for 23″ wide insulation. For the 15″ wide insulation, multiply the total square feet by .90. This is the total square feet of insulation you will need. Buy enough to equal this amount or go over it by as little as possible.

CAUTION: Most flexible insulation used today is fiberglass. This material is harmful to skin and breathing passages. Wear gloves, long pants, and a long-sleeved shirt to protect your skin. You should also wear a filter mask so that you do not breathe in any fibers.

To install flexible insulation, you need the following tools: a sharp utility knife, a zigzag ruler, a light source, some pieces of plywood or boards thick enough to support your weight, a pair of work gloves, and a mask. Follow these steps:

1. Take all the tools, boards, and insulation up into the attic so that you do not have to make trips up and down. Place the plywood or boards across the joists so that you have a place on which to walk or kneel while you are working. CAUTION: Walk only on the catwalk or boards. Do not step between the joists as you may go through the ceiling below.
2. Start on one end of the attic space. If

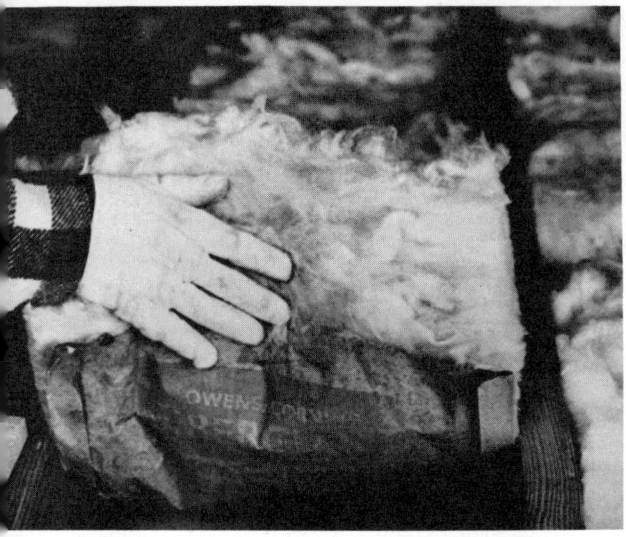

Owens Corning Fiberglas Corp.

16-3. Install the insulation with the vapor barrier next to the ceiling.

Owens Corning Fiberglas Corp.

16-4. Installing fiberglass insulation in an attic.

you are using batts, fill in the space with full batts until you reach the last one. Measure the remaining space and cut a batt to fit. Save the leftover batt for use later.

If you are using rolled insulation blankets, measure the length that you need. Roll out the insulation and cut off the length that you need.

To cut insulation, place it on a piece of scrap plywood or wallboard. Compress the insulation with one hand and use a sharp utility knife to cut through the material. If the insulation has a vapor barrier, cut it with the barrier facing up toward you.

3. The batts or blankets are placed between the joists. Do not compress them by pushing them down. They do not have to be stapled in place. Fill in any small uncovered areas with the leftover pieces of insulation, stuffing them into cracks. Fig. 16-4.

4. When you install the insulation, do not cover the attic vents in the soffits, any exhaust fan motors that protrude into the attic, or recessed lighting fixtures. Trim the insulation to fit around these areas.

Attic Insulation—Loose Fill

To install loose fill insulation, follow these steps:

1. Install vapor barrier material between the joists. (This is not necessary if there is already some insulation present.)
2. Pour the insulation into place.
3. Use a leveling board to obtain a consistent insulation thickness. Fig. 16-5.

Installing Wall Insulation

Installing insulation in various walls of your home can help to give you a tight, well-insulated house. Basement walls can be insulated with $3\frac{1}{2}''$ thick fiberglass batts or blankets placed between 2 x 4 furring strips. Exterior sidewalls where windows

16-5. Use of a leveling board.

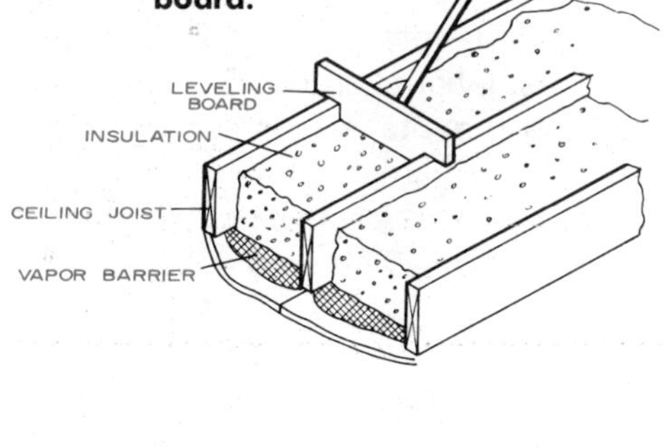

have been replaced, doorways closed up or installed, or other changes made may need new or additional insulation.

To install flexible insulation between the existing wall studs or newly installed furring strips, you will need the following items: a sharp utility knife, a zigzag ruler, a pencil, a staple gun with a supply of 1/4″ staples, a pair of work gloves, and a filter mask. The gloves will protect your hands from the fiberglass, and the filter mask will prevent you from inhaling any of the fibers. A piece of scrap plywood will serve as a board for cutting the insulation to length.

1. Assemble all the tools and materials in the area where you will work. Wear long pants and a long-sleeved shirt to protect your skin from the fiberglass.

2. Measure the height of the first space between two exposed 2 x 4s with your zigzag ruler. Roll out the insulation blanket and mark off the correct length with a pencil. Cut off the length that you need by placing the insulation, vapor barrier up, on the piece of scrap plywood. Compress the insulation with one hand and cut through the vapor barrier and insulation with one or two strokes of your utility knife.

16-6. Push the insulation into the space between two studs. The vapor barrier must face the room. You should wear a mask to avoid breathing the glass fibers.

Owens Corning Fiberglas Corp.

3. Pick up the cut piece of insulation and push it into the space between the two studs as shown in Fig. 16-6. *Make sure the vapor barrier is facing toward the room.* There are flanges on the edges of the blanket which are used to staple the insulation in place. You could leave the blanket forced between the studs, but the insulation might eventually sag, leaving an uninsulated area on the wall up near the ceiling. It is better to staple the flanges to the inside surfaces of the 2 x 4s so that the edges of the flanges are flush with the outside surfaces of the studs. Use the staple gun and 1/4″ staples to fasten the blanket every 8″. Be sure to staple at the top of the blanket and also along the bottom edge where the insulation meets the plate or horizontal 2 x 4.

4. If there are ducts or pipes between the studs, push the insulation behind them so that the blanket or batt touches the outside wall.

5. Do each cavity between the studs the same way. If you are using batts (which are already cut to length) instead of blankets, fill in each cavity with as many precut batts as necessary. Then measure the remaining uninsulated space and cut a batt to length as described in Step 2. Put this batt in place without compressing it. Staple the flanges on the batts to the studs as described in Step 3.

6. Save all the scrap pieces of insulation. These should be used to stuff small spaces around window and door frames to prevent drafts. Use a thin object, such as a putty knife, to force insulation into narrow spaces.

7. If you are using blankets that have no vapor barrier on them, you will have to add a vapor barrier. Cut the blankets to length

and push them into place. Then cover them with a sheet of 2-mil thick polyethylene. Unroll a sheet of this material to cover the entire wall area from floor to ceiling. Staple it to the top and bottom plates (horizontal 2 x 4s) as shown in Fig. 16-7. Cut it to length with a utility knife. Then staple it to the end studs and around the window and door openings. Cut out the window and door openings with a knife. Staple every 8″ to be sure that the plastic sheeting stays on the top, bottom, and end studs.

Owens Corning Fiberglas Corp.

16-7. Staple the polyethylene vapor barrier to the top and bottom plates.

WEATHERIZING

Besides insulating, there are other measures you can take to help block the flow of heat into or out of your home.

• Check all windows in your home. On a cold day hold a lighted candle near windows and door frames to see whether cold air is leaking in. You can also use the palm of your hand to detect a blast of cold air. Caulk all cracks around window and door frames, chimneys, etc. (See Chapter 11.)

• In cold climates, the fewer windows the better. Windows are a source of heat loss. All windows should have storm windows or insulated double or triple glazing.

• Install inside storm windows. These may be glass or rigid plastic. The storms are held to metal windows with magnets. On wooden windows steel strips are installed so that the magnets on the storm windows will hold. Inexpensive polyethylene can be used over inside windows. It is held with tape or molding strips.

• Shutters or lined draperies help keep window heat loss to a minimum.

• Plug leaks around exterior light fixtures, exterior electrical outlets, mail chutes, etc., with permanent (silicone) caulking. (See Chapter 11.)

• Repair cracks and breaks in roofing and siding. Keep a good coat of exterior paint on the sides of your house.

• Make sure that basement windows and doors fit tightly and are weather-stripped. Repair broken window panes.

• Check the masonry on your house. Fill in chinks and cracks. If mortar is missing between bricks, have them pointed up (old mortar removed and new material put in joints).

• Use weather stripping around doors and windows. (See Chapters 9 and 10.)

• Install storm windows and doors early in the heating season. If your home has central air conditioning, you can leave most of the storm windows on year-round. Remove the storm sash from a few windows during the summer for ventilation.

• If you have a fireplace, close the

damper when the fireplace is not in use. Otherwise, heat from the room will escape through the chimney, and the furnace will have to work harder. A glass screen can help prevent heat loss after the fire burns down.

• Vent dryers to the outdoors. This helps keep the house cool in summer and helps prevent moisture problems year-round.

• Close off spare rooms in winter. However, do not let the room temperature go below 40 °F (4 °C). Low temperatures will damage walls and water pipes.

• Wrap heat ducts in unheated areas with special insulation made for that purpose.

• Insulate all water pipes in crawl spaces.

• Crawl space vents should be closed in winter unless the heating unit is in the crawl space or there is a moisture problem. During summer, vents should be open.

• If you live in a mobile home, install skirt boards around the foundation.

• If your home's basement is used only for storage, insulate the ceiling and keep the basement at the lowest practical temperature. During the summer, close the basement registers if you have central air conditioning.

• Keep attic vents open to prevent moisture problems, but make sure that the attic is well insulated.

CHECKUP

1. What is the purpose of thermal insulation?
2. What are some common types of insulation?
3. What are the disadvantages of using a fireplace to heat a room?

CHAPTER 17

Setting Up a Workshop at Home

A workshop is the base of operations for the do-it-yourselfer. It provides an area to work away from the main traffic in the home. Thus you can work there without having to worry about making a mess or disturbing others. Also it is a place to store tools and supplies.

The workshop can be as elaborate as you wish it to be. It should be designed and built to suit the needs of those who work there. It can be a place where one person works alone, or where two or more family members work on various repair projects.

SELECTING AN AREA FOR THE WORKSHOP

Shop Considerations

Before you set up a workshop at home, you have to decide why you are setting it up. Questions you may ask yourself are:

- How much repair is my home likely to need in the foreseeable future?
- How much of the repair work will I be doing myself?
- Will my shop be used for other purposes besides home repairs?

If you do most of the repair work around the house yourself, then you will need an extensive workshop. If you plan to use the shop only occasionally, for emergency repairs, you will not need so large an area or so much equipment. If your shop will have other uses—perhaps as a hobby center—then those uses will help determine the layout and equipment.

Thus your interest in making repairs and your mechanical capabilities will determine the layout of your home workshop. Your ability to make repairs may be limited by inexperience when you first move into a private house. After a time, the periodic maintenance jobs around the house and the difficulty in obtaining mechanics to make adequate repairs may lead you to attempt tasks that you have never tried before. It is often helpful to talk to other homeowners and friends to learn from their experiences. Reading can also increase your knowledge of home repairs.

When you feel that you need and want a home workshop, you must consider the space available for one in your home. Some of the possibilities for workshop space are:

- The basement.
- The garage (attached or unattached).
- An outside shed or barn.
- A spare room.

After you examine each available area in your home, a decision must be made based on the suitability of each. The area must offer enough room for you to have all the equipment that you want in your shop. You must be able to get into the shop area easily. (It may be necessary to bring in large items once in a while.) As you work in your shop, the noise of hammering and sawing or power tools should not disturb the other members of the family or the neighbors.

The size of your shop will depend on the type of work you will be doing. If you plan to do a lot of woodworking, you will need to allow enough space so that large sheets of plywood and long boards can be easily handled. If you plan to use a table saw or a radial-arm saw, you will need an area where long pieces of wood can be ripped or crosscut without interference.

If you plan to use only portable power tools, the shop area can be smaller. These tools can be stored away when not in use, and large pieces of wood can be cut outside before they are brought into the workshop. Stationary power tools require a large area for installation and work space. If you start out with a few tools but expect to enlarge your tool collection as time goes on, then you will need to include room for expansion. If all you desire for a workshop area is a workbench and some shelves, then all you will need is a corner of the basement or the garage.

The physical setup of the shop can be simple or elaborate. In addition to tool boards and assorted shelf areas, used kitchen cabinets or chests of drawers can be used for storing tools and hardware.

Essentials of the Workshop

It is important that a shop have adequate lighting. The area should be wired prior to use, so that lighting can be installed. You can install different kinds of overhead lighting and use spotlights for particular areas, or you can use fluorescent lighting throughout the shop. Natural light from windows is also good, but not absolutely necessary. An example of sufficient lighting for a small workshop would be two twin-bulb, 4′ long fluorescent light fixtures running along the center of the shop ceiling. Fig. 17-1. There must be a switch for them at the entrance to the shop.

The workshop must have adequate electrical outlets for the power tools that you own or will purchase in the future. For portable power tools, a power strip or multiple grounded outlets near the workbench are sufficient. Fig. 17-2. Stationary power tools, such as a table saw, require an outlet with a separate circuit breaker or fuse. This is necessary because some power tools draw a lot of amperage when in use. If they are connected to an electrical line with other

17-1. Fluorescent light fixtures in the center of the workshop ceiling.

17-2. Multiple grounded outlets on the wall over the workbench are convenient for portable power tools.

household appliances operating at the same time, they will overload the circuit. The result will be a blown fuse or a tripped circuit breaker.

Adequate ventilation is important in a home shop. Sawdust and paint fumes in the shop require good ventilation to protect your health and safety. Where poor ventilating systems exist, a small electric fan will improve the circulation of air in the work area. Proper ventilation also improves comfort during hot or humid weather.

The workshop area should also be heated so that it is comfortable during cold weather. Heat also helps to dry newly painted or varnished items. Certain products, such as glazing compound, varnish, shellac, lacquer, and all types of paint, require a minimum temperature for their successful use.

BUILDING A WORKBENCH

An essential piece of equipment in any home workshop is the workbench. Fig. 17-3. It must be sturdy enough to take rough treatment and large enough to accommodate big materials. A workbench can be purchased as a complete unit, or the various parts for it can be bought separately. For example, steel workbench legs can be purchased in sets, and a laminated top can be added to complete the bench. Additional metal tool racks and drawers for the bench are sold separately and can be installed on any part of the bench.

17-3. A workbench for a home workshop.

If you want to build your own workbench, the following drawings and instructions will be helpful to you. Fig. 17-4. To build this type of workbench, you will need just a few hand tools. The top of this bench will measure 2′ 6″ x 6′ (762 mm x 1829 mm). The height of the bench depends upon the height of the person who is going to use it. The top of the bench should be about the height of your waist; so you may have to change the length of the legs mentioned in the instructions. A bench that is too low requires you to bend over when you are working at it and can become uncomfortable to use.

Materials and Tools

Fig. 17-5 lists the materials you will need to build the workbench. Note that both customary and metric sizes are given. In the column of metric dimensions, standard customary sizes have been changed to the probable standard metric sizes. For example, 2 x 4s are listed as 40 x 90 mm. Dimensions that would be cut to size at the lumberyard or at home are given metric equivalents to the nearest millimeter. For example, one inch equals 25.4 millimeters. The length of the bench legs is therefore given as 864 mm (34″ x 25.4 = 863.6, or 864 mm). Since metric standards for wood fasteners have not been developed, no metric equivalents are given for the bolts, screws, and so forth.

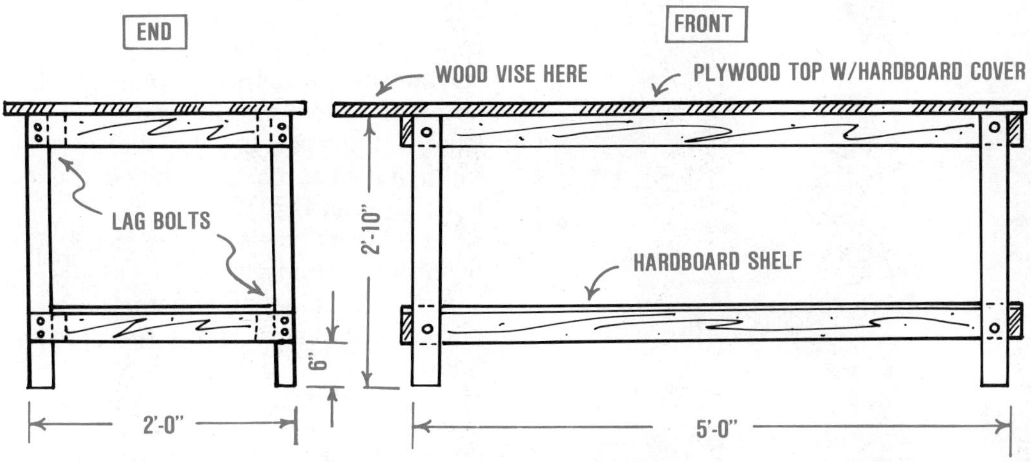

Customary	Metric
6″	152 mm
2′0″	610 mm
2′10″	864 mm
5′0″	1524 mm

17-4 Front and end views of the workbench.

17-5. This table lists the materials you will need to construct the workbench shown in Fig. 17-4.

MATERIALS LIST FOR WORKBENCH

Materials	Size (customary)	Size (metric)
4 legs	2″ x 4″ x 2′ 10″	40 x 90 x 864 mm
4 end crosspieces	2″ x 4″ x 2′ 0″	40 x 90 x 610 mm
4 crosspieces	2″ x 4″ x 5′ 0″	40 x 90 x 1524 mm
1 top (plywood or particle board)	¾″ x 2′ 6″ x 6′ 0″	20 x 762 x 1829 mm
1 top cover (hardboard)	⅛″ x 2′ 6″ x 6′ 0″	3 x 762 x 1829 mm
1 shelf (plywood or hardboard)	¼″ x 1′ 9″ x 5′ 0″	6 x 838 x 1524 mm
8 carriage bolts with nuts	½″ x 4″	
8 washers for bolts	½″	
12 flathead wood screws	1½″ No. 8	
16 lag bolts	⅜″ x 2½″	
brads	¾″	

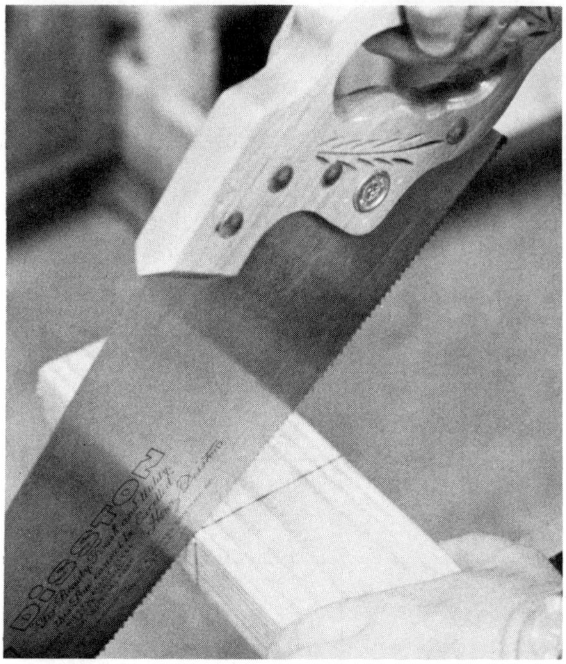

17-6. Cutting the 2 x 4s with a handsaw. Notice the pencil guide lines made with a square.

17-7. Legs and end crosspieces are assembled using lag bolts.

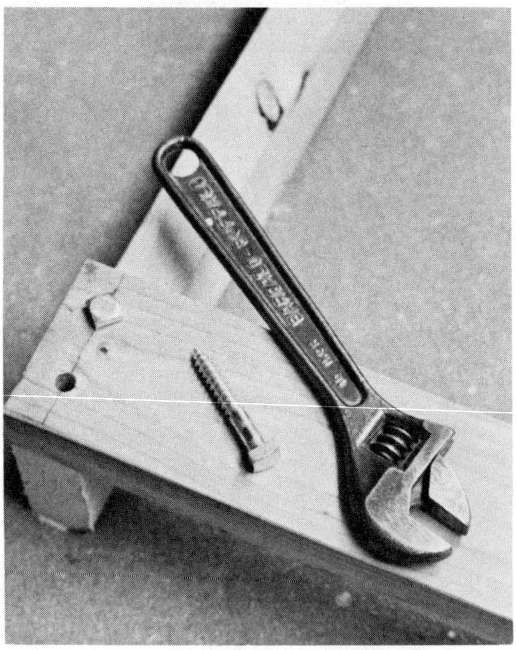

To gain practice in using the metric system, you may want to build the bench according to metric measurements. You can still buy the standard sizes of material, such as 2 x 4s or 3/4″ thick plywood. Then cut the length of the 2 x 4s, and the length and width of the boards, according to the metric sizes given in Fig. 17-5.

In addition to the materials listed, you will need the following tools:

- 12″ combination square.
- 6′ push-pull or zigzag ruler (or metric ruler).
- Crosscut saw, 26″, 10 points.
- Claw hammer, 13-ounce.
- Bit brace.
- 3/8″ auger bit.
- 1/2″ auger bit.
- Hand drill, 1/4″ chuck.
- Set of twist drills, 1/16″ to 1/4″.
- Countersink, 1/4″ shank.
- 10″ adjustable open-end wrench.
- 2 C-clamps, 6″.
- Screwdriver with regular blade, 4″ or 6″.

Constructing the Bench

1. Measure and cut all the pieces of 2 x 4s as called for in the list of materials. Be sure to square a line across the wood with a combination square before you make each cut so that you will cut the pieces squarely. Fig. 17-6.

2. Gather two legs and two end crosspieces. Assemble them as shown in Fig. 17-4. Use two lag bolts for each joint. Fig. 17-7. Clearance holes (3/8″) and pilot holes must be drilled for each fastener. Use the wrench to tighten the lag bolts. Fig. 17-8. Do the same with the other two legs and two end crosspieces.

3. Lay out the spots for the 1/2″ bolt holes in the four legs, using the measurements shown in Fig. 17-9. After the layout is completed, use the bit brace and the 1/2″ auger bit to drill the two holes in each leg. Fig. 17-10.

4. Put the assembled legs on their sides as shown in Fig. 17-11. Put a 5′ crosspiece

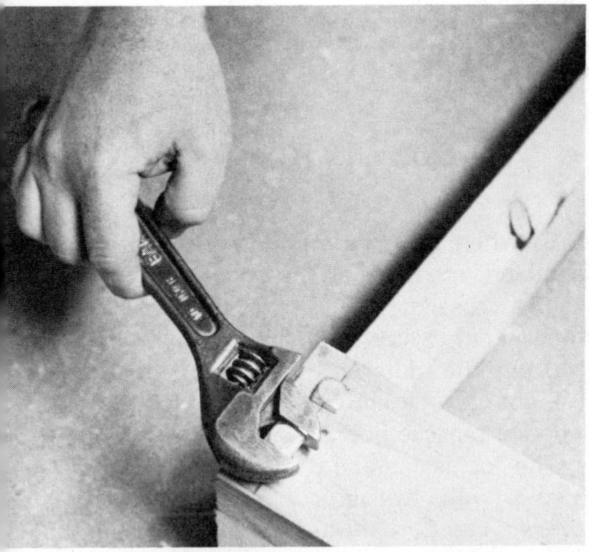

17-8. Using an adjustable open-end wrench to tighten the lag bolts.

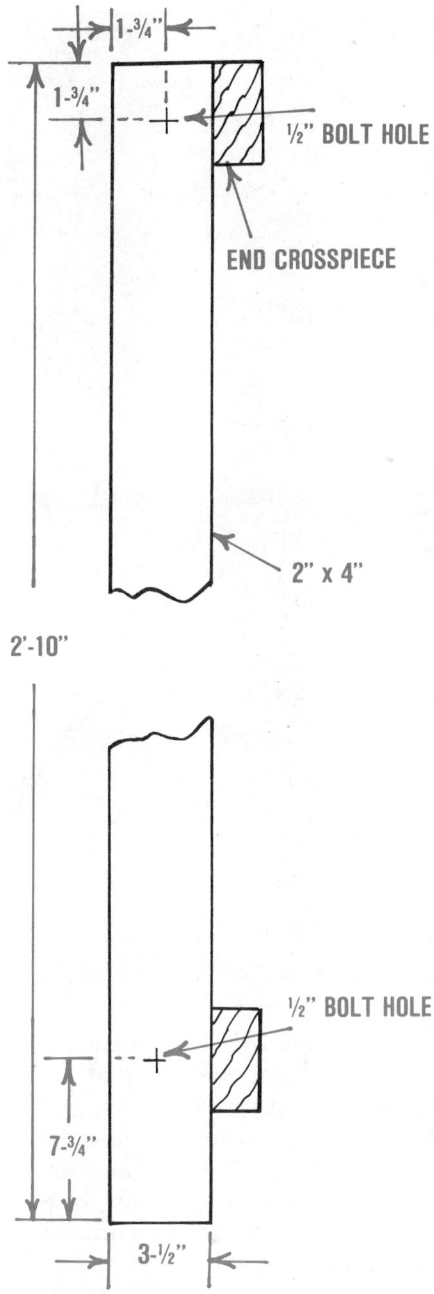

17-9. The layout of the ½″ bolt holes in the legs.

17-10. Drilling the ½″ bolt holes with a brace and an auger bit.

Customary	Metric
$1\frac{3}{4}''$	44.4 mm
$2'' \times 4''$	40 x 90 mm
$3\frac{1}{2}''$	88.9 mm
$7\frac{3}{4}''$	196.8 mm
2′10″	864 mm

17-11. The assembled legs are put on their sides. A 5′ crosspiece is held in place with C-clamps while the holes are drilled.

in place and use two C-clamps to hold it to the leg assemblies, one clamp at each end. Using the previously drilled holes in the legs as a pattern, drill holes in the crosspieces while they are in place. Do all four crosspieces, holding each one at the place where it will be put in the final assembling of the bench.

5. After drilling the holes, fasten each crosspiece in place with carriage bolts. Figs. 17-12, 17-13. Drive the bolts through the holes from the outside with the hammer until they are tight. Fig. 17-14. Then put a washer and a nut on each bolt and tighten it with an adjustable wrench. Make sure that each crosspiece is square with the legs to which it is fastened.

6. When the frame of the bench is assembled, measure and cut the top to size with a crosscut saw. It is possible to have the top cut to size at the lumberyard where you buy the materials. (Some lumberyards will charge a small amount to cut the plywood or particle board to your dimensions).

The top is fastened to the upper crosspieces with twelve 1½″ flathead wood screws. Fig. 17-12. After placing the top on the frame, lay out the places for the screw holes. There should be two screws on each end and four screws along each side. The wood screws will go through the top and into the crosspieces underneath. Drill the holes for the screws. Be sure to countersink the screw holes on top so that the screw heads will be even with the top surface.

The top on the bench shown in these illustrations was fastened even with one end of the frame. The other end has a 9″ overhang for a woodworking vise.

7. You should cover the top of the bench with a piece of hardboard to protect it. This ⅛″ hardboard is fastened in place with small brads.

8. If you want to cover the bottom crosspieces to form a shelf, use a piece of hardboard or plywood at least ¼″ thick. The shelf is held in place with ¾″ brads.

Alternate Procedures

The workbench can be nailed together with ten-penny (10d) common nails. Carriage bolts and lag bolts are recommended, though, because they will hold the bench together without the possibility of working loose.

The top of the bench can be made of other materials than those mentioned. It can be made of 2″ lumber by gluing together three straight, dry 2″ x 10″ x 6′

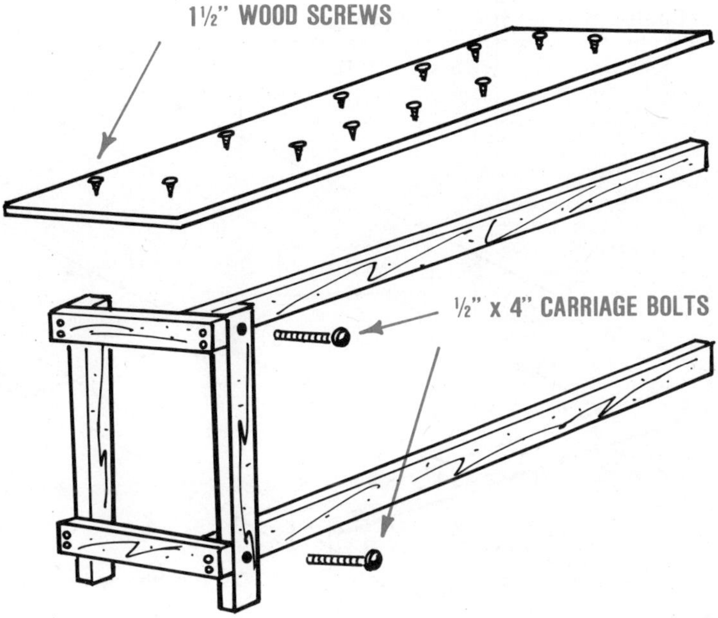

17-12. An exploded view of the workbench showing how the carriage bolts go through the legs into the crosspieces. This also shows how the top is fastened down with wood screws.

17-13. The carriage bolt, nut, and washer ready to be put into the bolt holes in the leg and crosspiece.

17-14. Driving the carriage bolt in tight with a hammer.

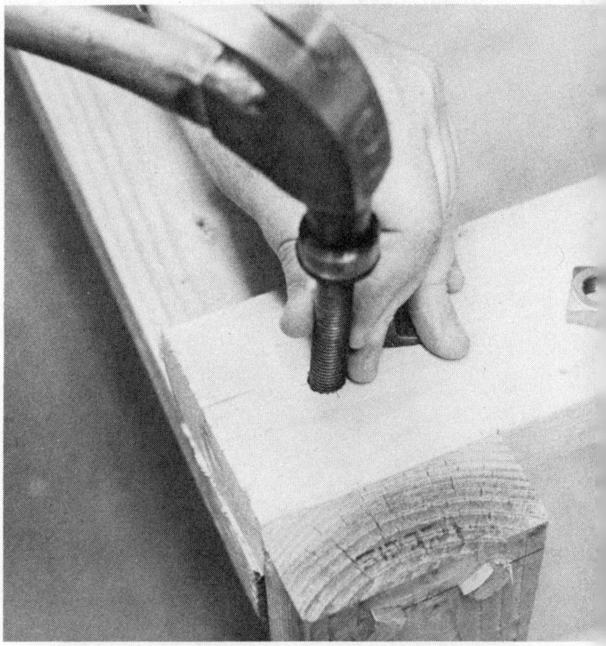

Customary	Metric
1″ x 3″ 2″ x 10″	25 x 76 mm 38 x 235 mm (dry)

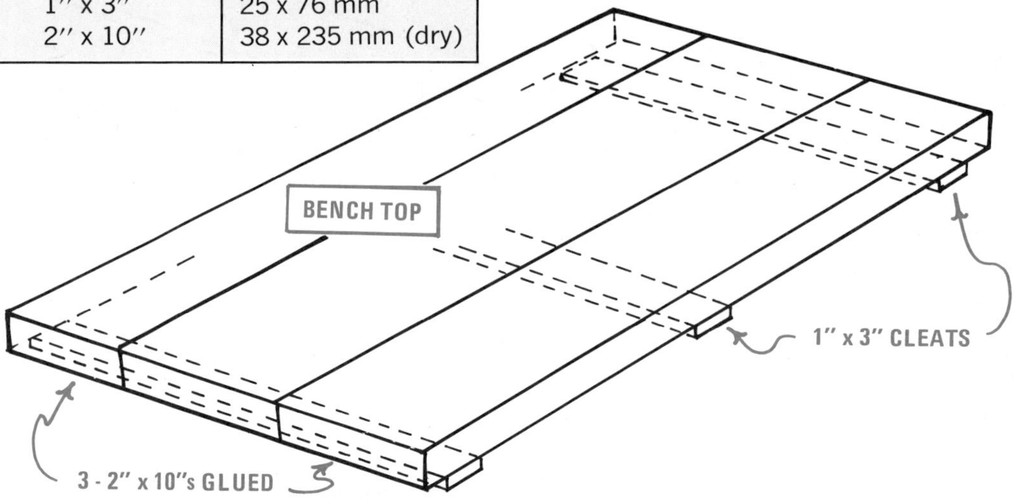

17-15. A bench top made of 2″ x 10″ lumber with cleats fastened underneath.

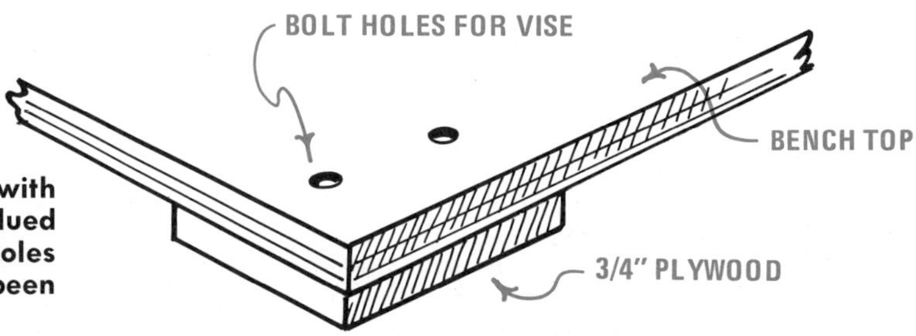

17-16. The bench top with a piece of plywood glued underneath. The bolt holes for the vise have been drilled.

17-17. The woodworking vise in place on the bench top. A piece of plywood was used to build up the thickness of the top.

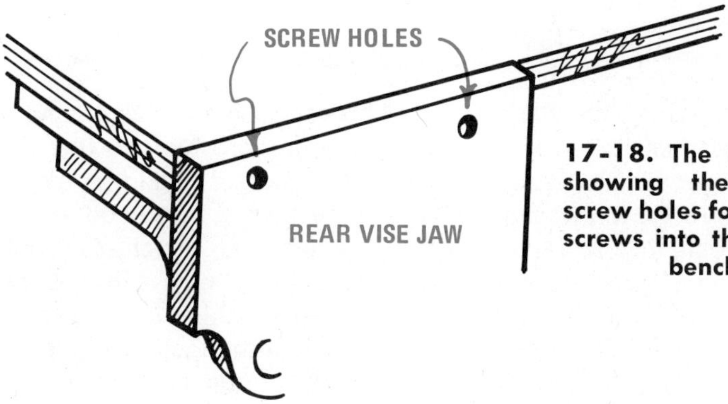

17-18. The rear vise jaw showing the location of screw holes for driving wood screws into the edge of the bench top.

(38 x 235 x 1829 mm) pieces of wood. They are glued edge to edge and 1″ x 3″ (25 x 76 mm) cleats are fastened across the three pieces with glue and screws as shown in Fig. 17-15.

Two or three pieces of particle board can be glued together face to face to form a thicker top. For example, two ¾″ thick pieces will form a top that is 1½″ (38 mm) thick.

Installing a Vise on the Bench

When the bench is finished, vises or other accessories can be installed on it. A metal-working vise can be bolted to the bench top near the front edge. It is usually put close to an outside corner. Place the vise where it will be handy and mark the layout of the holes in the base with a pencil. Drill the holes in the bench top with a ⅜″ auger bit. Fasten the vise in place with ⅜″ machine head bolts. Use a washer and a nut on each bolt. Tighten them with an adjustable open-end wrench.

A woodworking vise is installed in a different way:

1. Measure the height of the rear vise jaw to see how thick the bench top must be to allow the top of the jaws to be even with the top of the bench. Using some of the scrap plywood or particle board left from making the bench top, cut one or two 6″ x 9″ pieces. Glue them to the underside of the top where the vise will go. Fig. 17-16. This will increase the thickness of the top so that the vise will be even. Clamp them in place overnight until the glue is dry. A piece of hardboard can also be used to help get that section of the bench top to the proper thickness.

2. Using the template that comes with the vise or the vise itself, mark the location of the bolt holes on the top surface of the bench. Select flathead bolts of the same diameter as the holes in the vise to fasten the vise to the bench top.

3. Drill the proper size holes where you have marked their location, using a bit brace and an auger bit. Countersink the holes on top so that the bolt heads will be flush with the top surface of the bench.

4. Put the vise in place under the bench top and insert one of the bolts through the holes from the top down. Put a washer and a nut on the bolt loosely to hold the vise. Do the same with the other bolt and tighten them with a wrench. Fig. 17-17.

5. Some woodworking vises have holes in the rear jaw. On these you can drive two long, flathead screws through the jaw and into the edge of the bench top to make the vise more stable. Use at least 1½″ wood screws with flat heads. Fig. 17-18.

6. It is a good idea to fasten auxiliary hardwood jaws to the insides of the metal vise jaws. This will protect anything that you clamp in the vise from being marred by the metal jaws. The wooden jaws are held in place with flathead wood screws or machine screws, depending upon the way that the vise is designed. Cut them to the measurements of the inside of the metal jaws.

TOOL STORAGE

Your tools should be stored in an orderly way so that you can find them when you need them. Proper storage will also keep them from getting dull or rusty. Many people prefer to store their tools in a tool box. This is not a recommended practice because the tools rub together and can get dull or damaged.

Drawers are good storage places for tools in your workshop. The drawers may be on the workbench or in a discarded dresser. Drawers work well for portable power tools and some hand tools that have no cutting edges on them. Auger bits and twist drills can be stored in drawers if you make or buy individual cases to protect them so that they stay sharp. If the points and cutting edges are not protected, you will have to resharpen them often.

The best way to store tools so that they will remain in good condition is on a tool board in a dry place. If you have many tools, you may need more than one tool board. To make a tool board, buy a piece of $\frac{1}{8}''$ pegboard which measures 2′ x 4′. Hang it on the wall of your workshop in some convenient place. Fig. 17-19. All types of pegboard hooks and tool holders are available. Arrange your tools any way you like on this tool board. You can move the hooks around as you add more tools to the board.

Another way of making a tool board is to buy a piece of $\frac{3}{4}''$ plywood and hang it on the wall near your bench. You could also use an old solid door as a tool board. Use *L*-hooks or nails to hold the tools in place. To keep track of the tools on the board, draw a silhouette around each tool with a felt-tip marker. In that way you can quickly see if any tools are missing from the board. The silhouettes will also help you to hang the tools back up in the same place.

Many of your small hand tools—such as chisels, screwdrivers, pliers, and drill bits—can be stored in a tool rack attached to your workbench. Such a rack made of metal can be bought at any large hardware store, but you can make your own quite easily. Build an *L*-shaped rack of $\frac{3}{4}''$ wood and fasten it to the back of your workbench with screws. The *L* should be turned upside down and face your bench as shown in Fig. 17-20. The rack can be as long as the bench. Drill holes in the horizontal piece of wood for the tools. The rack should be high enough off the bench top so that tools hang freely in the holes without touching the bench.

17-19. A shop tool board made of pegboard.

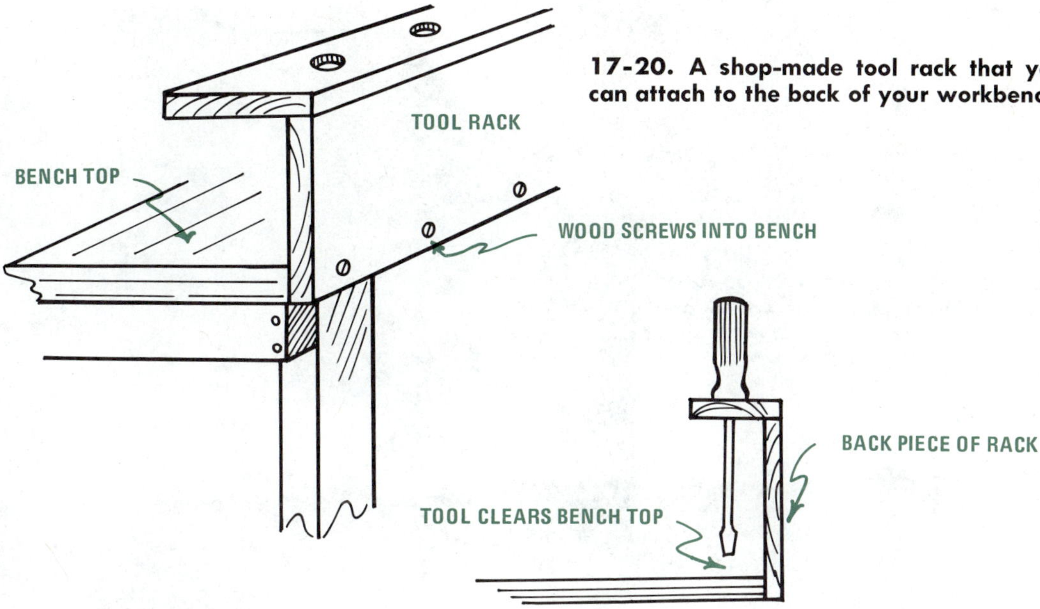

17-20. A shop-made tool rack that you can attach to the back of your workbench.

ORGANIZING SUPPLIES AND MATERIALS

Hardware and Parts

As you begin to fix things around your home, you will need to keep handy various kinds of hardware and other supplies. You can use shelves to store all these items. If you can obtain some old kitchen cabinets that are in good condition, these can be hung on the shop walls. Fig. 17-21. Cabinets help keep supplies dust-free and neatly organized. As you do repair work around the house, you will begin to collect extra screws, bolts, nails, and other fasteners. These can be kept organized in plastic containers, baby food jars, or even small cans. Label each container with a felt-tip marker or a piece of labeling tape. Stores that sell hardware items also sell small plastic or metal cabinets with numerous drawers. These are ideal for storing small items, and each cabinet comes with drawer dividers and labels.

Large Item Storage

You will also have building materials left over from repair jobs. These extra pieces of wood, pipe, and metal can be useful for other repair jobs; so you will want to store them in the shop where they will be available when needed. The type of storage rack you make will depend upon how much room you have and where you have set up your shop.

A shop that has a lot of space will allow you to store spare materials against one wall. If your shop is in the basement and the

17-21. An old kitchen cabinet used to store hardware and supplies in the workshop.

17-22. Exposed heating ducts on the basement ceiling can be used to store short pieces of wood and molding.

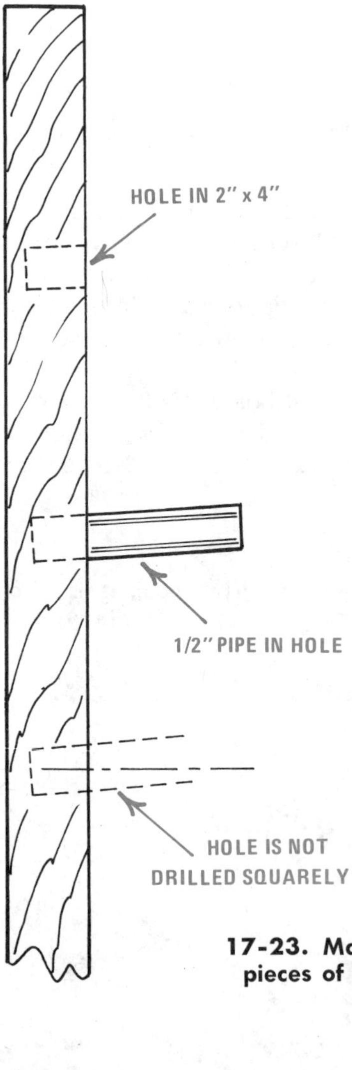

17-23. Making holes in a 2 x 4 to hold pieces of pipe for a lumber storage rack.

beams overhead (floor joists) are uncovered, you can use them for storage space. By nailing a couple of wooden strips across two beams, you can use the space between the joists to store long pieces of wood, pipe, and molding.

If the walls of your shop have exposed studs (2" x 4" beams), you can nail two strips of wood across two or three studs to make an upright lumber rack. Either long or short pieces of material can be kept in this type of rack if you nail one of the wooden strips across the studs about one foot off the floor. Basement heating ducts that are exposed can be used to store short pieces of wood, screening, and other odd items as shown in Fig. 17-22.

You may want to build a horizontal lumber storage rack. It can be as simple as two upright 2″ x 4″ studs nailed in place with holes drilled in them to accommodate pieces of ½″ diameter pipe. The pieces of pipe stick out at varying lengths to hold up long boards or pieces of molding. The holes in each beam are marked so that they are exactly the same as the holes in the other beam. The result is a pair of pipes at the same height to hold up the material. The holes should not be drilled into the wood squarely, but instead on a slight upward slant. This will allow the pipe lengths to slant up and will keep the boards from accidentally slipping off the rack. Fig. 17-23.

CHECKUP

1. Do you have a home workshop? If so, are there improvements that could make the workshop more efficient?
2. What places in and around a house could be used for a workshop?
3. Why are adequate heat, light, and ventilation important for a workshop?

CHAPTER 18

Related Careers

By now you have had some practice in common household repairs and maintenance. Perhaps you found that you have a special interest or ability in a certain area, such as painting or electrical work, for example. Many people make their living in trades that are related to the building, repair, and maintenance of homes. This chapter will tell you about some of these trades. Your special ability and interest may lead you to choose one of these trades as your career.

SKILLED TRADES

Plumber

Plumbers install, alter, and repair pipe systems and plumbing fixtures. In house construction, plumbers "rough in" the pipe system during early stages. Later, they install the plumbing fixtures. (Bathtubs, however, are installed with the rough-in, before the walls are finished.)

Most plumbers work for contractors on new construction. Others are self-employed or work for contractors making repairs or alterations. Many belong to a union.

Plasterer

Plasterers finish interior walls and ceilings with plaster coatings. They apply cement plasters or stucco to exterior surfaces.

The plaster is applied in two or three coats. First, a backing or lath, is applied to the framing. The lath—which may be gypsum, fiberboard, or metal—acts as a base to hold the first coat of plaster. The remaining coat or coats are applied over the first.

Plasterers also cast ornamental designs in plaster. Public buildings are sometimes decorated with such designs.

Most plasterers work for contractors. Some are self-employed. Many plasterers belong to a union.

Dry-Wall Installer and Finisher

Because of the savings in time and money, most homes built today have dry wall instead of plaster. Two trades are involved: that of the installer and the finisher.

Dry-wall installers cut the panels to shape and attach them with nails and glue to the wall and ceiling framework. Dry-wall finishers prepare the panels for painting. They apply joint cement and perforated tape to the nailheads and to the joints between the panels. These areas are then sanded to make them level with the rest of the wall.

Dry-wall installers join the carpenters' union, while finishers are part of the painters' union. Sometimes carpenters install dry wall, and painters finish it.

Painter

Painters prepare a building surface and then apply paint, varnish, or other finishes to protect and beautify it.

Some painters are self-employed. The rest work for contractors. Many belong to a union. Often a painter also works as a paperhanger.

Paperhanger

Paperhangers apply wallcoverings after properly preparing the surface. The preparation often includes minor repairs of plaster or dry wall.

This is a small field, but it is growing somewhat. Many paperhangers are self-employed. Others belong to a union.

Floorcovering Installer

Floorcovering installers are also known as floorcovering mechanics. It is their job to install and replace resilient tile, linoleum and vinyl sheets, and carpeting. Usually they specialize in either resilient floorcoverings or carpeting, but some install both.

Floorcovering installers prepare the floor for installation of the covering (see Chapter 7). The floor may be made of wood, concrete, or some other material, and the installer must know what type of covering to use and how it should be fastened to the floor.

These workers may be employed by flooring contractors or retailers, or they may be self-employed. Many belong to a union.

Construction Glazier

These workers install the different kinds of glass used in homes, such as window glass, shower doors, bathtub enclosures, and mirrors. Most work for contractors and belong to a union.

Carpenter

A variety of construction work is done by carpenters. Most carpenters stay in one field of construction, such as home building. Carpenters are involved in almost every phase of house construction. They build the forms for receiving concrete, erect the framework of the house, install windows and doors, build stairs, lay floors, and install paneling and cabinets. Some carpenters specialize in one type of job. Fig. 18-1.

Besides working on new construction, carpenters repair and remodel existing buildings. Hourly wages are high, but bad weather can cause loss of worktime and earnings. Most carpenters work for contractors and are members of a union.

18-1. Carpenters make up almost one-third of all workers in the construction trades.
U.S. Dept. of Labor

Cement Mason (Cement and Concrete Finisher)

On construction projects, laborers spread concrete and cement masons finish it. That is, the masons make the concrete level and work it to obtain the proper consistency and the desired finish. Cement masons must know their materials and the effects of heat, cold, and wind on the curing of cement.

In home building, the mason's work may involve finishing a concrete slab on which a house will be built or finishing a patio or driveway.

Most masons work for contractors and belong to unions. Most work is outdoors.

Roofer

Roofers apply the finishing material (composition roofing, metal, tile) to the roof of buildings. They also waterproof and dampproof walls and other surfaces of buildings. Fig. 18-2.

Most roofers work on construction or repair jobs for roofing contractors. Many belong to a union.

18-2. This roofer is applying wood shakes to the roof of a new building.

U.S. Dept. of Labor

Tilesetter

Tilesetters install tile on walls, floors, and ceilings. Although most of their work is nonresidential, they may be employed to install tile in kitchens and bathrooms.

Some tilesetters are self-employed. Wages are good, and the work is mostly indoors. Tilesetters may belong to one of several unions.

Electrician

Electricians assemble, install, and wire electrical systems. They may work on new construction or existing buildings. For safety reasons, their work must conform to the National Electrical Code and the local codes.

Most work is indoors. Wages are above the average for building trades workers. Most electricians belong to a union.

Air-Conditioning, Refrigeration, and Heating Mechanic

This field includes air-conditioning and refrigeration mechanics, furnace installers, oil burner mechanics, and gas burner mechanics.

- Air-conditioning and refrigeration mechanics install and repair equipment that ranges in size from window units to central air-conditioning or refrigeration systems.
- Furnace installers install oil, gas, and electric heating units.
- Oil burner mechanics service oil-fueled heating systems.
- Gas burner mechanics service gas-fueled heating systems. They also repair gas stoves, clothes dryers, and hot water heaters.

Training

One way to learn a trade is by working as a helper for someone who is experienced. You begin with simple tasks and gradually develop the skills needed for that trade.

Today many men and women learn their trades through a formal apprenticeship program. An apprenticeship program includes both on-the-job and classroom training. On the job, you learn to use the tools, equipment, and materials of the trade. In class, you learn subjects related to your trade, such as blueprint reading, mathematics for layout work, or drafting. Most apprenticeship programs last 2–4 years, depending on the trade.

Whether you learn your trade informally on the job or in a formal apprenticeship program, a high school or vocational school diploma is important. Courses taken in school can help prepare you for a trade. For example, if you plan to become a carpenter, courses in shop, mechanical drawing, and general mathematics will be useful.

SOURCES OF CAREER INFORMATION

In addition to the trades already discussed, there are many other jobs related to home maintenance. There is the field of appliance repair, for example. There are also careers in retailing—hardware, lumber, paint, plumbing supplies, and so forth.

The purpose of this book has been to help you learn to take care of your home. Every home requires minor repairs from time to time. Knowing how to make everyday repairs can save you time and money. There is also a sense of accomplishment and independence when you have the skills to handle those repair tasks.

Perhaps this book has also helped you to discover your special interest or skills. This chapter has described some of the careers related to home building and maintenance. You may want to find out more about these careers. Information is available from local construction firms and employer associations, trade unions, the local office of the state employment service or state apprenticeship agency, or from the local office of the Bureau of Apprenticeship and Training, U. S. Department of Labor.

CHECKUP

1. How do people in the skilled trades train for their occupations?
2. What are some sources for information about careers in home building and maintenance?
3. How might practice in household repairs and maintenance help a person decide on a career?

Index